Benjamin Franklin

&

The Politics of Liberty

David Martin, *Benjamin Franklin*, 1767.
Courtesy the Pennsylvania Academy of the Fine Arts.

Benjamin Franklin

&

The Politics of Liberty

A Biography with Readings

BY THOMAS WENDEL

Professor of History,

San Jose State University
California

Shapers of History Series

Kenneth C. Colegrove, Editor

Barron's Educational Series, Inc.

WOODBURY, NEW YORK

© Copyright 1974 by Barron's Educational Series, Inc.

All inquiries should be addressed to:
Barron's Educational Series, Inc.
113 Crossways Park Drive
Woodbury, New York 11797

Library of Congress Catalog Card No. 73–7133

Paper Edition
International Standard Book No. 0–8120–0459-0

PRINTED IN THE UNITED STATES OF AMERICA

PHOTO CREDITS
Page ii   Pennsylvania Academy of the Fine Arts
Page 106   Historical Society of Pennsylvania
Page 218   Philadelphia Museum of Art
Page 250   The Henry Francis du Pont Winterthur Museum
Page 278   American Philosophical Society

for HAL *and* DAVID

Table of Contents

Appendix

Illustrations

> *The German bleeds & bears the Furs*
> *Of Quaker Lords & savage Curs*
>
> *Th' Hibernian frets with new Disaster*
> *And kicks to fling his broad brim'd Master*
>
> *But help at hand Resolves to hold down*
> *Th' Hibernian's Head or tumble all down*

Franklin, as Speaker of the Pennsylvania Assembly
during the election of 1764, represents the "help at
hand." But instead of help, he holds a unanimous Assembly resolve that states the proprietor is a knave and
tyrant and the governor, ditto. The broad-brimmed
Quaker riding the back of a Scotch-Irish "Hibernian"
leads a blindfolded, i.e. duped, German by the nose. On
the German's back rides an Indian bearing furs belonging to Israel Pemberton (I.P.), leader of the pacifist
Quakers. The fox between Franklin's legs represents
the Quaker Joseph Fox, who with Pemberton effected
to pacify rather than defy the Indians. The bodies
strewn on the ground and the Indian lurking in the
bushes represent the results of the Quaker dominated
Assembly's alleged neglect of frontier defense.

> *He snatched the lightning from the sky,*
> *And the sceptre from tyrants.*

Turgot's famous epigram describing Franklin provides the motif for Fragonard's design. With his left arm, Franklin directs Minerva to turn aside the lightning. His right hand directs Mars to destroy Avarice and Tyranny. America, under Franklin's protection, sits at his side in confident repose.

> *Figures included are Franklin, John Jay, John Adams, Henry Laurens, and William Temple Franklin.*

The popularity of America's revolutionary heroes was such that in their haste to meet the demand, old world craftsmen sometimes made mistakes. This fourteen inch high Franklin is identified as General Washington, an inadvertently amusing tribute to both men.

Editor's Foreword

THE BIOGRAPHY OF BENJAMIN FRANKLIN by Professor Wendel follows the system of the Shapers of History Series in offering a biography of a statesman who contributed much to the world in which we live. A chapter in this biography is devoted to the history of the public image of Benjamin Franklin in the decades following his career. And the final chapter gives the author's appraisal of the man and a summary of his career. The appendix includes a selected bibliography and a collection of documents illustrative of Franklin's place in American and world history.

Many biographies of Benjamin Franklin have neglected the influence of the great intellectual movement of the Enlightenment upon the American colonies as well as the contribution of such Americans as Franklin to the Enlightenment both in Europe and the Americas. Professor Wendel fully covers this important subject, showing Franklin's contributions to learning, science, literature, public education and the struggle for human freedom. Dr. Wendel's discussion of Franklin's objections to chattel slavery in an age when Voltaire, Diderot and other intellectuals gave little attention to this subject is particularly pertinent.

The author, Thomas Wendel, is a native of Portland, Oregon. He took his bachelor of arts degree at Yale University in 1949, and his doctorate of philosophy at the University of Washington in 1964. He is now Professor of History at San Jose State University. He is presently engaged in a study of the office of speaker of the house in the popular assemblies of the English colonies in America. Dr. Wendel is also an accomplished musician, and this love of music is reflected in the fluid quality of his writing.

KENNETH COLEGROVE

Author's Preface

FRANKLIN'S POLITICAL CAREER, the primary emphasis of this study, cannot be separated from his several other careers. As a civic leader, he entered Pennsylvania politics. His printing and publishing business opened up continental opportunities and helped to gain him an intercolonial reputation. His scientific achievements, for which he won world renown, provided the backdrop for his prominence in England as a patriot leader and later, for his success in France as a diplomat. For these reasons I have interwoven Franklin's other careers with his political biography. Franklin's life, though multifarious, had about it a grand unity. Civic leader, scientist, moralist, politician, these are all facets of the "amazing Benjamin Franklin," a veritable human synthesis of the Century of Enlightenment.

I wish to express my indebtedness to the many scholars whose knowledge and insight have helped me to understand Franklin and his times. Some are acknowledged in footnotes particularly where modern scholarship has called for new interpretations. They and others are listed in the bibliography which unfortunately can only indicate my more immediate debts. The influence of a myriad scholars of early American history, of past teachers and present students cannot be specified, but is no less real. I have leaned most heavily on the profound scholarship of Leonard Labaree and his associates, whose edition of the *Papers of Benjamin Franklin,* presently in progress, is a model of editorial skill.

I also wish to express thanks to the several publishers who granted permission to quote from their works as follows: American Philosophical Society (I. Bernard Cohen, *Franklin and Newton*), The Belknap Press of Harvard University Press

(Lyman Butterfield, ed., *Adams Family Correspondence* and Gottlieb Mittelberger, *Journey to Pennsylvania,* ed. by Oscar Handlin and John Clive) Harvard University Press (J. A. Cochrane: *Dr. Johnson's Printer: The Life of William Strahan*), Harper & Row (Richard B. Morris, *The Peacemakers*), Indiana University Press (Samuel Flagg Bemis, *The Diplomacy of the American Revolution*), International Publishers (Karl Marx, *Capital,* ed. by Frederick Engels, trans. by Samuel Moore and Edward Aveling), J. B. Lippincott (Alfred Owen Aldridge, *Benjamin Franklin: Philosopher and Man*), Little, Brown and Co. (Verner Crane, *Benjamin Franklin and a Rising People*), W. W. Norton & Co. (Edmund Cody Burnett, *The Continental Congress*), G. P. Putnam's Sons (Harvey Wish, ed., *Ante-Bellum*), Charles Scribner's Sons (Max Weber, *The Protestant Ethic and the Spirit of Capitalism,* trans. by Talcott Parsons, and Dixon Wecter, *The Hero in America*), University of California Press (Leonard Labaree *et al.,* eds., *Autobiography of Benjamin Franklin*), University of Nebraska Press (Jack Sosin, *Whitehall and Wilderness*), University of North Carolina Press (Verner Crane, Benjamin Franklin's Letters to the Press: 1785–1775), Viking Press, Inc. (Harold Laski, *The American Democracy* and Carl Van Doren, *Benjamin Franklin,* and *Benjamin Franklin's Autobiographical Writings*), John Wiley & Sons (Richard W. Van Alstyne, *Empire and Independence*), Yale University Press (Leonard Labaree et al., *The Autobiography of Benjamin Franklin* and *The Papers of Benjamin Franklin*).

I am grateful finally to several individuals who read parts of the manuscript and gave me the benefit of their expert counsel. These include Professor Otis Pease of the University of Washington; my colleagues Professors Lawrence Lee, James High, and Linda Kerber; and Mrs. George Greene. Listing my wife Charlotte last belies my special debt to her for her unflagging patience as well as help and encouragement during our Franklin years.

THOMAS H. WENDEL

San Jose State University
San Jose, California

I Apprentice

THE LIFE OF Benjamin Franklin, spanning the eighteenth century, is illustrative of the opportunities open to talent in colonial America. A new society had need of abilities of every sort, particularly technical skills such as printing in which Franklin became a master. He benefitted also in that he grew to maturity in the innovating atmosphere of the eighteenth century Enlightenment. The period's reliance upon reason to break through the inhibiting conventions of tradition had singular appeal to the young American. Franklin was a philosopher and a budding man of letters by the time he was a teenager. The ease with which he made his way through life resulted in part from his rigorous self-training of both mind and body for a successful career. It was also a consequence of the influence of new ideas upon the relatively unstructured society of the New World.

Franklin was not the only colonial to take advantage of the immense scope offered the enterprising along the frontier of the British Empire. The complementary relationship between ideas and social reality, in fact, led an entire generation to prosecute a war of independence against the mother country. But Franklin stood at the focal point where the influence of the American environment converged with the stimulation of liberating ideas. His life testified to the dynamic potential of these forces. So did the founding of the American nation in which he played a crucial role.

Circumstances and ability go far to explain Franklin's rise to world fame. Heredity may explain his inexhaustible physical vitality. Franklin was descended from a long line of blacksmith-ancestors stretching back into the mists of time in the little village of Ecton, sixty-six miles north of London. These

Ecton Franklins displayed a streak of independent-minded-
ness in their "Zeal against Popery," as Franklin expressed
it, during the mid-sixteenth century when Queen Mary I
labored to bring England back within the folds of the Roman
Catholic Church. One of Franklin's more immediate forebears, his uncle Thomas, also showed traits similar to that
of his famous nephew. Rising to local prominence in parish
affairs, Thomas was well known for his inventiveness and
public spirit. Another uncle, Benjamin, had something of his
namesake's bookish interests. From England, when Franklin
was a boy, this uncle sent him avuncular advice in didactic
rhyme. Franklin's father Josiah was a silk dyer by trade and
a religious nonconformist. Long before the birth of his famous son, during the persecuting days of the later Stuart
Kings, he took sail with his wife Anne and their three children for Boston.

After the death of Anne following the birth of her seventh
child, Josiah married Abiah Folger of Nantucket. By this
marriage, Josiah's progeny was increased to the grand total
of seventeen of which Benjamin, the last son, would be number fifteen. Abiah's father, Peter, was one of the earliest settlers of the island. A friend to the Indian whom he schooled
in reading and writing, Peter Folger was equally an enemy
of religious bigotry. His poem, "A Looking-Glass for the
Times," criticised the Massachusetts ministry for the "sin of
persecution." Peter Folger, like his grandson Benjamin
Franklin, practiced the gospel of toleration in times less
propitious for freedom than those in which the latter lived.

When Benjamin Franklin was born in Boston in 1706, the
last of the Stuart monarchs sat upon the English throne while
on the continent there raged the War of the Spanish Succession. That very year Louis XIV suffered a horrendous defeat
at Ramillies. Two years previously, the war, spilling over into
America, had eventuated in the bloody Deerfield massacre.

In 1706, the English were still almost a half a century away from accepting the Gregorian calendar, so that the birth of Franklin may be recorded as January 6, 1705, old style, or January 17, 1706, new style.

The Massachusetts Bay Colony at the time of Franklin's birth was less than one generation past the witchcraft delusion at Salem. The Mathers, father and son, still struggled to preserve the ancient admonition of Governor John Winthrop to his people to build "a City upon a Hill." Yet Boston was a rapidly growing seaport of nine thousand people, whose eyes were less on the hereafter than on the main chance. Boston's merchant ships plied the seven seas in a vast and complicated commerce. This commerce made Boston the first city on the American continent until Philadelphia after midcentury surpassed her. To young men of ambition and spirit, the sea provided opportunity and adventure. To them, she sang her eternal siren song.

One of Ben's older brothers, to his father's "great vexation," as Ben put it, had listened and succumbed. Seeing a similar faraway look in his younger boy's eyes, Josiah Franklin hastened to find him a trade. This boy from the beginning had been a precocious lad. Josiah Franklin's first thought was for Ben to prepare for Harvard and a church career, but he changed his mind after observing the impoverished circumstances of the ministry. Instead, after two years of schooling during which he excelled in letters but failed in mathematics, the ten year old Ben entered his father's shop to learn Josiah's new trade of a tallow chandler and soap boiler. But cutting wicks for candles could not compensate for hoped-for adventure across the seas. Ben hated the work, and Josiah had the wisdom again to seek new alternatives.

Another brother James, returning to Boston from London where he had acquired a certain worldliness, in 1717 set himself up as a printer. Ben's proclivity for books indicated

that this might be the right road for him as well. To forestall
his wanderlust, Ben was apprenticed to James for a term of
nine years. In return for his room and board, Ben was to work
for his brother from whom he would learn the printer's trade.
At the age of twelve, Benjamin Franklin found his vocation.

In these early years, the future statesman had rapidly
matured. His father's crowded household afforded Ben, not
unlike the biblical Benjamin, the security of love and the
spirit of sociability. Ben could remember thirteen sitting at
one time at his father's table. Josiah frequently included, he
recalled, "some sensible Friend or Neighbor, to converse with
and always took care to start some ingenious or useful Topic
for Discourse, which might tend to improve the Minds of his
Children." The sagacious Josiah, though too burdened with
domestic responsibilities to cut a figure in politics, was nevertheless sought out by others for advice, as Franklin put it,
"in prudential matters, both in private and publick affairs." [1]

Franklin never forgot his father's prudential wisdom. A
half a century later, when he sat down to begin his memoirs,
he recounted how he as a boy led his friends in the construction of a wharf, using stone intended for a new house in the
neighborhood. When upbraided by his father for using that
which was not his, Ben replied that the wharf was useful. But
the father soon convinced his son, "that nothing was useful
that was not honest." From his earliest years, Ben absorbed
from his father a homely philosophy of practical morality
which he would later raise to the stature of a science.

Young Ben early proved himself a leader among his
friends. He became an excellent swimmer, an activity to
which he was devoted all his life. Indeed, as a young man in
England, he nearly gave up his career to become a swimming
instructor to the sons of the gentry. His expertise at water
sports included his great ability in handling boats. "When in
a Boat or Canoe with other Boys," he recalled, "I was com-

monly allowed to govern, especially in any case of Difficulty; and upon other Occasions I was generally a Leader among the Boys, and sometimes led them into Scrapes. . . ." [2] But Ben's activities, sometimes misguided as in the case of the pilfered stone, were, as in that case, generally directed toward useful purposes.

Of all his interests, he found reading the most beguiling. He must have discovered this pleasure very young, for he could not later recall a time when he was unable to read. Although his father's library was weighted with sermons and theological works which proved of little value to the boy, there were also available Daniel Defoe's *Essay on Projects* and Cotton Mather's *Essays To Do Good.* Franklin read both with much pleasure. His future to a large extent would seem a fulfillment of these works. Defoe suggested to the boy the rich possibilities of social action for the betterment of mankind. Likewise Mather, pillar of the old order and leading intellectual of the Bay Colony, insisted upon the obligation of philanthropy and the duty of each man to do good toward his fellow men. Ignoring Mather's religious philosophy, the young boy absorbed from him the Puritan ethic minus its theological foundations. Utilizing the pseudonym Silence Dogood in his first essays, Franklin poked gentle fun at the not-so-silent Mather. He was also acknowledging the profound influence exercised upon him by the older man.

If Defoe and Mather were prime influences on Franklin, so were Plutarch and Bunyan, whose *Pilgrim's Progress* delighted him with its mingling of narrative and dialogue. Stylistically less pleasing, but full of exciting tales of history and romance, of science and biography, was Burton's *Historical Collections.* Franklin purchased these forty small volumes by selling his collection of Bunyan's works. Another more eccentric book, Thomas Tryon's *The Way to Health,* confirmed the young man, who was something of a health faddist, in a belief in vegetarianism. His forswearance of meat not only complied with the new doctrine, but allowed him to live more frugally so that he had more money for books. By the time of his apprenticeship, Franklin was well advanced in self-education, if not in formal schooling. His new position, although time consuming, did not discourage him.

Although books provided Franklin with his chief nourishment, he learned also through conversation with his peers. He took great delight in disputation with another bookish lad, his friend John Collins. When the two boys decided to put their differences in writing, although Ben usually made the better points, young Collins showed a rhetorical advantage. Ben thereupon set himself to improve his prose style. Seizing time on Sundays when others were at church, or during lunch hours instead of tarrying over food and drink, Franklin schooled himself in prose composition. His method was to emulate that palladium of eighteenth century elegance, the *Spectator*. Published in London by Joseph Addison and Richard Steele, this periodical taught London's ambitious middle class the grace and manners of proper discourse. Franklin would cast some of the *Spectator*'s pieces into poetry and then back into prose, thereby enlarging his vocabulary and enriching his style. He would make a haphazard list of the themes of a particular essay and then rearrange them to teach himself order and continuity in the flow of ideas. Franklin later attributed his successful career to his mastery of the language in which he would have no superiors and few peers in the colonial period.

Although prose was Franklin's medium, his first public exercises were two poetic ballads composed at about the age of thirteen, which he later denominated "wretched Stuff." One, entitled the *Lighthouse Tragedy,* memorialized the recent drowning of "Captain Worthilake, with his Two Daughters." The other celebrated the demise of Blackbeard the pirate. James set up the two pieces and had Ben hawk them about town. The *Lighthouse Tragedy* sold wonderfully, "the Event being recent, having made a great Noise," as Franklin recalled. Its success considerably puffed up the young author. But he was soon deflated by his prudent father who ridiculed his poetic performances and explained to Ben that "Verse-makers were generally Beggars." [3]

The self-education of Benjamin Franklin meanwhile continued. Perusing a book purporting to refute deistic attacks upon the Christian religion, the sixteen year old Ben found the refutations less convincing than the antichristian arguments. The works of Anthony Collins, an infamous name to the orthodox, further schooled Franklin in rational theology. Likewise, the essays of the third Earl of Shaftesbury, who like Collins could not accept the miracles of the Bible, confirmed Franklin's faith in reason against revelation, and in works as against faith. The young reader became a disciple of the English Enlightenment. For the terrible Jehovah of the Old Testament, he would substitute a divine creator of a rational universe in which miracles were impossible transgressions against natural law. For the Christian God of love who sent his son Jesus to live and die among men, Franklin would substitute a moral imperative: to do good toward all mankind. Accepting Christian ethics, Franklin, to the horror of many good Boston folk, rejected the formalities of organized religion.

Another of Franklin's instructors was that preceptor of Athenian youth, Socrates. It was less Socrates the sage that influenced Ben than Socrates the sophist. Heretofore, in disputation Franklin would present his case with "abrupt Contradiction and positive Argumentation." Now, having absorbed the Socratic method, he "put on the humble Enquirer and Doubter." He found it safest to expound his antichristian ideas in this way, frequently tricking others into dialectical traps he quietly prepared for them. Although he would forgo this method over the years, he never gave up the Socratic manner. Indirection, wit, and feigned humility became the media through which he would influence his world.

As Franklin matured intellectually—his studies included arithmetic which he finally mastered, navigation, and Lockean psychology—he also gave intimations of the inventiveness that would be so characteristic of his genius. To improve his swimming speed he fashioned paddles affixed to his hands and feet, giving him greater power in the water. He also utilized a kite to pull him across the water as he floated on his back while holding the kite string. During these early years, Franklin also gained considerable mechanical ability which later enabled him to fashion his own tools and equipment necessary for perfecting and testing his inventions and scientific hypotheses. The many-sidedness which became Franklin's hallmark was manifest while he was still a boy.

Foremost of Franklin's early abilities, however, was that with the pen. Ben's employer-brother James decided to begin a newspaper which, as Benjamin later not altogether accurately stated, was "the second that appeared in America." Although many persons tried to dissuade James from the undertaking, "one Newspaper being in their judgment enough for America," James, undaunted, brought out the first issue of the *New-England Courant,* actually the fourth colonial paper, on August 7, 1721.[4] It was a remarkable sheet for the time and place. In emulation of the *Spectator,* James printed light essays frequently satirizing either the clergy or the colony government. Young Ben had his chance when he anonymously left a letter from "Silence Dogood" under the office door. Ben was flattered when, not knowing the true identity of the author, James and his friends pronounced his composition admirable stuff and published it forthwith. In all, Franklin published fourteen Dogood letters, in one of which he had the temerity to take on that sacred cow Harvard College. Many of her graduates, wrote Franklin, "liv'd as poor as Church Mice, being unable to dig, and ashamed to beg, and to live by their Wits it was impossible." Franklin also showed a knowledge of men when he listed the way in which they tried to camouflage a certain condition. "They are seldom known to be *drunk,*" he wrote, "tho' they are very often,

> *cogey, tipsey, fox'd, merry, fuddl'd, groatable, Confound-edly cut, See two Moons, are among the Philistines, In a very good Humour, See the Sun, or The Sun has shown upon them; they Clip the king's English, are Almost froze, Feavourish, In their Altitudes, Pretty well enter'd, & c.*[5]

The *Courant's* antiministerial bias brought it vilification from both Cotton and Increase Mather. Its remarks upon the manners and morals of the times posed to the ministry the threat of competition: the clergy, not the press, was supposed to be the guardian of the peoples' morals. Nor did the politicians feel any the kindlier toward this paper which dared to criticize their administration of public affairs. Jailed once for a slur upon the government, James was supposed to be effectively silenced when the legislature ordered that "James Franklin should no longer print the paper called the *New England Courant.*" But James was not so easily defeated. In circumvention of the legislative order, he named Ben publisher of the *Courant.* At the same time, James publicly released Ben from his apprenticeship. Privately, however, he made Ben sign a new contract for the completion of his service.

Although this arrangement worked for a time, Ben resented his brother's short temper and his blows, and he chaffed at the secret indenture which seemed to be a sort of slavery. Knowing that James would not wish to divulge the contract by which he remained an apprentice, Ben informed his brother that he was quitting as "publisher" of the *Courant*. James was caught in a deception of his own making. He was forced to give Ben his freedom, but he saw to it that no other printer in Boston would offer the young man a position. The adventurous lad's father, moreover, sided with James in the dispute.

With the printing trade closed to him in Boston and with his father opposed to his position, Ben's prospects had suddenly declined. His reputation in the town, furthermore, was none of the best because of his heterodox religious opinions. It was time to try his luck elsewhere. Fearing his family would attempt to detain him, he kept his decision to leave to himself. He sold some of his books to raise a little money. Then, in September, 1723, he quietly slipped away from kinsmen, friends and neighbors to arrive in New York after a three-day journey. He was "near 300 Miles away from home, a Boy of but 17," he later wrote, "without the least Recommendation to or knowledge of any Person in the Place, and with very little Money in my Pocket." [6]

But he had a trade. Old William Bradford, pioneer publisher and printer first in Philadelphia and now in New York, was the sole pressman in the town of about seven thousand people. Bradford had no work for Ben, but suggested that the young man go on to Philadelphia, where his printer-son Andrew Bradford might need a hand. Ben accepted the opportunity with alacrity, although the one-hundred mile journey through wind and rain, by foot and leaky ship, proved arduous in the extreme.

When Franklin finally arrived in the Quaker city, wet, cold, tired, and hungry, pockets "stuff'd out with Shirts and Stockings," he cut a sorry figure indeed. Walking up Market Street from the wharf, he determined to buy some bread for his supper. Instead, because of his lack of familiarity with the Philadelphia bakers' lingo, he found himself encumbered with "three great Puffy Rolls." So accoutered, Ben trudged past the house of his future wife Deborah Read, who, "standing at the Door saw me, and thought I made as I certainly did a most awkward ridiculous Appearance." [7] At last, after returning to the river for a drink of water, the bedraggled lad fell in with a group of people who led him to the Quaker meeting house. In the evening he would find a room and the next day a job. But for the present, worn with the fatigue of his journey, enveloped by the reverent silence of the Quaker meeting, Philadelphia's future first citizen fell fast asleep.

II Printer

WHEN FRANKLIN ARRIVED in Pennsylvania in October, 1723, the colony appeared to have no more of a future than he did. An economic depression had descended upon the province. Recalling his arrival in the capital city, Franklin remembered seeing "most of the Houses in Walnut Street between Second and Front Streets with Bills on their Doors, to be let; and many likewise in Chestnut Street, and other Streets; which made me then think the Inhabitants of the City were one after another deserting it." [1] But the town, like the young tradesman, had a calling. As thousands of Europe's persecuted and improverished people poured into Pennsylvania, Philadelphia would become the principal entrepôt for Britain's American empire. Franklin and Philadelphia would rise together. Their achievements would signify the emergence of a unique American civilization of which Franklin would be its chief ornament and his adopted city its cultural center.

The depression that Franklin noted marked only a pause in the city's phenomenal growth. The year of Franklin's arrival, Philadelphia boasted some ten thousand of the forty thousand people of Pennsylvania. Granted by Charles II to William Penn in 1681, this proprietary colony had undergone none of the usual birth pangs of colonial settlement. Penn's exemplary attitude toward the Indians (he believed them to be of the "Hebrew race," possibly one of the lost tribes of Israel) guaranteed several generations of peace along the frontier. An early exponent of city planning, the founder mapped his city of brotherly love along a rational grid system. Between the Schuylkill and the Delaware Rivers were laid out nine broad streets with names drawn from the trees and fruits native to Pennsylvania. Twenty-one numbered streets crossed these at right angles. William Penn envisioned a quiet "green country town," at peace with itself and with the world. Pennsylvania's domestic politics, nevertheless, would be anything but peaceful. The colony, furthermore, could not remain immune from the wars of the mother country. Penn's capital, in fact, became the bustling metropolis of a flourishing agricultural domain, and the center of a world-wide seaborne commerce. The southern colonies and the West Indies particularly became dependent on the produce of Pennsylvania's fertile land. By mid-century, Philadelphia would be the second city of the British Empire, only London leading it in population.

William Penn had established his "Holy Experiment" principally as a haven for the persecuted Society of Friends, the Quakers of England. Franklin, though he could not share their theology, had much in common with Quaker beliefs. One of these was pacifism. The peace loving Quakers, however, were divided on the admissibility of defensive war. Franklin's position was very close to that of the so-called defense Quakers who, while hating war, were willing to participate in defensive measures. Another Quaker doctrine with which Franklin agreed was religious toleration. Another was Quaker repudiation of artificial social distinctions. Franklin, with the Quakers, believed in the basic equality of men. In all, the Boston boy found the Quaker atmosphere of Philadelphia entirely congenial.

Although Quakers may never have made up a numerical majority of the population (it was estimated in 1702 that they were but one-half the population; later immigration brought a preponderance of non-Quakers), they formed the economic and political elite of the colony. It was a tribute to Franklin's abilities that he, a non-Quaker, would assume the leadership of their party in the Assembly. A temperamentally antiauthoritarian people, the Quakers demanded of Penn from the beginning a more liberal constitution than he, constrained by the fears of many of his first purchasers of land, had originally granted.

In 1701, Penn at last acceded to the colonists' demands by granting Pennsylvania the famous Charter of Liberties, which would be Pennsylvania's constitution to 1776. Here was to be found the fundamental law under which Franklin would live and in the administration of which he was to become a key figure. By it, political power resided in the annually elected Assembly which was made up of the elected representatives of the city of Philadelphia and of the several counties of Pennsylvania. Unlike those of the other English colonies, the appointed Governor's Council had no legislative powers and could not participate in the lawmaking process other than to advise the Governor. That official was also appointed by William Penn (or after his death his heirs) to act as his deputy in the colony. In accordance with the proprietor's desires, usually formalized in written instructions, the Governor could either veto bills passed by the Assembly or sign them into law. As might be expected, the Assembly, which provided the Governor's salary, could usually bend him to its will, which was frequently contrary to the wishes of the proprietor. Just as the Assembly successfully curbed proprietary authority through its exercise of the power of the purse, so too it retained unusual immunity from royal supervision. By a peculiar quirk in the royal charter by which Penn received his princely domain, Pennsylvania's laws could stand a full five years before review by the Crown. If the Crown did not then act within six months, such laws were automatically confirmed.

Thus it was that Pennsylvania's legislative Assembly, in which Franklin would play a commanding role, was an all but autonomous governing body continually challenging the prerogatives of proprietor and Crown. Its quest for power was paralleled by a similar quest on the part of the assemblies of the other English North American colonies. These assemblies, in fact, were unique engines of government in the world of the eighteenth century. Although frequently led by an oligarchy of wealthy and talented men, the colonial assemblies provided a seedbed for democracy. Each was a miniature House of Commons, jealous of its dignity and protective of its privileges. In each colonial assembly, the office of speaker of the house to which Franklin would be elected in Pennsylvania, was the keystone in the edifice of colonial representative government. Republican forms were old in America many years before the Revolution. When the colonies became states, they had already practiced more than a measure of self-government. Pennsylvania's Assembly, unchecked by a legislative upper house and with its members representing a relatively broad electorate, was second to none in its assertion of freedom from outside control.

Pennsylvania's liberal religious and political institutions as well as economic opportunity invited the poor, the adventuring, and the oppressed from Europe. Although in 1723, when Franklin arrived, flood tide had not yet been reached, in the next decades thousands of persons from the Germanies, from Ulster, from England, Scotland and Wales, and to a lesser degree from the other countries of Europe would turn Pennsylvania into a melting pot of nations. The African came too, though not of his own volition, to help provide the labor in fields, mines and shops that produced the various products of Pennsylvania industry. The presence of slavery in the midst of a commonwealth that was supposed to be holy was a standing affront to many pious Quakers including the abolitionist John Woolman, but unfortunately not to all his coreligionists.

Pennsylvania then, in spite of economic setbacks that in

large part reflected changing conditions in the mother country, was a thriving young province. Her tolerance, openness, economic opportunity, impatience with restraint, her veritable babble of tongues and ideas all gave the young Franklin and many other Philadelphians abundant scope and opportunity to find fulfillment. Something of the spirit of the place in which Franklin would thrive was remarked by the teacher, Gottlieb Mittelberger, who, during his American sojourn, 1750–1754, recorded a saying he had heard: "Pennsylvania is heaven for farmers, paradise for artisans, and hell for officials and preachers." The system of liberty under which Pennsylvanians lived, Mittelberger observed, "makes them all equal." [2]

If equality means opportunities open to talent, Franklin's approach to Andrew Bradford the day after his arrival in the city seemed to disprove the rule. Like his father in New York, Andrew Bradford had no place for the young journeyman, but he sent him on to the printing shop of Samuel Keimer. This eccentric individual, part charlatan, part visionary, had recently arrived in Philadelphia following a stormy career in London, where he had several times been imprisoned for seditious libel. There was a place in Penn's province for an innovating printer. The "very illiterate" Bradford (Franklin's words) exercised a printing monopoly. But Keimer had neither the industry, the skill, nor the common sense to succeed in the undertaking. He had need of a lad of Franklin's expertise. "I endeavour'd to put his Press (which he had not yet us'd, and of which he understood nothing) into Order fit to be work'd with," Franklin recalled. [3] From this beginning, Franklin found permanent work and shortly became indispensable to Keimer, for whom he had little respect.

In the following weeks, Franklin found permanent lodging at the house of John Read, his future father-in-law, and made "acquaintance among the young People of the Town, that were Lovers of Reading with whom I spent my Evenings very pleasantly. . . ." [4] He lived frugally and, "forgetting Boston as much as I could," successfully began to carve a life for himself in his adopted city. But for the intercession of the provincial governor, Franklin might conceivably have settled prematurely into a comfortable life informed only through books of the marvellous stimulation of the English Enlightenment.

As it was, Governor Sir William Keith became the medium by which Franklin first travelled to England. At the time, Keith, an impecunious Scottish baronet, was locked in a struggle with the family of William Penn, who had died in 1718. The dispute concerned economic policies to deal with the depression in the colony. The Assembly desired to issue paper money to supply an adequate medium of exchange. It proposed a loan office that would loan out legal tender paper bills on the security of real or personal property such as silver plate. Keith supported this scheme against the instructions of the new proprietors, William Penn's heirs. They feared that paper money would decline in value and thereby reduce the value of their rents and other proprietary dues. They also distrusted the political power that would accrue to the Assembly were it permitted to exercise an independent economic role. The new proprietors' merchant friends in England likewise feared the deleterious effects of inflation. Keith, signing into law the Assembly's paper-money legislation, knew that he risked dismissal from the governorship, but he hoped to avoid this event by maintaining his popularity with the people. With the public behind him, Keith believed, the proprietors would not dare fire him. A remarkably modern politician, he recognized the power of the press, and it is in this connection that the young Franklin entered into his calculations.

Franklin's literary ability was early recognized by the Gov-

ernor to whom the young man's brother-in-law, shipmaster
Robert Holmes, had given a letter in which Franklin had
explained his reasons for leaving Boston. One day, to the
astonishment of Keimer and his workmen, Sir William himself paid a visit to the shop. Keimer naturally assumed that
the Governor had come to see him. What must have been
his diasppointment when the great man asked for Franklin!
Together the Governor and the journeyman left the shop for
the tavern to drink a glass of madeira, as Keimer stared, in
Franklin's words, "like a Pig poison'd." [5] Keith wanted to
set up Franklin as public printer. The only problem was
finding the money necessary to establish a printing shop. The
Governor believed that Franklin might borrow the funds
from his father, so Franklin soon found himself home again
with an appeal for funds from no less a person than the
governor of Pennsylvania.

Josiah Franklin, happy as he was to see the prodigal returned and pleased with Ben's progress, nevertheless suspected Keith's judgment in patronizing one so young. Ben,
he believed, was not yet ready for so great a responsibility;
he refused the loan. Josiah's doubts of Ben's maturity were
vindicated when, on the return voyage to Philadelphia, the
lad was very nearly ensnared by two attractive young women,
thieves as it turned out, whose charms he resisted only with
the earnest pleading of "a grave, sensible Matron-like Quaker-
Woman," who fortunately gave him timely warning.[6] Ben
showed his immaturity too when he agreed to receive a debt
in Pennsylvania owed to one Samuel Vernon of Newport,
Rhode Island. Ben did collect the money but instead of sending it to Vernon, he spent it. Vernon, fortunately, did not
immediately ask him for the money, but for several years Ben
lived in constant dread of its being called. His return trip to
Philadelphia was not, however, altogether disastrous. In New
York, Governor Burnet (son of the great Bishop-historian),

hearing of a bookish lad aboard ship, sent for Franklin, showed him his extensive library," and we had a good deal of Conversation about Books and Authors. This was the second Governor," Franklin noted, "who had done me the Honour to take Notice of me, which to a poor Boy like me was very pleasing." [7]

Back in Philadelphia with his father's refusal, Franklin found Governor Keith undaunted in his plans. The Governor would send the lad, equipped with letters of credit, to England to purchase the press, type and other equipment necessary to establish a small printing house. Meanwhile, while awaiting the sailing of his ship, Franklin would continue with Keimer. Returned with him to Philadelphia was his boyhood friend, John Collins. Unfortunately, the companion of his youth had become a dissolute and irresponsible drifter who begged money from Franklin only to spend it on drink. The break between the two youths came when one day on an outing in the river with several friends, Collins refused his turn at rowing. Angered at Franklin's insistence that he pull his share, Collins came at him as if to strike him. But the muscular Ben was ready. "I clapt my Hand under his Crutch, and rising pitch'd him head-foremost into the River." [8] After this day, the doubly sodden Collins soon accepted an offer as a tutor in the West Indies, never paying back to Franklin the money he had borrowed.

Young as he was, Franklin's strength and stability prepared him well for the coming London venture. So did his flexibility in adjusting philosophy to desire. On the voyage from Boston, the erstwhile vegetarian's mouth watered as the passengers prepared some cod freshly hauled in from New England waters. As the fish "came hot out of the Frying Pan," Franklin relates, "it smelt admirably well. I balanc'd some time between Principle and Inclination: till I recollected, that when the Fish were opened, I saw smaller Fish

taken out of their Stomachs: Then thought I, if you eat one
another, I don't see why we mayn't eat you. So I din'd upon
Cod very heartily. . . . So convenient a thing it is to be a
reasonable Creature, since it enables one to find or make a
Reason for every thing one has a mind to do." [9]

As the time for departure drew near, Franklin awaited the
promised letters of credit from his friend Governor Keith.
But Keith had meanwhile failed in his struggle with the proprietors who in England were effecting his replacement. Fatally embroiled with the proprietary leaders, Keith, with no
credit to give, became unavailable to his protégé who sailed
aboard the *London Hope* in November, 1724, in the mistaken
belief that his benefactor's letters were stowed aboard in the
ship's mail bags. After a seven-week passage, Franklin arrived in London. Once again, he was cast adrift in a strange
city. There were, however, some differences between his London and his Philadelphia beginnings. This time he left behind
not his family but the girl he hoped to marry, Deborah Read,
she who had stood in the doorway as he passed by on that
first day in Philadelphia. And this time, too, he had with him
a young companion, James Ralph, would-be poet who, aban-
doning wife and child, accompanied Franklin for the literary
opportunities of London.

Franklin seemed not to resent Governor Keith's failure to
provide the promised letters of credit. "Having little to give,
he gave expectations," wrote Franklin of the Pennsylvania
governor, whom he magnanimously further assessed as "a
good Governor for the People, tho' not for his Constituents
the Proprietaries, whose Instructions he sometimes disre-
garded." [10] But for Keith, who has the merit of early recogniz-
ing Franklin's genius, Franklin would not at age eighteen
have found himself in London—an experience which
markedly broadened his horizons and profoundly influenced
his future.

In the exhilarating year and a half which the provincial youth spent in the great city, he found work at two of the outstanding English printing firms, Palmer's and Watt's. It was London in the age of Pope and Defoe; Jonathan Swift in his Irish exile was about to loose Gulliver upon the world. It was the age of Walpole when the new wealth created a richly varied culture and the coffee houses abounded in wit and lively conversation. Caught up in the spirit of the place, Franklin gained minor notoriety when he published his *Dissertation on Liberty and Necessity.* His essay is a workmanlike example of the philosophical materialism which some radical thinkers deduced from the Newtonian concept of natural law. Man, according to the young Franklin, is an integral part of the universal machine. He is guided by two forces, pleasure and pain, that compliment one another in exact proportion. Pain and evil exist as the means toward equilibrium. It was a doctrine that could be used to justify questionable means to personal gratification of whatever sort. Franklin was soon to consider his temporary adherence to and dissemination of materialism to be, as to put it, one of the great *errata* of his life.

His *Dissertation,* however, was the means by which Franklin was introduced to the London literati, most notably to the famed cynic, Bernard Mandeville, whose *Fable of the Bees* showed civilization to be a product of man's vices rather than his virtues. Franklin also met Dr. Henry Pemberton, a collaborator of Sir Isaac Newton. Although Pemberton's promise to introduce him to Newton failed to materialize, Franklin did meet Sir Hans Sloane, president of the Royal College of Physicians. To Sloane, who soon succeeded Newton as president of the Royal Society, Franklin wrote a letter describing a curious asbestos purse which he had brought with him from "the Northern Parts of America." Sloane, who was an avid collector of curiosities, bought Franklin's purse. It can now

be seen in the British Museum, to which Sloane gave his
books and specimens as part of its original collection.

London not only furthered Franklin's intellectual growth,
but also offered other less ethereal opportunities. It was the
same London that in the next decade Dr. Johnson would view
with jaundiced eye:

> Here malice, rapine, accident, conspire
> And now a rabble rages, now a fire;
> Their ambush here relentless ruffians lay,
> And here the fell attorney prowls for prey;
> Here falling houses thunder on your head,
> And here a female atheist talks you dead.

There were of course, pleasanter pitfalls than death by chat-
ter. One example was the ease of opportunity for satisfaction
of "that hard-to-be govern'd Passion of Youth," as Franklin
put it, most indiscretely when he propositioned his friend
Ralph's mistress. Ralph, like Collins before him, had proved
a burden to the generous Franklin. But Franklin's indiscretion, Ralph believed, had cancelled his debts to the virile
philosopher. Amidst the temptations of cosmopolitan London, Franklin neglected Deborah Read, to whom he failed
to write. He was living the moral ambiguities of his neces-
sitarian pamphlet. He was restless and disatisfied. Should he
become a swimming instructor to the sons of the rich? Should
he travel about Europe supporting himself by his trade? The
Philadelphia Quaker Thomas Denham, a shipboard acquaintance on the passage out, advised him against these
plans. Denham was opening a store back home and offered
Franklin the position of clerk and bookkeeper. The young
man eagerly accepted. He left London without regret and in
high anticipation of being once again in his adopted Philadelphia.

On the long homeward voyage during the late summer of

1726, Franklin kept a journal in which he recorded several sober resolves that would, if obeyed, help restore greater moral balance to his so-far checkered career. Recalling the Vernon debt, he would be "extremely frugal . . . till I have paid what I owe." He would "aim at sincerity in every word and action—the most amiable excellence in a rational being." He would avoid "any foolish project of growing suddenly rich; for industry and patience are the surest means of plenty." And finally, "I resolve to speak ill of no man whatsoever. . . ." [11] These were not the commitments of a man wedded to an amoral philosophy. He was not only putting London behind him physically, but also leaving behind the philosophical mood in which he had lost his moral bearings.

The *Journal,* besides giving evidence of a moral regeneration, also evinces Franklin's interest in science. He calculated the ship's longitude from the magnitude and duration of an eclipse. He observed the "lustre and fine colours" of the dolphin and noted their loss when the animal was taken from the water; yet pieces cut from a living dolphin retained their color after the dolphin died. Most significantly, Franklin devised an experiment to discover if the tiny crabs he found among some sea weed were the result of a metamorphosis comparable to that undergone by silkworms and butterflies. Here was an example of patient testing of a theory, erroneous in this case, but the method of which would have astonishing results in later years in several fields of scientific endeavor.

The *Journal* closes with a "Thank God!" at his arrival in Philadelphia. Franklin and Denham set up their store with the goods they had brought with them. But before long, both men became sick; Denham died, while Franklin survived a near fatal attack of pleurisy. The new store closed its doors and Franklin, mourning the loss of his kindly benefactor, returned to his own trade as manager of the printing shop of Samuel Keimer, who himself minded the stationery end

of the business. As for Deborah Read, Franklin was cha-
grined to find that because of his neglect, she had married
another. She was now miserably unhappy, suspecting her
husband of bigamy and refusing to live with him. Feeling that
his "Giddiness and Inconstancy when in London" were partially responsible for her plight, Franklin would soon make
up the debt he believed he owed her.

The relationship between Keimer and his master printer
was a precarious one. Keimer was envious of Franklin's brilliance and ability, yet the young man was essential to Keimer's business, particularly when it garnered the lucrative job
of printing neighboring New Jersey's paper money. Franklin
contrived the first copperplate press in the country and
created the required cuts and type for ornamentation of the
bills. In New Jersey, much to Keimer's annoyance, it was
Franklin who was feted by the assemblymen and other important men of the province, men whose friendship, Franklin
wrote, was "afterwards of great Use to me, as I occasionally
was to some of them."

Franklin's opportunity to strike out on his own came when
the father of one of Keimer's journeymen, Hugh Meredith,
upon whom Franklin exercised a stabilizing influence, lent
the two young men the necessary funds to set up their own
printing establishment. Like his brother James in Boston,
Franklin determined to start a newspaper, the only other
such sheet in the colony being Bradford's lackluster *American
Weekly Mercury*. But before Franklin's plans could jell,
crafty Keimer heard of them and immediately started his own
paper with the grandiloquent title, *The Universal Instructor
in all Arts and Sciences: and Pennsylvania Gazette*. Franklin,
in retaliation, now lent his talents to Bradford in order to
brighten the *Mercury* and lessen Keimer's chances of success.
It was not difficult to satirize Keimer's foolish project of
serializing in his paper Chamber's *Encylopedia* from A to Z,

particularly when the fatuous editor early in the A's printed Chamber's article on abortion. "Martha Careful" and "Caelia Shortface," i.e. Franklin, huffily complained in the columns of the *Mercury*. Wrote "Martha Careful,"

> If [Keimer] proceed farther to Expose the Secrets of our Sex, in That audacious manner, as he hath done in his Gazette, No. 5. under the Letters, A.B.O. To be read in all *Taverns* and *Coffee-Houses,* and by the Vulgar: I say if he Publish any more of that kind. . . . my Sister Molly and my Self, with some others, are Resolved to run the Hazard of taking him by the Beard, at the next Place we meet him, and make an Example of him for his Immodesty.[12]

The popular success of Mesdames Careful and Shortface encouraged their creator to follow up with a series of essays from a Caelia-like character curiously named, "the Busy-Body." Franklin's new creation added considerable attraction to Bradford's hitherto grey paper. Keimer was one obvious target of the Busy-Body's satire. He was foolish enough to complain publicly which naturally increased the number of the Busy-Body's readers. The Busy-Body essays have an earthy humor similar to that of Henry Fielding, whose literary career, like Franklin's, was beginning at this time. The Busy-Body, for instance, receives a letter from "Patience," (Franklin) who complains of having to care for her thoughtless neighbor's children: "Thus, Sir, I have all the Trouble and Pesterment of Children, without the Pleasure of—calling them my own." [13] Philadelphia citizens were amused enough to forego Keimer's ponderous *Universal Instructor* for Bradford's *Mercury* with its waggish Busy-Body.

The result was that with his creditors closing in on him Keimer sold his newspaper to Franklin, who continued it as the *Pennsylvania Gazette.* Keimer's clumsy sheet immediately became the finest weekly published in the colonies. It was a preeminence which later would be seriously challenged as newspapers came to flourish in the busy port towns of America. But it was Franklin who first set the standard which later publishers would have to meet. The *Gazette* not only published extracts from the London journals, as did Bradford's *Mercury*, but also more local news and announcements, as well as advertisements, squibs and essays by local authors, most notably by the editor himself. One of these, occuring only in the second issue of the paper, helped Franklin and the *Gazette* to establish a wide readership. The matter concerned Governor Burnet, now of Massachusetts, who insisted that the Massachusetts Assembly provide him with a regular salary rather than make him annual grants as was the usual practice. Franklin took the Assembly's side, and in so doing, penned his first statement concerning colonial rights for which it seemed to him the Massachusetts Assembly was fighting. "Their happy Mother Country will perhaps observe with Pleasure," wrote Franklin,

> that tho' her gallant Cocks and matchless Dogs abate their native Fire and Intrepidity when transported to a Foreign Clime (as the common Notion is) yet her SONS in the remotest Part of the Earth, and even to the third and fourth Descent, still retain that ardent Spirit of Liberty, and that undaunted Courage in the Defence of it, which has in every Age so gloriously distinguished BRITONS and ENGLISHMEN from all the Rest of Mankind.

Commentary such as this soon gained for the *Gazette* a commanding lead over the *Mercury* even though Bradford as postmaster franked his paper while excluding Franklin's from the use of his post riders. The *Gazette*, a sober and dependable source of news, usually cautious in its comments upon established institutions, was nevertheless anything but dull. Its readers were delighted to come upon such items as the following:

> [Saturday last] an unhappy Man one Sturgis, upon some Difference with his Wife, determined to drown himself in the River; and she, (kind Wife) went with him, it seems, to see it faithfully performed and accordingly stood by silent and unconcerned during the whole Transaction: He jump'd in near Carpenter's Wharff, but was timely taken out again, before what he came about was thoroughly effected, so that they were both obliged to return home as they came, and put up for the Time with the Disappointment.

Or again:

> And sometime last Week, we are informed, that one Piles a Fiddler, with his Wife, were overset in a Canoo near Newtown Creek. The good Man, 'tis said, prudently secur'd his Fiddle, and let his Wife go to the Bottom.

If husbands and wives in colonial Pennsylvania had their difficulties, so did printers. "As your last Paper was reading in some Company where I was present," went one letter to the editor,

> these Words were taken Notice of in the Article concerning Governor Belcher, (*After which his Excellency, with the Gentlemen trading to New-England,* died *elegantly at Pontack's*). The Word *died* should doubtless have been *dined,* Pontack's being a noted Tavern and Eatinghouse in London. . . . Another related to us, that when the Company of Stationers in England had the Printing of the Bible in their Hands, the Word *(not)* was left out in the Seventh Commandment, and the whole edition was printed off with *Thou Shalt commit Adultery,* in-

stead of *Thou shalt not,* & c. The *Spectator's* Remark
upon this Story is, that he doubts many of our modern
Gentlemen have this faulty Edition by 'em, and are not
made sensible of the Mistake. . . . And lastly, a Mistake
of your Brother News-Printer was mentioned in *The
Speech of James Prouse written the Night before he was
to have been executed,* instead of *I die a Protestant,* he
has put it, *I died a Protestant.*[14]

The *Gazette* not only reflected its editor's wit, but also his
impulse to "do good," as it provided the medium through
which he furthered his many projects for civic betterment.
One of the greatest of American newspapers, the *Gazette*
would publish continuously from its founding in 1729 until
its demise in 1815.

Franklin soon became sole proprietor of the *New Printing-
Office* as well as the *Gazette* when he bought the ill-equipped
Meredith's share of the business with the aid of a welcome loan
from two friends. His position was also greatly enhanced
when he won the public printing from Bradford. This victory
was not only the result of the superior quality of his work,
but was also an award from the Assembly, whose program
for paper-money legislation was helped by Franklin's timely
pamphlet, *The Nature and Necessity of a Paper-Currency.* The
resultant issue of paper money—"coined land," he termed
it—did, as Franklin believed it would, benefit Pennsylvania's
economy.

By 1733, Franklin was ready to enter into the highly competitive almanac field. Several almanacs already enjoyed wide
circulation. Filled with a variety of information, astrological,
historical and meteorological, these little books helped the
farmer to decide when to sow and when to reap, and also
helped pierce the isolation of many a colonial's life. Franklin's *Poor Richard* followed the pattern; even its title was
probably suggested by James Franklin's *Poor Robin's Al-*

manack, printed in Newport. But although *Poor Richard* was not an original contribution, by its wit and comedy, it soon became the most popular almanac of all. Published by Franklin for twenty-six years, averaging an annual circulation of ten thousand, *Poor Richard* became a household word in English America. In his annual prefaces, Franklin created unforgettable characters in humorous Richard Saunders and his matronly wife Bridgit. In his aphorisms, some of Franklin's invention but most of them culled from innumerable sources and often improved over the original, the almanac hit a comic note in the usually sobersided world of colonial writing. Though most remembered for its words of prudent advice, such as "early to bed, early to rise, makes a man healthy, wealthy, and wise," there were also sayings of a different sort: "Sal laughs at every thing you say. Why? Because she has fine teeth," or "God heals, and the Doctor takes the Fees," or "Fish and Visitors stink in 3 days," or "There's more old Drunkards than old Doctors," or "Kings and Bears often worry their keepers," or "Where there's Marriage without Love, there will be Love without Marriage," or "Neither a Fortress nor a Maiden head will hold out long after they begin to parly," or "Marry your Son when you will, but your Daughter when you can," or "Three may keep a secret, if two of them are dead." Even prophecy, something the colonials took quite seriously, was treated with less than the solemnity befitting the subject:

Of the Diseases this Year

This Year the Stone-blind shall see but very little; the Deaf shall hear but poorly; and the Dumb shan't speak very plain. . . . Whole Flocks, Herds and Droves of Sheep, Swine and Oxen, Cocks and Hens, Ducks and Drakes, Geese and Ganders shall go to Pot; but the Mortality will not be altogether so great among Cats,

Dogs and Horses. As for old Age, 'twill be incurable this
Year, because of the Years past. . . . But the worst
Disease of all will be a certain most horrid, dreadful,
malignant, catching, perverse and odious Malady . . .
which is called . . . *Lacko'mony.*[15]

Poor Richard and the *Gazette* were but two aspects of
Franklin's multifarious printing business. His government
work which included printing the paper money and laws of
Pennsylvania and of several other colonies provided a major
source of income. So did his printing of theological tracts,
broadsides, essays and books. Franklin's edition of Samuel
Richardson's *Pamela,* whose heroine's virtue was cruelly be-
sieged through two volumes, was one of the first novels published in America (1744). Franklin was first to publish a
German hymn book. He published James Logan's *Cato's
Moral Distichs,* the first published American translation of
a classical author, as well as the same scholar-politician's
Cato Major. Among Franklin's many other publications was
the first Masonic book published in America.

Another first was the short-lived German newspaper, the
Philadelpia Zeitung (1732); and Franklin missed by only
three days in bringing out the first American magazine, the
General Magazine, one of his few business failures. Meanwhile he had begun to expand his interests outside of Pennsylvania through the establishment of several partnerships.
Franklin thereby instigated or had an interest in the *South
Carolina Gazette,* the *New-York Weekly Post-Boy* (later *Gazette*), the *Connecticut Gazette,* and newspapers on the islands
of Antigua and Dominica. Franklin also published the first
bilingual paper in the colonies, *Hoch Teutsche und Englische
Zeitung. The High Dutch and English Gazette.*

As if all this were not activity enough, Franklin ran a retail
store in conjunction with his printing business. He sold an

astonishing variety of wares including soap, compasses, quadrants, nuts, cheese, codfish, chocolate, sugar, coffee, goose feathers, sealing wax, Bibles, bottles and spectacles. He was also extremely active in the papermaking business. Over the years he bought hundreds of thousands of pounds of rags and sold them to paper mills. From the mills, he purchased paper and pasteboard to be sold up and down the coast including to the printers with whom he was in partnership. In connection with this trade, Franklin was responsible for establishing some eighteen paper mills. It is probable that at mid-century he was the largest paper dealer in the colonies.[16] Franklin's extraordinary success was due not only to his business acumen, but also to the exemplary image he projected, an image of hard work and industriousness. He was the model colonial tradesman: keeping store, working at his press late into the night, back at work early the next morning. Franklin was aware of the public relations value of his diligence which soon became proverbial among his contemporaries.

Although Franklin was now an established tradesman of the city, he needed a wife not only to complete the picture, but also to provide a mother for his newly born natural son William, another *erratum* of his early life. The identity of William's real mother remains a mystery; she may even have been Deborah Read Rogers, whose husband, pursued by his creditors, had disappeared. Not knowing whether Rogers were alive or dead, in 1730 she and Franklin entered into a common law marriage. Deborah had neither the education nor wit to provide Franklin with intellectual companionship. Yet, "she prov'd a good and faithful Helpmate," wrote Franklin, "assisted me much by attending the Shop, we throve together, and have ever mutually endeavour'd to make each other happy." Soon a son was born, Francis Folger, who died at age four. After forty years, the aggrieved father would

still say of little "Franky" that he was such as "I have seldom
seen equall'd in anything, and whom to this Day I cannot
think of without a Sigh." [17] In 1743, the Franklins had a
daughter Sarah, called "Sally." The delight of her doting
father, Sally, at twenty-four, married Richard Bache. The
Baches had eight children, the first of whom was named
Benjamin for his then famous grandfather. And so the Franklins did indeed, through tragedy and happiness, thrive
together.

Franklin's business success was assured. He paid Samuel
Vernon the money plus interest that he owed him, thereby
erasing another *erratum* of his early youth. By most stand-
ards, he was a successful man with a future of ever greater
returns. For Franklin, however, wealth was not an end in
itself. In 1748, retiring from business, he formed a partnership with master printer David Hall, recently from England.
To Hall, Franklin turned over the operation of the printing
house and the store. He was now free to devote all his time
and energy to intellectual pleasures and public affairs.

Posterity remembers Franklin as a scientist and statesman,
yet he honored the name of "printer" above all. Late in life,
he began his will, "I, Benjamin Franklin, Printer, late Minister Plenipotentiary from the United States of America to the
Court of France, now President of Pennsylvania . . . ."
Sometime probably in 1728, Franklin composed for himself
an epitaph:

The Body of
B. Franklin,
Printer;
Like the Cover of an old Book,
Its Contents torn out,
And stript of its Lettering and Gilding,
Lies here, Food for Worms.
But the Work shall not be wholly lost:

For it will, as he believ'd, appear once more,
In a new & more perfect Edition,
Corrected and amended
By the Author.[18]

III Citizen and Scientist

FRANKLIN'S DECISION TO break off a successful business career and retire at age forty-two indicates that the acquisition of material wealth was not his most important goal. Franklin appreciated life's creature comforts, but he viewed wealth as a means, not an end. Following his return from London in 1726, he worked out for himself a philosophy of life with which his business retirement was entirely consistent.

Through his London sojourn, Franklin's youth had been marked by independence, impulsiveness and rebellion against the accepted mores of his times. Boston was too confining for the freethinking young man. London was just the opposite; there he had free reign to do and say what he pleased. But Franklin was dissatisfied with the results of freethinking which he believed had led him into several errors. "I began to suspect that this Doctrine," he wrote, "tho' it might be true, was not very useful." He had come to feel the need of a system of values by which to live. Having discarded that of his forefathers, the twenty-two year old youth invented for himself a new theology that would provide direction for his so far wayward career.

English deism provided the taproot of Franklin's religion. Franklin's conception of God, however, differed from that of many deists who believed that the Supreme Being created the world-machine and then withdrew. For Franklin, reflecting his New England heritage, the God whom he worshipped "is not above caring for us, being pleas'd with our Praise, and offended when we slight Him, or neglect his Glory." And

Franklin, true to his Calvinist background, found a justification of material success as a reward for virtue and a sign of God's pleasure. "As I have Reason to hope and believe," he wrote,

> that the Goodness of my Heavenly Father will not withold from me a suitable Share of Temporal Blessings, if by a Virtuous and Holy Life I merit his Favour and Kindness, Therefore I presume not to ask such Things, but rather Humbly, and with a sincere Heart express my earnest Desires that he would graciously assist my Continual Endeavours and Resolutions of eschewing Vice and embracing Virtue.

Franklin's was not a gospel of wealth, but he did believe material success—"a suitable Share of Temporal Blessings"—to be an attribute of the Godly life.

In conformity with the Newtonian world view, Franklin's religion was polytheistic. Believing that one Supreme Creator was too remote to comprehend, Franklin theorized that the Supreme Being created lesser Gods for each planetary system in the universe. It was the God of our solar system whom Franklin "proposed for the Object of my Praise and Adoration." He believed that this God was a *"good being,"* who desired that man be virtuous for "without Virtue Man can have no Happiness in this World." In sharp contrast to the God of his Calvinist forefathers, Franklin believed that his God was "not offended when he sees his Children solace themselves in any manner of pleasant Exercises and innocent Delights, and I think no Pleasure innocent that is to Man Hurtful." [1]

Having conceived a religion whose most important command was that men be happy, Franklin next turned to the cultivation of virtue through which happiness could be obtained. Late in life when he sat down to write his memoirs, he smiled at his youthful presumption when at twenty-two he had "conceiv'd the bold and arduous Project of arriving at moral perfection. . . . As I knew, or thought I knew," Franklin recalled, "what was right and wrong, I did not see why I might not *always* do the one and avoid the other."

In order to help himself arrive at illusive perfection, Franklin worked out a canon of thirteen moral virtues including temperance, silence, order, resolution, frugality, industry, sincerity, justice, moderation, cleanliness, tranquility, chastity, and humility. Finding their collective practice too demanding, he assigned each a separate page in a little book in which he could record his progress. To each virtue, the young moral athlete affixed a short explanatory precept. The pages of the book were lined vertically for the days of the week. Across these columns, Franklin ruled thirteen lines, one for for each virtue, as in the following example:

TEMPERANCE							
Eat not to Dulness. *Drink not to Elevation.*							
	S	M	T	W	T	F	S
T							
S	..	.		.		.	
O	.	.	.		.	.	.
R			.			.	
F		.			.		
I			.				
S							
J							
M							
Cl.							
T							
Ch.							
H							

The scheme allowed him to practice each separate virtue for a week, and at the same time daily to grade himself with respect to the entire canon. In his earnestness, Franklin indicated that spiritually he had not left Boston so very far behind. His little book resembles nothing so much as one of the myriad diaries kept by New England puritans as they recorded their halting progress toward sainthood.

Franklin's puritan conscience, like his scientific bent, was not untypical of his times. In him, as in many of his contemporaries both in America and across the Atlantic, the puritan ethic survived the Deist assault on revealed religion. The theological dogmas of puritanism, however, were rejected, most notably the dogma of original sin. Enlightenment thought frequently resembled a secularized puritanism wherein God's grace was manifest in human reason. But all men, not just the few, possessed reason so that salvation was democratized. Human progress, not damnation, was predestined, and given the opportunity of liberalized political institutions—and in the case of the French Revolutionists perhaps a little persuasion—mankind would enter a new era of virtue.

Though Franklin believed that man would respond to improved social and political institutions, he never held that virtue could be enforced. He did think, however, that it was obtainable through practice. In his own case, though the goal remained illusive, he could later write that he was "by the Endeavour a better and happier Man than I otherwise should have been if I had not attempted it." [2] His faith in human betterment was in accord with eighteenth century optimism nowhere more impressively expressed than in the Frenchman Condorcet's *The Progress of the Human Spirit.*

Franklin's accord with the temper of the Enlightenment is particularly apparent in his project for founding a United Party for Virtue "by forming the Virtuous and good Men of all Nations into a regular Body." For his projected international society, Franklin designed a creed the central tenet of which was "that the most acceptable Service of God is doing Good to Man." Franklin never found time to work out this idea nor to write his projected book on the cultivation of moral virtue. But his retirement from business did give him time to put his concept of virtue into practice. The prayer which he daily addressed to God ended, "Accept my kind Office to thy other Children, as the only Return in my Power for thy continual Favours to me." [3] Service to others was the keystone of Franklin's philosophy.

Although Franklin never founded an international service society, he did make a beginning by establishing in 1727 a tradesmen's club in Philadelphia for the encouragement of moral and civic improvement. This was the famous Junto Club. "The Rules I drew up requir'd that every Member in his Turn should produce one or more Queries on any Point of Morals, Politics or Natural Philosophy, to be discuss'd by the Company, and once in three Months produce and read an Essay of his own Writing on any Subject he pleased." The Junto held weekly Friday night meetings which began with a ritual designed by Franklin. Made up of twenty-four "Standing Queries" punctuated by wine, the ritual was frequently supplemented by four qualifying questions directed at candidates for admission to the club. The "Standing Queries" and qualifying questions, indicate that the Junto emphasized religious freedom, love of truth, and service. "Do you think of any thing at present," went the eleventh query, "in which the Junto may be serviceable to *mankind?* to their country, to their friends, or to themselves?" [4] On all three counts, Franklin's Junto may be considered a success. In its meetings, the members helped one another in their various business careers. More importantly they worked out ideas for the improvement of life in Philadelphia and by extension America and mankind in general.

The first such idea resulted in the formation of the Library Company of Philadelphia, the original subscription library in America. Franklin suggested that the members pool their private libraries in the Junto meeting room so that each might have access to books other than his own. The arrangement proved to be too informal so that Franklin drew up proposals for the establishment of a Library Company, his "first Project," as he put it, "of a public Nature." With the help of his Junto friends, he procured fifty subscribers of forty shillings each and ten shillings annual dues. Later extended to one hundred subscribing members, the Library Company received a charter of incorporation from the Penns, who also gave a gift of land. Other libraries modelled on Franklin's plan appeared in Philadlephia and elsewhere, most notably the Redwood Library of Newport, Rhode Island, for which the noted architect Peter Harrison designed one of his most beautiful buildings. By 1769, Philadelphia's several small libraries merged with the original Library Company, resulting in a single strong institution well endowed with patrons, books, and financial support.

Another civic project which Franklin introduced in the Junto was his plan for an improved city watch. Heretofore a responsibility of the various ward constables, the city watch was inefficient and corrupt as householders paid the constables to be excused from this onerous duty. Franklin suggested the employment of regular watchmen who would be paid by a householders' tax. Franklin's friends approved of his idea as did the members of several new clubs which had sprung up in emulation of the Junto. It was not for several years, however, until Franklin's idea was finally passed into law by the Pennsylvania Assembly.

More immediately effective was another plan Franklin introduced in the Junto. In order to protect his city from frequent ravages caused by fire, he suggested the formation of a volunteer fire department. His suggestion resulted in the establishment of the famous Union Fire Company, the first voluntary fire association in Philadelphia. Each member of the Company was required to have fire buckets and other fire fighting equipment ready for action in case of a call. The Company, being a brainchild of Franklin's, was also a social club meeting once a month in a spirit of convivial fellowship. Franklin also suggested an insurance plan which resulted in the first fire insurance company in America. Over the next decades there appeared sixteen more fire companies and other insurance organizations. These companies were well equipped with fire engines, hooks and ladders so that, as Franklin proudly recounted, "I question whether there is a City in the World better provided with the Means of putting a Stop to beginning Conflagrations; and in fact since those Institutions, the City has never lost by Fire more than one or two Houses at a time. . . ."

Franklin also discussed in the Junto Philadelphia's need for street paving and lighting. "By talking and writing on the Subject," he recalled, "I was at length instrumental in getting the Street pav'd with Stone between the Market and the brick'd Foot-Pavement that was on each Side next the Houses." Following that success, Franklin next organized several householders to hire a man to sweep and carry away the dirt around the market. "All the Inhabitants of the City were delighted with the Cleanliness of the Pavement that surrounded the Market," wrote Franklin. They were therefore "more willing to pay a Tax for that purpose," a tax for which the Assembly finally provided in 1762. As for street lighting, the Assembly having made adequate provision, Franklin designed the now well-known lamp composed as he described it, "of four flat Panes, with a long Funnel above to draw up the Smoke, and Crevices admitting Air below to facilitate the Ascent of the Smoke." These were far more efficient than the lamps generally used in America or in the great cities of the old world.

Yet another institution in the origin of which the Junto

played a part was the present University of Pennsylvania. Franklin had long regretted that Philadelphia had no provision "for a compleat Education of Youth. . . . The first Step I took," he wrote, "was to associate in the Design a Number of active Friends, of which the Junto furnished a good Part; the next was to write and publish a Pamphlet intitled, *Proposals relating to the Education of Youth in Pennsylvania.*"[5] Franklin's *Proposals* represented a compromise between his own conception of education and that of the many individuals, including some with aristocratic pretensions, whose interest he had to have to make the proposal a success. The key to his thinking lay in the careful phrasing of his suggested curriculum for the academy students:

> As to their STUDIES, it would be well if they could be taught *every Thing* that is useful, and *every Thing* that is ornamental: But Art is long, and their Time is short. It is therefore propos'd that they learn those Things that are likely to be *most useful* and *most ornamental,* Regard being had to the several Professions for which they are intended.

In other words, Franklin was willing to include such "ornamental" subjects as classical languages, but his true desire was to emphasize education for use and for professional competence.

Franklin accordingly emphasized English, both written and spoken, drawing, mathematics, history, geography, and science. It was his private opinion, still contested to this day, that it is better to begin language study with modern rather than ancient tongues. To keep the students in health "and to strengthen and render active their Bodies," he desired that they exercise frequently "in Running, Leaping, Wrestling, and Swimming."[6] Franklin's educational ideas anticipated the direction of modern secondary and higher education. But

the academy which he instigated and the college that grew
out of it fell under the control of more traditionalist sponsors.

Franklin's *Proposals* found immediate acceptance. Yet
from the beginning, Philadelphia's new educational institution displayed a split personality resulting from the antago-
nism between Franklin's educational principles and those of
many of the institution's financial backers. Under the "Constitution of the Publick Academy in the City of Philadelphia," drawn up in November, 1749, there were selected
twenty-four trustees including Franklin, who was elected
president. Within the academy were established two schools,
the Greek and Latin School and the English School. Though
to Franklin the English School was the heart of the academy,
a majority of the trustees disagreed. They named the master
of the Greek and Latin School Rector of the academy. They
also granted him twice the salary with half the work load as
that of the master of the English School.

Having organized the academy, the trustees next sought
out a suitable housing for the school. They soon set upon the
so-called New Building which had recently been erected for
the use of the spellbinding preacher George Whitefield, who
brought to America in the 1740's her first religious revival,
the Great Awakening. Through his printing business, Franklin and Whitefield became close friends, though Whitefield
despaired of Franklin's unorthodox religious views. (At one
time Whitefield presumed that "it was for Christ's sake" that
Franklin had tendered him his hospitality; Franklin replied,
"Don't let me be mistaken; it was not for Christ's sake, but
for your sake.") [7] The New Building, under the impetus of
the Great Awakening, had been built for nonsectarian religious services as well as to house a charity school, a typical
eighteenth century humanitarian project. But as religious
enthusiasm waned in the late forties, the building was little

used and the charity school failed to materialize. Franklin was a member of the board of trustees of the New Building as well as of the academy. He now effected an agreement between the two groups by which the New Building was ceded to the academy.

On Januray 7, 1751, amid pomp and circumstance, the governor of Pennsylvania and the trustees marching at the head of the procession, the academy with one hundred and forty-five pupils had its beginning. The next step was the expansion of the academy into a college, the first nondenominational institution of higher learning in America. Franklin invited the brilliant young Scotsman William Smith, soon to be ordained a minister of the Anglican church, as president or "provost"—a term introduced to America by Smith—of the combined academy and college. It was a fateful choice, for Smith, though leader of a nondenominational school, soon displayed an Anglican bias as well as a somewhat more conservative educational philosophy than that espoused by Franklin. During Smith's many years as provost, there grew up between him and Franklin a bitter enmity not only because of their differing educational views but also because they took opposite sides in Pennsylvania politics. They also took opposite sides on the issue of American independence. In 1779, the state legislature, reconstituting the college as the University of Pennsylvania, removed the tory-leaning Smith from his post as provost. Smith, nevertheless, would not down. In the next decade he returned as provost of the temporarily resurrected college,—it would shortly be reunited with the university—just in time to be chosen to deliver the eulogy on Franklin, who died in 1790. The choice of Smith was not altogether inappropriate, however, for Franklin at his death was once more serving as president of the college trustees whose minutes referred to "the Venerable Dr. Benjamin Franklin, the Father and one of the first Founders of the Institution."

The college, like the library, reflected one aspect of Franklin's civic consciousness: his desire to spread learning among the people. The Pennsylvania Hospital, another of Franklin's concerns, more nearly reflected his humanitarianism. Founding a hospital for the poor was not initially Franklin's idea. Rather, the idea originated with the eminent physician Dr. Thomas Bond. According to Bond, when he approached Philadelphia citizens for support, he was constantly asked, "Have you consulted Franklin on this business? and what does he think of it? And when I tell them that I have not, they do not subscribe, but say they will consider of it." With Franklin's aid, the public response was more generous. Franklin, nevertheless, believed the project warranted support of the Pennsylvania Assembly to which he submitted a petition. The country members, however, blocked support of a measure which would primarily benefit Philadelphia. Franklin thereupon submitted to the lawmakers a dollar-matching scheme whereby the Assembly would grant two thousand pounds to the hospital only when a like amount was privately raised. Since the members who opposed the hospital did not believe the necessary two thousand pounds could be raised, they "conceiv'd," Franklin wrote, "they might have the Credit of being charitable without the Expense," and passed his bill. But to their chagrin, Philadelphians, seeing that by law their donations would be doubled, oversubscribed their portion, "and we claim'd and receiv'd the Publick Gift, which enabled us to carry the Design into Execution." [8]

The hospital was a success. Franklin served as a manager for several years; he was the first secretary of the hospital's board of trustees, and its second president. He helped design the seal of the hospital and composed the inscription for the cornerstone of the building:

In the Year of Christ,
1755;
George the second happily reigning;
(For he sought the Happiness of his People)
Philadelphia flourishing,
(For its inhabitants were public-spirited),
This Building,
By the Bounty of the Government,
And of many private Persons,
Was piously founded,
For the Relief of the Sick and Miserable.
May the God of Mercies
Bless the Undertaking! [9]

Well might Franklin be pleased with the hospital whose record for healing far surpassed those of London and Paris hospitals. In its first twenty-five years, over one half of almost nine thousand persons admitted were completely cured. Franklin could be pardoned for pride in the accomplishment. Recalling his dollar-matching scheme by which the hospital was funded, he wrote, "I do not remember any of my political Manoeuvres the Success of which gave me at the time more Pleasure. Or that in after-thinking of it, I more easily excus'd my-self for having made some Use of Cunning." [10]

Of the many institutions Franklin helped found, none better illustrates his many-sidedness as well as does the American Philosophical Society, today the oldest learned society in America. It was the noted Philadelphia botanist John Bartram who first suggested to Franklin the idea of forming an intercolonial learned society. Franklin enthusiastically endorsed Bartram's idea and in 1743 drafted "A Proposal for Promoting Useful Knowledge." Situated in the geographical center of English America, Philadelphia appeared the perfect location for a society to which ingenious Americans would send notice of their discoveries which might otherwise be "lost to Mankind." The scope of the society's interests as

envisioned by Franklin gives some measure of the capacious-
ness of his mind. Its investigations should include:

> All new-discovered Plants, Herbs, Trees, Roots, &c.
> their Virtues, Uses, &c. Methods of Propagating them,
> and making such as are useful, but particular to some
> Plantations, more general. Improvements of vegetable
> Juices, as Cyders, Wines, &c. New Methods of Curing
> or Preventing Diseases. All new-discovered Fossils in
> different Countries, as Mines, Minerals, Quarries, &c.
> New and useful improvements in any Branch of Math-
> ematics. New Discoveries in Chemistry, such as Im-
> provements in Distillation, Brewing, Assaying of Ores,
> &c. New Mechanical Inventions for saving Labour; as
> Mills, Carriages, &c. and for Raising and Conveying of
> Water, Draining of Meadows, &c. All new Arts, Trades,
> Manufactures, &c. that may be proposed or thought of.
> Surveys, Maps and Charts of particular Parts of the
> Sea-coasts, or Inland Countries; Course and Junction of
> Rivers and great Roads, Situation of Lakes and Moun-
> tains, Nature of the Soil and Productions, &c. New
> Methods of Improving the Breed of useful Animals, In-
> troducing other Sorts from foreign Countries. New Im-
> provements in Planting, Gardening, clearing Land, &c.
> And all philosophical Experiments that let Light into the
> Nature of Things, tend to increase the Power of Man
> over Matter, and multiply the Conveniencies or Pleas-
> ures of Life.[11]

Franklin's proposal met with approbation in Pennsylvania
and several other colonies. A few meetings of the new society
followed but interest flagged. "The members of our Society
here are very idle gentlemen;" Franklin complained, "they
will take no pains." In spite of the efforts of Franklin, Bartram, and Dr. Bond, who helped found the hospital, the
society was moribund for two decades. In 1768, however,
the society was resurrected. Combined with another Philadelphia learned society recently begun by a group of younger
men, the newly constituted American Philosophical Society

elected Franklin, who was then in England, its first president, an office which he held until his death. An American counterpart of the English Royal Society, the American Philosophical Society, of which Thomas Jefferson was its third president, with its library, publications and annual research grants to scholars from a fund valued at over ten million dollars, is today perhaps the foremost memorial to Franklin's enormous energy and remarkable range of interests.

Franklin founded the American Philosophical Society "for the promotion of useful knowledge." Although his charge to the society was extremely broad in scope, its core was science, or "natural philosophy," as the men of the eighteenth century called it. The founding of the society was an aspect of Franklin's growing interest in this field. To Franklin, natural philosophy encompassed both practical and theoretical science. He had no particular interest in differentiating between these two approaches, but when he did think in such terms, he invariably chose science for use over what we today call "pure science." Franklin's contribution to both, nevertheless, was immense.

Franklin was unusual among scientists in combining a talent for abstract thought with a mechanical bent that led to his astonishing inventiveness. His first major invention was the Pennsylvanian fireplace, usually called the "Franklin stove." Utilizing the principle of heat convection, Franklin introduced an air box which was warmed before the heat and smoke were forced up the chimney. Constantly supplied by fresh air from below, the warm air circulated through shutters into the room. Franklin's fireplace was similar in principle to the modern hot air furnace. He introduced his invention characteristically with a brilliant promotional tract, concerning which one Franklin scholar, Sydney George Fisher, stated that "the test of literary genius is the ability to be fascinating about stoves." Though Pennsylvania's Governor Thomas offered Franklin a patent on his fireplace, he refused on the principle, "That as we enjoy great Advantages from the Inventions of others, we should be glad of an Opportunity to serve others by any Invention of ours, and this we should do freely and generously." [12] This was a principle from which Franklin never varied.

During the middle decades of the century, Franklin displayed a scientific virtuosity that would characterize him the rest of his life. His incisive mind encompassed an amazing variety of phenomena. In meteorology, for example, he was the first to observe the true path of cyclonic storms. A northeast storm, he discovered, originates in the southwest and moves in a direction opposite to that from which it blows. He also theorized on waterspouts and whirlwinds. He wrote on the circulation of the blood and body temperature. The discovery of fossils atop mountains led him, a century before Darwin, to ruminate on the geologic history of the Earth. To relieve his brother who was suffering from a painful disease, he devised the first flexible catheter in America. He was a sponsor of the first American Arctic expedition and his consideration of the time differential between eastern and western Atlantic crossings led him to the first scientific study of the Gulf Stream. He experimented with the relative abilities of various substances to conduct heat, and he studied the effects of atmospheric pressure on the boiling point of water, hitherto considered a constant in nature. He experimented with the raising of hemp and other aspects of modern agriculture on his New Jersey farm. He considered the nature of light and came close to the modern wave theory. He even conducted an experiment on the communicative abilities of ants! Nor was this all. He participated in the observation of the transit of Mercury and later of Venus. In part it was through his encouragement that John Bartram published his significant work in botany.

But of all Franklin's scientific achievements, none was as important as his experiments with electricity, experiments with which the science of electricity may be said to have had its beginning. Previous to Franklin, the peculiar properties of static electricity had long been familiar. The Greek philosopher Thales had noted the attractive powers of rubbed amber, a substance for which the Greek word was *electron*. In 1600, the English physician William Gilbert discovered other substances that had similar powers. That certain substances seemed to repel rather than attract led theorists to believe that they were dealing with two types of electricity which they named vitreous (after glass) and resinous (after amber). By Franklin's time, several ingenious machines for producing dramatic electrostatic phenomena had been invented and were frequently displayed by wandering practitioners of the seemingly weird and wonderful effects of the "electric fire."

In 1743 during a trip to Boston, Franklin had been fascinated by the electrical tricks of one of these travelling showmen, a certain Archibald Spencer (whom he mistakenly recalled as "Spence" in the *Autobiography*). In the next few years, Spencer gave his "Course of Experimental Philosophy" in Newport, New York, Philadelphia, and Williamsburg. Meanwhile, the Library Company's English friend and agent Peter Collinson sent to Philadelphia an electrostatic tube which produced electricity when rubbed with silk. Collinson's gift heightened Franklin's interest and he accordingly purchased Spencer's electrical apparatus. On March 28, 1747, he wrote Collinson,

> Your kind present of an electric tube . . . has put several of us on making electrical experiments, in which we have observed some particular phaenomena that we look upon to be new. . . . For my own part, I never was

before engaged in any study that so totally engrossed my
attention and my time as this has lately done. . . .

The "several of us" to whom Franklin referred included a
few Junto members and his principal electrical associate
Ebenezer Kinnersley, Baptist minister without a congregation. Kinnersley, like Archibald Spencer, gave demonstration
lectures, in part prepared by Franklin, before numerous audi-
ences. The "particular phaenomena that we look upon to be
new" to which Franklin referred was first, his discovery of
the "wonderful Effect of Points both in drawing off and
throwing off the Electrical Fire." Also, in contradiction to
the prevailing theory, Franklin had come to believe that "the
Electrical Fire was not created by Friction, but collected,
being an Element diffused among, and attracted by other
Matter. . . ." To describe a disequilibrium of electricity
within a body, Franklin coined the terms "positive" and
"negative" or "plus" and "minus," terms which have been
used in the science of electricity ever since.[13] These terms
referred to Franklin's major contribution to the science, his
single-fluid theory which contravened the then prevailing
dual theory.

In his work with electricity, Franklin displayed his great
ability to fabricate appropriate experiments with which to test
his hypotheses. His work with the newly discovered Leyden
jar, for example, proved that the electricity resided in the
glass rather than in the fluid contained in the jar. Having
established this fact, he went on to construct an "electrical
battery," introducing another basic term into the language.
Indeed, Franklin's experiments set forth the basic theoretical
structure and terminology (other terms introduced by Franklin include "charge," "discharge," "armature," "electric
shock," and "condenser") that have dominated electrical
science to our own time.

Franklin's experiments became known to the world

through a series of letters he wrote to Collinson, who in England introduced them to the Royal Society and in 1751 had them published as *Experiments and Observations on Electricity,* with a preface by the noted Quaker physician Dr. John Fothergill. During Franklin's lifetime, there appeared five English editions of this most important scientific book to come out of colonial America. There were also many European translations which, like the later English editions, included Franklin's revisions and supplementary writings on electricity, as well as his many diverse writings on other aspects of "natural philosophy." Although Franklin's theoretical conceptions alone made him the leader in the new electrical science, it was his suggestion of an experiment to prove the identity of lightning and electricity that catapulted him to world fame.

In April, 1749, Franklin had noted the several similarities between lightning and an electric spark. Though he was not the first to see such an identity, he was the first scientist to suggest a means by which the hypothesis could be tested. Utilizing his "doctrine of points" and the knowledge he had gained of the importance of grounding, he described in his book his "sentry box" experiment by which a man stationed high on a tower or steeple could test the electrification of a high pointed rod affixed to the stand as clouds passed overhead. "Let the experiment be made," he had written. The challenge was first successfully met in May, 1752, by Thomas-François Dalibard, scientist, and French translator of Franklin's letters on electricity. A few weeks later, believing there was no building high enough in Philadelphia for his experiment, Franklin worked out his ingenious kite device which substitued for the sentry box and rod. Months later he posted a short notice in the *Gazette* of the kite experiment's success, and the notice was then transmitted to Collinson and the Royal Society.

Franklin, meanwhile, had characteristically turned the

now proven identity of lightning and electricity to use. Even before the success of the sentry box and kite experiments, Franklin had suggested that if the identity could be proven, then high pointed rods erected over houses and other structures would protect the buildings from the destructive effects of lightning. In September, 1752, he erected a lightning rod over his own house. The rod was so constructed that whenever the atmosphere became electrified, connecting bells in his house would automatically ring. Slowly the lightning rod, Franklin's most famous invention, began to appear in cities other than Philadelphia in America, and in England and Europe. In far-off Geneva, the famous Voltaire was among the first to utilize Franklin's invention. But in spite of mounting acceptance, lightning rods had to make their way against religious prejudices as well as the objections of a few scientists. The religiously inclined believed that the stealing of God's fire was blasphemy. They blamed earthquakes on Franklin's rods which seemed to store the fire within the earth. Scientific objections, based mainly against the single-fluid theory of electricity, were published in France. They were immediately answered, however, by the Italian scientist Father Giambatista Beccaria, who thereby relieved Franklin of composing his own defense.

Franklin's invention of the lightning rod all but submerged his contributions to electrical theory of which the rod was a byproduct. He was now a famous man; his name was mentioned in the same breath with that of Newton. Adherents of his theory were called Franklinists. Europeans were particularly charmed that the great scientist was an American, for without instruction at the ancient European seats of learning and far from the culture of the old world, he proved that man's untrammelled intelligence could unlock the secrets of the universe. Europeans were even more delighted with Franklin when they discovered that he was a moralist as well as a scientist and that his scientific interests ranged far beyond electricity.

Recognition of his achievements came swiftly. Louis XV of France proferred Franklin his congratulations. In 1753, Franklin was awarded the prestigious Copley Medal of the Royal Society, to which in 1756 he was unanimously elected. Harvard, Yale, and William and Mary conferred honorary degrees upon him. Although the experimental proof of the identity between lightning and electricity and the resulting lightning rod formed the basis of Franklin's contemporary fame, his more fundamental contributions have had even greater impact. Franklin's electrical theories, wrote the Nobel Prize winner Robert A. Millikan, "laid the real foundation on which the whole superstructure of electrical theory and interpretation has been erected." Millikan named Franklin one of "the fourteen most influential scientists who have lived since Copernicus was born in 1473." [14]

It has already been pointed out that Franklin's achievement was not an isolated phenomenon. He was always careful to acknowledge the work of his associates such as Ebenezer Kinnersley and Philip Syng, who invented a convenient friction machine for producing electricity, and Robert Grace, metallurgist, who not only assisted in his electrical experiments but also cast the plates for Franklin's fireplace. Philadelphia could also boast of James Logan, mathematician, classicist and pioneer student of plant reproduction, who, previous to Franklin, was the city's outstanding scientist. Logan, as well as Franklin, encouraged John Bartram in his botanical investigations. These men were but a few of the many Philadelphians whose work in natural philosophy created the milieu in which Franklin's genius found fruition. Outside Pennsylvania there was the historian-doctor-natural philosopher Cadwallader Colden of New York. Colden's *An Explication of the First Causes of Action in Matter* (1745) was one of the significant philosophical works produced by a colonial American. His son David, also a correspondent of Franklin, contributed some original proofs of Franklin's electrical theory. In Connecticut, there was Jared Eliot, an important agriculturalist with whom Franklin corresponded on modern farming methods as well as meteorology and other natural phenomena.

Across the seas, English philosophers gave essential encouragement to their American brethren. Foremost among these men was the Quaker merchant-botanist Peter Collinson, member of the Royal Society and contributor of books and scientific instruments to the Library Company. To Collinson, Franklin addressed his most important letters concerning electricity, and through Collinson these letters were presented to the Royal Society and published. William Watson, outstanding English electrician, though he disagreed with some of Franklin's ideas, nevertheless also was instrumental in giving Franklin a hearing. There was also John Canton, like Franklin a selfmade tradesman, who was the first Englishman successfully to perform Franklin's experiment proving the identity of lightning and electricity.

All of these men—Americans, Englishmen, and their European correspondents—shared a common faith in an ordered universe whose laws were not only beneficial to man but also discoverable by him. John Bartram somewhat naively spoke their creed when he wrote, "It is through the telescope I see God in his glory." Bartram spoke for a common Atlantic Civilization that spanned the ocean from Philadelphia to London and the great cities of Europe. Franklin's book, *Experiments and Observations on Electricity,* was one of the highest achievements of that civilization.

Franklin's civic and scientific contributions seemed to justify the faith of the Enlightenment in the power of reason to improve the life of man. Progress demanded that aristocratic forms and formalized religions be replaced by natural equality and a religion of nature. God, to the men of the Enlightenment, created a universe whose immutable laws, harmonious and benign, were discoverable by men freed from social, religious and political restraints. In the words of Alexander Pope,

> Nature and Nature's Laws lay hid in night:
> God said, Let Newton be! and all was light.

Herein lay the explanation for Franklin's great fame. Like Newton, through the application of reason, he laid bare nature's laws. His experiments which led to the invention of the lightning rod lent credence to the eighteenth century faith that the discovery of natural laws would lead to the enhancement and perfection of the life of man.

To the eighteenth century deist, forms of religious worship were less important than the performance, as Franklin put it, of "real good Works, Works of Kindness, Charity, Mercy, and Publick Spirit." For Franklin, orthodox religions reversed priorities by emphasizing dogma before works. The minister's sermons, he commented, aimed "rather to make us Presbyterians than good Citizens." [15] "The Scriptures assure me," Franklin once wrote to his aged parents, "that at the last Day, we shall not be examin'd what we *thought,* but what we *did;* and our Recommendation will not be that we said *Lord, Lord,* but that we did GOOD to our Fellow Creatures." [16] Franklin's idea of establishing a United Society for Virtue was based in part on his philosophy of works over faith. His wide-ranging correspondence served as a kind of substitute for his projected society. So did Freemasonry to which Franklin adhered throughout his life.

Franklin joined Philadelphia's St. John's Lodge in 1734. Modern Masonry was born in London in the early eighteenth century and spread rapidly throughout the British Isles, Europe and America. The principles for which it stood included liberty, equality, freedom of conscience, and justice. In its recruitment of members, the order emphasized ability over social standing. Masonry, fostering a spirit of sociability and brotherhood, appealed to the rising middle class that would create in the latter half of the century the Age of the Democratic Revolution. A large proportion of the founders of both the American and French republics were men such as Franklin and Washington, who found Masonry congenial to the new era of freedom.

Franklin moved rapidly upwards in Masonry's ranks soon to become Provincial Grand Master of Pennsylvania. In Masonry, Franklin found an international society that gave institutional form to values which he shared with like-minded men throughout the western world. The Masonic constitution, drawn up in England in 1723 and first published in America by Franklin, obligated its members only "to that Religion in which all Men agree, leaving their particular Opinions to themselves, that is to be *good Men and true. . . .*" It was an obligation that Franklin had long since accepted.

Although Franklin would attain world fame as a statesman, he had already gained a worldwide reputation by the middle decades of the eighteenth century. These were the years when he gave concrete form to his humane faith. Almost a half a century later, a month before he died, Franklin received a query as to his religious beliefs from Ezra Stiles, Congregational minister and one-time President of Yale. Avoiding allusion to, or perhaps having foregone his polytheism, Franklin replied with the essentials of the belief he had evolved as a young printer in Philadelphia:

> Here is my creed. I believe in one God, Creator of the Universe. That he governs it by his Providence. That he

ought to be worshipped. That the most acceptable Service we render to him is doing good to his other Children. That the soul of Man is immortal, and will be treated with Justice in another Life respecting its Conduct in this. These I take to be the fundamental Principles of all sound Religion, and I regard them as you do in whatever Sect I meet with them.

As to Jesus of Nazareth, . . . I think the System of Morals and his Religion, as he left them to us, the best the World ever saw or is likely to see; but I apprehend it has received various corrupting Changes, and I have, with most of the present Dissenters in England, some Doubts as to his Divinity. . . .[17]

In the latter half of Franklin's life, politics would increasingly monopolize his time. But in helping to found the library, the hospital, the university, and the American Philosophical Society and in the pursuit of science, he best embodied the faith of the Age of Reason: that to serve man was to serve God.

IV Tribune of the People

FRANKLIN'S METEORIC CAREER in Pennsylvania politics, culminating in the decade of the 1750's, sprang in large measure from the reputation he had gained through his journalistic, philanthropic and scientific accomplishments of previous years. As a man of means, early retired from a successful business career, Franklin had provided far-seeing leadership in intellectual and civic affairs. These broad achievements formed the backdrop to his emergence in provincial politics, which in turn schooled him for the part he would play on the national and international scene.

Yet it is not altogether accurate to view Franklin's political career as beginning only after he had become established as a nabob of the city. Politics, in fact, played a part in his early success as a businessman, just as that success later enhanced his political opportunities. As early as 1736, the Pennsylvania Assembly appointed Franklin its clerk, a position he held for fifteen years. That office, he wrote, "was the more agreeable to me, as besides the Pay for immediate Service as Clerk, the Place gave me a better Opportunity of keeping up an Interest among the Members, which secur'd to me the Business of Printing the Votes, Laws, Paper Money, and other occasional Jobbs for the Public, that on the whole were very profitable."

The year after Franklin went to work for the Assembly, he was appointed postmaster of Philadelphia. Here again, as with the position of clerk, Franklin found the postmastership economically as well as politically profitable. "Tho' the Salary was small," he wrote, "it facilitated the Correspondence that improv'd my Newspaper, encreas'd the Number demanded, as well as the Advertisements to be inserted, so that it came to afford me a very considerable Income." [1] Unlike Andrew Bradford, the previous publisher-postmaster who had refused to allow his competitors the services of his post riders, Franklin's post was open to all. His success in the operation of the Philadelphia postoffice was a strong recommendation for his appointment in 1753 as joint deputy postmaster-general of North America with William Hunter, Virginia printer and publisher of the *Virginia Gazette*.

During Franklin's long tenure in the postoffice—he retained his position until the eve of the Revolution—the colonial postal service was vastly improved. He set up businesslike procedures, standardized postal bookkeeping, established the first dead letter office in America, and saw to the construction of new roads. In 1761, for the first time the colonial postoffice showed a profit. Under Franklin's management, distances were shortened. For example, it had previously taken three weeks from the request to the reply between Philadelphia and Boston. Franklin reduced the time to six days. Improved communications undoubtedly helped to unify the colonies and thereby stimulated intercolonial cooperation against Britain in the years leading to the Revolution.

Franklin's appointment as head of the colonial postoffice resulted in part from the patronage of the proprietors of Pennsylvania: Thomas Penn, who inherited three-fourths of his father's estate, and Thomas' brother Richard, who owned the remaining part. Thomas, who by virtue of his larger holdings was the chief proprietor, has not been kindly treated in histories of early America. An apostate from Quakerism, he became an Anglican in 1751. He had the further misfortune with regard to his future reputation, of earning the enmity of Franklin. Admirers of both Quakerism and Franklin have consequently been harsh in their judgment of Thomas Penn, who lived in London far from the Quaker city his father had founded, but where, at the center of empire, he could guard his American interests against interference by the British government. In Pennsylvania, Penn acted through his deputy governor whom he bound tightly with penal bonds to allow no legislative interference with the proprietary estates. Penn hoped as well for support from the leading men of the colony. It was for these reasons that he cultivated such men as Franklin across the water, and sought the friendship in London of members of the British government and merchants in the American trade.

Although Penn's courting of Franklin would end in failure, there were individuals in Pennsylvania upon whom the proprietor could generally depend. Among Penn's friends were Pennsylvania's successive deputy governors who owed their appointment and tenure to the proprietors. The governors' power of appointment and their licensing authority created a proprietary faction in the colony, a faction made up of those persons and their dependents who were the beneficiaries of proprietary patronage. Also in the proprietary camp were such men as the wealthy William Allen, long-time Chief Justice of the Pennsylvania Supreme Court, who both as a Presbyterian and an aristocrat preferred proprietary prerogative to Quaker rule. There were also proprietary appointees such as the Reverend Richard Peters, secretary to the governor's council. Finally, there was William Smith, provost of the college, whose vitriolic writings in support of Penn and against the Assembly caused a split between himself and his erstwhile patron, Franklin.

Down to the 1750's, Franklin remained largely independent of the proprietary faction and of the Quakers who dominated the Assembly. But the midcentury renewal of the French and Indian wars intensified the inherent division between the executive branch of the government which Penn controlled and the Quaker dominated legislature. Renewed

warfare meant that Pennsylvania's government would have
to contribute to the defense of the colonies. Providing funds
for defense, however, not only posed a challenge to Quaker
pacifism, but also gave rise to the question of the proprietors'
rights with regard to the raising of moneys. These issues first
emerged in a deadlock between the legislature and the executive with regard to the passage of a militia bill, even though
France and England were at war. Franklin, who ultimately
had to choose between the Assembly and the Penns, came
up with a solution to the militia problem which not only
enhanced his political reputation, but by which he also temporarily maintained his political independence.

The immediate cause of the crisis in Pennsylvania affairs
was the War of the Austrian Succession, known in America
as King George's War. Beginning in Europe in 1740, this war
heralded the renewal of the Anglo-French conflict for world
hegemony. In the past, Pennsylvania had remained relatively
free from involvement, since New England and New York
received the brunt of the attacks from Canada. Furthermore,
Pennsylvania's Indian policy had generally been such as to
retain the respect of her western neighbors. With the northern border once more aflame, however, Pennsylvanians harbored the uneasy feeling that they could not forever remain
immune. Nor was their coast immune from French and Spanish privateers who played havoc with their commerce and
even landed a raiding party in Delaware to plunder and lay
waste the surrounding countryside. The Pennsylvania Assembly, nevertheless, remained deaf to Governor Thomas'
plea for defense measures, though it did vote funds in support
of New England's successful attack on Ft. Louisbourg, the
French bastion on Cape Breton Island.

Support of New England did nothing, though, to allay the
fear that seized Philadelphians at the thought of their un-
protected sea defenses. With the people in a state of near

panic and the government deadlocked, Franklin in November, 1747, came forth with his famous pamphlet *Plain Truth,* which cogently argued the need for a voluntary military association. If the Assembly refused to act, the people could form their own military organization without leave of the government. The tone of *Plain Truth* was perfectly attuned to "the middling People, the Farmers, Shopkeepers, and Tradesmen of this City and Country," as Franklin expressed it, appealing both to their interest and their patriotism. And their response was overwhelming. Franklin was immediately immersed in organizing the province into military companies and founding a lottery for raising funds for supplies. At the request of the governor's council, which appreciated Franklin's clever alternative to a regular militia, he drew upon his boyhood experiences in New England to draft an order for Pennsylvania's first general fast which lent the sanction of religion to the Association. He also travelled to New York to borrow cannon from Governor Clinton. That worthy first refused, "but at a Dinner with his Council where there was great Drinking of Madeira Wine," Franklin later recalled, "he soften'd by degrees, and said he would lend us Six. After a few more Bumpers he advanc'd to Ten. And at length he very good-naturedly conceded Eighteen." [2]

In spite of the approbation of New York's Governor Clinton and the government of Pennsylvania, Franklin's Association was an extralegal military force. Though on the one hand it saved Thomas Penn from embarrassment over his colony's lack of defense, it was also a kind of democratic threat against his authority. Reluctantly, the proprietor contributed moneys for cannon which arrived in Pennsylvania after the treaty of peace between France and England had been signed. But his resentment against Franklin and his Association, "founded on a Contempt of Government," was great. Penn believed the Association to be a "Military Common Wealth" in the heart of his province, and he disapproved of the popular election of Association officers, even though the governor issued the officers' commissions. The Association, to Penn, smacked of treason, and *Plain Truth* seemed to be an open invitation to insurrection. He particularly resented Franklin's statement that *"Protection* is as truly due from the Government to the People, as *Obedience* from the People to the Government." Such a doctrine, Penn believed, "is not fit to be always in the heads of the Wild unthinking Multitude." Franklin "is a dangerous Man," concluded the proprietor, but "as he is a Sort of Tribune of the People, he must be treated with regard." [3]

Thomas Penn's conclusion stated the proprietary attitude toward Franklin as it would stand for the next five or six years. Though Penn and his friends deeply distrusted this "Tribune of the People," they feared to alienate him. Their policy of wary cordiality was furthered when the Treaty of Aix-la-Chappelle of 1748 brought an uneasy truce between France and England. With the coming of peace, the Association dissolved. As the problem of defense receded, so politics became less abrasive, particularly as Penn appointed the popular Pennsylvanian James Hamilton (whose father had defended freedom of the press in the Zenger case) to be his lieutenant governor.

But the success of the Association made Franklin a marked man. "The Publick," he wrote, "now considering me as a Man of Leisure, laid hold of me for their Purposes." The same year as the peace treaty, Franklin was appointed to the Philadelphia common council and later to the board of aldermen which by virtue of the proprietary charter held exclusive control of the city's administrative machinery. These city offices were essentially proprietary strongholds. The next year Governor Hamilton appointed Franklin as a justice of the peace. Then in 1751, Franklin took his seat in the Assembly as an elected member for Philadelphia. His position was unique. Enjoying the confidence of the people, as well as the reluctant patronage of the proprietor, he could play an independent role. Reelected by his constituents for the next thirteen years, Franklin would emerge as the leader of the antiproprietary forces in the mid-fifties when the renewal of the Anglo-French struggle again divided the colony on the issue of defense.

Until that time Franklin plunged into the day-by-day work of the Assembly without regard to partisanship. On the very first day of his attendance as a legislator—his son William had taken his place as Assembly clerk—he became involved in imperial politics. From time immemorial the colonists had objected to the deportation of English convicts into America, a grievance that was to be included in the Declaration of Independence. The Assembly appointed Franklin to a committee for the framing of a bill to control this practice. Two years before, Franklin had stated the colonial case in the *Gazette*. There, in a pointed satire, he suggested that in return for the "Thieves and Villains introduc'd among us," Americans send rattlesnakes to Britain for distribution in St. James's Park . . . and other Places of Pleasure about London; in the Gardens of all the Nobility and Gentry throughout the Nation; but particulary in the Gardens of the *Prime Ministers,* the *Lords of Trade* and *Members of Parliament;* for to them we are *most particularly* obligated." [4] Pennsylvania, however, had been comparatively successful in limiting the importation of convicts, and Franklin's committee now framed a new bill, accepted by the Assembly and governor, that would answer this purpose without raising constitutional objections in England.

During these first years of Franklin's legislative career, he dealt with many matters that were less spectacular than laws for curbing the commerce in convicts. For example, he worked on finding the proper location for a bridge over the Schuylkill River, he helped draft a new law regulating the weight and price of bakers' loaves, and he acted on a citizen's petition for the regulation of stray dogs. Perhaps his most congenial task was preparing a "Report on the State of the Currency," a historical review of Pennsylvania's economy calculated to persuade the governor to favor a renewed issue of paper money. Franklin's lengthy and detailed report reached back to the 1720's when under Governor Sir William Keith, Pennsylvania's successful experiment with paper money was launched. Franklin himself had contributed to its continuation with his 1729 essay in favour of a paper currency.

In spite of Franklin's exhaustive report on the successful history of Pennsylvania's paper money, neither the English government nor Pennsylvania's proprietors looked kindly upon renewed issues. Thomas Penn was not blind to the problem facing his colony with regard to finding an adequate medium of exchange. But he distrusted the political power that paper-money laws gave to the Assembly, which insisted upon the exclusion of the governor from participation in the appropriation or disbursement of funds. Equally fearful of Parliamentary interference with his colony, Thomas Penn labored for Pennsylvania's exclusion from the Parliamentary ban on paper money in the northern colonies, a ban enacted in 1751. At the same time, he instructed Governor Hamilton to veto any paper-money bill in his colony that did not give him a share in its administration. The Assembly, however, sure of its constitutional supremacy in financial affairs, passed just such a measure. The resultant dispute between Assembly and governor soon meshed with the renewed necessity of financing defensive measures as England and France prepared to enter upon the Great War for Empire.

In America, the Treaty of Aix-la-Chappelle had proved to

be but a breathing space between wars. To the disgust of most Americans, England traded Fort Louisbourg on Cape Breton Island, which the New Englanders had taken, for Madras in India. In the next war it would take nine thousand British regulars and forty warships to retake the French bastion. Until that time, Louisbourg remained a threat to New England commerce. The French were also determined to connect Canada and Louisiana thereby effectively cutting off English expansion into the Mississippi Valley. The English colonies, on the other hand, were equally determined to make good their claims to the transmontane region, claims that were based in part on the sea-to-sea grants made in several of their original royal charters. Virginia was among the first of the colonies to intrude into the contested area when in 1749 a group of planter-speculators joined by certain London merchants received a royal grant involving some 500,000 acres in the Ohio Valley. Futhermore, at Logstown the year previously, Pennsylvania had negotiated a treaty for trade in the area with Indians previously allied with the French.

France at first replied to these incursions with a futile, if picturesque gesture. From Montreal, a party of two hundred Frenchmen made a circuit of the valley to bury at intervals leaden plates proclaiming Bourbon sovereignty in the Ohio country. Three years later, in 1752, the French turned from gesture to action. At Pickawillany (Piqua, Ohio), two hundred French-led Indians destroyed the village, captured the English traders with their goods, and boiled and ate the pro-English Indian chief who for his loyalty had been named "Old Britain." In the next year, Canada's Governor Duquesne erected several forts in the contested area.

The result of these actions was disaster for the English interest in the Ohio Valley. Fear gripped the frontier as the western Indians rushed to embrace the French, whose power they came suddenly to respect. The English colonists, for

their part, were now confronted with the spectre of a dangerous enemy at their backs, locking them in between the sea
and the mountains, and rendering their very existence inse-
cure. Even the usually unruffled Pennsylvania Assembly hastily voted a grant to the bereaved Indians of 600 pounds for
"the Necessities of Life" (Quaker for guns) as well as another
200 pounds for condolences. In September, the Ohio Indians
arrived at Carlisle, 100 miles west of Philadelphia, to receive
the gifts. Governor Hamilton immediately commissioned
Speaker of the House Isaac Norris, proprietary secretary
Richard Peters and Franklin "to hold a Treaty with these
Indians agreeable to their Request."

Franklin's earliest venture in diplomacy took place the first
three days in October, 1753. It was clear that French aggressiveness had loosened the Indian alliance with the English.
There was little the commissioners could do except to listen
sympathetically to the Indians' complaints which mainly
concerned the brutal practices of the English traders. With
rum and chicanery, the traders weakened the resistance of
the Indians and stole their possessions. The commissioners,
upon their return to Philadelphia, made a report to the governor which condemned the sale of liquor to the Indians and
suggested governmental regulation of the traders, lest "by
their own Intemperance, unfair Dealings, and Irregularities,"
they will "entirely estrange the Affections of the Indians from
the English." [5] Franklin furthermore introduced legislation
based on that of his native Massachusetts by which the Indian
trade was taken out of the hands of individuals and administered by government-operated trading posts. The result was
that after five years of disputation with the proprietors over
control of Indian affairs, the Assembly passed a bill that
severely curbed free enterprise in the fur trade by establishing
fixed prices as well as a government monopoly of the trade
beyond the Alleghenies.

The role that Franklin played in the effort to hold the Indians to the English interest reflected his conviction that the transmontane west held the future of the British Empire. Two years before the Carlisle Treaty, and before many other colonials had considered the wider implications of the Anglo-French confrontation in the Ohio Valley, Franklin gave expression to his imperial vision in what would become one of his most famous essays, *Observations concerning the Increase of Mankind*. Franklin correctly calculated that given a continent in which to expand, the American population would double every twenty-five years. Soon therefore, America's population would overtake that of England, whose people were limited to the resources of an island. The thought of western empire caused the usually temperate Franklin to wax rhapsodic: "What an Accession of Power to the British Empire by Sea as well as Land! What Increase of Trade and Navigation! What Numbers of Ships and Seamen!" For the attainment of these goals, the West must be secured for English America, "since on the Room depends so much the Increase of her People." [6]

Franklin's projected estimate of America's future population later influenced Thomas Malthus' theory of the geometric rate of population growth as against the arithmetic rate of increase of the means of subsistence. Principally through Malthus, Franklin's views entered into the mainstream of nineteenth century economic thought. More immediately, the *Observations concerning the Increase of Mankind* laid down the theoretical framework for Franklin's idea of the necessity of colonial union in the face of French and Indian attacks. Without such a union, the French could block western expansion and hence frustrate the attainment of western empire. Franklin therefore proposed an Anglo-American confederation made up of "a general Council form'd by all the Colonies, and a general Governor appointed by the Crown to preside in that Council." [7] An excise tax on liquor in all the colonies would provide for a common treasury. Representation in the Council would be proportioned to each colony's contribution to the treasury. Though Franklin's plan of confederation was directed toward solving the problem of defense, the military situation in 1751, the year of his proposal, was not yet serious enough for his plan to receive a general hearing.

In the next few years, however, the French pursued their intention of making good their claims to the west. In response to the French construction of forts throughout the Ohio country, Virginia's Governor Dinwiddie sent Major George Washington with a small force to protect the English workmen hastily building a fort at the forks of the Ohio, site of present-day Pittsburgh. But before Washington arrived, the work party was driven off by a French force which immediately began construction of Ft. Duquesne. Franklin's *Gazette* published the news. "The Confidence of the French, in this Undertaking," he wrote, "seems well-grounded on the present disunited State of the British Colonies. . . ." There followed the famous emblem of the disjointed snake, the first American political cartoon:

JOIN, or DIE.

In the deepening crisis, Franklin was not alone in his feeling that intercolonial cooperation was essential to the security of America. Several of his correspondents shared his imperial vision, as did many of the royal governors. London, too, had become alarmed that French incursions were influencing the Indians from their English alliance. In consequence, the impetus for an intercolonial meeting came from the Lords Commissioners of Trade and Plantations, better known as the Board of Trade. The Board, which was the Crown's advisory and policy making body for the colonies, in September, 1753, requested that an intercolonial conference be held to forge "one general Treaty to be made in his Majesty's Name." Plans were therefore made for an Indian conference to be held at Albany in June. Governor Hamilton named Franklin one of Pennsylvania's four commissioners to attend the conference to which commissioners were also appointed from Massachusetts, New York, New Hampshire, Connecticut, Rhode Island and Maryland. Although the Board of Trade made no mention of a plan of union, many of the conference participants viewed the Albany meeting as an opportunity to form such a plan.

Franklin had originally believed that a union could be formed on the voluntary consent of each colony. But although the French had militantly challenged English control of the West, individual colonial assemblies seemed to have little concern for the general welfare beyond the security of their own colonies. In 1751, Franklin had underestimated the force of colonial particularism. Now, with the crisis assuming ever greater proportions, he changed his mind. "The best public Measures," he had come to believe, "are seldom *adopted from previous Wisdom,* but *forc'd by the Occasion.*"[8] In line with this philosophy, he prepared notes toward a colonial union that were based upon his previous suggestion, but with the significant change that union would have to be established by an act of Parliament.

Franklin's notes formed the basis for the famous Albany Plan of Union, agreed to by the Congress on July 10, 1754. The plan provided for a President General, appointed by the King. There was also to be a representative Grand Council that with the concurrence of the President General would direct all Indian treaties, declare war and make peace, regulate the Indian trade, purchase land, establish new colonies, raise a military force ("but they shall not Impress Men in any Colonies, without the Consent of its Legislature"), and for these purposes the President General and Grand Council would have the power to levy taxes in the several colonies. Although the President General was given the veto power over acts passed by the Grand Council, unlike other royal governors, he could neither prorogue nor dissolve the Council.

It is clear that the framers of the Albany plan attempted to cleave a middle ground between the claims of the royal prerogative and the rights of the colonial assemblies. But this first essay in federalism proved to be premature. To Franklin's mortification, none of the colonial assemblies to which the plan was submitted agreed to it. Resentment was added to mortification when Speaker Norris contrived to present the plan in the Pennsylvania Assembly at a time when Franklin could not be present. "Every Body cries a Union is absolutely necessary," wrote Franklin, "But when they come to the Manner and Form of the Union, their weak Noddles are presently distracted." Nor did the plan fare any the better at the hands of the British ministry from whom he had hoped for effective implementation.

Disappointing as the failure of the Albany Plan was, Franklin was not ready to accept a curtailment of colonial rights in return for colonial union. Following the Albany Conference, Governor Shirley of Massachusetts showed Franklin an alternative plan of union which took the taxing power out of the hands of the representatives of the people.

Franklin's comments on this plan in the form of three closely reasoned letters later became famous as one of the earliest defenses of American rights. The colonists believe, wrote Franklin, "that it is suppos'd an undoubted Right of Englishmen not to be taxed but by their own consent given thro' their Representatives. . . . To propose taxing them by Parliament . . . shews a Suspicion . . . of their Common Sense and Understanding, which they have not deserv'd." The colonists have not objected to "Secondary Taxes" such as restraints on their manufactures and the requirement that a "great Part of our Produce," be shipped only to England. But direct taxes laid on the colonists by other than their own representatives will seem hard "to Englishmen, who cannot conceive, that by hazarding their Lives and Fortunes in subduing and settling new Countries . . . they have forfeited the native Rights of Britons. . . ."

Though Franklin was unwilling to compromise American liberties for the sake of union, he nevertheless believed for the rest of his life that had a reasonable plan been adopted in 1754, the course of history might have been different. After the Revolution, Franklin reminisced that with colonial union in 1754 there would have been no reason for Britain to send armies for American defense. There would consequently have been no pretense for Parliamentary taxation of the colonies, and the Revolution might therefore have been avoided, "so that the different Parts of the Empire might still have remained in Peace and Union. But the fate of [the Albany] Plan was singular," Franklin continued. Although the Albany congress had unanimously agreed to it, "the Crown disapprov'd it, as having plac'd too much Weight in the democratic Part of the Constitution; and every Assembly as having allow'd too much to Prerogative. So it was totally rejected." [9]

Franklin's plan, nevertheless, was the most significant step in the development of the federal concept that had yet appeared. As such, it formed an important precedent for later still-born plans of imperial union such as that of Joseph Galloway, who during the First Continental Congress consciously modeled his plan on the union agreed upon at Albany. Furthermore, Franklin's ideas entered into the Articles of Confederation and through them, the Federal Constitution. Finally, there was more than a hint in the Albany Plan for a design for western settlement that would later come to fruition in Jefferson's Northwest Ordinance of 1787. In the Ordinance as in the Albany Plan, new settlements would be under the aegis of the central government until such time as they would be erected into states, or in the latter case, colonies.

Western settlement, in spite of the failure of the Albany Plan, still aroused Franklin's enthusiasm. Late in 1754, he composed his "Plan for Settling two Western Colonies," which envisioned buffer states against the French, one between the Allegheny River and the south shore of Lake Erie near present-day Cleveland, and the other to the west along the Scioto River. Franklin urged liberal governments for these colonys, "for extraordinary privileges and liberties, with lands on easy terms, are strong inducements to people to hazard their persons and fortunes in settling new countries." As for raising the monies to purchase the designated lands from the Indians, Franklin believed there were many Americans "who would be glad of any opportunity . . . to secure land for their children, which might in a few years become very valuable." [10] Needless to say, Franklin was prepared to include himself in any such speculative venture.

Plans such as these, however, fell by the wayside as France and England inexorably headed for war. Even as the commissioners at Albany were debating the plan of union, George Washington, now a lieutenant colonel, was defeated by the French at the hastily constructed Fort Necessity, some fifty

miles south of Ft. Duquesne. As a result, Governor Dinwiddie asked England for help, which arrived in February, 1755,
in the person of Major General Edward Braddock with two
incomplete Irish regiments to be supplemented from American enlistments. Braddock's arrival marked the emergence
of a grand strategy to reduce the French power in America.
Braddock was to march to the forks of the Ohio to bring
about the capitulation of Ft. Duquesne. At the same time,
Massachusetts Governor Shirley, now a major general, was
to attack Ft. Niagara, while William Johnson, New York
councilman, and Indian agent, would take Ft. St. Frédérick
at Crown Point.

In support of the Crown Point venture, commissioners
from Massachusetts traveled to New York, New Jersey and
Pennsylvania to obtain aid from their respective assemblies.
Josiah Quincy, wealthy Boston merchant, arrived in Philadelphia when the problem of defense had renewed the bitter
struggle between the Pennsylvania Assembly and the proprietors now represented by Governor Robert Morris, who had
replaced Governor Hamilton in 1754. Indeed, during Franklin's absence at Albany and his following tour of the northern
postoffices, Governor Morris' vetoes of the Assembly's paper-
money bills had so angered the legislators that they had sent
a petition of grievances to the King. Franklin believed that
the Assembly's action was unwise, and he did not like the
governor's conduct any better. "The Assembly ride restive,"
Franklin commented, "and the Governor, tho' he spurs with
both Heels, at the same time reins-in with both Hands, so that
the Publick Business can never move forward; and he remains
like St. George in the Sign, always a Horseback, and never
going on."

With the legislature and the executive at deadlock, Franklin, having resumed his seat in the Assembly, strove to find
"a Method of doing business without the Governor." He

finally hit upon a scheme whereby the Assembly issued against the Loan Office orders that would not be payable for a year and that would bear five percent interest. In this way the necessity for raising immediate sums was avoided while suppliers of foodstuffs for the armies were assured of future payment plus interest. Though Governor Morris was miffed at having been bypassed, Josiah Quincy "went home highly pleas'd with the Success of his Embassy, and ever after bore for me," wrote Franklin, "the most cordial and affectionate Friendship." [11]

Franklin's stratagem in effect postponed the showdown between Assembly and governor over taxation and paper money. Meanwhile, there were more pressing matters at hand. Major General Braddock, now encamped at Frederick, Maryland, had met disappointment in his expectation that the colonies would find the necessary wagons, horses and foodstuffs for his attack on Ft. Duquesne. His anger was particularly turned against the Pennsylvania Quakers who, he believed, were the principle obstructors of military preparedness. Blustering and fuming, the major general threatened to impress men and materials into his service; there were even rumors that he intended to turn his forces against the stubborn Pennsylvanians rather than against the French. In this crisis, the Pennsylvania Assembly sent Franklin as its representative to meet with and reassure the general as to its readiness to assist him. "It was a pity," Franklin told Braddock, that "he had not been landed rather in Pennsylvania, as in that Country almost every Farmer had his Waggon." Eagerly, Braddock commissioned Franklin to contract with the Pennsylvania back-countrymen for the necessary supplies.

Travelling to Lancaster, some sixty miles west of Philadelphia, Franklin posted an artful advertisement that appealed both to the farmers' pocketbooks and to their fears:

"If you are really, as I believe you are, good and loyal Subjects to His Majesty," Franklin addressed the farmers,

> you may now do a most acceptable Service, and make it easy for yourselves. . . . But if you do not this Service to your King and Country voluntarily, when such good Pay and reasonable Terms are offered you, your loyalty will be strongly suspected; the King's Business must be done . . . violent Measures will probably be used; and you will be to seek for a Recompense where you can find it, and your Case perhaps be little pitied or regarded."

Distributed in German as well as English, Franklin's broadside was an immediate success. In fact, the response was so overwhelming that Franklin, having expended the money given him by Braddock, personally "advanc'd upwards of 200 pounds more, and in two Weeks, the 150 Waggons with 259 carrying Horses were on their March for the Camp." Franklin had promised the farmers that Braddock would pay for any damage to or loss of the wagons and horses, but the farmers insisted upon his bond to that effect. The amount came to twenty thousand pounds which had it not been honored by the government, "to pay would have ruined me." On top of this, Franklin managed to have the Assembly make a handsome gift to Braddock's officers of such items as "Jamaica Spirits," madeira, tea, cheese, ham, coffee and sugar.

Needless to say, Braddock was delighted with Pennsylvania, which as he put it, had promised nothing and done everything, whereas Virginia and Maryland had promised everything and done nothing. As for Franklin, Braddock wrote home to the ministry that the Pennsylvanian's activities constituted "almost the only Instance of Ability and Honesty I have known in these Provinces. His Waggons and Horses . . . are indeed my whole Dependence. . . ." It was unfortunate for the general that he did not think as highly of Franklin's military acumen. "The only Danger I apprehend of Obstruction to your March," Franklin told Braddock, "is from Ambuscades of Indians. . . . And the slender Line near four Miles long, which your Army must make, may expose it to be attack'd by Surprize in its Flanks, and to be cut like a Thread into several Pieces. . . ." It was a surprisingly accurate forecast. But, as Franklin put it, Braddock "smil'd at my Ignorance." It was impossible, the general replied, that the Indians "should make any Impression upon the King's regular and disciplin'd Troops. . . ." Braddock's praise of Franklin, in spite of the American's pessimism, was equalled by that of the Pennsylvania Assembly, which voted Franklin its thanks. Meanwhile, Governor Morris, whom Franklin considered "half a Madman," utilized the most exasperating tactics in his effort to bend the Assembly to the proprietary will.[12] Morris' instransigence reflected, Franklin believed, the unconstitutional and greedy demands of the Penns. The politically independent philosopher would soon become the leader of the antiproprietary party.

The turning point for Franklin came after the disaster that overtook Braddock in the valley of the Monongahela. On July 9, 1755, only some ten miles from Ft. Duquesne the general was killed, as was his secretary, the young son of Governor Shirley. Out of fourteen hundred troops, there were a thousand casualties; sixty-three of Braddock's eighty-six officers were killed or wounded. George Washington miraculously escaped injury, having his clothing ripped by bullets and two horses shot out from under him. The attacks on Ft. Niagara and Ft. St. Frédérick at Crown Point were likewise failures. Now if ever, there was reason for the colonies to close ranks in support of the common cause. But Pennsylvania remained ensnarled in the endless struggle between the Assembly and the proprietor.

Two weeks following the disaster along the Monongahela, the Assembly passed a tax measure to raise 50,000 pounds for defense. The measure provided for a tax on all estates, including those of the greatest landholders of all, the proprietors. Thomas Penn believed however, that as chief governor of the colony, his estates should be immune from taxation. Furthermore, collections of quitrents due him were disastrously in arears, and although on paper Penn was a rich man, he was constantly embarrassed for want of cash. Finally, Penn believed that with agents of the Assembly in charge of the assessment of values for purposes of taxation, he would be destroyed. He therefore instructed Governor Morris that on no account was he to sign a tax bill that included the proprietary estates. The issue was joined. Throughout the fall of 1755, when the fate of the colonies seemed to hang in the balance, the Assembly, with Franklin as its chief penman, entered into bitter dispute with Governor Morris, who took an immovable stance on the proprietary instructions.

To Franklin, the proprietor's attitude reflected an "incredible Meanness." He was already angered by Thomas Penn's insistence that his governor have a say in the expenditure of funds raised by the Assembly. Penn's claim threatened the natural right of the people to grant and dispose of their own money. Now Penn's claimed exemption from taxation meant that the people of Pennsylvania alone were expected to provide for the defense of estates whose owners would contribute nothing. Meanwhile, because of such defense measures, the value of the proprietary estates would be increased at the expense of the people. "This is not merely Vassalage," wrote Franklin for the Assembly, "it is something we have no adequate Name for; it is more slavish than Slavery itself." To the Assembly, the issue represented more than a matter of money; the proprietary attitude involved a denial of the ancient rights of Englishmen. "Those who would give up essential Liberty, to purchase a little temporary Safety," wrote Franklin, "deserve neither Liberty nor Safety." [13]

Franklin's leadership of the Assembly infuriated the proprietary party. In England, Thomas Penn tried to have Franklin removed from his deputy-postmastership. At home, as Franklin put it, "Those who caress'd me a few Months since, are now endeavoring to defame me every where by base Art." And while her government remained locked in dispute, Pennsylvania's long history of amicable Indian relations came to an end. French successes emboldened the Indians against the English, but there was a more immediate reason for the sudden attack upon the Quaker colony. At the Albany Conference, with incredibly poor timing, the proprietary representatives purchased most of western Pennsylvania from the Iroquois, who acted as overlords of the Ohio Valley. Profoundly disturbed by the steady encroachment upon their lands, the once friendly Delaware and other Ohio tribes savagely attacked along the Pennsylvania frontier. In October, 1775, they massacred eight families near the site of present-day Sunbury, some one hundred miles northwest of Philadelphia.

"We are all in Flames," wrote Franklin describing the political situation. The phrase also fit the situation in the west. In November, a band of angry frontiersmen marched to Philadelphia to demand protection from the government. At the same time, to break the legislative deadlock but again postponing solution of the basic issues, the proprietor made a free gift of five thousand pounds to the colony for defense. The Assembly, bowing to expediency, capitulated and passed a fifty-five thousand pound revenue measure that excluded the proprietary estates from taxation.

The money problem now temporarily in abeyance, the government next divided on the mode of raising troops. Following the Albany Conference Governor Morris asked the Assembly for a militia bill. After eleven months, the Assembly finally passed a bill personally drafted by Franklin, instead of by a committee which was the usual procedure. Franklin based his bill on the Association of 1747. Conscientious Quakers and other pacifists were excused from service. The bill provided for a voluntary militia, the members of which would elect their own officers who would be commissioned by the governor. Only four Quaker Assemblymen dissented while the governor reluctantly signed the measure, which he believed to be hopelessly inadequate and too democratic. To Franklin, however, this first militia bill ever passed in Pennsylvania was "agreeable to the Liberty and Genius of our Constitution." In retaliation, the governor instituted "independent companies," ironically based upon Franklin's earlier Association, except that the companies would be under the control of the supporters of Thomas Penn. With the Assembly militia and the proprietary companies staging competitive military exercises, it was fortunate that the colony was not plunged into civil war.

With the passage of the money and the militia bills, Franklin's brief military career had its beginning. He was elected colonel of the Philadelphia City Regiment, which, in an excess of military ardor, fired several rounds before Franklin's door. Less than pleased with the affectionate display, Franklin later ruefully complained that the resulting concussion "shook down and broke several Glasses of my Electrical Apparatus." [14] Governor Morris felt obliged to grant Franklin his commission, but he feared that the popular assemblyman might attempt a military takeover of the colony. Particularly galling to Thomas Penn was an incident during which Franklin was given a military escort by mounted guards, swords drawn, "as if he had been a member of the Royal Family or Majesty itself," wrote Richard Peters to the proprietor. Franklin was both flattered and embarrassed. "The

People happen to love me," he wrote. "Perhaps that's my Fault. . . . I, who am totally ignorant of military Ceremonies, and above all things averse to making Show and Parade . . . suffer'd at the Time much more Pain than I enjoy'd Pleasure. . . ." [15]

This "silly Affair," as Franklin called it, although important in further alienating Thomas Penn, had occurred after Franklin returned from his command of the northeastern frontier. There he had overseen the expenditure of moneys for arms and the building of forts in the Lehigh Valley in hitherto defenseless Northampton County. On the strenuous march from Bethlehem to Gnadenhütten (present-day Weissport on the Lehigh River), "General" Franklin, as the Bethlehem Germans called him, and his men spent the rain-soaked night of January 17, 1756, his fiftieth birthday, "all huddled together as wet as Water could make us." [16] At Gnadenhütten, which had been desolated by the Indians, Franklin and his men set to work constructing a fort which he named Ft. Allen. Some fifteen miles on either side of this fort were constructed Forts Norris and Franklin. Franklin's service on the frontier lasted fifty days; he was back at work in the Assembly the first week of February. As a result of his efforts the northeastern frontier was more secure; yet Indian attacks continued, and in the fall, Franklin returned once more to help draw up an Indian treaty at Easton. This treaty plus the victory of Colonel John Armstrong over the Indians at Kittanning on the Allegheny River helped quiet the Indians until finally in 1758, the fall of Ft. Duquesne (renamed Ft. Pitt) to the English brought peace to the Pennsylvania frontier.

Pennsylvania's Indian relations, like the taxation issue, were complicated by the political struggle between her Assembly and the proprietors. The Quakers viewed Indian unrest as a result of the present proprietors' reversal of William Penn's benign policies. The proprietors, preferring to deal with the Iroquois, had not only neglected such tribes as the Delaware, with whom the founder had originally drawn his great treaty, but they had defrauded these Indians of their lands most notoriously in the illfamed Walking Purchase of 1737. Having agreed to a purchase of land whose bounds were to be set by the distance a man could walk in a day and a half, the proprietors had hired "walkers,"—runners would be a more exact term—who, after cutting paths through the woods, were able to cover sixty-four miles in the allotted time. Thus, while the proprietors in England blamed Quaker pacifism as inviting Indian incursions, Pennsylvania's Quakers placed the blame on proprietary chicanery.

For its part, the proprietary faction made strenuous efforts to tarnish the reputation of the Quakers and the Germans, whose votes helped continue Quaker supremacy in the Assembly. Though Franklin did not at the time suspect its authorship, William Smith penned a *Brief State of the Province of Pennsylvania,* which was a devastating attack upon the Quaker party. Smith blamed Quaker pacificism for Pennsylvania's lack of adequate defense measures, and he accused the Germans of a secret alliance with the French. The work was designed as a political tract whose main purpose was to influence Parliament to curb Quaker participation in government. The proprietors also managed to have Franklin's militia bill disallowed by the Crown, thereby cancelling his colonelcy. In Pennsylvania, in order to ward off the threatened Parliamentary attack, thirteen pacifist Quakers gave up their seats in the Assembly. They were supplanted by men whose religious principles did not include pacifism, but whose political creed was as antiproprietary as that of the Quakers whom they replaced. The newly elected Assembly, including the brilliant Joseph Galloway, who became Franklin's legislative lieutenant, not only continued its attack on proprietary

Indian policy, but also voted a tax measure which, as usual, included the proprietary estates. When Governor Denny, who had superseded Robert Morris, reported that he would send the supply bill to the King with his reasons for opposing it, the Assembly promptly appointed Franklin its agent to go to London "to solicit a Redress of our Grievances."

So it was that only six years after Franklin had first entered the Assembly, he now found himself named to be Pennsylvania's chief representative in England. He had become one of the foremost political figures in Pennsylvania. His position was unique: a successful politician who was admired by the public. At about the time when he was selected the Assembly's London agent, there appeared an anonymous poem that was indicative of his popularity in Pennsylvania. In his eulogistic verses, the poet managed to sum up Franklin's political and scientific achievements as well as to mention the philanthropic ventures which he had initiated:

> Dear patriot muse that honest man behold
> Record his Acts in characters of gold.

> Who plann'd the Scheme the Associates to unite?
> Who wrote *plain truth* to bring that scheme to light?
> Who bid Yon Academick structure rise?
> "Behold the Man!" each lisping babe replies.
> Who schemed Yon Hospital for the helpless poor?
> And op'd to charitable use each folding door.
> Our Countrys cause, what senator defends?
> Void of all partial, or all private ends.

> Who to his publick trust has firmly stood?
> And built Fort Allen for his Countrys good.
> Who form'd a Law our Forces to unite?
> And deign'd to execute that Law aright.
> Who found out means our Treasury to supply?
> Who would not suffer publick faith to die?

Who was the Man brave Braddock, did record?
"The only man that with him keep his word."

'Twas He, whose name, the good and just all sound,
While patriot deeds on faithful records stand.

Great thy reward for all thy Labours done,
And at the great Tribunal will be known.
There will thy Genius other worlds survey,
And there adore the glorious God of day.
There Bacon Newton will our F——lin greet.
And place him in his Electrisic seat.
'Ore Uurope, Asia, Affrick's, science'd Fame,
The Royal Medal will exalt thy name;
Transfer the Palm by thy great genius won,
And proudly own America's great son.
If then thy sphere, to Electerise above,
Dart me one ray in pitty and in love.
Oh! send thy influence, if permitted, send,
To guide my soul to my beloved Friend.[17]

Franklin's popularity worried proprietary secretary Richard Peters, who warned Thomas Penn "that B. F.'s view is to effect a change of Government, and considering the popularity of his character and the reputation gained by his Electrical Discoveries which will introduce him into all sorts of Company he may prove a Dangerous Enemy." Penn, however, remained unimpressed. "Mr. Franklin's popularity is nothing here," he wrote. "He will be looked very coldly upon by great People." It will not be those who know of his electrical experiments with whom Franklin will have to deal, "but it is quite another sort of People, who are to determine the Dispute between us."[18]

Thomas Penn, in unguarded moments, may have indulged himself in the not unpleasant thought of Franklin finding himself agent to the court of King Neptune rather than to that of King George. An ocean crossing that spring of 1757 was a particularly hazardous undertaking. In June, England

and France formalized a state of war that in fact had begun two years before on the American frontier. The Seven Years' War as it is sometimes called, or the more aptly named Great War for the Empire would rage in America, Europe, Asia, Africa, and on the high seas until England would finally emerge victorious, the veritable ruler of the world. But whether or not Penn entertained wistful visions of Franklin's ship helplessly flying before the guns of a French man-of-war, Franklin himself, in spite of the danger, was anxious to be off. Deborah, who feared the sea, remained at home to look after her husband's business affairs. In early April, 1757, she bade him farewell. Accompanied by his son, Franklin travelled to New York to await the sailing of the convoy.

Months passed, however, before the convoy was ready to leave. It was the most inactive period of Franklin's life. He used the time to catch up on his scientific correspondence for which politics over the past years had given little leisure. He also applied to Lord Loudon, who had replaced Governor Shirley as the British Commander in America, for the balance of moneys still due him for his aid to General Braddock. Loudon, who wished to keep his accounts separate from those of his predecessors, referred him to London, but so far as is known, Franklin never received full compensation. Also during these months of waiting, Franklin commissioned James Parker, with whom in 1742 he had entered into business partnership, to act on his behalf as deputy postmaster-general. Parker, who with Franklin's help had established the *New York Weekly Post Boy* in 1743, was given broad authority, but he was to write frequently of his proceedings and to inform Franklin of matters that required his counsel.

It was a great relief to the Franklins when the procrastinating Loudon on June 20 finally allowed the convoy to sail. Although French privateers gave chase to his ship, Franklin's equanimity was such that he spent the voyage composing what proved to be in his own time his most popular work. This was the preface to his last almanac. In it he composed a kind of morality play in which an old man recites the best of Poor Richard's prudential maxims. Since its first publication in 1758, *The Way to Wealth,* has been republished hundreds of times in a dozen different languages. Even before the end of the eighteenth century there were some 144 reprintings, including 28 in French, 11 in Italian, 3 in German and one each in Dutch, Gaelic, and Swedish.

If as Father Abraham of the preface, Franklin assumed the guise of a didactic old maxim monger, he was more himself in his letters to friends. "Look out sharp," he had written to the London publisher William Strahan, "and if a fat old Fellow should come to your Printing House, . . . depend upon it, 'tis Your affectionate Friend." [19] Much to the delight of his London correspondents, Franklin and his son safely arrived at Falmouth on July 17. Ten days later, stopping once briefly to see Stonehenge, they were in London, where thirty years before, the now famous Franklin had sought work as a printer's boy.

V Franklin Versus the Penns: England and America

FRANKLIN'S ARRIVAL IN London on July 26, 1757, must have given him pause to reflect upon his present situation in comparison to that of his first London visit in 1724. At that time, he and his friend James Ralph had arrived penniless and friendless in the great city. Now Franklin had numerous friends and although he would meet most of them for the first time, they had become intimate through years of fruitful correspondence. He was a member of the prestigious Royal Society. He was the first electrician of the age. As deputy postmaster-general he was a royal official. And he now came on an important mission as the duly appointed agent of the legislative Assembly of Pennsylvania.

The institution of the colonial agency was nothing new when Franklin assumed his commission. Indeed, the Pennsylvania Assembly, like the legislatures of the other colonies, had long maintained an agent in London to look after its interests. The agents acted a role somewhere between that of lobbyist and ambassador. One of their most important functions was to oversee the passage of colonial laws through the gamut of inspection by the Board of Trade and the Privy Council. They lobbied for or against certain Parliamentary measures concerning America. They worked for bounties on some American products and for the reduction of duties on others. They had become an important adjunct of the imperial constitution, and they helped introduce the colonists to the arts of diplomacy. Franklin, for instance, was Pennsylvania's special ambassador to London before he was American minister to France. His experiences at the one court helped prepare him to meet the exigencies of the other. On the other hand, the assemblies frequently appointed members of Parliament as their agents. Such men for obvious reasons could be of great aid to their American constitutents.

Franklin's agency was supplementary to that of Pennsylvania's regular agent Robert Charles, with whom he worked closely during these years. He was to seek a redress of grievances from the proprietors, but if they remained recalcitrant, he would appeal his case to the king. But preliminary to these activities, he and his son had to find living quarters in the great city. During their first week in London, they were treated to the hospitality of Franklin's longtime correspondent Peter Collinson, who many years before had contributed to the fledgling Library Company and ever since then had acted as Franklin's principal literary and scientific representative in England. Soon, Franklin settled in at No. 7, Craven Street, presided over by his landlady Mrs. Margaret Stevenson. The location was both convenient and pleasant. His Craven Street house was not far from Whitehall, and the widow Stevenson and her eighteen year old daughter Mary adopted Franklin as one of the family. Among the Stevensons, their acquaintances, and Franklin there grew a lifelong friendship. To Polly, as Mary was familiarly known, Franklin through the years wrote some of his finest letters on various subjects including science about which she had as great a curiosity as her mentor had knowledge.

The Craven Street house was to be Franklin's home away from home during all his years in England. But Franklin was to have little time for relaxation. Arrangements had been made for an immediate meeting with the President of the King's Privy Council, Lord Granville, with whom Franklin had a significant interview. To his dismay, Franklin found that Granville believed that instructions to the governors had the effect of legislation in the colonies. To this, Franklin replied, "I had always understood from our Charters, that our Laws were to be made by our Assemblies, to be presented indeed to the King for his royal assent, but that once given the King could not repeal or alter them." [1] Inconclusive as the interview with Granville was, it served as a kind of forewarning of the difficulties with which Franklin would cope in his dealings with Thomas Penn. Granville's attitude also indicated that between the English government and the colonies, there had developed antithetical conceptions of the nature of the British Empire.

Shortly after the Granville interview, Franklin presented to Thomas Penn a paper listing the grievances of the Pennsylvania Assembly. The proprietor took immediate umbrage to Franklin's "Heads of Complaint," because it was not formally addressed to "the true and absolute Proprietaries of the Province of Pennsylvania." Nor did he like the complaints any better. The paper listed as particular grievances first, that proprietary instructions to the governors hampered legislation; next, "That the indubitable Right of the Assembly, to judge of the Mode, Measure and Time of Granting Supplies, is infringed," by instructions denying this right; and finally that the proprietor's insistence that his estates be exempt from taxation was "both unjust and cruel." Much as Penn disliked the "Heads of Complaint," he thought even worse of its bearer. Franklin looked, thought Penn, "like a malicious Villain." He was none the happier when the contents of a letter of Franklin's was reported to him by Pennsylvania friends. Penn talked, Franklin had written, "as a low Jockey might do when a Purchaser complained that He had cheated him in a Horse." Franklin's meetings with the proprietors only bore out his previous conviction that "The Spirit that makes them so ardently aim at the Disposition of Money not their own, is the same with that which inclines lesser Knaves to rob and pick Pockets." [2] It is little wonder that the Pennsylvania agent and the proprietors were unable to compromise their differences.

The solution of these differences, however, was soon taken out of the hands of the immediate protaganists. Under the pressure of successive British commanders in America, Pennsylvania Governor Denny signed money bills which included taxation of the proprietary estates as well as several other bills that were obnoxious to the Penns. The proprietors, therefore, appealed to the King against these measures, and so it was that the English government would finally adjudicate the issue. Franklin carefully prepared the Assembly case. He engaged lawyers to argue before the Board of Trade and the Privy Council, and he saw to the publication of two works designed to blacken the proprietors' reputation. The first of these was his friend Charles Thomson's book, *An Enquiry into the Causes of the Alienation of the . . . Indians.* Thomson detailed the alleged defrauding of the Indians by the proprietors and their agents. Next appeared the London barrister Richard Jackson's *An Historical Review of the Constitution of Pennsylvania,* for which Franklin supplied much of the material. Franklin believed, none too charitably, that as a result of this work, "the proprietors will be gibbeted up as they deserve, to rot and stink in the Nostrils of Posterity." [3]

It was not until June of 1760 when the Board of Trade finally made its detailed report on the eleven different Assembly bills that the proprietors hoped to have disallowed. The Board's report, a disappointment to Franklin in that it upheld most of the Penns' objections to the bills, was next appealed to the Privy Council and here Franklin fared better. The key bill, passed in Pennsylvania in the previous year provided for taxation of the proprietary estates. After Franklin and Pennsylvania's permanent agent Robert Charles promised to make personal indemnification to the proprietors if their estates were unfairly assessed, the Privy Council allowed the act to stand. Here was a signal victory for Franklin and the Assembly. The highest imperial authority had admitted the principle of the liability of the proprietary estates to taxation. For his part, Thomas Penn achieved the disallowance of several important acts including one which would have severely curbed his power to appoint judges of the Pennsylvania courts. He did not, however, achieve the disallowance of an act empowering Franklin to collect Pennsylvania's share of the 200,000 pound Parliamentary grant to the colonies for their aid during the war with France.

The grant of moneys to the colonies reflected the policy of Secretary of State William Pitt, whose brilliant leadership turned the tide of war in England's favor. His desire to win greater cooperation from the colonies was eminently successful. During the Great Year of 1759, on the Plains of Abraham where both Montcalm and Wolfe were fatally wounded, French Canada fell to the English. That year saw also the capture of the French sugar island of Guadaloupe, the conquest of India, the defeat of the French army at Minden, and of her fleet in the battle of Quiberon Bay. Pennsylvania's share of the Parliamentary grant passed at Pitt's request came to 26,618 pounds which was given to Franklin in November, 1760. The sequel to this aspect of Franklin's agency brought him close to financial and political disaster.

By the terms of the act of the Pennsylvania Assembly empowering Franklin to receive the moneys, he was to bank Pennsylvania's share of the Parliamentary grant. The Assembly then would write drafts against him personally, drafts which he would honor by withdrawals of the funds as needed.

In September, 1760, when prospects for an advantageous peace with France looked particulary bright, the Assembly, in a flush of speculative fever, instructed Franklin to withdraw the funds and invest them in his own name in the stock market. Franklin hastily complied. Unfortunately, it was at this juncture that the peace talks between France and England failed. Rumors circulated of Spain's secret decision to enter the war, and the great Minister William Pitt resigned when his colleagues refused to agree with him on an immediate strike against the new enemy. With stocks tumbling, the Pennsylvania Assembly called upon Franklin to make good on several drafts. Unfortunately, the drafts totalled more than the present value of his investments. Here was a fine triumph for the proprietors: not only would the credit of the Assembly be destroyed, but so would that of their nemesis Franklin. But the proprietary triumph was shortlived. As a testimony to the esteem in which he was held, two London bankers informed Franklin that they would pay the Assembly drafts against him "without desiring any other Security from you, than that which we know we have in your Character. . . ." [4] It was a close call. The Assembly did not blame Franklin for the losses it incurred from the sale of stock, and although the proprietors' Pennsylvania friends attacked his handling of the Parliamentary grant, he emerged from the affair as popular as ever.

The intricate manouverings surrounding the Parliamentary grant served to hold Franklin in England for two years following the hearing before the Privy Council, when the principle of the taxation of proprietary estates had been established. The slowness with which official business was carried on allowed him leisure for writing and for the scientific and philosophic studies in which he took so much pleasure. It also allowed him time for travel, particularly during the late summer months when the public offices were closed and the members of the government left for their estates in the country. In the summer of 1758, he and his son travelled to the English Midlands to visit Ecton and other places where his forebears had lived, and where there still were relatives with whom the two men made acquaintance. In the next year, they travelled to Scotland, where Franklin was granted a doctor of laws degree from St. Andrews University, and where he became a close friend of the eminent jurist Henry Home, Lord Kames, with whom he spent "Six Weeks of the *densest* Happiness I have met with in any Part of my Life." Once again in 1761, father and son in the company of Richard Jackson travelled to the Austrian and Dutch Netherlands (present-day Belgium and Holland) where Franklin met one of the discoverers of the Leyden jar, Professor Pieter van Musschenbroek, with whom he had previously corresponded. "Nobody," Musschenbroek had written Franklin in reply to his request for a list of European electricians, "has discovered more recondite mysteries of electricity than Franklin." The older man believed that the American "shall certainly find things which have been hidden to natural philosophers throughout the space of centuries." [5]

Though Franklin's major electrical discoveries were behind him, during these English years he continued his investigations into electrical phenomena. He also experimented with the cooling effects of evaporation, and pursued his interest in medicine and other aspects of natural philosophy. One of these concerned the differing abilities of various colors to absorb heat for which he had years before designed an ingenious experiment which he now described to Polly Stevenson:

> My Experiment was this. I took a number of little Square Pieces of Broad Cloth from a Taylor's Pattern Card, of various Colours. There were Black, deep Blue, lighter Blue, Green, Purple, Red, Yellow, White, and other

Colours or Shades of Colours. I laid them all out upon
the Snow in a bright Sunshiny Morning. In a few Hours
(I cannot now be exact as to the Time) the Black being
warm'd most by the Sun was sunk so low as to be below
the Stroke of the Sun's Rays; the dark Blue almost as
low, the lighter Blue not quite so much as the dark, the
other Colours less as they were lighter; and the quite
White remain'd on the Surface of the Snow, not having
entred it at all.

Franklin followed his description with several questions.
"What signifies philosophy that does not apply to some Use
. . . ? May we not learn that black Cloaths are not so fit to
wear in a hot Sunny Climate or Season as white ones . . . ?
That Soldiers and Seamen who must march and labour in the
Sun, should in the East or West Indies have an Uniform of
White?" [6] Unfortunately, it was a century before Europeans
learned to wear light-colored clothing in the tropics.

Franklin followed up another one of his earlier interests
when in 1758 he improved the efficiency of fire places with
the invention of the "Sliding Plate," or damper which became
very popular in London. Among his other mechanical con-
trivances of this period was a three wheel clock concerning
which a friend published an account. Years later in Paris,
Franklin was delighted to find several such clocks that had
been manufactured in England.

Perhaps his most famous invention of this time, however,
was the celebrated glass armonica, or harmonica as it frequently is called. Franklin utilized the well known principle
that when the dampened rim of a glass container is gently
rubbed, it gives off a musical sound. He created a tapered
series of thirty-seven glass hemispheres affixed to a horizontal
spindle. A treadle operated by the foot of the player caused
the glass hemispheres to revolve. As they turned, they were
dampened by a sponge, while the player lightly touched

them with his fingers. Franklin's armonica enjoyed great popularity throughout the latter part of the eighteenth century. Mozart wrote several works for it, and Beethoven used it to accompany the words of a melodrama for which he composed the incidental music. Franklin, who frequently delighted his visitors by performing on the armonica, carried one with him back to Philadelphia—along with extra glasses. The fragility of the armonica seems to be one of the causes of its passing from the musical scene in the early decades of the nineteenth century, though not before Donizetti scored the "Mad Scene" from *Lucia* to the accompaniment of Franklin's instrument.

Franklin's travels and his philosophical achievements refreshed him from the ardors of his continuing struggle with the Penn family. But for all his activities, he also found time to develop his theory of the British Empire and to attempt to influence the peace negotiations as the Great War for the Empire drew to a close. With the English conquest of both Guadaloupe in the West Indies and Canada there arose a great debate concerning which of these should be retained following the conclusion of hostilities. Guadaloupe appealed to many as the immediate source of sugar, an essential raw material. For others like Franklin, who viewed America as a vast market for English goods, Canada seemed the more valuable prize. Franklin, as a colonial, had also in mind the security of the mainland colonies. More fundamentally, as he had indicated earlier in his pioneering essay in demography, *Observations concerning the Increase of Mankind,* he was convinced that the future of the British Empire lay in the American West.

It was in support of this idea that Franklin entered the pamphlet war over what should be the spoils of the shooting war then drawing to a close. In April, 1760, he published his lengthy *The Interest of Great Britain Considered, With Re-*

gard to her Colonies, And the Acquisition of Canada and Guadaloupe. To it, he appended his *Observations concerning the Increase of Mankind* with its impressive projection of America's population growth. The two essays together formed a striking argument for the retention of Canada instead of Guadaloupe.

Franklin viewed the British Empire as one united whole. "Our North American colonies," he wrote, "are to be considered as the frontier of the British empire on that side." It is therefore to England's interest to see that frontier secured. "If ever there was a *national war,* this is truly such a one: a war in which the interest of the *whole* nation is directly and fundamentally concerned." Let not the English be afraid that the annexation of Canada will render America so powerful as to become a danger to her interests. It is true, "that with Canada in our possession, our people in America will increase amazingly." Yet, "the growth of the children tends to encrease the growth of the mother. . . ." Franklin could assure his readers from his own experience that a union of the colonies in opposition to England was impossible without, he added, "the most grievous tyranny and oppression. . . . While the government is mild and just, while important civil and religious rights are secure, such subjects will be dutiful and obedient. The waves do not rise, but when the winds blow." [7]

Franklin could hardly have known how prescient were these remarks, for in the next decade the winds would blow up a mighty storm between England and her colonies. It is impossible to assess the influence of Franklin's pamphlet, but he must have been highly pleased when at the conclusion of the Great War for the Empire, the Treaty of Paris provided for the cession of Canada to England while France retained Guadaloupe.

Franklin's many interests, of which international diplomacy was one, kept him busy during the months of waiting upon official business. But with the completion of the matter of the Parliamentary grant, there was no longer need for him to be in England. In all, his five years there had been a political and personal success. Though he had been unable to win every point of the Assembly's grievances against the proprietors, he had been successful in winning the Assembly's right to include the proprietary estates in general tax measures.

And personal honors continued to accrue. Shortly before Franklin sailed in August, 1762, he received his second doctorate from a British University, this time Oxford. Something of the esteem felt for him by the men of the European Enlightenment was expressed by the historian-philosopher David Hume, who heard of Franklin's impending departure. "America has sent us many good things," wrote Hume, "Gold, Silver, Sugar, Tobacco, Indigo, etc.: But you are the first Philosopher, and indeed the first Great Man of Letters for whom we are beholden to her." Hume, along with many other of Franklin's friends pressed him to stay in England. To his publisher friend William Strahan he explained why he must leave. His mission in England was completed. "I feel," he wrote, "like a thing out of its place, and useless because it is out of place. How then can I any longer be happy in England? You have great powers of persuasion, and might easily prevail on me to do any thing: but not any longer to do nothing. I must go home." [8]

Franklin's son William did not accompany his father on the return journey. To the annoyance of the Penns and the chagrin of Franklin's political enemies at home, the ministry appointed William royal governor of New Jersey. Franklin may have influenced the appointment through his friendship with Sir John Pringle, physician to the first minister the Earl of Bute. In any case, the appointment was a singular mark of favor to the American philosopher. William, of course, had actively sought governmental patronage, though this pursuit had evidently not monopolized his time. Sometime in 1760 he had fathered an illegitimate son whom he named William Temple Franklin. Shortly thereafter, the wayward governor-elect became engaged to be married. Since the ceremony was scheduled after the elder Franklin's date of departure, and since William had not yet been granted his governor's commission, he and his new wife remained in England until the following November.

Franklin arrived in Philadelphia on November 1, three weeks before his son and new daughter-in-law took ship from England. He found, as he wrote to William Strahan, "my little family perfectly well." Franklin furthermore discovered that rumors of his unpopularity circulated by William Smith and other proprietary friends while he was in England were untrue. "My House," Franklin told Strahan, "has been full of a Succession of my Friends from Morning to Night. . . ." [9] He had been chosen for the Assembly every year while he had been in "Happy England," for which he now felt a keen nostalgia. But although he hinted in his letters that he might return to spend his last years there, he and Deborah laid plans for their new house to be built on Market Street. It would be the first home that they owned, for previously they had always lived in rented quarters.

When the Assembly met in January, Franklin was present to take his seat for the first time in almost six years. In the warm glow of victory over the French, political strife in Pennsylvania was momentarily muffled. The proprietors' friends attempted to stir the pot with accusations that Franklin had wasted the province's money while he was in England, but the Assembly promptly indicated its confidence in him by voting him a handsome sum that more than covered his expenses. With the money, the Assembly also voted Franklin its thanks "for the faithful Discharge of his Duty to this Province in particular, as for the many and important Services done America in general, during his Residence in Great Britain."

Franklin did not remain long in Philadelphia to bask in popularity. Postal affairs demanded his attention. His colleague William Hunter, deputy postmaster for the southern colonies had died in 1761, and Franklin wished to confer with Hunter's replacement John Foxcroft, also of Virginia. The two men made an extensive inspection trip of postal facilities from Virginia north to New England. In five months, Franklin covered over 1100 miles. He extended the service to newly acquired Montreal and Quebec, and he improved communications between Philadelphia, New York and Boston by adding night carriers. He also visited in the northern colonies his many friends as well as such officials as Governor Monckton of New York and General Amherst, commander of the British forces in America. With these men Franklin discussed the ominous news of Indian uprisings in the west.

The aftermath of the Great War for the Empire in America was not peace, but one of the bloodiest Indian wars of the colonial period. Pontiac's Rebellion, as it is called after the charismatic leader of the Ottawa Indians, burst forth in full fury in May, 1763, just before Franklin and Foxcroft left Philadelphia for their northern tour. The basic cause of the uprising was the steady treck of western pioneers over the mountains into lands claimed by the Indians. To this general cause was added the alarm spread among the western tribes when they heard of the Treaty of Paris, by which the French ceded not only Canada, but also the vast area between the Appalachians and the Mississippi River. Furthermore, General Amherst, who at one time entertained the idea of sending to the Indians blankets infected with smallpox, had refused to continue the policy of giving to the tribes presents, including ammunition upon which they were dependent for hunting. The Indians considered such presents not as charity but as compensation for British forts in their territory. Before the Indian rebellion was put down, innumerable whites along the Virginia, Maryland, and Pennsylvania frontiers had been captured or killed.

The immediate result of Pontiac's Rebellion was renewed political turbulence in Pennsylvania. No people had suffered greater Indian depredations than the Scotch-Irish pioneers who inhabited the frontier regions of the colony. And yet while they faced a savagely revengeful foe in a war of mutual extermination, their government was once more locked in dispute over taxation and defense. Not only that, but Philadelphia had given refuge to the so-called Moravian Indians of Bethlehem, upon whom the pioneers would vent their hatred. The Scotch-Irish Presbyterians blamed their woes upon the Quakers, who dominated the government. In their accusations that the proprietors had defrauded the Indians of their lands, the Quakers had seemingly encouraged the red men to take up the hatchet. Adding insult to injury, the three eastern Pennsylvania counties had twice the representation in the Assembly as did the five counties to the west.

Although the frontiersmen had legitimate complaints, their stand was severely compromised by the grim violence of some of their younger men. At Conestoga, fifty miles west of Philadelphia, lived the remnants of the small tribe of Conestoga Indians, who from the time of William Penn had been at peace and amity with the people of Pennsylvania. Utterly impoverished, these helpless Indians survived by begging or selling baskets and brooms. One December morning, when most of the Indians were out selling their wares, some fifty men from Paxton township rode into Conestoga, burst into the Indians' huts and butchered the remaining three men, two women and a child. One of the men was the venerable Shehaes, who had attended a treaty with William Penn in 1701. The fourteen remaining Indians, having beheld their dismembered kinsmen, fled to neighboring Lancaster, where the authorities placed them in the ruggedly built workhouse for their protection. Nevertheless, the Paxton Boys, who professed to believe that these Indians had given assistance to Pontiac's warriors, rode into Lancaster, burst open the workhouse door and slaughtered the defenseless men, women and children, leaving their bodies strewn about the yard. They then gathered a greater force and rode toward Philadelphia in order to extirpate the Moravian Indians there in protective custody.

Philadelphia was immediately thrown into a panic greater by far than that caused years before by French incursions up the Delaware River. Once more, Franklin, who had returned from the north in early November, sparked the preparations for defense. He formed a new military association. John Penn, the new governor and grandson of the founder, offered Franklin command of the troops, which he refused, and used his house for military headquarters. The colony balanced on the edge of civil war. By the first week of February, the rioters, "Hickory Boys" as they called themselves, arrived only a few miles from Philadelphia at Germantown, where clothed as Indians they terrorized the people. Governor Penn named Franklin to the commission to ride out to parley with the invaders. At Germantown, Franklin, finding the westerners satisfied that they had dramatically demonstrated their feelings, promised their leaders to present their grievances to the Assembly. The westerners' ardor may also have been cooled by the formidable military preparations in Philadelphia, for they quickly disbanded to return to their homes. None of the Conestoga murderers was apprehended and ultimately they accomplished their mission against the Moravian

Indians, who, returned to the frontier in 1765, were destroyed during the turmoil of the American Revolution.

Franklin had not only promoted the defense of the city and turned back the rioters, but he was also profoundly moved by the fate of the Conestoga Indians. In January, he penned his *Narrative of the Late Massacres in Lancaster County.* Burning with moral indignation, Franklin castigated the "Christian White Savages" of Pennsylvania. "What had little Boys and Girls done? What could Children of a Year old, Babes at the Breast, what could they do, that they too must be shot and hatcheted? Horrid to relate! And in their Parents Arms! . . . We have seen, that they would have been safer among the ancient *Heathens,* with whom the Rites of Hospitality were *sacred.*" Yes, Indians too had committed murders, but,

> If an Indian injures me, does it follow that I may revenge that Injury on all Indians? It is well known, that Indians are of different Tribes, Nations and Languages, as well as the White People. In Europe, if the French, who are White People, should injure the Dutch, are they to revenge it on the English, because they too are White People? The only Crime of these poor Wretches seems to have been, that they had a reddish-brown Skin, and black Hair; and some People of that Sort, it seems, had murdered some of our Relations. If it be right to kill Men for such a Reason, then, should any Man, with a freckled Face and red Hair, kill a Wife or Child of mine, it would be right for me to revenge it by killing all the freckled red-haired men, Women and Children, I could afterwards anywhere meet with.[10]

Franklin's pamphlet helped rally Philadelphians against the threat from the west. It was also a powerful appeal for continued protection of the Moravian Indians. Nevertheless, it was soon used against him in the virulent political strife that boiled up in the wake of the sectional conflict. An alliance emerged between the proprietor's followers and the west. Both blamed the Assembly for insufficient defense measures, for coddling the Indians, and for the inequitable representation of the newer counties. The Assembly party on the other hand blamed the proprietors for their failure to keep order in the colony. Furthermore, in spite of the Privy Council order of 1759 with regard to the taxation of proprietary estates, the issue now reappeared in a dispute over the proper interpretation of that order. Governor Penn not only refused to sign a new tax measure of the Assembly, but he also vetoed a militia bill which provided as before for the election of officers.

Thoroughly exasperated, the Assembly having elevated Franklin to the Speaker's chair, now turned to a solution to which he had given long consideration. That was to petition the Crown to royalize Pennsylvania. Royalization would get to the root of the problem. The proprietors could no longer obstruct needed legislation; their private interests would no longer take precedence over the public interest. In *Cool Thoughts on the Present Situation of Our Public Affairs,* Franklin made the Assembly's case. "At present we are in a wretched Situation," he wrote. "The Government that ought to keep all in Order, is itself weak, and has scarce Authority enough to keep the common Peace." It does not dare to lift a finger against the Paxton murderers, while,

> honest Citizens, threatened in their Lives and Fortunes flie the Province, as having no Confidence in the Publick Protection. . . . There seems to remain, then, but one Remedy for our Evils, a Remedy approved by Experience, and which has been tried with Success by other Provinces; I mean that of an immediate *Royal Government,* without the Intervention of Proprietary Powers, which, like unnecessary Springs and Movements in a Machine are so apt to produce Disorder.[11]

Proprietary versus royal government became the central issue in the election of 1764, an election in spite of Franklin's *Cool Thoughts* the most heated in colonial Pennsylvania history. Westerners and the friends of the Penns came together in a Presbyterian-proprietary alliance designated as the New Ticket. The Old Ticket, with Franklin and Galloway its leaders, appealed to the artisans and shopkeepers of the city, the Quakers and their German allies, and to all who had cause to dislike the proprietors. Accusations and counter accusations flew. Proprietary defenders accused Franklin of desiring to be the first royal governor of Pennsylvania, while Galloway allegedly wanted to be chief justice. The Old Ticket, it was alleged, wanted control of the two hundred justices of the peace appointed by the proprietors. Its leaders, furthermore, were portrayed as hungry for the loot available from proprietary fees such as the licensing of taverns.

Particularly damaging to Franklin was the first edition of his *Observations concerning the Increase of Mankind,* in which he had expressed alarm at the increasing German population of Pennsylvania. "Why should the Palatine Boors," he had asked, "be suffered to swarm into our Settlements? . . . Why should Pennsylvania, founded by the English, become a Colony of *Aliens,* who will shortly be so numerous as to Germanize us instead of our Anglifying them . . . ?" [12] Franklin evidently regretted this outburst as being neither generous nor politic. He excised the passage from the subsequent editions of the *Observations,* but the New Ticket nevertheless saw to its distribution among the German voters. Much print was spilled over whether "boor" meant "clown," or "peasant." Furthermore, the city's Presbyterians were not allowed to forget that Franklin had called their western coreligionists "Christian white Savages." Some of the proprietors' aristocratic supporters voiced contempt for Franklin's humble origins, nor was the origin of his illegitimate son, the governor of New Jersey, overlooked. The scurrilous attack on Franklin's morals was accompanied with a denigration of his scientific reputation: he had copied the ideas of other men. One would-be proprietary rhymster had Franklin gloating over the political turbulence of the times:

> Fight dog, fight bear, you're all my friends;
> By you I shall attain my ends;
> For I can never be content
> Till I have got the government;
> But if from this attempt I fail,
> Then let the devil take you all! [13]

The Old Ticket, for its part, was not idle. One pamphleteer showed the members of the proprietary party to be descended from London fishwives and convicts. Petitions for royalization were circulated among the people and Governor Penn noted that for one of them Franklin's party had "procur'd some names by the Assistance of Punch and Beer for they kept open house at first at a Tavern for all the Blackguards in Town, by which means a few Ship Carpenters and some of the lowest sort of people were prevailed upon to sign it." Franklin himself composed a lengthy reply to one proprietary pamphlet which drew from the records of the Assembly words of praise for the first proprietor who had granted liberal privileges to the original settlers. Going to the same sources, he composed a similar sketch for the sons:

> They,
> Foolishly and cruelly,
> Taking Advantage of public Distress,
> Have extorted from the Posterity of those Settlers;
> And are daily endeavouring to reduce them
> To the most abject Slavery;
> Tho' to the Virtue and Industry of those People
> In improving their Country,

Political caricature, 1764.
Courtesy of the Historical Society of Pennsylvania.

They owe all that they possess and enjoy.
                    A striking Instance
           Of human Depravity and Ingratitude;
             And as irrefragable Proof,
             That Wisdom and Goodness
       Do not descend with an Inheritance;
                     But that ineffable Meanness
May be connected with unbounded Fortune.[14]

The results of the October 1 election turned upon the extraordinary unity of the Presbyterians to which was added Quaker disunity over the issue of royalization. Many Friends, much as they hated Thomas Penn, preferred his government to that of the Crown, under whom their religious privileges might be compromised. Royalization, it was feared, might result in the establishment of the Anglican Church in Pennsylvania. When the votes were counted, the Old Ticket still maintained control of the Assembly, but its two leaders, Franklin and Galloway, were defeated by the narrow margin of twenty-five votes out of four thousand cast. "Mr. Franklin died like a philosopher," wrote one observer. "But Mr. Galloway agonized in death, like a mortal deist who has no hopes of a future existence."

Shortly after the convening of the new Assembly, Franklin was appointed to return to England with the petition for royalization. Proprietary spokesmen loudly proclaimed against this flouting of the people's will: had not both Franklin and Galloway, principal promoters of royalization, been defeated by the voters? Though there was point to the argument, there was a certain logic in the Assembly's action. Franklin's presence in England might intimidate Thomas Penn into granting further concessions to the Assembly. Above all, the Assembly desired that Penn free his deputy in Pennsylvania from binding instructions, instructions that limited his—and the Assembly's—legislative independence.

If the threat of royalization failed to convince Thomas Penn, Franklin could then attempt to make the threat a reality. Royalization was but a possible means to the attainment of the Assembly's true goal: self-rule.[15]

Franklin's appointment, nevertheless, resulted in renewed pamphlet warfare. The proprietary leaders, in a public protest, blamed him for the disorders in the province; they pointed to his defeat as a mandate against his policies in the recent election; they alluded to Franklin's "fixed Enmity to the Proprietors;" and they charged Franklin with mismanagement of the Parliamentary grant while he was in London.

To this protest, Franklin published a point for point reply. As to his share in the Assembly's antiproprietary measures, he believed them "such as will in time do Honour to all that were concerned in them." His narrow defeat was purchased by "double Tickets, and whole Boxes of forged Votes," and by stirring "up against me those religious Bigots, who are of all Savages the most brutish." "And why do you think I have a fixed Enmity to the Proprietaries?" asked Franklin. "Let them do Justice to the People of *Pennsylvania,* act honourably by the Citizens of *Philadelphia,* and become honest Men; my Enmity, if that's of any Consequence, ceases from the *'very Moment,'* and, as soon as I possibly can, I promise to love, honour, and respect them." As to the *"high* Charge," of malfeasance with regard to the Parliamentary grant, Franklin showed that even the signers of the Protest, some of whom were at the time members of the committee for examining his accounts, "found them just . . . ." If the protesters' accusation were true, why did not the Assembly demand recompense? "The Reason is, This Accusation was not then invented. . . . I am now to take Leave (perhaps a last Leave) of the Country I love," Franklin concluded. "I wish every kind of Prosperity to my Friends; and I forgive my Enemies." [16]

If these unctious last words pleased Franklin and confounded his enemies ("God has blessed me with two or
three," he had written, "to keep me in order"), he was even
more delighted and his enemies annoyed when several merchants in the city, the Assembly coffers being then empty,
came up with the money for his voyage to England. Little
could he have realized that during his second agency for the
Pennsylvania Assembly, its struggle with the Penns would
be wholly overshadowed by the growing dispute between
England and America. His experiences over the past years,
however, meant that he would face a new and unprecedented
crisis as a seasoned politician, ready to assume the mantle of
international statesman.

Though by 1764 such British legislation as the Sugar Act
and the announced intention of a colonial stamp tax presaged
the storm to come, as he prepared for the ocean crossing,
Franklin saw only the continuing crisis between the Assembly and the Penns. He had little faith that renewed negotiation would heal the breach: the Assembly would insist upon
its privileges, the proprietors on their prerogatives. Nor did
Franklin share Quaker fears concerning royalization. The
English government was in the process of reorganizing the
imperial structure. Over the past years all the proprietary
governments with the exception of Maryland and Pennsylvania had been royalized. Indeed, back in 1712, William Penn
himself had begun the sale of his government to the Crown.
Now Franklin had only to see to the consumation of this
much-to-be-desired transaction. Pennsylvanians, he had written, "are chiefly people of *three Countries:*

> *British* Spirits can no longer bear the Treatment they
> have received, nor will they put on the Chains prepared
> for them by a Fellow Subject. And the *Irish* and the
> *Germans* have felt too severely the Oppressions of *hard-*

> *hearted Landlords and arbitrary Princes,* to wish to see, in the Proprietaries of *Pennsylvania,* both the one and the other united."

Franklin looked forward to the time "when the direct and immediate Rays of Majesty benignly and mildly shine on all around us," rather than being "transmitted and thrown upon us thro' the Burning-Glass of Proprietary Government." [17] Little did he realize that "Rays of Majesty" would burn more severely than those of the proprietors. And those rays would burn not only Pennsylvania, but all of America as well.

VI The Stamp Act

PENNSYLVANIA'S INTERNAL POLITICAL STRUGGLE between proprietary and Assembly factions coincided with developments elsewhere that would have far greater significance for the peace of America. The Treaty of Paris of 1763 placed England at an apogee of world power. Yet ironically, the Treaty also marked the beginning of the end of the old British Empire. France and Spain sullenly awaited a chance to revenge their humiliating defeat. The colonies' dependence upon the mother country was lessened by the removal of the French threat from Canada. They emerged from the Great War for the Empire with a proud consciousness of their own strength and maturity. Finally, the war left England with a catastrophic national debt and a newly won world-wide empire to rule. All of these factors combined to make her moment of victory a herald of future defeat.

England's fateful dispute with her colonies was a result of her efforts to solve her postwar financial and administrative problems. Though previous Anglo-American relations had been marked by many quarrels, now for the first time the colonies would be united by common grievances. The Crown itself contributed to American unity when it insisted that American defense was the collective responsibility of all the colonies. From this principle, it followed that all thirteen colonies should help pay the costs of victory. These included the maintenance of English troops in the new American territories of Canada, the Floridas, and the transmontane west.

George Grenville, who became Chancellor of the Exchequer and First Lord of the Treasury in 1763, was the perfect embodiment of these ideas. Member of Parliament for over twenty years, brother-in-law to the great William Pitt, the new first minister was a conscientious, hard working and able financier, whose major fault was his failure to understand that the American colonies had matured beyond England's ability to discipline them. England, he believed, had carried the major burden of the war; yet the colonies were the real beneficiaries. With a cash register concept of empire, Grenville had tallied up the cost in pounds and pence. Like an eighteenth century Coolidge, his understanding never went beyond the narrow principle of cash on the line for benefits received.

Similarly to the Europeans who in the nineteen twenties believed Uncle Sam to be parsimonious, Franklin and other colonials resented the imputation that the colonies had gained the most while paying the least. The war, they pointed out, had been fought for English trade, for English predominance in the West Indies, Africa, and India, and for the security of Nova Scotia. The colonies, furthermore, had contributed much in men, material, and money. Nevertheless, in spite of such arguments, Grenville, believing that England would bear no further financial burden, determined to impose revenue taxes on the American colonies.

Grenville was aware that his plan to tax the colonies would be viewed in America as a baneful innovation. Yet he believed that the right had always existed, though it might not ever have been exercised. But the colonists denied that Parliament ever had authority to tax the colonies. They spoke not of the rights of Parliament, but of the rights of Englishmen, and ultimately of the rights of man. Grenville had been warned that it would be well to consider the constitutional implications of parliamentary taxation of the colonies. What, for instance, was the constitutional place of the powerful colonial assemblies in the British Empire? Were they not true legislative bodies, and if so could Parliament legislate for the colonies? Can the taxing power lie with any but the direct representatives of the people? Franklin had raised such questions as early as 1754 in his letters to Governor Shirley. Now Grenville would answer them by the disingenuous doctrine that the colonists were "virtually represented" in Parliament. It followed that there could be no legitimate objections to Parliamentary taxation. Convinced of his own rectitude, Grenville instituted his imperial reforms.

First there was the reordering of the customs service, including authorization for use of the navy in revenue collections. Then came passage of the so-called Sugar Act, though by virtue of its comprehensiveness it might be better termed the American Act. Reducing the old unenforceable molasses duty by half, Parliament provided new and stringent mechanisms for its collection as well as for the collection of numerous new duties on various articles from cloth to wine. For the first time, the all-important colonial coastwise and river trade was put under customs surveillance. The act also introduced the questionable doctrine of "guilty till proved innocent." It placed the burden of proof not on the arresting naval or customs officer, but upon the ship owner to prove he was not in violation of this or any other of the multifarious acts of navigation and trade. Finally, the act contravened the ancient British doctrine that an accused man be tried by his peers where the alleged crime took place. Instead, a new admiralty court was established in Halifax, Nova Scotia, to which accused American merchants and ship captains could be taken for trial.

Grenville also secured a new currency act which extended to the rest of the colonies the prohibition against paper money applicable in New England since 1751. The Currency Act seemed to the Americans to be peculiarly punitive in that the new sugar duties were to be paid in hard money only, thereby further exacerbating a chronic drain of specie from America to the old world. Franklin, whose first political pamphlet was a defense of Pennsylvania currency, had long ago recognized the necessity of paper money. Parliament's restrictive policy, enacted in spite of serious colonial objections, indicated it had little understanding of the colonial economy.

Grenville also proposed a new quartering act by which the Americans were required to billet and provision British regulars stationed in the colonies. The act was not passed until 1765, by which time Franklin had arrived in England and was able to modify its terms with respect to private houses. There was also the Proclamation Line of 1763 by which the Crown hoped to stop colonial emigration into the Ohio and Mississippi valleys. The line was proclaimed in part to mollify the Indians and also to allow time for the planning of orderly western settlement. It officially closed off an enormous area west of the Appalachian Mountains from Georgia to Quebec. To both actual settlers and land speculators, of whom Franklin was one, the line represented a policy that seemed to deny them the fruits of the recent victory over the French. Finally, the new first minister proposed the levying of a stamp tax on the colonies. To make it more palatable, he offered a one year period of grace, ostensibly to allow the colonies time to come up with alternative plans. But in fact, Grenville used the time to work out the many details of the stamp scheme.

With the exception of the Quartering Act, Grenville's program had been enacted before Franklin left on his second official mission to England. Deeply convinced as he was of the virtues of royal as against proprietary government, he failed to show much concern at these new policies. "There is scarce anything you can do that may be hurtful to us," wrote Franklin to an English correspondent, "but will be as much or more so to you . . . . What you get from us in Taxes," he went on, "you must lose in Trade. . . . In time perhaps Mankind may be wise enough to let Trade take its own course . . ." As a forecast of Adam Smith's doctrines,

Franklin's comments were impressive. As responses to a serious political challenge, they were irrelevant. But he was in a mood to take the long view. Nature would win over policy. "Consider *the rate of our Increase,*" he wrote. The future belongs to America regardless of the machinations of selfish politicians.[1]

In early November, 1764, only a few weeks after his election as agent, Franklin prepared for England. He bade farewell to Deborah: he could not have known it would be their final parting. The Old Ticket made of his departure a triumphant political demonstration. Three hundred mounted horsemen escorted him the fifteen miles to his ship at Chester. There, to the tune of *God Save the King,* they sang an anthem especially composed for the occasion:

> O Lord our God arise,
> Scatter our enemies,
>   And make them fall.
> Confound their Politicks,
> Frustrate such Hypocrites,
> *Franklin,* on Thee we fix,
> God Save us all.[2]

From shipboard, Franklin wrote his daughter that "the affectionate leave taken of me by so many friends at Chester was very endearing. God bless them and all Pennsylvania." [3]

Though Franklin had been sent once more across the ocean to do battle with Thomas Penn, he was sure that regardless of the outcome, the future belonged to Pennsylvania and America. Britain's American colonies were no longer feeble enclaves located on inhospitable coasts. They had become states with unique traditions of their own. Virginia's House of Burgesses, dating from 1619, was one of the oldest representative bodies in the world. Massachusetts Bay, from its inception as a self-governing corporation in 1629 to its royalization in 1691, had developed a tradition of independence to which it stubbornly adhered throughout the colonial period. Pennsylvania, with a more mixed white population than either of these, prided itself on its liberal institutions and developing economy and culture. Neither these nor the other colonies would take kindly to a permanent status of subservience to a mother country that had mothered fewer colonists with every passing generation.

It was ironic that England chose to strengthen her authority in America at a time when the colonies had become conscious of their cultural and economic maturation. No colonial with the opportunities Franklin had had to observe the scene could have been unaware of America's tremendous potential. In the bustling coastal cities, skilled artisans and laborers helped swell a population that demanded an increasing number of complex services. The resulting growth of manufacturing and industry prefigured the later development particularly of Franklin's adopted colony. Pennsylvania was preeminent in the manufacture of such diverse items as glass, rifles, barrels, and flour. Pennsylvania and New Jersey were the center of the colonial iron industry, which by the time of the Revolution contributed one-seventh of the world's iron output. Philadelphia itself was the center of the colonial paper industry in which Franklin had played so significant a role.

Initiative such as Franklin's had carried other colonials to success in a wide variety of enterprises. Commerce played a predominant part in the colonial economy. By the Revolution, one-third of England's trade would be carried in colonial-built ships. In the year 1770, for example, 800 ships cleared from the port of Boston, 769 from Philadelphia, 612 from New York, 541 from Charleston: in all, well over three thousand vessels sailed out of American ports, while somewhat more than this entered from overseas or neighboring colonies.

Whether Americans were exporting flour (Pennsylvania in the seventies annually shipped 350,000 barrels); rum (as early as 1750, Massachusetts shipped two million gallons); or the products of the southern colonies (in 1774, Virginia and Maryland shipped fifty-four and a half million pounds of tobacco; South Carolina and Georgia exported some seventy-six million pounds of rice); their commerce made up a significant part of Britain's imperial stature. The colonies had come of age. Only at extreme peril would Britain fail to recognize that fact.

Franklin arrived in England after a remarkably short voyage of thirty days. Once more he settled into the warmly hospitable house of Margaret Stevenson on Craven Street. His immediate purpose was negotiations with the Penns. These were pursued through intermediaries: Franklin and Thomas Penn were no longer on speaking terms. Meanwhile, the Pennsylvania Assembly elections of October, 1765, swept the Quaker party leaders including Joseph Galloway back into power. Franklin took the election defeat of the proprietary party to mean that the people would gladly be rid of proprietary government. Therefore, with the foreordained failure of the negotiations with Thomas Penn—Penn insisted upon his right to delimit his deputy governor's legislative independence—Franklin carried the Assembly petition for royalization before the Privy Council. To his dismay, the Council found legal obstacles and postponed the petition indefinitely. Franklin had miscalculated the willingness of the British government to take the Assembly's side in its struggle with Thomas Penn. He also had failed seriously to consider the threat inherent in the ministry's attitude toward America. The ocean voyage had not lessened his philosophic detachment from the reality of Grenville's colonial program.

The reasons for Franklin's bland attitude were many and complex. Since Grenville's legislation was all but complete before Franklin set foot in England, he believed it too late for effective opposition. Furthermore, he did not wish needlessly to antagonize the new ministry and thereby jeopardize the Pennsylvania petition. Also as a land speculator, he had personal reasons for maintaining the confidence of a ministry from whom he desired cooperation in broaching the Proclamation line. Besides these public and personal considerations, there was also the fact that Postmaster General Franklin was, after all, an officer of the Crown, to whom his son also was beholden as Royal Governor of New Jersey. Franklin was still an imperialist who believed the future greatness of the English nation to be dependent upon the vast potential of the American continent. He loved old England, the mother country that had conferred such high honors upon her humble son, the island which at times he had considered making his final home. But for whatever reasons, Franklin's mild response to the challenge of 1764, and particularly to Grenville's suggestion of a colonial stamp tax, nearly destroyed his career.

The idea of extending the long-endured English stamp duty to the colonies did not originate with George Grenville. Many years before the Grenville administration, Franklin's would-be patron Sir William Keith had suggested the scheme to the then first minister, Robert Walpole. At that time, Walpole, who was near the end of his administration, had opposed the idea. Old England was against him, he said; he would not have New England against him too. Grenville had no such scruples, nor was Franklin greatly concerned. He had brought with him a mild protest from the Pennsylvania Assembly. He also brought with him a new plan of taxation which he hoped he could convince Grenville to substitute for the stamp tax. This ingenious scheme would have Parliament authorize a colonial loan office, similar to Pennsylvania's loan office, which would solve the colonial currency problem. The interest accruing from paper-money loans would be utilized for whatever imperial purposes Parliament saw fit. The implied admission of Parliament's right to raise moneys in America indicated that Franklin, at this time, was willing to forgo the principles he had proclaimed in 1754 in his letters to Governor Shirley. Had his currency proposal been publicized in America, his political reputation there would probably have been ruined.

As it was, Franklin found Grenville "besotted with his Stamp Scheme." Neither his arguments nor those of such colonials as James Otis and Daniel Dulany could influence the ministry. Otis, in *The Rights of the British Colonies Asserted and Proved,* denied Parliament's right to tax the colonies unless they were represented there. Dulany's *Considerations on the Propriety of imposing Taxes in the British Colonies* . . . . attempted to draw a line between Parliament's right to regulate trade and her right to tax the colonies. He admitted the former, but denied the latter. His distinction between raising a revenue and regulating trade would be simplified and somewhat obscured by later spokesmen as a distinction between internal and external taxation. As such, Dulany's formulation would soon be used by both friends and foes of America.

Although Dulany did not publish his views until after passage of the Stamp Act, several colonial assemblies embodied similar views in petitions to Parliament, which convened in January, 1765. New York, for example, arguing upon the high ground of natural rights, denied Parliament's authority to impose taxes upon America. Arguments such as these, however, appeared to English officials as representing a challenge to Parliamentary supremacy, the keystone of the British constitution. To the economic arguments for an American stamp tax was therefore added a political argument: the colonial challenge to Parliamentary supremacy must be answered by the exercise of Parliamentary authority. Therefore, when Grenvill placed his stamp bill before the House, debate was brief, though highlighted by Colonel Isaac Barré's impassioned defense of the colonials whom he designated, "Sons of Liberty." Thus when the act became law on March 22, 1765, the Americans not only had a new grievance, but also a name for their emerging revolutionary associations.

The preamble to the act, like that to the Sugar Act of 1764, frankly stated that its purpose was to raise revenue in the colonies. The act required stamped paper at denominations from as little as three pence for court pleas to ten pounds for attorney's licenses. College degrees and diplomas were taxed at two pounds. Newspapers, pamphlets and almanacs (Poor Richard surely would take note) were taxed, as were dice, playing cards and licenses for the retailing of wines and liquor. Real estate contracts were taxed an amount relative to the number of acres purchased. Likewise there were taxes on commercial contracts from bills of sale to bonds. Stamped paper could be purchased only by hard money, a particularly resented aspect of the act. The colonists, at this time, were suffering from an economic depression caused, they believed, by a dwindling money supply. The Stamp Act, like the Sugar Act which had a similar provision, would further drain specie from America. It was an argument, incidentally, that the ministry denied, pointing out that moneys raised by the Stamp Act were to be expended only in America.

As if its economic aspects did not render the Stamp Act satisfactorily exhaustive, Parliament also ventured into the social realm. To encourage the Anglicization of German and other non-English colonists, the act doubled the tax on all non-English instruments for which stamps were required. Finally, similar to the Sugar Act, the Stamp Act provided for admiralty, rather than common-law jurisdiction over violations of its provisions.

Had Grenville set out to alienate all the most articulate members of colonial society, he could hardly have found a better formula than this act. The act laid heavy burdens on newspaper editors, merchants, students, lawyers, land speculators—in fact on all the most influential groups in colonial society. Yet while America seethed, Franklin remained singularly calm. "We might as well have hindered the sun's setting," he wrote to a friend in Pennsylvania. "But since 'tis down," he continued in philosophical vein, "and it may be long before it rises again, let us make as good a night of it as we can. We may still light candles." [4] Franklin, for once, had badly misjudged the temper of his countrymen.

The colonial agents could not of course be immediately apprised of the American reaction to the passage of the act. They faltered badly when they accepted Grenville's artful suggestion that they nominate persons at home to be distributors of the stamped paper sent from England. Franklin believed that Grenville's approaching him for names, rather than the Penns, was a blow against the proprietary family. He would have been wiser to let the Penns designate one of their party. Instead, he picked his loyal friend John Hughes, who thereby became in Pennsylvania the hapless symbol of the hated act. Hughes was fortunate that it was only his career that was wrecked. Some luckless stamp agents in other colonies saw their property destroyed and their very lives endangered.

The Stamp Act proved a boon to the proprietary party in Pennsylvania. Now the Penns could be made to appear as a bulwark against Parliamentary tyranny. Conversely, Franklin, who had appointed Hughes as a stamp agent, was portrayed as an accomplice of those who had conceived the hated act. So effective was proprietary propaganda that the Philadelphia mob not only forced Hughes to resign his post, but even threatened to burn down Franklin's house. The threat was real enough for Deborah to take arms, and with some friends and her son who hastened from New Jersey, she barricaded herself against attack. Fortunately, it never came.

While mob action against the stamp agents and other royal officials occurred in Pennsylvania and elsewhere, the Virginia House of Burgesses held an extraordinary session during which it approved Patrick Henry's flaming resolves. These were published with additional resolves not passed by the Assembly but accepted outside Virginia as representing her stand. One of these read,

> *Resolved,* That any person who shall, by speaking or writing, assert or maintain that any person or persons other than the General Assembly of this Colony, have any right or power to impose or lay any taxation on the people here, shall be deemed an enemy to His Majesty's Colony.[5]

By this resolve, the carrying out of Parliament's purpose in Virginia would be committing treason against the colony. Shortly, other colonial assemblies, followed Virginia's lead in framing similar, though usually less radical resolves. All of this legislative activity finally culminated in the intercolonial Stamp Act Congress, which met in New York in October, 1765. Representatives from nine colonies drafted a statement of colonial rights and instigated an effective agreement not to import British goods until the odious act had been repealed. In the meantime, Americans would carry on their business without stamps, effectively nullifying the act.

Franklin was stunned by the news. "The Rashness of the Assembly in Virginia is amazing!" he wrote to the luckless Hughes in Philadelphia. "A firm Loyalty to the Crown and faithful Adherence to the Government of this Nation," he continued, will always be the wisest Course for you and I to take, whatever may be the Madness of the Populace or their blind Leaders, who can only bring themselves and Country into Trouble and draw on greater Burthens by Acts of rebellious Tendency.[6]

Franklin now found himself in a difficult dilemma. He would either have to attack the Stamp Act and the ministry with which he hoped to gain favor, or put his American career in serious jeopardy. Fortunately, circumstances came to his aid. Grenville fell into royal disfavor for reasons other than the Stamp Act. A ministry formed by the young Marquis of Rockingham, though wavering at first, finally sought the act's repeal. In furthering this cause, Franklin could at one and the same time ingratiate himself with the new ministry and win back his popularity in America. Once more the philosopher found himself in the congenial position of finding his principles in conformity with his interests.

Repeal became the goal. An overwhelming combination of forces pressed in upon the new ministers who, not having originated the Stamp Act, had no personal interest in its continuance. America was on the edge of revolt. Her refusal to import British goods was crippling England's economy. Powerful British merchants, who feared repudiation of the enormous debts owed them by the colonists, agitated for relief. And not the least of these influences was the activity of Benjamin Franklin, who, released from theoretical and personal reservations, threw himself wholeheartedly into the movement.

Franklin served chiefly as press agent for repeal. Not only did he see to the publication of essays against the Stamp Act by English and American correspondents, but also he wrote and published some thirteen articles of his own for dissemination in the British press. During the early months of 1766, he also personally lobbied for repeal among governmental leaders. "He is forever with one member of Parliament or another," wrote his publisher friend William Strahan. "All this while, too," Strahan continued, "He hath been throwing out Hints in the Public Papers, and giving answers to such Letters as have appeared in them, that required or deserved an answer. In this manner is he now employed with very little Intermission, Night and Day." [7] Publication of letters such as this in Pennsylvania began to refurbish Franklin's reputation there. Soon, Franklin's activities would make him not only a hero in his home colony, but he would be recognized from Maine to Georgia as the leading spokesman for American rights. Once a Pennsylvanian, he now became a statesman for the continent.

Among Franklin's most effective writings were his letters to Governor Shirley of 1754, which he published with a new introduction to show America's attitude toward Parliamentary taxation *"before* the late restraints on their Commerce . . . ." [8] The letters were widely reprinted in England and shortly became the classic exposition of the American cause. Friends saw to their American publication which further secured Franklin's political reputation.

Franklin's essays utilized comedy as well as polemics. English ignorance of America, for example, gave him good material for satire. It had been suggested in the British press that the colonies were about to establish a cod and whale fishery in the Great Lakes as well as woolen manufactures. Could this imminent threat to British trade safely be ignored? Forecasting later American humor, Franklin utilized exaggeration to ridicule British fears. "The very Tails of the American sheep," he wrote,

> are so laden with Wool, that each has a Car or Waggon on four little Wheels to support and keep it from trailing

on the Ground. Would [the Americans] caulk their Ships? would they fill their Beds? would they even litter their Horses with Wool, if it was not both plenty and cheap?

The climax to this foolishness was to follow. Davy Crockett would do no better:

> Ignorant People may object that the Upper Lakes are fresh, and that Cod and Whale are Salt-water Fish: But let them know, Sir, that Cod, like other Fish, when attacked by their Enemies, fly into any Water where they think they can be safest; that Whales, when they have a Mind to eat Cod, pursue them wherever they fly; and that the grand Leap of the Whale in that Chace up the Fall of Niagra is esteemed by all who have seen it, as one of the finest Spectacles in Nature! [9]

Franklin evidently believed that if the English could not be talked out of the Stamp Act, they might be laughed out of it.

While Franklin busily utilized his abundant resources of pen and persuasion in the cause of repeal, he was rethinking his position on the relationship between the colonies and the mother country. He had at hand the writings of Otis and Dulany, both of whom provided provocative theories of the imperial constitution. Even more significant, Franklin had read the rigorous pamphlet of Virginia's foremost constitutional theorist, Richard Bland. In his *An Inquiry into the Rights of the British Colonies,* Bland allowed that the colonies are subordinate to Parliament "in Degree, but not absolutely so." [10] Franklin, preferring practical to theoretical considerations such as these, would just as soon Parliament effectively repeal the Stamp Act by the simple expedient of not enforcing it. The tactic of suspension could lead to the quiet demise of the act without confrontation with the colonies over the extent of Parliamentary sovereignty. But as this plan seemed unlikely, the conundrum of the colonies' relationship to Parliament would have to be faced. It was at this point that Franklin, possibly influenced by Bland, evolved his particular theory of the British Empire.

Although he was not yet ready to proclaim his views publicly, Franklin, going beyond Bland, came to the conclusion that the colonies were dominions of the Crown and not at all subject to Parliamentary legislation. In private memoranda he wrote, "The sovereignty of the Crown I understand. The Sovereignty of the British Legislature out of Britain, I do not understand. . . . We are different States. Subject to the King." [11] Earlier than any other colonial leader, Franklin clearly foresaw the terms of the coming struggle. His formulation of 1766 was the basis ten years later of the Declaration of Independence, which cut the only colonial tie then recognized by the patriots—the tie to the Crown.

The Stamp Act crisis had brought Franklin to a conception of the British Empire far ahead of its time: Canada would not gain dominion status, for example, until 1867. Franklin was aware that his imperial conception was visionary. The Parliament of England which had only recently won its preeminent place in the British constitution, was hardly ready to relinquish its legislative authority in the colonies to the prerogative of the Crown. Always practical, Franklin, in spite of his private convictions, still hoped to avoid confrontation. The rapid growth of America, not theoretical argumentation over the nature of the Empire, would ultimately prove the correctness of his views.

In the hopes of reconciliation, then, Franklin continued to suggest plans designed to avoid the explosive constitutional issue. With the new ministry, he pursued his colonial loan office scheme. He also toyed with the idea of a "consolidating union" of the British Empire either along lines he had urged at Albany in 1754, or, as Otis had suggested, by colonial representation in Parliament. There was still the simple expedient of nonenforcement of the Stamp Act. Yet all of these ideas seemed impractical for one reason or another. Before repeal was possible, the colonies would have to prove to England the inexpediency of Parliamentary taxation of America.

And indeed, nonimportation proclaimed by the Stamp Act Congress, was taking its toll. Surpluses mounted in British warehouses; there were tumultuous riots by the unemployed. For the first time, merchants trading to the West Indies, the tobacco merchants, and traders to the middle and northern colonies supported a common cause. The value of exports of manufactured goods from London to the port of New York alone had fallen from a high in 1764 of over 336,000 pounds to a low in 1766 of something under 200,000 pounds. Although this precipitous decline could not entirely be laid to nonimportation which was abandoned by midyear, nonimportation was responsible for upwards of a twenty percent reduction in British exports to America.

Upon the convening of Parliament early in 1766, debate centered upon the American question. Repeal received far greater attention than did the original passage of the Stamp Act. As merchants' petitions poured in, George Grenville, no longer a minister of the Crown, but still a leader in the House of Commons manfully defended his colonial policies and warned of the consequences of allowing colonial insubordination to go unpunished. Had he had his way, the American Revolution might have occurred in 1766 rather than ten years later.

That Grenville did not get his way resulted in part from the position taken during the debate by William Pitt, still the most popular man in Britain. No one knew which way he would go, for he had up until now kept his counsel. He rose.

"I speak not with respect to parties," he said. "I stand up in this place single and unconnected." Then, turning toward Grenville, "As to the late ministry, every capital measure they have taken has been entirely wrong!" Pitt urged "That the Stamp Act be repealed absolutely, totally, and immediately." At the same time, he would assert the "Sovereign authority of this country over the colonies" in "every point of legislation . . . except that of taking their money without their consent." [12]

If Pitt's speech and the merchants' petitions convinced the Rockingham leadership to press for repeal, the climax of the campaign occurred in February when Franklin appeared to testify before the House of Commons. Here was a measure of the distance travelled by the penniless youth who forty years previously had slipped away from his father's house and now stood before the supreme legislature of the British Empire.

"What is your name and place of abode?" he was asked.
"Franklin, of Philadelphia."

The reply summed up a career; its unpretentiousness must have startled the Parliamentary array of Britain's great. From this moment, the philosopher became the spokesman for America.

He had prepared his case well. Leading questions from sympathetic members were worked out beforehand, but there could be no controlling of questions from Grenville and other opposition members. The friends of repeal drew from Franklin a statement of America's present attitude as contrasted to that before 1763. Then, said Franklin, "the temper of America towards Great Britain" was "the best in the world." The Americans "considered the Parliament as the great bulwark and security of their liberties and privileges . . . ." But now, respect for Parliament "is greatly lessened." Will the Americans submit to a modified stamp tax? "No; they will never submit to it." If a military force were sent to command submission, "they will not find a rebellion," but, prophesied Franklin, "They may indeed make one."

In an effort to save something of Parliament's authority in the colonies, Franklin turned to Daniel Dulany's distinction between regulation and taxation. The stamp tax was not an external tax for purposes of regulating trade, a form of taxation the colonies had long endured, but an internal tax. That the argument was flimsy was seen by several proponents of the act. Could not the colonies, Franklin was queried, by the same logic with which they objected to internal taxation, also "object to Parliament's right of external taxation?" Franklin's reply was adroit and prophetic.

> They have never hitherto. Many arguments have been lately used here to show them that there is no difference, and that, if you have no right to tax them internally, you have none to tax them externally, or make any other law to bind them. At present they do not reason so; but in time they may possibly be convinced by these arguments.[13]

Franklin was already so convinced. It would not be long before thousands of colonists would, with him, be ready to deny any American authority to Parliament at all.

Franklin's examination in published form proved to be his most influential political writing. It was used in Pennsylvania to prove his loyalty, in the other colonies for its arsenal of arguments, in England by friends and foes alike as a powerful statement of the American point of view, and in Europe as a palladium of wisdom. Its immediate effect was overwhelming. "You cannot conceive what Impression his Replies made upon the House," wrote William Strahan. "From that very day, the *Repeal* was generally and absolutely determined . . . . Happy Man!" he continued. "In truth, I almost envy him the inward Pleasure, as well as the outward Fame, he must derive from having in his Power to do his Country such eminent and seasonable Service." [14]

The Stamp Act was repealed on March 18, 1766, shortly after Franklin's performance. But the action, following Pitt's earlier suggestion, was accompanied by the passage of a Declaratory Act setting forth Parliament's legislative authority over America "in all cases whatsoever." Pitt's stipulation that this authority over the colonies did not include "taking their money without their consent" was notably absent. The near unanimity with which Parliament expressed its supremacy was in ominous contrast to the deep division over repeal. The Declaratory Act was also in stark contrast to Franklin's private thoughts denying Parliament any authority in America at all. Yet on this issue, Parliament's victory was only rhetorical. The actual victory went to the Americans, who had forced Parliament to back down.

Franklin shared with his compatriots across the seas a sense of relief at the passing of the crisis. So long as deeds did not follow words, the Declaratory Act would remain merely a face-saving gesture. The empire survived the Stamp Act. Provided constitutional issues could be avoided, it might well fulfill Franklin's imperial vision of continental expansion.

Nevertheless, in spite of repeal, difficulties remained. The Currency and Quartering Acts stayed on the books. There were also new revenue measures modifying Grenville's legislation which, although further decreasing the molasses duty, included onerous regulatory and trade provisions. There was the proclamation line, which Americans believed unfairly deprived them of the fruits of victory over France. There was cause for optimism in repeal, but optimism would be qualified by a large amount of caution.

The Stamp Act proved to be but the first of many crises leading to the War of Independence. The constitutional question at the crux of the dispute would not down. At one time Franklin believed a "consolidating union" to be the solution to the imperial problem. Yet at the height of the Stamp Act crisis, he had become wary. "The time has been," he wrote, "when the colonies would have esteemed it a great advantage, as well as honour to be permitted to send members to Parliament . . . . The time is now come," he continued, "when they are indifferent about it . . . . And the time will come, when they will certainly refuse it." [15] The alternative would be a federal, not a consolidating union. But this alternative to which Franklin had already privately come, was unacceptable to Parliament. In laying bare this dilemma, the Stamp Act crisis had forced Franklin to choose between England and America. From then on, there could be little doubt as to which way he would go.

VII The Widening Breach

FRANKLIN'S DECISION to throw himself wholeheartedly into the struggle for repeal of the Stamp Act was influenced in no small degree by the fall from power of George Grenville. Of a pragmatic temperament, Franklin during Grenville's ministry, was willing to bend with the wind. Time was on America's side. He became the most avid American, however, when the Marquis of Rockingham, who favored repeal, came to power. Franklin's wavering was not due to confusion of principle, for he believed that America's future was ordained no matter what England might do. Rather, it was a matter of tactics. Franklin had much to gain by staying in the good graces of the British government. He would stay on good terms, if possible, with both the colonies and the mother country. If such a balancing act proved impossible, he would cast his lot with the former.

Franklin's acrobatic performance was rendered particularly dubious, however, by hardening attitudes on both sides of the Atlantic. The English continued to believe that the ungrateful Americans were refusing to pay for their own defense. For their part, the Americans felt no gratitude for the repeal of an unjust law, and they continued to insist, in spite of the Declaratory Act, that Parliament had no right to tax them. They paid little heed to Franklin's advice, written on the eve of repeal:

> I trust the Behaviour of the Americans on the occasion will be so prudent, decent, and grateful, as that their Friends here will have no reason to be ashamed, and that our enemies, who predict that the Indulgence of Parlia-

ment will only make us more insolent and ungovernable, may find themselves, and be found, false Prophets.[1]

Certainly American prudence would make Franklin's position easier. But the Americans would prove no more tractable than would their English cousins.

The heroes of repeal in the minds of the Americans were William Pitt, the Marquis of Rockingham, and Benjamin Franklin. Statues of Pitt and the king were erected in various colonies, although in New York, that of the king was a distinct afterthought. Later, the leaden Pitt and king, melted into bullets, would offer a hot greeting to the invading redcoats. While the colonial assemblies showed little repentance for their past obduracy, the New York merchants were so ungrateful as to author a lengthy petition to Parliament, a petition in which the Boston merchants concurred, calling into question much of the navigation system. To Pitt, the petition was "grossly falacious and offensive." He and Rockingham and other English friends of America now had, in Franklin's words, "reason to be ashamed." Further reasons were supplied by the several colonies that refused compensation, demanded by Parliament, for persons who lost property during the Stamp Act riots. The colonies remained restive also under the restrictions of the Currency Act, and the Pennsylvania Assembly instructed Franklin to work for its repeal.

But of all the signs of ingratitude, none so angered Parliament as New York's refusal to comply with the Quartering Act. As headquarters of the North American British Army command under General Gage, New York would bear the major burden of the act's provisions for local quartering and provisioning of the troops. The Assembly viewed the Quartering Act as another example of "taxation without representation." New York's attitude resulted in a new constitutional challenge more ominous than Parliamentary taxation. After the fall of the Rockingham ministry and in complete disregard of colonial notions of legislative autonomy, Parliament suspended the New York Assembly until its demands were met. It was clear, in spite of Franklin's hope for mutual restraint, that the repeal of the Stamp Act did not end the conflict between America and the mother country.

The change of ministry that occurred in July, 1766, reflected a major weakness in the English system that would contribute to the breakdown of the structure of the Empire. When George III became king in 1760, a period of marked instability began in the English government. Thirty years of experience represented by such men as the politically wise Duke of Newcastle now gave way as the new king tried to form a ministry in which he would have confidence and which could maintain a Parliamentary majority. Whether or not, as the story went, his mother admonished him, "George, be a King," it was clear that George III intended to rule as well as reign. For ten years following his accession to the throne, England had almost as many governing ministries. The times called for vision and consistency; England offered instead factional politics and inconsistency.

Yet that was in the future. When he assumed his royal office, the twenty-two year old monarch was the toast of the Empire. Franklin was not alone in his admiration of the new king, an admiration that may have contributed to his philosophic detachment at the time of the passage of the Stamp Act. "I am of opinion," he wrote in 1763,

> that the King's Virtue and the Consciousness of his sincere Intentions to make his People happy will give him Firmness and Steadiness in his measures . . . . Faction will dissolve and be dissipated like a Morning Fog before the rising Sun. Such . . . . will be the future course of his Majesty's Reign, which I predict will be happy and truly glorious.[2]

That this was one of the philosopher's less successful predictions was soon clear to the electrical doctor. The "Morning Fog" of faction blocked out the sun for twenty years and glory was not to be this monarch's particular distinction.

Constitutionally empowered to select his own ministers, George III was determined not to become the prisoner of any one particular interest. He was as opposed to party government as his great opponent George Washington would prove to be. Yet finally his efforts to destroy the "hydra faction," ended in the creation of a new faction, the "king's party." His efforts to reassert the royal prerogatives that had moldered under his predecessors (George I could not speak English; George II could, but also like his father, preferred Hanover to England) could be made to appear usurpation rather than assertion. Thus it was that to many of the Old Whigs in Parliament and to those not of the "king's friends," (by conscience or by hire), America's struggle seemed their own. When the showdown came, King George III led a disunited people into war.

Both the Americans and their friends in England chose to call the king's followers tories, thereby implying that they favored absolute monarchy rather than the constitutional form settled by the Glorious Revolution of 1688-89. Yet in actuality, the true Tories had dwindled to insignificance. The several ministries under George III were all made up of one or another grouping of Whig factions. Their rapid rise and fall made it extremely difficult for the colonial agents, just as for ambassadors from foreign countries, to do business. During the Stamp Act crisis, Franklin had attempted to trim sail to the prevailing ministerial winds. But he learned his lesson. He would not, as he put it, "change my political Opinions every time his Majesty thought fit to change his Ministers." [3] Franklin's faith in the new king's ability to dispel factionalism rapidly declined. "New men, and perhaps new measures, are often expected and apprehended," he wrote in 1767,

> whence arise continual cabals, factions, and intrigues among the outs and ins, that keep every thing in confusion. And when affairs will mend is very uncertain. . . . The whole seems to be wasted in party contentions about places of power and profit, in court intrigues and cabals, and in abusing one another.[4]

Franklin's admiration for everything English was rapidly eroding as he observed at close hand the workings of a government in disarray.

From the time of the Stamp Act crisis, Franklin saw first ministers come and go before the king in 1770 settled upon the luckless Lord North, who commanded a Parliamentary majority long enough to wreck the British Empire. At the time in 1767 when Franklin was expressing his disgust at the ministerial "cabals, factions and intrigues," the king had turned to William Pitt, who during the debates on the Stamp Act sonorously rose to America's defense. But Pitt now proved to be a disappointment. Accepting an earldom, the erstwhile Great Commoner moved to the Lords, where his popularity and influence swiftly waned as his gout waxed strong. Government was left in the hands of the urbane and witty Charles Townshend, Chancellor of the Exchequer. "Champagne Charlie," who had voted both for the Stamp Act and its repeal, cheerfully offered to satisfy both Grenville and the great landowners upon whom the rising land tax had fallen. He would raise a painless revenue in America. Since the Americans, including Franklin in his examination, had evidently admitted Parliament's right to levy "external taxes," external taxes it would be. But the purpose would be revenue and not the regulation of trade for which Daniel

Dulany and Franklin himself had admitted Parliamentary authority.

Townshend's irresponsible plan involved the levying of duties at the port of entry on paper, lead, glass, paint, and (fatefully) tea. The proceeds, like those of the Stamp Act to be collected in specie, were to be applied to the American service. Further, according to the preamble of the act, the Townshend duties were to defray "the charge of the administration of justice, and the support of civil government, in such provinces as it shall be found necessary." [4] The result would be a revolution in the colonial constitution. After years of struggle, the assemblies had won the power of the purse whereby they gained some control over their governors and the judiciary. These officers, however, would be rendered independent of local control if their salaries were to be provided from the new taxes.

Although Townshend, to his credit, did not follow Grenville's demand that the members of the colonial legislatures be required to take an oath of allegiance to the Parliament, his was, in Franklin's words, a "Grenvillianized Ministry." Not only did he suspend the New York Assembly for noncompliance with the Quartering Act, but also, with an ineptness bordering on genius, he established a new board of customs commissioners to be located in Boston, the very epicenter of American dissent. As if this were not enough, Townshend also established in the colonies several new Admiralty Courts, to which Parliament granted original as well as appellate jurisdiction. Having now thoroughly justified the Declaratory Act, and in so doing pushed the Empire nearer to dissolution, Townshend died before he could view the wreckage he had wrought.

During the debates on the Townshend acts, Franklin had clearly foreseen the fateful consequences of these measures. To Lord Kames he had written of the colonies that "every act of oppression will sour their tempers . . . and hasten their final revolt," adding eloquently, "for the seeds of liberty are universally found there, and nothing can eradicate them." [5] The American response to the Townshend acts bore out the truth of Franklin's warning. If, as some English politicians believed, the American Sons of Liberty were seeking reasons to make trouble, the Parliament could hardly have offered greater cooperation. As news of the Townshend program arrived, Americans aired their protests in the press, in town meetings, in Assembly resolves and in the reinstitution of nonimportation agreements among the merchants.

More fatefully, the colonies were once again unified as they responded to a circular letter emanating from the Massachusetts Assembly and authored by Sam Adams. To Lord Hillsborough, who in 1768 became the first secretary of the newly created American Department, the circular letter was not only illegal, but also incendiary and seditious. He therefore instructed the colonial governors that their assemblies must disavow the letter on pain of dissolution. Meanwhile the seizure of the popular John Hancock's ship the *Liberty* for alleged smuggling activities resulted in such mob fury that the new customs commissioners were forced to seek refuge aboard the fifty-gun British frigate, the *Romney*. As a result General Gage sent two regiments to Boston from Nova Scotia while two more regiments sailed from England. It did not take a prophet to foresee the results of these actions. As Franklin put it, "I have been in constant Pain since I heard of Troops assembling at Boston, lest the Madness of Mobs, or the Insolence of Soldiers, or both, should, when too near each other, occassion some Mischief difficult to be prevented or repaired, and which might spread far and wide." [6] There could be no better description, though written before the fact, of the Boston Massacre. On March 5, 1770, the British troops opened fire on a taunting mob whose actions balanced on the edge of violence. Five Americans died. Further bloodshed was averted only by the timely withdrawal of the troops to Castle William in Boston harbor.

With the colonies once more presenting a united front, and with Boston on the edge of anarchy, America found a new spokesman in the Philadelphia attorney John Dickinson, whose *Letters from a Farmer in Pennsylvania* clearly exposed the sham of Townshend's pretending to levy "external taxes" only. Franklin, once again America's press agent for repeal, saw to the publication of the *Letters*, to which he added a special preface. As with the struggle for repeal of the Stamp Act, Franklin also contributed numerous original press essays including the important *Causes of the American Discontents before 1768*, and the eleven numbers of *The Colonist's Advocate*, his most sustained political writing.

In essays such as these, Franklin could lightly attribute the imperial crisis to the "Evil Genius of England," who "whispered in the Ear of a certain Gentleman [Grenville], 'George! be a Financier.' " But at the same time that he employed humor and irony in his attack on the Townshend program, he also edged closer to a public announcement of the philosophy of empire to which he had come during the Stamp Act crisis. It may have been the *Farmer's Letters* that brought Franklin to sharpen his concept. In spite of the fact that he saw to their publication in England, the *Letters*, Franklin believed, did not offer an adequate solution to the imperial problem. To his son, Franklin wrote that it is "difficult to draw lines between duties for regulation and those for revenue," as Dickinson attempts to do. "The more I have thought and read on the subject," Franklin continued,

> the more I find myself confirmed in opinion, that no middle doctrine can be well maintained, I mean not clearly with intelligible arguments. Something might be

made of either of the extremes; that Parliament has a power to make *all laws* for us, or that it has a power to make *no laws* for us; and I think the arguments for the latter more numerous and weighty, than those for the former. Supposing that doctrine established, the colonies would then be so many separate states, only subject to the same king. . . .[7]

Here was the dominion concept again. It was ironic that Franklin chose to express his ideas to his son, who shortly would become a loyalist leader and a refugee from revolutionary America.

That Parliament was anything but ready for such a doctrine was clear from the debates on repeal of the Townshend duties that began, coincidentally, on the day of the Boston Massacre. Under the leadership of Lord North, who had formed a new ministry in January, Parliament once more found itself in the humiliating situation of finding a way to back down without losing its claim of supremacy. The Stamp Act had been repealed on the basis of expediency only, and the repeal had been accompanied by the face saving Declaratory Act. In the case of the Townshend duties, Franklin estimated that they brought in some 3,500 pounds. But the political crisis caused by American discontent occasioned a five-percent decline on the London stock market, a decline that Franklin calculated cost British stockholders 7,250,000 pounds.[8] The duties were plainly inexpedient, if not actually ruinous. It was easy to show, too, that the duties on articles such as paper, glass and painters' colors were hindrances to the export of British manufactured goods. Such duties denied the very object for which the Empire had been brought into being.

With these considerations in mind, the North Ministry proposed repeal of the "anti-commercial" duties. The duty on tea would remain, however, not because it brought in significant revenue, but as a symbol of Parliamentary supremacy. The tea duty, in effect, played the same face saving role in the repeal of the Townshend duties as did the Declaratory Act following repeal of the Stamp Act. The tea duty, furthermore, retained "that obnoxious preamble," as Franklin put it, stating the purpose to be to raise a revenue to pay the salaries of governors and judges. "Methinks that in drinking Tea," Franklin mused,

> a true American, reflecting that by every Cup he contributed to the Salaries, Pensions, and Rewards of the Enemies and Persecutors of his Country, would be half choak'd at the Thought, and find no Quantity of Sugar sufficient to make the nauseous Draught go down.

And as for the policy of partial repeal, Franklin found it "bad policy; . . . as it is bad surgery to leave splinters in a wound, which must prevent its healing, or in time occasion it to open afresh."

Although Franklin's prophecy ultimately proved all too true, the immediate result of partial repeal was a cooling of tempers on both sides of the Atlantic. The events of the past years, however, had made him wary of undo optimism. "History shows," he wrote, "that . . . great empires have crumbled heretofore; and," he continued.

> the late transactions we have so much cause to complain of show, that we are in the same train, and that, without a greater share of prudence and wisdom, than we have seen both sides to be possessed of, we shall probably come to the same conclusion.[9]

Nevertheless, in spite of his doubts about the future, the improved atmosphere brought about by repeal, he hoped, might yet be conducive to the conclusion of some of the matters for which he had come to London in the first place.

These included the Pennsylvania petition for royalization and the promotion of his land schemes.

As for the petition, its postponement by the Privy Council in 1765 had not at first dampened Franklin's enthusiasm. He wrote optimistically of its future success to Joseph Galloway and other leaders of the Quaker party at home. In response, they tried to aid the cause by keeping Pennsylvania's reaction to the Stamp and Townshend Acts within bounds. If Pennsylvania behaved itself, they believed, the Crown would gladly take the colony from the control of the Penns and into its own care.

With the passage of time, however, Franklin lost his enthusiasm for royal government. "I have urged over and over the necessity of the change we desire," Franklin wrote to a correspondent in Pennsylvania. "But this country," he continued, "itself being at present in a situation very little better, weakens our argument that a royal government would be better managed, and safer to live under, than that of a proprietary." It was all but impossible, Franklin pointed out, that "the ministry, divided in their counsels, with little regard for each other, worried by perpetual oppositions, in continual apprehension of changes, intent on securing popularity in case they should lose favour," should "attend to our small affairs, whose remoteness makes them appear still smaller." [10] Even though he had lost faith in royal government, Franklin's hatred of the Penns kept his hopes alive. Therefore, when in August, 1768, Secretary Hillsborough informed him that the petition had no chance of success, Franklin was disturbed by their apparent victory. But the rebuff carried less sting than had the Privy Council's postponement of the petition three years before when he still entertained high regard for the government of the Crown. In any case, Hillsborough's statement meant the end of the long quest for the royalization of Pennsylvania.

If Pennsylvania's "small affairs" were lost in the forest of ministerial intrigue, so the far larger affair of new colonies in the west also foundered on the shoals of governmental instability and indecision. For more than a decade, Franklin had encouraged the British government to foster western expansion. At the time of the Albany Conference of 1754, he had drawn up an elaborate plan for the establishment of two barrier colonies against the French. Two years later, in a letter to his old friend the Reverend George Whitefield, Franklin indicated his personal interest in such a venture. "I sometimes wish, that you and I were jointly employ'd by the Crown to settle a Colony on the Ohio," he wrote. "What a glorious Thing it would be, to settle in that fine Country a large Strong Body of Religious and Industrious People!" As he dwelled on the theme, the philosopher waxed enthusiastic:

> Life, like a dramatic Piece, should not only be conducted with Regularity, but methinks it should finish handsomely. Being now in the last Act [Franklin was then in his fiftieth year], I begin to cast about for something fit to end with. . . . In such an Enterprize I could spend the Remainder of Life with Pleasure; and I firmly believe God would bless us with Success, if we undertook it with a sincere Regard to his Honour, the Service of our gracious King, and (which is the same thing) the Publick Good.[11]

To Franklin, western settlement was another great public project which, like the library, the college and the hospital, furthered the general welfare. Sensing that America's future lay to the west, Franklin believed that the greatness of the British Empire would rest solidly on the almost infinite resources of the American hinterland.

Seven years later, to an England exhausted by war and faced with financial catastrophe, however, plans such as these appeared visionary in the extreme. Following the Treaty of Paris of 1763, expediency, if not statesmanship, dictated that the newly won west be secured with as little financial drain as possible. England's immediate policy was therefore one of restriction, not expansion. For this reason, in the same year as the treaty, the king closed the trans-Allegheny west to future settlement. Royal superintendents for Indian affairs would regulate the Indian trade and carry out the purchase of Indian lands on behalf of the Crown. A few military posts would secure the interior. The costs of these establishments would be borne by the colonies through such measures as the stamp or Townshend duties. Yet, as it turned out, England's restrictive western design was no more successful than were her efforts to have the colonies pay the bill.

Franklin's interest in the west, like that of George Washington and many other colonial leaders, was not wholly theoretical. At a time when land was a principal measure of wealth, Americans, as well as Englishmen, dreamed of the riches that lay beyond the proclamation line. For those who got there first, there would be undreamed-of wealth as increasing population would cause land values to soar. Already the flow of pioneers across the mountains had begun in spite of the imaginary line. Land speculation began as a temptation and developed in the 60's and 70's in both England and America into a raging fever. Unfortunately, the plans of settlers and speculators alike conflicted with the policy of the English government, which viewed these activities as incitement to Indian wars. The result could only be a ruinous drain on England's already strained finances.

Nevertheless, in spite of official policy, Franklin's interest remained unabated. At about the time of the Treaty of Paris, when the Crown was preparing to halt western settlement, Franklin discussed with Colonel Henry Bouquet, the British commander at Ft. Pitt, the possibility of their settling a mili-

tary colony on the Scioto River in the Ohio country. This
dream evaporated when Bouquet, who favored the establishment of such colonies in order to pacify the Indians, died
suddenly in Pensacola in 1765.

Perhaps because British policy made such efforts difficult,
Franklin momentarily turned toward the north rather than
the west. With Philadelphia merchants John Baynton and
Thomas and Samuel Wharton, he invested in some lands in
Quebec. Also in concert with many "principal persons in
Philadelphia," Franklin applied for and received a grant of
land in Nova Scotia.[12] John Hughes, whom Franklin had
named as a stamp commissioner during the Stamp Act crisis,
was equally unfortunate in his management of this affair. The
settlers had been unprepared for the Nova Scotian winter and
in consequence suffered from the bitter cold, while Hughes
lacked the resources to provide them with adequate supplies.

Although the Nova Scotian adventure ended in failure,
Franklin's interest in the settlement of new colonies made it
inevitable that in England he would attempt to further the
cause of western expansion. He would represent not only the
Pennsylvania Assembly, but he would act as agent also for
various individuals and companies at home involved in western land schemes. The most important of these was the Philadelphia firm of Baynton, Wharton and Morgan, with whom
Franklin had already purchased lands in Quebec. With the
Philadelphia firm as a nucleus, the Illinois Company was
formed in 1766 at the suggestion of the Pennsylvania Indian
agent George Croghan. Besides Baynton, Wharton and Morgan, the new company included Sir William Johnson, who
was the Indian Superintendent for the district north of the
Ohio River, Franklin's political allies Joseph Galloway and
John Hughes, Croghan, Franklin, his son Governor William
Franklin of New Jersey, and later, Governor Sir Henry
Moore of New York. The purpose of the company was to buy

up lands of French settlers in the Illinois country and to establish a colony there. Their eagerness for royal approbation of new colonies stemmed in part from the fact that Virginia, by her royal charter of 1609, laid claim to much of the land in which they were interested. The memberships of Johnson and the younger Franklin were kept secret so that their concurrence in the plan as seemingly disinterested experts would have more weight with the authorities in England. The elder Franklin was to promote the proposed colony with the ministry which was already committed to oppose such schemes.

At this time, however, a friend and admirer of Franklin's, the Earl of Shelburne, was Secretary of State for the Southern Department, which included not altogether logically, Europe and the American colonies. As a follower of William Pitt, Shelburne desired to reduce colonial expenses and thereby remove the necessity of raising an American revenue. Although this policy would seem to preclude the erection of new colonies, Franklin, with supporting letters from Croghan, Sir William Johnson, Governor Franklin and others finally convinced the secretary of the necessity of orderly western settlement. The alternative, according to Franklin and his friends, would be expensive Indian wars brought on by the unfair practices of illicit traders.

But if Shelburne was convinced, the Board of Trade presented a new hurdle. Presided over during the negotiations by the unfriendly Lord Hillsborough and later by the hesitant Lord Clare, the Board finally agreed only to a westward revision of the proclamation line of 1763. Although the Board rejected Shelburne's suggestion of new colonies, the revised boundary line represented a victory for the land speculators. Prepared for such a contingency, the members of the Illinois Company had been involved in purchasing the reparation claims of traders who had suffered Indian depredations in past wars. Calling themselves the "suffering traders," and having obtained the interested cooperation of Sir William Johnson, they received a compensatory grant of land from the Iroquois in the area of Ft. Pitt. Since the grant was west of the proclamation line, it was to their interest to have that line revised in their favor.

Franklin in England and his friends in America were quick to capitalize on their partial victory. At Ft. Stanwix on the Mohawk River in October, 1768, Sir William Johnson managed an agreement with the Iroquois, who ceded an area even greater than that approved by the Board of Trade. The cession to the Crown was at the same time made contingent on a ratification of the special grant to the "suffering traders." All that was needed now was for Franklin to gain acceptance of the Ft. Stanwix agreement in England. Unfortunately his task was rendered impossible by a renewed change of ministers which brought the obdurate Lord Hillsborough to the new office of Secretary of State for the colonies. Hillsborough was far more concerned with the turbulence in the coastal towns of America resulting from the Townshend Acts than he was with the west. He refused approbation of the Ft. Stanwix accords and reprimanded Johnson for allowing the private grant to the "suffering traders" to be made a condition of the Indian grant to the Crown. Also, Hillsborough was adamantly opposed to the establishment of western colonies. He feared the probable expense and as a landlord with large holdings in Ireland, he feared a "dispeopling" of his lands in favor of America.

Franklin felt keenly disappointed at the new turn of events. To his son, he wrote of his plans to see Lord Hillsborough with regard to the Illinois Company grant, "so long solicited, and perhaps still to be solicited, in vain." [13] Franklin had underestimated the tenacity of his friends at home. In a few months Samuel Wharton sailed from Philadelphia to England with plans to form a new company for the purpose of purchasing from the Crown the lands granted by the Indians at Ft. Stanwix. Wharton proved to be a spectacular success in promoting his scheme among many of the foremost politicians and merchants in England. Named the Walpole Company after the London banker Thomas Walpole, the new syndicate represented by Wharton, Franklin and several other leading members placed its offer before the Privy Council to purchase some 2,500,000 acres of land ceded by the Iroquois at Ft. Stanwix. To their amazement, Hillsborough, once again First Lord of the Board of Trade as well as Colonial Secretary, urged them to extend their request for enough land to establish a new colony. Franklin's despair turned to elation as the Treasury Board accepted the company's original offer for eight times the amount of land in the original request.

Hillsborough's volte-face may have sprung from his hope that the Walpole Company would be unable to support so large an undertaking. He may also have wished to spite Franklin, who had publicly stated that Hillsborough would "never let them have it." [14] In any case, the Walpole Company, now called the Grand Ohio Company, went forward with its plans for a royal charter for a colony covering present-day West Virginia and about a third of Kentucky. The new colony would be called Vandalia after the Queen who, it was said, sprang from an ancient line of Vandals. Franklin was genuinely hopeful of success. "Mr. Wharton has been indefatiguable," he wrote to his son. "If the present Ministry stand a little longer, I think it will be completed to our Satisfaction. . . . I would, however, advise you not to say anything of our Prospect of Success, till the Event appears, for many things happen between the Cup and the Lip." [15]

Franklin's closing caution proved all too correct. Among the "many things" that happened was the adjudication of

innumerable conflicting claims of such powerful interests as
the Ohio Company, which included among other notables,
Virginia luminaries Governor Dinwiddie and George Washington. Months passed before such issues were settled. Then,
having advised the grant in the first place, Hillsborough now
issued a lengthy report against it. Replete with mercantilist
concepts of the advantages of seaboard colonies as markets
for British manufactured goods, Hillsborough was answered
by a lengthy reply drawn up by Wharton with the probable
assistance of Franklin. Thereafter the Privy Council, many
of whose members were interested in the company, overruled
Hillsborough, who promptly resigned from the ministry to
the relief of Franklin and his associates. Into office now came
the new Colonial Secretary, the Earl of Dartmouth, friendly
to both America and the speculators. The man after whom
an Indian college in New Hampshire was named forwarded
the Vandalia charter to the Crown lawyers for affixation of
the Great Seal.

But now there were further delays. The Crown lawyers,
Attorney-General Thurlow and Solicitor-General Wedderburn found fault with various aspects of the charter. "I do
not clearly yet see land," Franklin wrote to Joseph Galloway
in 1773. "I begin to be a little of the Sailor's Mind," he
continued,

> when they were handing a Cable out of a Store into a
> Ship, and one of 'em said: ' 'Tis a long, heavy Cable. I
> wish we could see the End of it.' 'D—n me,' says an-
> other, 'if I believe it has any End; somebody has cut it
> of.' [16]

By the next year, when the colonial crisis was about to explode into war, Franklin, although he kept his shares of stock,
publicly resigned from the company in order that his being
"too much of an American" would not hinder its progress.

Even so, delay followed delay and Vandalia was soon lost in the smoke of battle.

The delays and procrastination to which the Americans were subjected, and the final demise of Vandalia and other plans for western settlement contributed to the growing colonial disaffection from the mother country. The Americans were anxious to exploit the great trans-Allegheny west, but their designs were frustrated by new obstacles at every turn. The problem of the disposition of America's landed heritage would soon be transferred from Whitehall to the new American Congress. There the lobbyists would renew their efforts. The ghost of Vandalia would not soon be laid to rest.

Franklin's disappointment unquestionably influenced his attitude toward the English government. Not only was the failure a personal defeat, but also it indicated a lack of vision on the part of the various ministries and crown officers with whom he had to deal. Plainly, they did not share his expansive view of the significance of the American west for the future of the Empire. Their parsimony, combined with their ill-judged and heavy handed efforts to squeeze money out of America through what was to him the unconstitutional device of Parliamentary taxation, had thoroughly alienated the philosopher from the England he once had loved. To his son he expressed his disillusionment upon the occasion of the Parliamentary elections of 1768. "*Four thousand pounds* is now the *market price* for a borough," he wrote, continuing,

> In short, this whole venal nation is now at market, will be sold for about two millions, and might be bought out of the hands of the present bidders (if he would offer half a million more) by the very Devil himself.[17]

It is significant that in this same letter Franklin expressed his concern over the lack of progress of the Illinois Company grant, "perhaps still to be solicited in vain."

Nevertheless, in spite of, or more probably because of his increasingly partisan attitude, his reputation as a statesman grew. The Assembly of Georgia, concerned over the growing crisis brought about by the Townshend Acts, appointed him its agent in 1768. In 1769, the philosopher was appointed by New Jersey, which now had a Franklin for agent as well as for governor. The elder Franklin was particularly instructed by the New Jersey Assembly to seek repeal of the Currency Act, an act that was later relaxed, but too late to mollify the Americans. Franklin's most important appointment, however, was his selection by the Massachusetts Assembly as its agent in 1770. In choosing Franklin, Massachusetts offended Virginia's Dr. Arthur Lee, who at the time was also in England. Lee, whom Massachusetts appointed a sort of deputy under Franklin, was the author of flaming pro-American letters which he signed "Junius Americanus." He believed himself morally superior and politically more able than Franklin, for whom he developed an enmity which would later endanger the two men's diplomatic mission in France.

The Massachusetts Assembly chose Franklin over Lee in part because of Franklin's greater prestige. But the Assembly, dominated by Samuel Adams and other radicals also took particular note of Franklin when, almost alone among prominent Americans, he urged continuance of nonimportation after the partial repeal of the Townshend duties. His advanced ideas of the nature of the empire also contributed to his stature in Massachusetts. In letters to the Boston clergyman Samuel Cooper, the philosopher had at last publicized his views. "That the Colonies originally were constituted distinct States . . . is clear to me from a thorough Consideration of their original Charters," wrote Franklin. "I could wish," he continued, "that such Expressions as the *Supreme Authority of Parliament, the Subordinacy of our Assemblies to the Parliament,* and the like . . . were no more seen in our publick Pieces." [18] With his avowed doctrine of the political autonomy of the colonial assemblies, and with his Massachusetts appointment, Franklin became the patriot ambassador from America.

And it was as an ambassador that Franklin now began to conceive his role. His concept of the empire as expressed to Samuel Cooper was reflected in his idea of the agency. Were the colonies considered "distinct states . . . as I conceive they really are," wrote Franklin, "their agents may be treated with more respect, and considered more as public ministers." [19] Yet by this time, Franklin must have known that the British government would never consider the colonies as "distinct states." More likely, it viewed their agents not as "public ministers," but as public nuisances. Yet Franklin was generally treated with respect. But respect was accorded for his attainments, not, as he would have preferred, for what he represented.

Indeed, the ministry had not been unaware of his possible value as an ally. There were rumors in 1768 that Franklin would be appointed undersecretary to Lord Hillsborough in the American department. Such a position would have been ideal for carrying out his western plans, but Franklin remained skeptical. There is "little likelihood," of the appointment, Franklin wrote, adding, "as it is a settled point here, that I am too much of an American." On the other hand, there was also talk stemming from the same "settled point" that Franklin might be relieved of his Postmaster-Generalship. "We may be either promoted or discarded," Franklin advised his son. Yet the issue seemed no longer important:

> I am myself grown so old as to feel much less than formerly the spur of ambition, and if it were not for the flattering expectation, that by being fixed here I might more effectually serve my country, I should certainly

determine for retirement, without a moment's hesitation.

The note of weariness and disillusionment was plain. So was Franklin's clear differentiation between England and "my country." By 1768, anticipating an attitude that would be common to post-Revolutionary America, Franklin had come to view the Old World as morally inferior to the New. The English people seemed "intent on nothing but luxury, licentiousness, power, places, pensions, and plunder." [20] From this time on, Franklin consistently complained of the "corruptness" of the Parliament and the venality of the English people. His growing estrangement from England was well known to the ministry. By 1770, as a result of his published letters urging the Americans to continue nonimportation, he was pilloried in the London press as "Dr. Doubleface," and "the Judas of Craven Street."

Besides press attacks against him, and the possibility that he might lose his postoffice appointment, Franklin was pointedly snubbed by Hillsborough, to whom he wished to announce his new appointment as agent of the Massachusetts Assembly. The Colonial Secretary refused to recognize Franklin's appointment because it had not been signed by Governor Hutchinson. Franklin urged that he represented the people, whereas the governor was an agent of the king. But it did not matter, Franklin told Hillsborough, whether "the appointment is acknowledged or not, for I have not the least conception that an agent can *at present* be of any use to any of the colonies." Following this stormy interview, Franklin heard that Hillsborough interpreted his remarks as meaning "that the Colonies could expect neither Favour nor Justice during his Administration. I find that he did not mistake me." [21]

Franklin's bitterness took a lighter form in the public press.

At about the time of the Hillsborough interview, there appeared in the London papers his anonymous New Fables, *humbly inscribed to the* s—y *of* St—e *for the* American Department. One of them went as follows:

> A Lion's Whelp was put on board a Guinea Ship bound to America as a Present to a Friend in that Country: It was tame and harmelss as a Kitten, and therefore not confined, but suffered to walk about the Ship at Pleasure. A stately, full-grown English Mastiff, belonging to the Captain, despising the Weakness of the young Lion, frequently took its *Food* by Force, and often turned it out of its Lodging Box, when he had a mind to repose therein himself. The young Lion nevertheless grew daily in Size and Strength, and the Voyage being long, he became at last a more equal Match for the Mastiff; who continuing his Insults, received a stunning Blow from the Lion's Paw that fetched his Skin over his Ears, and deterred him from any future Contest with such growing Strength; regretting that he had not rather secured its Friendship than provoked its Enmity.[22]

There was no need, in the manner of Aesop, to draw a moral. Parliamentary taxation of America, ministerial interference with the colonial governments, imperial restrictions on colonial trade, royal interdiction of westward expansion—all of these as well as other colonial grievances had taken their toll of American patience. In Franklin's fable, Britain was fairly warned. The lion had come of age.

VIII The Mind of an American

THE YEARS OF Franklin's second mission to England coincided with the period during which, as John Adams put it, "the real American Revolution" occurred. Looking back as an old man, the ex-president ruminated on the nature of the events in which he, like Dr. Franklin himself, had taken so great a part. "The Revolution," he said, "was effected before the war commenced. The Revolution was in the minds and hearts of the people . . . . This radical change in the principles, opinions, sentiments, and affections of the people, was the real American Revolution." Franklin's thought as revealed in his letters and essays reflects the truth of Adams' formulation. Formerly devoted to the mother country, Franklin's admiration of England during the course of his agency, gradually turned to contempt. At the same time his American patriotism grew. As agent in the British capital for four colonies after 1770, Franklin was at the crux of the imperial dispute. He lived in the eye of the storm.

Yet astonishingly, Franklin found time during these years for "leisure to enjoy life and my friends," as he put it at the time of his retirement from business. And as before, his formula meant travel, sharing a convivial cup with stimulating friends, and the pursuit of science. It also meant the luxury of close human relationships with those among whom he lived. Politics, even during these years of crisis, could never satisfy the remarkable energy of this versatile man.

From his earliest years when he thought he might take to the sea, travel had enormous appeal for Franklin. Compared to most colonials who rarely if ever left their homes and farms, the peripatetic deputy postmaster-general who at seventeen came from Boston to Philadelphia and shortly thereafter sailed to England for the first of three such trips, was an extremely well-travelled man. Nor did his journeying cease during his years as a colonial agent in London. But now there were new pleasures in travel, for Franklin had become a famous man. His reputation preceded him wherever he went.

First, accompanied by his close friend Dr. John Pringle, now physician to the Queen, there was a trip to Germany and Holland following the repeal of the Stamp Act. At Göttingen both men were elected to the Royal Society of Sciences. In 1767 and again 1769, Franklin and Pringle travelled to France. As in Germany, Franklin's work in electricity was well known. Now at Versailles, he conversed with Louis XV. As a leading scientist in an age of science, Franklin was welcomed at court as well as in the academy.

But Franklin was also beginning to be known as a states-man. Frenchmen were familiar with his examination before the House of Commons at the time of the Stamp Act debates. In consequence, he was taken up by a group of men who in their opposition to mercantilism became known as physio-crats. These promulgators of laissez-faire economics included the physician to the king Francois Quesnay; Dupont de Nemours, who later founded an American financial dynasty; the Marquis de Mirabeau, father of the French revolutionist; Anne Robert Jacques Turgot, who in 1774 became French minister of finance; and Dr. Jacques Barbeu Dubourg, who would be the first translator of Franklin's complete works into French. Their doctrine which influenced Adam Smith as well as Franklin held that agriculture, which must not be trammeled by governmental restraints, was the only true source of wealth. Industry, on the other hand, was fundamentally unproductive and must be secondary to agriculture. No wonder then that to these men, America, paradise of farmers, was superior to industrializing England. And it is little wonder that Franklin was drawn to them, and they to him.

The physiocrats, for their part, believed they saw in the city-bred Franklin, the perfect example of their pastoral philosophy. Eagerly they published in their journal, the *Ephémérides,* various of his writings which they believed agreed with their philosophy. On his part, Franklin delighted in the physiocratic notion of the superiority of agriculture to industry. Not long after his second trip to France, he published a short essay on national wealth, for the acquirement of which, he wrote, there are but three ways:

> The first is by *war,* as the Romans did, in plundering their conquered neighbors. This is *robbery.* The second by *commerce,* which is generally *cheating.* The third by *agriculture,* the only *honest way,* wherein man receives a real increase of the seed thrown into the ground, in a kind of continual miracle, wrought by the hand of God in his favour, as a reward for his innocent life and his virtuous industry.[1]

Here, by the fruits of physiocracy (this essay was published in the *Ephémérides*), Franklin summarized the dispute between commercial England and agricultural America. It was clear which of the disputants reflected the higher moral values.

The lessons of political economy could also be applied to Ireland, to which Franklin travelled in the company of Richard Jackson in the fall of 1771. The Emerald Isle was in much the same situation with regard to England as was America. At the time of Franklin's visit, an Irish patriot party, similar to its American counterparts, struggled to gain legislative freedom from the Parliament of England. The Irish Parliament, like the American assemblies, resented the English

Poyning's law by which, as with the American suspending
clause, no bills could become law in Ireland without previous
review by the Privy Council. Furthermore, in another
similarity to the American situation, there had long been on
the English statute books a Declaratory Act for Ireland.

It was little wonder then that Franklin received a warm
welcome in Dublin. At the convening of the Irish Parliament,
Franklin's companion Richard Jackson, himself a member
of the English Parliament, was allowed the privilege of the
floor. Franklin, supposing he would sit in the visitors' gallery,
was pleased and flattered when, as he later related it,

> The Speaker stood up, and acquainted the House, that
> he understood there was in Town an American Gentle-
> man of (as he was please'd to say) distinguish'd Charac-
> ter and Merit, a Member or Delegate of some of the
> Parliaments of that Country, who was desirous of being
> present at the Debates of this House . . . .

Yet there was a rule, the Speaker continued, for the admission
of members of the English Parliament, and "he did suppose
the House would consider the American Assemblies as English Parliaments." On this point the Speaker asked for a vote
and "the whole House gave a loud unanimous Aye; when two
Members came to me without the Bar where I was standing,
led me in, and placed me very honourably." [2] It was an
unusual honor and, as he put it, a "mark of respect" not only
for himself, but also for the American colonies whose legislatures Franklin also believed to be "English Parliaments."

Politically, then, Franklin found the situation of Ireland
and America to be similar. But socially he found the Irish
woefully behind his native country. "The appearances," he
wrote,

> of general extreme poverty among the lower people are
> amazing. They live in wretched hovels of mud and straw,

are clothed in rags, and subsist chiefly on potatoes. Our
New England farmers, of the poorest sort, in regard to
the Enjoyment of all the comforts of life, are princes
when compared to them.

The social condition of the Irish people was an object lesson
for other colonial peoples. The impoverishment of the Irish
peasant, Franklin thought,

> is the effect of the discouragements of industry, the non-
> residence not only of pensioners, but of many original
> landlords, who lease their lands in gross to undertakers
> that rack the tenants and fleece them skin and all to
> make estates themselves, while the first rents, as well as
> most of the pensions, are spent out of the country.[3]

From Ireland, Franklin traveled on to Scotland where he
visited his friends David Hume and Lord Kames. There was
time for good talk and side trips to observe various industries.
Likewise there was time for Franklin to reflect further on the
social differences between the old world and the new. In
Scotland as in Ireland, he found a few "Landlords, great
Noblemen, and Gentlemen, extremely opulent, living in the
highest Affluence and Magnificence." Yet the "Bulk of the
People . . . lived in the most sordid Wretchedness . . . ."[4]
As Franklin viewed the yawning chasm between rich and
poor, he "thought often of the Happiness of New England,
where every Man is a Freeholder, has a Vote in publick
Affairs, lives in a tidy, warm House, has plenty of good Food
and Fewel," and is cloathed "from Head to Foot, the Manufacture perhaps of his own Family." Franklin's travels, during which he saw with his own eyes the misery of the majority
of the population, contributed to his disenchantment with old
England. "Had I never been in the American Colonies," he
wrote,

> but was to form my Judgment of Civil Society by what
> I have lately seen, I should never advise a Nation of
> Savages to admit of Civilization: For . . . compar'd to
> these People every Indian is a Gentleman: And the
> Effect of this kind of Civil Society seems only to be, the
> depressing Multitudes below the Savage State that a few
> may be rais'd above it.[5]

Plainly, America possessed a superior "Civil Society," where
the disfiguring gap between rich and poor was less in evidence
and very much narrower.

Nevertheless the American social landscape was disfigured
by the blight of slavery. Franklin was acutely conscious of
the high irony of the Americans talking of liberty when at
the same time they countenanced human bondage. On the
eve of the Revolution, the Tory Dr. Johnson put it succinctly.
"How is it," he asked, "that we hear the loudest yelps for
liberty among the drivers of Negroes?" For several years the
English had justifiably taunted the Americans with this para-
dox. In a "Conversation on Slavery," published in the London press in 1770, Franklin attempted a defense. Slavery,
Franklin wrote, was not general throughout the colonies;
"many thousands there abhor the Slave Trade." British merchants tempt the Americans by bringing "stolen Men" to
their ports. "I do not justify our falling into Temptation,"
but, *"the Thief is as bad as the Receiver."* Besides, the coal
miners of Scotland and impressed British seamen are as much
slavery's victims as are the Negroes of America.[6]

Franklin's published answer to America's English critics
contained not a little bit of sophistry. But while at the same
time he attempted to defend the colonies from the blame for
the institution of slavery, Franklin became a part of the movement for the institution's abolition. He may have been influenced by the Quaker antislavery leader Anthony Benezet,
who, writing from Philadelphia, asked Franklin's help in

having published in England some statistics on the evils of the slave trade. Franklin complied, with some elaborations of his own. "It is to be wished," he wrote, that a law be obtained, for abolishing the African commerce in Slaves, and declaring the children of present Slaves free after they become of age." Then, in allusion to the valuable West Indian cane fields: "Can sweetening our tea, etc. with sugar, be a circumstance of such absolute necessity? Can the petty pleasure thence arising to the taste, compensate for so much misery produced among our fellow creatures, and such a constant butchery of the human species by this pestilential detestable traffic in the bodies and souls of men?" [7] Franklin, far ahead of his time, believed that Negroes "are not deficient in natural Understanding, but they have not the Advantage of Education." [8] As for this deficiency, since 1757 Franklin had been associated with efforts to establish schools in America for Negro youth.

But short of an agricultural revolution, there was no way to assuage the grinding poverty of the people of Ireland and Scotland. Franklin's journeys there led to further disenchantment with the mother country and ever greater appreciation for America. Yet not all of Franklin's trips were so extensive nor so arduous as those to Paris, Dublin and Edinburgh. Perhaps his favorite retreat was some fifty miles southeast of London, at Twyford, where resided (far from his church in Wales) Jonathan Shipley, Bishop of St. Asaph. Franklin might have met Shipley through his brother William, founder of the Royal Society of Arts, of which the American philosopher was a member. But in any case the Bishop and the philosopher became fast friends. Shipley, possibly through the influence of Franklin, was one of the few high Churchmen who took America's part in her dispute with England, most notably during debates in the House of Lords.

At Twyford, Shipley, with his wife and five daughters,

treated Franklin as one of the family. It was in this congenial and relaxed atmosphere that the sixty-five year old statesman in the late summer of 1771 sat down, as he later expressed it, "to do a little scribbling in the garden study." Written in the form of a letter to his son, the world's best-known autobiography was half completed in little more than one week. "Having emerg'd from the Poverty and Obscurity in which I was born and bred," the book begins,

> to a State of Affluence and some degree of Reputation in the World, and having gone so far thro' Life with a considerable Share of Felicity, the conducting Means I made use of, which, with the Blessing of God, so well succeeded, my Posterity may like to know, as they may find some of them suitable to their own Situations, and therefore fit to be imitated.

Here was introduced a new literary genre: the success story of the self-made man. The *Autobiography* is a kind of secular *Pilgrim's Progress.* It had few precedents and has had innumerable successors. It is the first significant landmark in the history of American literature.

Franklin ended the portion of the work written at Twyford with his marriage to Deborah and the beginning of the Library Company, which, he believed, with its many imitators throughout America, "contributed in some degree to the Stand so generally made throughout the Colonies in Defense of their Privileges." [9] Even in writing his memoirs, America's cause was not far from Franklin's thoughts. Yet this was not a political essay, but rather a picaresque tale, the ease and quiet humor of which reflected the happy atmosphere of the Shipley household.

Twyford was particularly pleasant for Franklin because it offered the two conditions for which he had the greatest need: a change of scene, and warm human relationships. And he

had a particular way with children. For the Shipley girls
Franklin procured from America a grey squirrel that, escaping from its cage, was killed by a dog. The girls' grief must
have been lightened when their old friend, the famous author
of political and scientific essays, penned the following epitaph
for their pet:

> Here Skugg
> Lies snug,
> As a bug
> In a rug.[10]

With the Shipley children, Franklin assumed one of his favorite roles, that of the wise and humorous uncle.

Back in the city, Franklin was paterfamilias of another
close family, that of his landlady Mrs. Stevenson. Here too
there were children, including William Franklin's illegitimate
son William Temple, who frequently stayed with his grandfather; thirteen year old Sally Franklin, a cousin who lived at
Craven Street during her schooling in London; and Mrs.
Stevenson's new grandson William, for whom Franklin was
godfather. To Polly, the little boy's mother, Franklin was
friend, advisor and witty confidante. Her friends were his
friends and for them at one time he composed a daily newspaper, the *Craven Street Gazette,* in the mode of numerous
London sheets reporting court gossip. His numerous references to himself are among the *Gazette's* highlights: "Dr.
Fatsides made four hundred and sixty-nine turns in his dining-room . . . ;" "We hear, that the great person (so called
from his enormous size) . . . could hardly be comforted this
morning, though the new ministry promised him a roasted
shoulder of mutton and potatoes for his dinner;" "This evening there was high play at Craven Street House. The great
person lost money . . . ." There was other miscellaneous
news:

MARRIAGES, none since our last;—but Puss begins to go a Courting.

DEATHS, In the back Closet and elsewhere, many poor Mice.

STOCKS, Biscuit—very low. Buckwheat & Indian Meal—both sour.

TEA, lowering daily—in the Canister. Wine, shut.[11]

Franklin's Craven Street home helps explain his willingness to stay so many years in London. There, the Stevenson household not only gave him warmth, but also the intellectual companionship upon which he throve. For Deborah in Philadelphia, he would hardly have written a Market Street Gazette.

Nor could Philadelphia, cosmopolitan as it had by then become, compete with the multitudinous occasions offered by London for congenial friendships and intellectual stimulation. Though Franklin celebrated in prose the "innocent life" of husbandry, he was in fact the perfect burgher. The eighteenth century was the time of the club when every tavern, alehouse and coffeehouse had its special group of habitués. Franklin, with his Junto, had begun the first tradesman's club in Philadelphia. Now, an inveterate joiner, he frequented some half dozen such clubs in London. Each had its particular coterie. Yet there was considerable repetition of clientele in that the members of a scientific club were frequently also interested in politics or the arts, which would be the particular interest of another club. Franklin regularly attended the Royal Society Club at the Mitre Tavern on Fleet Street. Then there was the Monday Club, meeting at the George and Vulture Tavern, and the Thursday club, which met at St. Paul's Coffeehouse. The former was made up of successful merchants some of whom, like Franklin, were not only self-made men, but also contributors to science and charitable schemes for the betterment of the city. The Monday Club

seemed particularly an extension of the Junto. Besides
Franklin, several other members were also Fellows of the
Royal Society. One of these, Captain Cook, would make his
last Pacific voyage during the Revolution. Franklin, then in
France, issued orders to American naval officers for Cook's
safe-conduct. He was unaware that a month previously, the
explorer had been killed in the Hawaiian Islands.

The Thursday Club, called by Franklin his Club of Honest
Whigs, was probably his favorite. Its founder, John Canton,
was twice awarded the Royal Society's Copley medal. He was
known not only as the first Englishman to verify Franklin's
electrical experiments, but also for his work on magnetism,
the electrification of air, the compressibility of water, and as
the discoverer of a phosphorescent substance that is luminous
in the dark. Canton had gathered round him at St. Paul's
Coffeehouse such outstanding men as Richard Price and Joseph Priestly. Price, liberal theologian, political philosopher
and pioneer in annuities and life insurance, mentions in one
of his books a Dutch institution for providing housing for the
aged, an institution about which he had learned from
Franklin, who had observed it in Holland. Priestly, another
liberal minister and discoverer of oxygen, published in 1767
in his history of the science of electricity the first detailed
account of Franklin's kite experiment. More than any of
Franklin's clubs, the Club of Honest Whigs illustrates the
pervasive interconnection between religious dissent, humanitarian reform, science, and liberal politics in the eighteenth
century.

There were also clubs more directly connected with American affairs. The Pennsylvania Coffeehouse saw gatherings of
merchants and traders to Franklin's home colony. Then,
meeting at the Dog Tavern, there was a Thursday dinner club
which Franklin had helped found for resident Americans and
Englishmen with American interests. There was also an

American Club, which met at the New England Coffeehouse. For all the tremendous variety of clubs available to Franklin in London, he never forgot the Junto. " 'Tis now perhaps one of the *oldest* Clubs," Franklin wrote in 1765 to a Philadelphia friend, "as I think it was formerly one of the *best,* in the King's Dominions." But whether in Philadelphia or London, Franklin loved "Company, Chat, a Laugh, a Glass, and even a Song, . . ." and he relished "the grave Observations and wise Sentences of old Men's Conversation . . . ." [12] Here was Franklin's definition of the good life, a mode of living for which London offered abundant opportunity.

In the Philadelphia Junto as well as in the London clubs, science remained a basic common denominator. In this sense, the Royal Society itself provided yet another club in which Franklin could share with like-minded men his scientific interests. Here were some of Franklin's closest friends: his travelling companion Dr. Pringle, President of the Society; his long-time friend and correspondent Peter Collinson; and Dr. John Fothergill, who had written the preface to Franklin's book on electricity; also there were John Canton and Joseph Priestly of the Thursday Club; and the portrait painter-chemist-electrician Benjamin Wilson, whose championing of round knobs rather than Franklin's points for lightning rods later caused a break between the two men.

In the stimulating atmosphere provided by friends such as these, Franklin found time to contribute to an incredible array of scientific and allied subjects. Perhaps his most publicized experiment was that of the effects of oil on stilling the turbulent waters off Portsmouth on the south coast of England. He also wrote much on the cause of the common cold. One of his five propositions suggesting the cause of colds comes close to the modern view: "By particular Effluvia in the Air, from some unkown Cause. . . . By being in a Coach close, or small Room with a Person having a cold." Franklin prescribed sensible diet and fresh air, both of which, but particularly the latter, were heresies in his day. "People," Franklin noticed, "often do not get Cold when they think they do, and do when they think they do not." [13]

Franklin also hypothesized on methods for embalming living creatures over a long period of time so that they could be revived many years later. He claimed that flies, seemingly drowned in Madeira wine, could after many months be brought back to life. Meditating on this strange effect, Franklin allowed his imagination to cross the seas. He wished it were possible, to be "recalled to life at any period, however distant; for having a very ardent desire to see and observe the state of America a hundred years hence, I should prefer to any ordinary death, the being immersed in a cask of Madeira wine, with a few friends, till that time, to be then recalled to life by the solar warmth of my dear country!" [14] Even in a state of suspended animation, Franklin preferred being with friends.

Franklin of course continued to turn science to useful purposes. He supervised the erection of pointed rods over St. Paul's and advised the Board of Ordnance on the protection of the powder magazines. The latter was the occasion of Franklin's dispute with Benjamin Wilson. With the commencement of the Revolution, the King ordered Franklin's points to be replaced by Wilson's round knobs, proving that not even science is safe from politics. Franklin also sent a report to Boston on the heating and ventilation of a new church there. He also advised the House of Commons on a new heating system.

Electricity and heat were old interests of Franklin's. So was his work on the gulf stream for which he now devised a chart. But there was always something new: he meditated on sun spots and considered the causes of lead poisoning; he constructed a model of a canal with which to test the effect of the water's depth on the passage of a boat; he devised a new mode of phonetic spelling in which many years later he tried to interest the young American lexicographer Noah Webster; and he wrote on the theory of music.

And honors continued to accrue. In 1769, he was made President in abstentia of the American Philosophical Society. In 1772, he was made a foreign member of the Royal Academy of Sciences of Paris, the last American so honored for a century. Another indication of Franklin's great reputation was the invitation he received to dine with King Christian VII of Denmark when that monarch visited London in 1768. Five years later, Franklin's physiocratic friend Barbeu Dubourg brought out his edition of Franklin's works. Here, in an English translation, Franklin's countrymen for the first time read his letters on swimming. Franklin himself saw to the publication of a fourth English edition of his works including not only his electrical letters, but also his writings on such subjects as geology, tides, waterspouts and whirlwinds, absorption of heat by colors, and demography.

Franklin's writings concerning colds and diet would indicate that he was something of a health addict. Although he was not notably abstemious in eating or drinking, he did rise early in the morning for his hour's air or "tonic bath," which involved his sitting nude in his room with the windows open. He also exercised with dumbbells and when weather allowed pursued his favorite recreation, swimming. Travel too he believed necessary for his health, as he frequently explained to Deborah, who might think that if he had time for France and Ireland, he might also have time for Pennsylvania. Although she may have felt neglected, she was not lonely, for Sally and her husband Richard Bache came to live with her and in 1769 was born her first grandchild Benjamin Franklin

Bache. To her husband, she wrote detailed accounts of little Benny's progress, accounts which gave Franklin the greatest pleasure.

And yet for all Franklin's innumerable pleasures—travel, the Stevenson household, his clubs and friends, science, and the many honors which came to him—politics demanded constant attention. Usually business and pleasure were mixed, as when in the same letter to Joseph Galloway he told of his successful efforts to modify yet another quartering act, and also mentioned his preparations for packing and sending a telescope to the American Philosophical Society. Likewise business and pleasure would mix at his clubs, where conversation easily slid from the effect of oil on water to that of oiling the rusty machinery of empire. Many of Franklin's closest friends were political liberals who, like Richard Price, Priestly, the Bishop of St. Asaph, and innumerable others took America's side during the struggle between England and her colonies.

It was this struggle that to a large extent formed the context in which Franklin lived and worked in England from 1764 until his return to Pennsylvania in 1775. His growing estrangement from the England he had loved exemplifies John Adams' belief that the real revolution was "in the minds and hearts of the people." A thorough empire man in 1764, Franklin became an American patriot. He came to see America as a nation apart, fortunate in its physical separation from England, to which it was superior not only in size and resources, but in character as well. It was not only acts of Parliament or disappointment in his western land schemes that changed his "sentiments and affections." It was also the sight of colonialism at work in Ireland and Scotland, the stimulating doctrines of the physiocrats, and the libertarian views of many of his coworkers in science that influenced his thinking. Nor would Parliament's shortsighted effort in 1773 to relieve the financial embarrassment of the East India Tea Company render him any the less of an American.

"When I consider the extreme Corruption prevalent among all Orders of Men in this old rotten State, and the glorious publick Virtue so predominant in our rising Country," Franklin wrote in 1775, "I cannot but apprehend more Mischief than Benefit from a closer Union." [15] Though this was written only two months before Lexington, it was not a sudden revelation. Rather it was the product of a decade's experience and reflection by the one man who in the view of the Old World, had come to symbolize the New.

IX The Final Break

PREVIOUS TO HIS DISILLUSIONMENT with English institutions, Franklin held a generous view of the British Empire. He had believed that England and America would together form an imposing edifice of freedom for as long as wisdom prevailed. "The *foundations of the future grandeur and stability of the British Empire,*" he wrote, *"lie in America."* Such foundations are "broad and strong enough to support the greatest political structure human wisdom ever yet erected." But during the years of his second London agency, Franklin found little enough of wisdom in an England that looked upon her colonies as children to be chastised rather than as equal partners. The establishment of the subordination of America to the mother country became the cornerstone of English colonial policy. Many years later, Franklin looked back and wondered how his friends in the Club of Honest Whigs "came to be such good Creatures in the midst of so perverse a Generation." [1]

Yet the next great crisis in Anglo-American relations came less from British perversity than through inadvertance. The partial repeal of the Townshend duties had gone a long way toward smoothing over the ominous divisions created by Townshend's colonial program. Nonimportation, in spite of Franklin's urging that it be continued, gave way as hungry merchants sought a return to normal trade relations. English tea, the remaining Townshend duty notwithstanding, found a ready market even in Boston, much to the embarrassment of the patriot leaders there. In spite of the many onerous regulations still on the books after 1770, American imports from England in 1771 reached their greatest peak in the entire colonial period, at a value in excess of four million pounds. It is little wonder that the English government turned its attention away from American problems to those of India, where the East India Company was in serious financial difficulties.

The crisis that threatened this greatest of England's chartered companies resulted from its dependence upon one product: tea. Faced with a surplus of 18,000,000 pounds of the amiable leaves, the ancient company sought governmental help in staving off bankruptcy. The government, politically and financially intertwined with the company—the Crown itself was in investor in its stock, and the company represented Britain's hold on India—was ready to help. The most logical medicine, as Franklin pointed out, was to repeal the Towhshend duty on tea. Repeal would lower the price of the East India product in America, whereby it would be more competitive with tea illegally supplied from Dutch sources. But this eminently sensible solution seemed politically impossible to the North ministry to whom the tea duty represented England's legislative supremacy over the colonies.

The solution chosen, therefore, was to reduce the cost of the tea through means other than the repeal of the Townshend duty. The company, heretofore, had been required to sell its tea at public auction in England before its transhipment overseas. Now the ministry proposed that the tea be shipped directly to company agents in the colonies. Relieved of duties charged at entry into England and bypassing the middlemen there, the tea, including the remaining Townshend duty levied in America, would undersell all competitors, smugglers and legitimate importers alike. The ministry, having turned its attention to India, gave little thought to a possibly adverse American reaction. The colonists had been drinking dutied tea; now such tea, with all encumbrances except the Townshend duty removed, would be cheaper than ever. The East India Company would reduce its surplus through increased American sales.

While Parliament was evidently convinced that the Americans would happily swallow the Townshend duty with their tea, Franklin knew better. "It was thought at the beginning of the Session," he wrote,

> that the American Duty on Tea would be taken off. But now the wise Scheme is to take off so much Duty here, as will make Tea cheaper in America than Foreigners can supply us, and to confine the Duty there to keep up the Exercise of the Right. They have no Idea that any People can act from any other Principle but that of Interest; and they believe, that 3d in a lb of Tea, of which one does not perhaps drink 10 in a Year, is sufficient to overcome all the Patriotism of an American.[2]

The "wise scheme" was passed by Parliament in May, 1773. Though not directed against the colonies, it came at precisely the right time to rekindle all of the anger and resentment in America that had lain just beneath the surface since 1770. There was the threat of monopoly posed by the government backed East India Company. Furthermore, if the Americans rose to the bait, paid the duty, and bought the cheapened tea, a considerable revenue might be raised. Such revenue would enhance the ministry's plan to render the colonial judges and governors independent of their assemblies.

The ministry, in fact, had already begun to put this plan into effect. When the newly appointed Governor Hutchinson and Lieutenant-Governor Oliver of Massachusetts took office in 1770, their salaries were provided from the duty on tea. Two years later, the judges of the Massachusetts Supreme Court were placed on the civil list. The result of this latter action was the formation in Massachusetts of town committees of correspondence which, under the leadership of Samuel Adams, adopted a lengthy platform listing colonial grievances and stating colonial rights. Franklin in England published the Massachusetts statement to which he affixed a special preface. Governor Hutchinson believed Franklin to be responsible for the ideas contained in the Massachusetts pamphlet. Its authors, wrote Hutchinson, "had little more to do than to make the necessary alterations in the arrangement of materials prepared for them by their great director in England, whose counsels they obeyed, and in whose wisdom and dexterity they had an implicit faith." [3] The "great director" of course was Franklin, but he was not the author of the Massachusetts petition as Hutchinson implied. It is true that the petition expressed ideas with which Franklin agreed, but he disagreed with its timing as well as with the inflammatory tactics used by some of the Massachusetts patriot leaders.

Franklin questioned Hutchinson's tactics too. The governor unwisely chose to begin a great debate with the Massachusetts Assembly at its opening session in 1773. The British Parliament is supreme throughout the empire, said the governor. "It is impossible," he continued, "there should be two independent legislatures in one and the same state . . . ." Samuel Adams for the Massachusetts Assembly replied with Franklin's dictum that the colonies had no tie but to the Crown. When Parliament attempted to legislate for them, Parliament was acting in an unconstitutional manner. Franklin regretted Hutchinson's "imprudence" in forcing debate on what had become an irreconcilable issue. Nor was the ministry any the happier for the opportunity given by Hutchinson for the Massachusetts Assembly to express its independence of Parliament.

The governor of Massachusetts was also imprudent in his handling of the crisis brought about by passage of the Tea Act. To the surprise of the North Ministry, the act was deeply resented in the colonies as an infringement of American liberties both in its threat of monopoly and because of the tea duty, an example of taxation without representation. Such resentment was intensified in Massachusetts where Hutchinson's two sons, Thomas and Elisha, were named as two of the agents for receiving the tea. The patriot leaders of Massachusetts were determined that the tea would not be landed in their colony. Governor Hutchinson was equally determined that the Tea Act, which represented the will of the British Parliament, would be enforced.

Hutchinson badly misjudged the temper of the Massachusetts patriots whose zeal was all but matched in the other colonies as well. By September, 1773, some 600,000 pounds of the East India Company's unsold tea were loaded for shipment to Boston, New York, Philadelphia, and Charleston. Pennsylvania's reaction signified the political changes that had followed the failure of the royalization movement. Joseph Galloway and his followers previously had exercised moderation to please the Crown, whose favor they solicited. Now, particularly in Philadelphia, the old Quaker party had been considerably weakened. The result was that Franklin's town was the first to force the appointed tea agents to resign. When the tea finally arrived in December, the ship with no agents to receive the cargo turned about and sailed back to England. The story was similar in New York and Charleston, although in the latter port, the tea was landed, warehoused, and ironically, was later sold to support the Revolution. But in Boston the colonial governor refused to allow the tea ships to sail away and insisted that the tea be landed.

The result was that on the night of December 16, 1773, Boston harbor became a giant teapot as 340 chests of dutied tea worth some 9000 pounds were hurled into the dark waters. So well planned was the operation that to this day not even the number of participants, let alone their identity, is definitely known. Some were disguised as Mohawk Indians, but whether there were thirty or sixty participants, their action, in the words of John Adams, "so bold, so daring, so firm, intrepid, and inflexible," was indeed "an Epocha in History."[4]

When the news of the "Epocha" reached England, Franklin's reaction, similar to his reaction upon hearing of the Stamp Act riots, was dismay. To the official notification of the tea party which Franklin received from Samuel Adams and others, he replied, "I am truly concern'd as I believe all considerate Men are with you, that there should seem to any a Necessity for carrying Matters to such Extremity, as, in a Dispute about Publick Rights, to destroy private Property." He urged that full compensation for the destroyed tea be made to the East India Company so that "if War is finally to be made upon us . . . an Act of violent Injustice on our part, unrectified may not give a colourable Pretence for it."[5] Franklin's advice was out of step with patriot feeling in America, where it was believed that the East India Company had willingly acted as a tool of the ministry in its plans to "enslave" the colonists.

Franklin's doubts of the wisdom of radical action in America, however, in no way reflected a softening of his attitude. Indeed, his contributions to the press between the passage of the Tea Act and the Boston Tea Party served as a kind of catalyst to patriot feeling. In September, 1773, within eleven days of each other appeared his two finest satires. Facetiously addressing the ministry, the first of these, *Rules by which a Great Empire May Be Reduced to a Small One*, begins, "In the first place, gentlemen, you are to consider, that a great empire, like a great cake, is most easily diminished at the edges. Turn your attention, therefore, first to your *remotest* provinces; that, as you get rid of them, the next may follow in order." There follow twenty "rules," each pinpointing one of the many acts concerning America passed since 1763.[6]

An *Edict by the King of Prussia,* the second of Franklin's two satires, has King Frederick declare that "Whereas it is well known to all the world, that the first German settlements made in the Island of Britain, were by colonies of people, subject to our renowned ducal ancestors," that, "for the use of us and our successors," duties shall be levied on all goods shipped to and from Britain. All inward and outward ships must therefore "touch at our port of Koningsberg, there to be unladen, searched, and charged with the said duties." There follow further details of a navigation system by which England's commerce is subordinated to that of the "mother" country. English manufactures that compete with those of Prussia are to be discouraged. Finally, the thieves, murderers and other villains "whom we, in our great clemency, do not think fit here to hang, shall be emptied out of our goals into the said island of Great Britain, for the better peopling of that country." [7]

The *Edict,* similarly to the *Rules,* managed to touch upon most of the grievances of the colonies. The two pieces were "designed," as Franklin put it, "to expose the conduct of this country towards the colonies in a short, comprehensive, and striking view, and stated, therefore, in out-of-the-way forms, as most likely to take the general attention." Perhaps the English even then were slow to catch a joke. Franklin delightedly told of a friend's taking the *Edict* seriously. *"Damn his impudence,"* exclaimed the shocked Englishman of the Prussian king. *"I dare say,"* he went on, *"we shall hear by next post that he is upon his march with one hundred thousand men to back this."* But then he looked at Franklin; the light dawned: *"I'll be hanged if this is not some of your American jokes on us."* [8]

Although the *Edict* was a joke, the constitutional crisis

brought about by American resistance to the Tea Act was a matter of most serious moment. Furthermore, by a peculiar chain of events, Franklin himself became in the eyes of the ministry an immediately assailable scapegoat for the insubordination of the colonists 3000 miles away. The immediate cause of Franklin's disgrace involved Massachusetts Governor Hutchinson and Lieutenant-Governor Oliver. Several years previously, when Hutchinson was chief justice and lieutenant-governor of Massachusetts and Oliver secretary of the colony, these officials had written a series of letters to Thomas Whately, a follower of George Grenville, whose treasury secretary he had been during his patron's ministry. Whately had been instrumental in drafting the Stamp Act, but at the time of the correspondence he was, like Grenville, an opposition member of Parliament.

The letters of Hutchinson and Oliver, both of whom suffered grievously at the hands of angry mobs during the Stamp Act crisis, consisted of a continuing round of complaints at the increasing radicalism of the popular leaders of the colony. "Ignorant as they may be," wrote Hutchinson to Whately, "yet the heads of a Boston town-meeting, influence all public measures." "There must be an abridgement of what are called English liberties," Hutchinson wrote in another letter. For the good of the colony, he continued, "I wish to see some further restraint of liberty, rather than the connexion with the parent state should be broken. . . . I must beg the favour of you," Hutchinson admonished Whately, "to keep secret everything I write . . . ."

Andrew Oliver, for his part, urged upon Whately the necessity of the Crown's providing fixed salaries for royal officials such as the governor, lieutenant-governor and secretary. If the Americans retaliated with nonimportation against British manufactures, the government should guarantee the affected British merchants a payment to cover their losses "and then the game would be over." Oliver further suggested the creation in Massachusetts of an "order of Patricians," from which the Council would be royally appointed instead of, as presently constituted, elected by the Assembly. The Council would then be more like Britain's House of Lords. One of the letters, not by Hutchinson or Oliver but by one Charles Paxton, a royal customs official, writing from his sanctuary aboard the frigate *Romney,* urged that England send to Boston "two or three regiments." [9]

These letters, written during the years 1767–1769, had been read by Grenville and perhaps by members of the ministry and other members of Parliament. When Thomas Whately followed his leader Grenville to the grave in 1772, the letters somehow fell into the hands of Franklin, who never divulged the "channel" through which he obtained them. Franklin evidently believed that if the letters could be read by the patriot leaders in Massachusetts, they might see that the recent acts of Parliament concerning America were instigated not by the ministry, but by their own Crown officers. He felt no qualms in exposing the deceased Whately's correspondence, for he believed that the letters "were not of the nature of *private* letters between friends." Rather, "They were written by public officers to persons in public stations, on public affairs, and intended to procure public measures." His only restriction on the use of the letters, a restriction required by his secret intermediary, was that they not be copied or published; they could, however, be shown "to a few of the leading People of the Government." [10]

Franklin may have been naive in expecting that the Hutchinson-Oliver letters would not be published in Massachusetts, or that they would contribute to a lessening of the tension between that colony and the mother country. In fact, the letters were published, and they led to the Assembly's sending through Franklin a petition to the king for the removal of Hutchinson and Oliver from their posts. Franklin preferred, since publication of the letters broke his promise to his intermediary, that if possible ("tho' I hardly expect it") his name also be kept secret.

Meanwhile, William Whately, the executor of his deceased brother's estate, had accused one John Temple, a kinsman of Grenville and official of the customs service, of stealing the letters. Temple vociferously, and finally militantly denied any part in the matter; he met Whately on the dueling ground and with sword and pistol wounded his accuser. The match, however, was inconclusive, for Whately recovered and promised to continue the battle. Franklin had not been aware of the duel. When shortly he heard about it and of the promise of further bloodshed, he promptly published a statement in the newspapers that he, and not Temple, had obtained and sent the letters to America. Immediately, Franklin became the focus of governmental resentment against the colonies. Through him had come the Massachusetts petition for removal of Hutchinson and Oliver, men who so far as the ministry was concerned, should be rewarded, not punished, for stating the truth and doing their duty. News was already filtering through on the American reception of the Tea Act. And now the author of the *Rules* and the *Edict,* the publisher of the Massachusetts statement of grievances, and he whom Governor Hutchinson had designated as the "great director in England," had admittedly conspired against the peace of his majesty's colony of Massachusetts.

From the moment Franklin on Christmas day, 1773, made known that he was responsible for sending the letters to America, he became a marked man. "Hints were given me," Franklin later wrote, "that there was some thought of apprehending me, seizing my papers, and sending me to Newgate." The London papers, as he put it, "were filled with invectives against me." [11] "Thou base, ungrateful, cunning, upstart thing!" began one such invective in rhyme,

> False to thy country first, then to thy King;
> To gain thy selfish and ambitious ends,
> Betraying secret letters writ to friends:
> May no more letters through thy hands be past,
> But may thy last year's office be thy last. [12]

The stage setting for the public disgrace of the American philosopher was provided by the Massachusetts petition to remove Hutchinson and Oliver. A hearing was suddenly granted, an unusual procedure in itself. Petitions from America—the Pennsylvania petition for royalization is an example—were frequently shunted aside, and this one had been collecting dust for months. Franklin was ordered to appear before the Lords of the Committee for Plantation Affairs on January 11, the same day, by coincidence, that the public was treated to the doggerel denunciation of Franklin in the press.

On January 10, Franklin was advised that Governor Hutchinson would the next day be represented by counsel. Franklin was surprised, for he considered the hearing to concern a political, not a legal matter. It was a question of the wisdom, not the legality of the Privy Council's retaining a royal governor in whom the populace had lost confidence. At the hearing, where Soliciter-General Alexander Wedderburn appeared as Hutchinson's counsel, Franklin asked for and received a postponement during which time he too could obtain counsel and prepare his and the Assembly's case. Fearing that the disfavor into which he had fallen would adversely reflect upon his business confederates, it was at this time that Franklin publicly proffered his resignation from the Grand

Ohio Company, whose Vandalia grant Wedderburn opposed.

By the day of the final hearing, January 29, Franklin labored under a triple disadvantage. First, he was obligated not to reveal how he had obtained the Hutchinson-Oliver letters. Second, William Whately, possibly at the suggestion of the ministry as Franklin suspected, filed a chancery suit against him. This suit, though it was never prosecuted, effectively silenced him as he put it, from "answering . . . to charges trying in another court." And finally, only days before the hearing, news arrived in London of the Boston Tea Party. Property, with life and liberty most sacred to the mind of the eighteenth century, had been destroyed. Boston had at last breached even British patience.

Thirty-six privy councillors, including the Archbishop of Canterbury and the Bishop of London, attended at the Cockpit (a block of buildings opposite Whitehall and erected over an old cockfighting site wherein were housed the treasury and privy council offices) to hear the vitriolic Wedderburn condemn the Massachusetts agent and the cause he represented. "All the courtiers were invited," wrote Franklin, "as to an entertainment, and there never was such an appearance of privy counsellors on any occasion . . ." [13] A very few of the "immense crowd of other auditors" were friends or admirers of Franklin. These included Joseph Priestly, Edmund Burke, and Shelburne with his young protégé Jeremy Bentham. The sixty-eight year old Franklin stood for over an hour as Wedderburn, moving from a lengthy history of Massachusetts over the past ten years, turned to excoriate the silent philosopher. Wedderburn himself had particular reason for plying his rhetoric with double vengeance. He was first the officer of an affronted Crown; second, he had been a close personal friend of the deceased Thomas Whately, whose correspondence had been violated by the defiant Americans.

According to the soliciter-general, the purloined letters, as well as the recent history of Massachusetts, offered "the strongest proofs of Mr. Hutchinson's good sense, his great moderation, and his sincere regard to the welfare of that his native province." Far from Hutchinson's influencing the ministry to oppressive acts, it was Franklin, who "first made the Assembly *his* Agents in carrying on his secret designs . . . ." The ideas contained in the Massachusetts statement of rights and grievances of 1772 "are the lessons taught in Dr. Franklin's school of Politics . . . . It is not very likely," Wedderburn continued, "that any of the Doctor's scholars at Boston, should attempt to draw up such a state of rights and grievances, when the *great man,* their master, had given them notice that he should himself set about such a work . . . ."

Wedderburn became increasingly abusive. Franklin was a thief ("Men will watch him with a jealous eye; they will hide their papers from him and lock up their escritoires,") and he had treasonous ambitions ("Dr. Franklin's mind may have been so possessed with the idea of a Great American Republic that he may easily slide into the language of the minister of a foreign independent state.") Perhaps Franklin wanted the governorship for himself! Franklin was the "prime conductor" of the plot against Hutchinson and Oliver, an apt metaphor for the inventor of the lightning rod. Through all Wedderburn's storm of vituperation, Franklin stood immobile while most of the king's privy councillors and other spectators clapped their hands in encouragement of the royal prosecutor.[14]

It was a foregone conclusion that the council which had applauded Wedderburn would deny the Massachusetts petition. It was clear too that Franklin's tenure as deputy postmaster-general of America was considerably foreshortened; as expected, the day following the hearing he was notified of his removal from his post. Feeling that his usefulness as agent of the Massachusetts Assembly was irretrievably impaired, Franklin resigned that office to Arthur Lee. Lee, however, left England for a tour of Europe, so Franklin, against his better judgment, continued to represent the Bay colony. In America, news of Wedderburn's tirade made Franklin more of a hero than ever. There, to the satisfaction of Franklin's compatriots, his scientific colleague Dr. Kinnersley set electrical fire to effigies of Wedderburn and Hutchinson.

The period from the Boston Tea Party, December 16, 1773, to Franklin's disgrace, January 29, 1774, marks a pivotal point in Anglo-American history. Boston had thrown down the gauntlet. In the attempt to destroy Franklin, the ministry proved it had at last accepted the challenge. From now on there could be no turning back. "The die is now cast," wrote George III. "The colonies must either submit or triumph."

The members of Lord North's administration agreed with the king. Boston must be punished and, if possible, the instigators of the tea party be brought to justice. The government's only hesitation was whether to pursue its objectives through the issuance of executive orders, or the more drastic alternative of seeking punitive legislation from Parliament. After a month of fruitless searching for witnesses necessary for a treason trial, the ministry finally turned to the legislature, and in doing so invited the final confrontation between an angry Parliament and the recalcitrant Americans.

Parliament responded with the passage of four measures designed not only to punish Massachusetts, but also to safeguard against further colonial insubordination. Three of them dealt specifically with the Bay colony. The first of these Coercive, or Intolerable Acts as the Americans called them, was the Boston Port Bill, by which Boston was closed to all oceanic shipping. Even coastal imports of food and fuel were jealously guarded by the armed might of Britain. Next came the Massachusetts Government Act, which overthrew the

Massachusetts Charter. Substituting a military for a civilian governor, the act severely restricted the ancient town meetings and provided for appointive rather than elective councillors. The third measure, the Administration of Justice Act, effected to protect royal officials in America, who, running afoul of local authority in their efforts to enforce the acts of trade, might be brought to trial before "persons who do not acknowledge the validity of the laws." Such officials might now be tried in another colony or in England. Finally, Parliament passed a new Quartering Act, applicable in all the colonies. It provided for the quartering of troops in buildings such as unoccupied dwellings where barracks were unavailable.

Taken as a whole, the Coercive Acts represented to the colonists a massive onslaught on their liberties. The Boston Port Bill punished the innocent along with the guilty. The Massachusetts Government Act, in altering the royal charter of 1691, destroyed something far more valuable than a mere cargo of tea. The Charter, the people believed, was a superior kind of property: a contract that by right could be broken only by proper judicial process. The Administration of Justice Act seemed to grant to royal officials special immunity from the ordinary courts of justice. The Quartering Act raised age-old fears of standing armies in times of peace.

At the same time that Parliament asserted its authority over the colonies, it also passed the Quebec Act, which extended the southern boundary of Quebec down to the Ohio River and granted recognition to the Catholic Church and French legal practices in that province. Though a statesmanlike act and not intended to be a punitive measure, the Quebec Act's timing was unfortunate. The Americans considered it another coercive act. They were now blocked off from the Ohio country. Furthermore, to the heated minds of the New England patriots, Parliament was not only encouraging "popery" at their back door, but also was denying to the people of Quebec, most of whom were French Catholic peasants, the rights of Englishmen, such as trial by jury and the right to make their own laws in a representative legislature.

The Quebec Act, long in the making, was not passed in response to the American challenge. But the Coercive Acts were meant as punishment, and as such their passage was subject to heated debate in Parliament. The friends of America, however—Burke, Chatham, Barré, and others—represented only a small minority of a legislature that believed the time for strong measures had arrived. Though not all agreed with the member who believed that like Carthage, Boston, a "nest of locusts," ought to be burned to the ground, they were ready to apply military force to bring the rebellious colonists to heel. Even Barré, who during the Stamp Act crisis had coined the phrase, "sons of liberty," voted for the Boston Port Bill, and such moderates as Burke and Chatham were devoted to the sentiments expressed in the Declaratory Act. Rhetoric was on their side, but divided and on the defensive, the opposition members could do little to stem the tide.

Yet it was the hope that these men might come to power that held Franklin in England during this time. He was aware that his decision to remain involved some danger. But "the worst that can happen to me," he believed, "will be an Imprisonment on Suspicion . . . ." [15] Shortly there was a new reason for him to stay: America had responded to the Coercive Acts with a Continental Congress, which instituted a Continental Association to boycott British goods and published a Declaration of Rights and Resolves. The Congress also sent a petition to the king. With the colonies now acting in concert, a conjuncture Franklin had long desired, they had need of representation in England. Franklin, although without direct contact with the ministry since the affair of the Hutchinson letters, could fulfill this role. He was now more than ever an American ambassador.

As such, in the fall and winter of 1774–75, Franklin became the object of circuitous diplomacy as the government clandestinely sounded him out on a basis for a "treaty," as he put it, with America. One evening, Lady Howe, sister of Lord Howe, who was a member of Parliament and a rear admiral in the royal navy, invited Franklin to a game of chess, a game for which the American had a known weakness. A pleasant evening led to others. Soon Lady Howe introduced Franklin to her brother and the game of chess became a game of diplomacy. The Howes' advances coincided with a parallel approach by the merchant David Barclay and the American Secretary Lord Dartmouth's personal physican, Dr. John Fothergill, member of the Royal Society and longtime friend of Franklin. Lord Howe hinted at the possibility of personal reward if Franklin would mediate the American dispute. Barclay, too, suggested that if he would take a moderate position, he "might expect," as Franklin later wrote his son, "not only Restoration of my old Place, but almost any other I could wish for . . . . I need not tell you," Franklin continued, "how improper and disgusting this language was to me . . . . I reply'd that the Ministry, I was sure, would rather give me place in a Cart to Tyburn [the gallows], than any other Place whatever." [16] But Franklin was willing, at Barclay's request, to draw up a list of American demands as a basis for negotiation.

Franklin's list contained 17 points as *Hints for Conversation upon the Subject of Terms that might probably produce a durable Union between Britain and the Colonies*. The *Hints* were conveyed by Barclay to Howe, who expressed disappointment in them and asked for a new plan less rigorous in its demands. Fundamentally both the *Hints* and the second paper that Franklin drew up for Lord Howe echoed the American Congress' insistence that Parliament repeal almost every act regarding the colonies passed since 1763. It was a position Franklin had artfully argued in the press over a year previously. "Place the Americans," he then wrote, in the same Individual Situation they were in before that di—cal, unconstitutional, oppressive Revenue Act was formed and endeavoured to be carried into Execution by Mr. Grenville; repeal the odious Tax on Tea; supersede the Board of Commissioners; let the Governors and Judges be appointed by the Crown, and paid by the People as usual; recall the Troops, except what are absolutely necessary for the Preservation of the new-acquired Provinces; in fine, put everything on its ancient Footing.[17]

Now, putting "everything on its ancient Footing" included also the repeal of the Coercive Acts. As for the destroyed tea, although Franklin believed that the Boston Port Bill alone had cost Massachusetts many more times than the loss suffered by the East India Company, he offered "to engage for that Payment, if the Massachusetts Acts were to be repeal'd; an Engagement in which I must have risqu'd my whole Fortune, which I thought few beside me would have done." [18]

Franklin's extraordinary offer personally to pay for the tea, conditional as it was on the repeal of the Coercive Acts, was unacceptable to the British government. The king's ministers were determined not to emulate their predecessors by backing down. That policy, they believed, had only encouraged the Americans to greater disobedience. The opposition, nevertheless, continued its ineffectual efforts to avert disaster. Exactly one year to the day after Wedderburn's verbal attack on Franklin, William Pitt, Earl of Chatham, pulled up in his carriage in front of the American's Craven Street house. Chatham's visit was in connection with a bill he would present in the House of Lords for reconciliation with America. The great man invited Franklin to attend the upper house on the day he presented his plan, which fell short of American demands, though it did admit to the inviolability of the colonial charters. Franklin himself became an object of debate when the Earl of Sandwich, first lord of the admiralty, suggested that Chatham's bill had been devised by the American. Franklin, according to the Earl, was "one of the bitterest and most mischievous Enemies this Country had ever known." Chatham replied that "he should not be asham'd of publickly calling to his Assistance a Person so perfectly acquainted with the whole of American Affairs . . . ; one, he was pleased to say, whom all Europe held in high Estimation for his Knowledge and Wisdom, and rank'd with our Boyles and Newtons; who was an Honour, not to the English Nation only, but to Human Nature." "I found it harder," Franklin wrote, "to stand this extravagant Compliment than the preceding equally extravagant Abuse." [19]

Because Chatham's plan renounced Parliament's right to tax the colonies, it failed in the Lords, and because it insisted on Parliamentary supremacy, it failed to mollify the Americans. Later that February, Parliament declared that New England was in a state of rebellion. The North government also urged upon Parliament an act to restrain the colonies from trade with foreign nations. In order to weaken the Parliamentary opposition to the restraining measure, North also introduced a new plan of reconciliation. The plan provided for Parliament's renunciation of American taxation. In return, the Americans would legislate permanent salaries for colonial governors and other royal officials. They would also contribute supplies in time of war. This plan had the appearance, but lacked the substance of moderation. Its primary purpose was to disarm the opposition and to help passage of the restraining bill. Franklin compared North's proposal for reconciliation to that "of a Highwayman, who presents his Pistol and Hat at a Coach Window, demanding no specific Sum, but if you will give all your Money or what he is pleas'd to think sufficient, he will civilly omit putting his own Hands into your Pockets; if not, there is his Pistol." [20] Friends of America in Parliament agreed with Franklin, but they could not muster the votes to reverse the decision to coerce the colonies.

The restraining measure, along with the meaningless "reconciliation" bill, passed by clear majorities. At the same time, the ministry determined to strengthen General Gage's hand by sending 6000 more troops, and Lord Dartmouth instructed the general to arrest the principal leaders of the American Congress.

It was during this time of mounting crisis that Franklin received the news from home that Deborah had died in December. She had been "a good and faithful wife" for forty-three years, the last sixteen of which she had seen little of her husband. She had been afraid to cross the seas, and she may also have feared the society of her husband's English friends. The semiliterate Deborah was unable to share her husband's intellectual life. Yet Franklin's "dear child," as he frequently addressed her, had helped him in his business career and during his absence had loyally seen to his affairs. The sudden news of her passing led Franklin to thoughts of home. His remaining in England could serve no further purpose. Personal matters in Pennsylvania might now need his attendance.

Politics as well as time had taken their toll. Not only was Deborah gone, but William had become a tory. As America and England drew further apart, so did the gulf widen between father and son. William had justified the Boston Port Bill. His father had replied, "You, who are a thorough Courtier, see every thing with Government Eyes." [21] Old friendships, too, were strained. Joseph Galloway, who would also become a loyalist, had proposed in the Continental Congress a new plan of union with England. But Franklin had gone well beyond his friend's hopes for such a solution. It was in respect to Galloway's plan that Franklin had expressed his view of "The extreme Corruption prevalent among all Orders in this old rotten State . . . . To unite us intimately," he replied to Galloway, "will only be to corrupt and poison us also." [22]

After ten years in England, Franklin, with his grandson William Temple, sailed for home on March 21, 1775. During the six weeks voyage he composed his lengthy *Account of Negotiations in London,* concerning his part in the diplomacy of the last six months. He also continued his study of the Gulf Stream, carefully recording the temperature of the water several times daily. He arrived in Philadelphia on May 5. Two weeks before, while Franklin and his grandson were in mid-Atlantic, the War of the American Revolution began at Lexington.

X Member of Congress

FRANKLIN ARRIVED in Pennsylvania to find the Quaker colony in arms. News of Lexington and Concord had enkindled a martial spirit so that the streets of the City of Brotherly Love resounded to the sounds of military drill, shouted orders, and all the bustle of a roused populace preparing for battle. He had one night in his new Market Street house—new to him but built in 1765—when the next day the Pennsylvania Assembly unanimously elected him a delegate to the second Continental Congress scheduled to begin its deliberations in the Statehouse on May 10. The next month the Assembly appointed him to the Pennsylvania Committee of Safety, which was charged with preparing the defense of the colony and of which he became the presiding officer. From 6 till 9 o'clock in the morning, Franklin was with this committee designing river obstructions against the British navy, obtaining supplies for the militia, and coping generally with the problems of readying a defense against a possible attack. From 9 until 4 o'clock in the afternoon, Franklin attended the Congress. In the fall, he was elected to the Pennsylvania Assembly. During the year and a half he spent in America—from May, 1775, to October, 1776—Franklin became intimately connected with the destinies of both his own colony and of the rising new nation of which it would be a part.

Among the distinguished members of the Continental Congress, Franklin was the best known and most venerated. His presence lent the prestige of his great name to an assemblage whose very legality was denied by the mother country. Franklin was not a debator, nor did he stand forth as a public speaker. Jefferson compared Franklin to Washington: "I never heard either of them speak ten minutes at a time . . . . They laid their shoulders to the great points, knowing that the little ones would follow of themselves." Rather than enter into lengthy debate, Franklin preferred to expend his energies in the numerous committees to which Congress appointed him. In fact, he became so involved on the larger stage that in February, 1776, he resigned from the Pennsylvania Assembly and Committee of Safety. He continued, nevertheless, to play a part in colony affairs.

Franklin's Congressional duties were many and varied. As chairman of the postoffice committee, he established the nation's first postal system over which Congress appointed him postmaster general. He turned his postmaster's salary of $1,000 a year over to the relief of soldiers wounded in battle. His knowledge of science led to his appointment on a committee for the manufacture of saltpetre used in producing gunpowder. Likewise, he turned his knowledge of printing to the designing of the new continental currency. He also helped draft George Washington's address to his troops upon taking command, and the Olive Branch Petition to the king, mainly the work of John Dickinson, which Congress adopted July 8, three weeks after the battle of Bunker Hill.

These last responsibilities pointed up the dilemma facing the Congress in the fourteen months between Lexington and the Declaration of Independence. Congress on the one hand directed an increasingly bitter war against the erstwhile mother country; at the same time it sought a reconciliation. On May 10, the day of Congress' first meeting, occurred Ethan Allen's and Benedict Arnold's capture of Fort Ticonderoga followed by that of Crown Point, keys to the Canadian invasion routes and depositories of much needed armaments. Cannon, dragged overland from there, provided the necessary muscle to break the siege of Boston after Bunker Hill and to force the British to withdraw to Halifax, Nova Scotia. In October, meanwhile, British Admiral Graves began to carry out his intention to despoil the coastal towns of America, attacking Bristol, Rhode Island and destroying Falmouth (Portland), Maine. In Virginia, on New Year's Day, 1776, Governor Dunmore, who had attempted to raise a slave rebellion, bombarded Norfolk from his refuge aboard a British warship while a landing party set fire to the town. In the far north, the Americans secured Montreal, but Montgomery's and Arnold's expedition against Quebec proved a disaster. Montgomery was killed, and Arnold's bedraggled army maintained a tenuous seige of the citadel until forced to retreat in the spring of 1776.

War, then, had become a stark reality; reconciliation an increasingly idle dream. Although Franklin and particularly the delegates from Massachusetts and Virginia were willing to face the logic of events, men such as John Dickinson and other conservatives still held back. As for independence, wrote Franklin, "the novelty of the thing deters some, the doubt of success, others, the vain hope of reconciliation, many." Yet England was inadvertently removing "these obstacles . . . since every day furnishes us with new causes of increasing enmity, and new reasons for wishing an eternal separation." [1]

From the time of the Stamp Act crisis, Franklin had foreseen that the question of Parliament's power in America was fraught with peril. Now that this question had led to armed conflict there seemed little alternative between abject submission and independence. Following the news of Bunker Hill when the little town of Charlestown was burned by the British, Franklin wrote to Bishop Shipley that "perhaps ministers may think this a means of disposing us to reconciliation. I feel and see everywhere the reverse. . . . You see I am warm," Franklin continued, "and if a temper naturally cool

and phlegmatic can, in old age, which often cools the warm-
est, be thus heated, you will judge by that of the general
temper here, which is now little short of madness." [2] Something of this anger of the people was reflected in a celebrated
letter which Franklin addressed but never sent to his old
friend William Strahan, now a member of Parliament. "Mr.
Strahan," wrote Franklin,

> You are a Member of Parliament, and one of that
> Majority which has doomed my Country to Destruc-
> tion.—You have begun to burn our Towns, and murder
> our People.—Look upon your Hands! They are stained
> with the Blood of your Relations!—You and I were long
> Friends:—You are now my Enemy,—and I am
>   Yours,
>   B. Franklin [3]

Franklin's steadiness in the cause momentarily commended him even to the hypercritical John Adams, who
generally saw little good in his fellow man. To his wife Abi-
gail, Adams penned a picture of the doctor which reveals
something of the temperament of both men:

> Dr. Franklin has been very constant in his Attendance
> on Congress from the Beginning. His Conduct has been
> composed and grave and in the Opinion of many Gentle-
> men very reserved. He has not assumed any Thing, nor
> affected to take the lead; but has seemed to choose that
> the Congress should pursue their own Principles and
> sentiments and adopt their own Plans: Yet he has not
> been backward; has been very usefull, on many occa-
> sions, and discovered a disposition entirely American.
> He does not hesitate at our boldest Measures, but rather
> seems to think us, too irresolute, and backward. He
> thinks us at present in an odd State, neither in Peace nor
> War, neither dependent nor independent. But he thinks
> that We shall soon assume a Character more decisive.

He thinks, that We have the Power of preserving ourselves, and that even if We should be driven to the disa-
greeable Necessity of assuming a total Independency,
and set up a separate state, We could maintain it. The
People of England, have thought that the Opposition in
America, was wholly owing to Dr. Franklin: and I suppose their scribblers will attribute the Temper, and Proceedings of this Congress to him: but there cannot be
a greater Mistake. He has had but little share farther
than to cooperate and assist. He is however a great and
good Man. I wish his Colleagues from this City were All
like him, particularly one, whose Abilities and Virtues,
formerly trumpeted so much in America, have been
found wanting.[4]

The "one" to whom Adams referred was John Dickinson,
whose *Farmer's Letters* had made him a hero at the time of
the Townshend Acts. Even then, Franklin had regretted
Dickinson's admission of Parliamentary authority in
America, though Dickinson had attempted to limit that authority to the regulation of commerce. Dickinson, in fact, had
maintained the position he had taken in 1767, while Franklin,
like John Adams, had advanced to a more radical posture.

Adams wrote his description of Franklin in late July.
Franklin did "cooperate and assist," and he also frequently
took the lead. At about the time of the Adams letter, Franklin
startled the Congress by presenting two momentous proposals. The first suggested that America throw open her ports
to the commerce of the world; the second urged Congress'
consideration of a plan of union which he had drafted. Both
proposals, if acted upon, would have carried America far
along the road to independence. But Congress in the summer
of 1775 was not yet ready to consider such plans. The port
proposal, which Franklin offered in concert with a similar
proposal by Richard Henry Lee, was indefinitely postponed.
As for Franklin's plan of union, it seemed so radical to the

majority of delegates that it was not even reported in the Congressional Journals.

Nevertheless, Franklin's *Articles of Confederation and Perpetual Union,* though officially ignored in 1775, helped lay the basis for the Articles of Confederation as ratified in 1781. Franklin's plan was particularly noteworthy in that it was more national than federal. Representatives in Congress would be apportioned by population and they would vote not by state, but as individuals, as in the House of Representatives today. Amendments offered by the Congress could be ratified by a majority of the colonies, rather than by the almost impossible unanimous approval required by the Articles of Confederation or the cumbersome three-fourths of the states as now constituted. Franklin would have invited into the American confederation Quebec, the West Indies and other British North American possessions as well as Ireland across the Atlantic. There in 1771, he had viewed Ireland's struggle for autonomy as essentially similar to that of the American colonies. The memory of the hospitality shown him then by the Irish Parliament perhaps inspired him to encourage the Irish people to join the American revolt.

Franklin's proposed articles of confederation, similar to his previous Albany Plan of Union, allocated to the central government the responsibility of "the Planting of new Colonies." [5] There could be little question that disposition of America's landed heritage would better be the responsibility of the nation rather than of the individual states. Some of these, nevertheless, maintained "sea to sea" claims based on ancient royal charters. Such claims, of which Virginia's were the most extensive, posed a formidable obstacle to confederation. They also posed a formidable obstacle to the speculative plans of individuals in the so-called landless states. Previously, Franklin and his associates had attempted to bypass the Chesapeake colony by influencing the British government to create new colonies which would nullify her claims. Now they staked their hopes in the newly emerging central government in Philadelphia.

Congress became a battleground for the competing land companies. Franklin, for example, upon the collapse of the Vandalia scheme had helped reorganize the Indiana Company, a speculative venture that had devolved from the old claims of Pennsylvania's "suffering traders." Throughout the war and Confederation period, he and others pressed their claims upon Congress, but to little avail. Virginia's 1781 cession of her western lands to Congress was conditional on the government's voiding prior claims in the area. Congress' acceptance of the cession in 1784 spelled the old speculators' ultimate defeat. A national domain was created. Jefferson's famous land ordinances provided for its disposal, and new men and new speculative schemes superseded the older groups.

Whether or not Franklin's alloting western settlement to the general government was entirely disinterested, the American Revolution had not dampened his long-cherished dream of western empire. Only now he saw that its realization would belong to America alone. " 'Tis a million pities," Franklin wrote to an English friend in 1775,

> so fair a plan as we have hitherto been engaged in, for increasing strength and empire with *public felicity,* should be destroyed by the mangling hands of a few blundering ministers. It will not be destroyed; God will protect and prosper it, you will only exclude yourselves from any share in it.[6]

Franklin rightly continued to envision the American west to be identical with the American future.

Just as Franklin's plan of confederation raised the question of the disposition of the west, so did it for the first time broach the problem of representation in the national legislature. Representation on the basis of population, as proposed by Franklin, plainly favored the large states, while at the same time it emphasized the nation at the expense of all the states. In the summer of 1776, when the Congress was finally willing to take up the subject of confederation, there ensued a great debate on this subject, a subject that would produce almost fatal divisions in the Constitutional Convention of 1787. The small states feared absorption by the larger if representation were to be based upon population. Arguing from history, Franklin pointed out that Scotland held similar fears at the time of union with England. But following union, the periodic predominance of Scottish statesmen in English affairs proved that "Jonah had swallowed the whale." As for the status of slaves with regard to representation and taxation, a southern member of Congress argued that slaves were property to be considered no differently than sheep. There is a difference, however, between slaves and sheep, replied the philosopher; "sheep will never make any insurrections."

Franklin's initiative toward confederation was a year ahead of its time. His efforts, however, to gain additional support for Washington's army bore more immediate fruit. In September, the general wrote Congress of his enormous difficulties. Winter was approaching and the men lacked proper clothing. Enlistments were drawing to a close. Blankets were in short supply; so were most other essentials, including money. Congress responded by appointing a three-man committee including Franklin, Thomas Lynch of South Carolina and Benjamin Harrison of Virginia to travel to Cambridge to confer with the commander. Arriving in mid-October, the committee conferred some ten days with Washington and other leaders. During this period, the Massachusetts Assembly paid Franklin his agent's salary which Governor Hutchinson had refused to allow. Back in Philadelphia, the committee composed a significant report recommending that the Congress comply with everything for which Washington asked. The committee convinced the Congress, as John Adams put it, "of several important points, which they and others doubted before." [7] There ensued a regeneration of the continental army, with standardized pay scales for officers and enlisted men and enlarged powers for the commander-in-chief. This reorganization, along with the timely arrival of the Ticonderoga cannon, eventuated in the British evacuation of Boston in March, 1776.

Franklin was ready to give the military every support it needed. "The freedom of America," he believed, "will be established in the surest foundation—its own ability to defend it." Of the so-called Hessians Franklin wrote, "The German Auxilliaries are certainly coming. It is our Business to prevent their Returning." To General Charles Lee, then commander at New York, Franklin made a recommendation that suggested the desperate situation created by lack of powder and effective weaponry. "I still wish with you," he wrote, "that pikes could be introduced, and I would add bows and arrows. These were good weapons, not wisely laid aside;

> 1st.   Because a man may shoot as truly with a bow as with a common musket.
>
> 2dly.   He can discharge four arrows in the time of charging and discharging one bullet.
>
> 3dly.   His object is not taken from his view by the smoke of his own side.
>
> 4thly.   A flight of arrows, seen coming upon them terrifies and disturbs the enemies' attention to their business.
>
> 5thly.   An arrow striking in any part of a man puts him *hors du combat* till it is extracted.

6thly.   Bow and arrows are more easily provided every-
          where than muskets and ammunition.[8]

Franklin's sixth point was the most compelling. Though Boston was not Agincourt nor Yorktown Crécy, he made a surprisingly cogent argument for the use of medieval weaponry.
The Pennsylvania Committee of Safety, in fact, designed
pikes for the use of the Pennsylvania militia against British
bayonets, but fortunately for America, more adequate military supplies were ultimately obtained, in part through
Franklin's later European diplomacy.

In his letter to Lee, who had a great military reputation,
Franklin expressed the wish that the general were in Canada.
There, the American effort had all but collapsed with General
Arnold maintaining a weakening seige of Quebec. Yet Congress believed it essential that Canada join the American
confederacy, for in enemy hands it offered a military threat
as it had during the French wars. For the purpose of persuad-
ing the Canadians away from their British allegiance, in
March, 1776, Congress selected a committee to go to Montreal, still in American possession. Though Franklin had
turned 70 in January, and though the north was frozen in
winter snow, Congress picked the ancient philosopher for a
trip that would tax men half his age. His companions for the
journey included the distinguished Maryland Catholic
Charles Carroll, his brother John, who was a Jesuit priest,
and Samuel Chase, one of Maryland's delegates to Congress.

According to John Adams, whose opinion of Franklin had
not yet soured, Congress chose the doctor because of his
"masterly Acquaintance with the French Language, his extensive Correspondence in France, his great Experience in
Life, his Wisdom, Prudence, Caution," as well as other characteristics which made him "the fittest Character for this
momentous Undertaking." [9] But not even Franklin's abilities

could overcome the tremendous obstacles in the way of a Canadian alliance. The Canadians, in the first place, doubted that they could be equal partners in a confederation some of whose members still denied to Catholics their civil rights. The Canadians also deeply resented the American response to the Quebec Act of 1774, which had guaranteed to Quebec religious freedom. The Congress, at that time, in its *Address to the People of Great Britain* had proclaimed: "Nor can we suppress our astonishment that a British Parliament should ever consent to establish in [Canada] a Religion that has deluged your Island in blood and dispersed impiety, bigotry, persecution, murder and rebellion through every part of the world." For the Yankees across the border to pronounce them bigots, seemed to the Canadians an astonishing reversal of the facts. American anti-Catholicism continued to show itself in the actions of the American soldiery who treated the Canadians with marked disrespect. Not only did the Americans disdain the Catholic religion, but they also commandeered supplies without paying for them. The army's behaviour hurt the patriot cause; the troops, furthermore, were demoralized as smallpox and other diseases took their toll, the result of a lack of proper food and exposure to the Canadian winter.

From the moment he arrived in Montreal on April 29 after an exhausting journey, Franklin realized that his commission was hopeless. Although his committee authorized the fortification of forts and the building of galleys, its members offering to pay the workmen from their own pockets, they could not convince the Canadians to join the American revolt. On May 11, Franklin, feeling his age, started for home which he believed he would never have made had it not been for the kindly ministrations of Father Carroll. Years later, on Franklin's recommendation, the pope chose Carroll to be the first Catholic bishop in America.

Back in Pennsylvania, Franklin retired to the country home of a friend to regain his strength. As for Congress, Franklin wrote to Washington, "I know little of what has pass'd there, except that a Declaration of Independence is preparing." [10] With these quiet words Franklin recorded the then most momentous business before the American people. Franklin had prophesied that the English would "furnish us with new causes of increasing enmity, and new reasons for wishing an eternal separation." The Olive Branch Petition, in which John Dickinson had placed such hopes, was ignored by the king. On August 23, 1775, George III proclaimed the thirteen colonies to be in a state of rebellion. In December, Parliament passed the Prohibitory Bill, by which all American trade with the outside world was subject to seizure by the British navy. John Adams thought this act to be tantamount to a British declaration of American independence, but Congress still held back.

It took Tom Paine in January, 1776, to convince the timid of the common sense of the matter. Paine had come to America in 1774 through the good offices of Franklin, who had recommended him to Philadelphians as an "ingenious, young man." Having himself arrived in Philadelphia the next year, Franklin suggested to Paine that he write a history of the "present transactions," and offered to supply him with the necessary materials. But unbeknownst to the Doctor, Paine was already at work on *Common Sense,* with which he surprised the older man by presenting him with the first copy to come off the press. American reconciliation, Paine wrote, was neither possible nor desirable. "All plans, proposals, &c. prior to the nineteenth of April, *i.e.* to the commencement of hostilities, are like the almanacks of last year; which tho' proper then, are superseded and useless now. . . . But Britain is the parent country, say some." To this, Paine answered, "Then the more shame upon her conduct. Even brutes do not devour their young, nor savages make war upon their families. . . . Europe, and not England, is the parent country of America. . . . There is something absurd," Paine argued, "in supposing a Continent to be perpetually governed by an island. . . . O ye that love mankind!" Paine concluded,

> Ye that dare oppose not only the tyranny but the tyrant, stand forth! Every spot of the old world is overrun with oppression. Freedom hath been hunted round the Globe. Asia and Africa have long expelled her. Europe regards her like a stranger, and England hath given her warning to depart. O! receive the fugitive, and prepare in time an asylum for mankind.[11]

The effect of these words was as electric as the lightning bolt that Franklin had caught with his kite. Within three months, 120,000 copies of *Common Sense* were sold. Washington spoke of its "sound doctrine and unanswerable reasoning." John Adams, who years later denied its influence, believed at the time that Paine's "Doctrines . . . will soon make the common Faith." The Virginia statesman Edmund Randolph attributed his colony's decision for independence to Paine's arguments.

Common Sense, however, did not convince the Pennsylvania Assembly. Though the old Quaker Party had been demoralized by the defeat of the petition for royalization, it still retained considerable influence, particularly in the country. Such men as Joseph Galloway fought to restrain the rise of a new city-based radical leadership that threatened their position. Proprietary leaders likewise opposed independence. Though John Dickinson had the opportunity to lead his colony to statehood, his fears of radical change typified the conservatism of Pennsylvania's established leadership. Unlike Massachusetts, where men such as Sam Adams and John Hancock were in firm control, radical agitation in

Pennsylvania was left to outsiders who rarely obtained seats in the Assembly. Quaker pacifism also contributed to Pennsylvania's conservative stance. Franklin, of course, was the outstanding exception among the older leaders. As his old political comrades in Pennsylvania struggled to maintain the status quo, his experiences in England had made him a patriot.

Because the old leadership held on almost to the last, when revolution finally came to Pennsylvania, it was more thoroughgoing than in the other colonies. At a suggestion from John Adams, who viewed the Pennsylvania Assembly as the greatest obstacle to independence, the Congress on May 10 not very subtly "recommended to the respective Assemblies . . . that where no Government sufficient to the exigencies of their affairs hath been hitherto established, to adopt such Government as shall . . . best conduce to the happiness and Safety of their Constituents." The preamble to the resolution argued that since the king was making war on the colonies, conscience would not allow an oath of loyalty to the present governments, therefore "every kind of Authority under the said Crown should be totally suppressed. . . ." Only five days following Congress' invitation, some 5,000 persons gathered in the Statehouse yard and demanded the overthrow of the Pennsylvania charter and a constitutional convention. Galloway, seeing the handwriting on the wall, had earlier retired to the country; his later years would be spent in England as a spokesman for the American tories. The last act of the old Assembly, bowing to popular pressure, was to withdraw its instructions to its Congressional delegation against independence.

The Congressional resolution leading to the overthrow of the Pennsylvania Assembly had occurred while Franklin was in Canada. He was recuperating from the ardors of the Canadian venture when Richard Henry Lee on June 7 offered his momentous resolutions in Congress that foreign alliances be sought, that articles of confederation be drawn up and ratified and that the United Colonies "are, and of right ought to be, free and independent States." In spite of his sickness, Franklin was appointed one of a committee of five, also including Thomas Jefferson, John Adams, Robert Livingston and Roger Sherman to frame a declaration in pursuance of the independence resolution. The burden of the work fell on Jefferson, who submitted his draft to Adams and Franklin, both of whom made several minor changes. (There is a tradition that Franklin would have been asked to draw up the declaration but for the fear that he might slip a joke into it.) Franklin may have been responsible for the term, "self-evident," in the phrase, "We hold these truths to be self-evident." Jefferson originally had written, "We hold these truths to be sacred and undeniable." In any case, the phrase as amended is not only more forceful, but also reflects Franklin's —and Jefferson's—scientific empiricism.

Jefferson's great paper was debated by Congress following its fateful vote for independence on July 2. For two days, Jefferson writhed as Congress deleted fully a quarter of the original document, including Jefferson's condemnation of the slave trade. Sensing his colleague's distress, Franklin diverted him with the amusing story of John Thompson, hatter, who underwent a similarly harrowing experience. "When I was a journeyman printer," Franklin began,

> one of my companions, an apprentice hatter, having served out his time was about to open shop for himself. His first concern was to have a handsome signboard with a proper inscription. He composed it in these words: 'John Thompson, hatter, makes and sells hats for ready money,' with a figure of a hat subjoined. But he thought he would submit it to his friends for their amendments. The first he showed it to thought the word "hatter"

tautologous, because followed by the words "makes hats" which show he was a hatter. It was struck out. The next observed that the word "makes" might as well be omitted, because the customers would not care who made the hats. If good and to their mind, they would buy, by whomsoever made. He struck it out. A third said he thought the words 'for ready money' were useless, as it was not the custom of the place to sell on credit. Everyone who purchased expected to pay. They were parted with, and the inscription now stood: 'John Thompson sells hats.' 'Sells hats?' says his next friend. 'Why, nobody will expect you to give them away. What then is the use of that word?' It was stricken out; and 'hats' followed it, the rather as there was one painted on the board. So his inscription was reduced ultimately to 'John Thompson' with the figure of a hat subjoined.[12]

Jefferson's Declaration of Independence, having withstood the scrutiny of his friends far better than did John Thompson's sign, was sent to Washington's command and to the states. Following action by the New York Assembly, the last state to ratify the document, the Declaration was engrossed on parchment and on August 2, signed by the members of Congress. Another tradition has grown up around the signing: John Hancock is said to have pleaded for unanamity, for "we must all hang together." "Yes," Franklin is supposed to have replied, "we must indeed all hang together, or most assuredly we shall all hang separately." Though there is no contemporary evidence for this famous quip, something of its mood may well have prevailed in Congress that day.

With the birth of the United States of America, the Pennsylvania revolution that had helped make it possible continued to run its course. On July 15, men who had heretofore been outside the ruling oligarchy met in convention, to which they elected Franklin president. The convention drafted a bill of rights and the most democratic constitution of any of the colonies-become-states. It was a constitution for which Franklin would be criticized by conservatives long after the event, although he appears to have had little to do with its drafting. The constitution, however, was in accord with Franklin's ideas. It provided for a plural executive and, similar to the Charter of Liberties of 1701, a unicameral legislature. It did away with the old property qualification for the vote, an institution deeply resented by the militiamen who believed that if they were qualified to fight, they were qualified to vote, a belief not unfamiliar to future generations of Americans. The convention also introduced a most unique institution in the Council of Censors, to be elected every seven years to examine into the working of the constitution and the laws. The final act of the convention was unanimously to resolve, "That the thanks of this Convention be given to the President for the honor he has done it by filling the chair during the debates on the most important parts of the Bill of Rights and frame of Government, and for his able and disinterested advice thereon."

Franklin, whose illness turned out to be nothing worse than an attack of gout, was occupied during much of the Pennsylvania Convention with national, rather than state affairs. Admiral Howe, brother of the chess-playing lady diplomatist, had arrived in June off Sandy Hook not only with a great fleet, but also with authorization to proffer conciliation with the Americans. Howe's mission in part reflected the Parliamentary opposition to the North administration's military policies in America. Howe, who of course did not recognize the Congress, wrote to Franklin a personal letter in which he sought the Doctor's help in "the Establishment of Peace and union with the Colonies." But Howe could only offer "pardon upon submission." With permission from Congress, Franklin tartly replied: "Directing Pardons to be offered to the Colonies, who are the very Parties injured, expresses indeed that Opinion of our Ignorance, Baseness, and Insensibility, which your uninform'd and proud Nation has long been pleased to entertain of us. . . . Long did I endeavour, with unfeigned and unwearied Zeal," Franklin continued, "to preserve from breaking that fine and noble China Vase, the British Empire." Howe had alluded to the "Necessity for preventing [America's] trade from passing into foreign channels." To this Franklin replied, "To me, it seems, that neither the Obtaining or Retaining of any trade, how valuable soever, is an Object for which men may justly spill each other's Blood." [13]

But Lord Howe was not easily rebuffed. His brother General William Howe soon drove Washington from Long Island; perhaps it was time to try again. Renewed negotiations led to Congress' picking a committee of three: Franklin, John Adams and Edward Rutledge to meet with the Admiral to assess the extent of his authority. On the way to Staten Island, the scene of the meeting, because of a lack of accomodations Franklin and Adams were forced to room together. Adams desired to sleep with the windows shut. Franklin insisted that they be open and proceeded to a long lecture on his theory of colds, a lecture which evidently had a soporific effect, for before it was over the younger man was asleep. He seemed however, to have suffered no ills from the night air.

The Staten Island Conference, September 11, 1776, was polite but fruitless. Howe had no power to treat with representatives of Congress, but only with individuals. Furthermore, the Declaration of Independence, ratified after Howe had received his instructions, had wholly altered the situation. The committee tried to impress Howe with the feasibility of England's having as great a commerce with the United States as she had before the Declaration, but Howe would have none of it. The failure of the conference served to strengthen America's resolve. It was now abundantly clear that independence could be maintained only upon the battle-field. And the war continued inexorably as General Howe forced Washington from New York and into retreat across New Jersey.

While the abortive Staten Island Conference was time consuming, Franklin and the Congress were harassed by a multitude of problems which involved not only supplying the armies but also grappling with a form of confederation and desperately seeking foreign aid. As early as the preceding November, Congress had established a Committee of Secret Correspondence, the forerunner of the American Department of State. Because of his European connections, the burden of the committee's work fell on Franklin. To the Spanish prince Don Gabriel of Bourbon, an admirer of his, Franklin wrote,

> "I think I see a powerful Dominion growing up here, whose Interest it will be, to form a close and firm Alliance with Spain, (their Territories bordering,) . . . . It seems, therefore, prudent on both sides to cultivate a good Understanding, that may hereafter be so useful to both; towards which a fair Foundation is already laid in our minds, by the well founded Popular Opinion entertained here of Spanish Integrity and Honor." [14]

To Professor Charles W. Dumas, an aquaintance he had made in Holland, Franklin wrote asking him to discover the attitude of the various European powers toward America and the possibility of their sending aid. Franklin also corresponded with his French translator Barbeu Dubourg, who tirelessly urged America's cause among leading Frenchmen.

Correspondence with European intermediaries, however, was not adequate to the winning of European support and recognition. It was essential that there be American representatives in Europe to purchase the matériel of war and to seek foreign alliances. Congress, therefore, decided to send Franklin as one member of a ministerial commission to Europe. Old as he was, he had regained his vigor, and no one in America had the prestige which Franklin's presence in the Old World would bring to the American cause. The other members of the commission were Thomas Jefferson and the Connecticut merchant-politician, Silas Deane, already in France procuring supplies for the patriot cause. The three members neatly reflected the sectional divisions in Congress: Deane from New England, Jefferson from the South, and Franklin from Pennsylvania, a middle state. Jefferson unfortunately, refused to go because of his wife's illness. His replacement, Arthur Lee of Virginia, brother of Richard Henry, retained the sectional, if not the emotional balance of the commission. Still resentful of Franklin's prestige by which the older man in 1770 had obtained the Massachusetts agency, Lee, irascible and suspicious, was to introduce dissension within the commission and even momentarily to ruffle the usually tranquil Franklin himself.

The commission's principal objective was an alliance with France. Franklin helped draw up the commissioners' instructions. "It is highly probable," he wrote,

> that France means not to let the United States sink in the present Contest [but may believe] we are able to support the War on our own Strength and Resources longer than, in fact, we can do. . . . It will be proper for you to press for the immediate and explicit declaration of France in our Favor, upon a Suggestion that a Reunion with Great Britain may be the Consequence of delay.[15]

The Congress hoped that the "explicit declaration of France in our favor," would take the form of her joining the United States in a treaty of amity and commerce. If obtainable, the desired treaty was to be based upon the "Plan of 1776," that had been drawn up by Franklin, Adams and other members of the committee for foreign affairs. The plan became the basis not only for the French alliance, but for all the treaties of the United States before 1800. It also expressed certain principles that were to remain basic throughout American history in the formulation of foreign policy. The plan carefully outlined the rights of neutrals in time of war; it laid down the traditional American doctrine of "free ships make free goods;" it narrowly restricted the definition of contraband to actual armaments; and it offered reciprocal commercial privileges including a most-favored nation stipulation by which American commerce would have privileges equal to any other trading nation.

Although a principal author of the "Plan of 1776" and unofficial chairman of the ministerial commission, Franklin voiced what was to become a chronic American distrust of foreign entanglements. He approached his new duties with some reservations. "A virgin state," he believed, "should preserve its virgin character, and not go about suitoring for alliances, but wait with decent dignity for the application of others." [16] A too eager approach might compromise American independence. The plan envisioned commercial relations only. Political alliances were to be avoided if at all possible.

Franklin was aware that French acceptance of a commercial treaty meant her recognition of the United States as a sovereign nation. The price to be paid by France for American commercial privileges would be war with England. Yet from the beginning of the Revolution, France had surreptitiously encouraged America by sending supplies for which the Americans paid by returning various raw materials. A free trade of sorts had sprung up to replace the old mercantilist system which had previously defined America's colonial status. Franklin's purpose in voyaging to France would be to bring that nation into an open avowal of a policy she secretly pursued.

XI The French Alliance

FOR THE SECOND TIME IN HIS LIFE, Benjamin Franklin would hazard an ocean crossing in time of war. The first time was during the Great War for the Empire—in 1757—when he left for England on his original agency for the Pennsylvania Assembly. Now he was headed on a far more important agency for the government of the United States of America, to which just before he sailed, he loaned "all the money he could raise, between three and four thousand pounds . . ." to encourage "others to lend their money in support of the cause."

With Franklin were his two grandsons, William Temple Franklin, age 16, and Benny Bache, age 7. They set sail aboard an armed sloop for Europe on October 27, 1776. Franklin included Temple, as he was known, on the voyage in part because his father, Governor William Franklin, had been arrested as a tory by the New Jersey Assembly. Temple would act as his grandfather's secretary. Young Benny, Franklin's daughter's son, would have the advantage of a European education. Though Franklin would later be accused of being overly fond of France, he sent Benny to school in Switzerland, "As he is destined to live in a Protestant Country, and a Republic, I thought it best to finish his Education where the proper Principles prevail." [1]

During the four week voyage, Franklin pursued his study of the Gulf Stream and, as before, took daily readings of the air and water temperatures. Had his ship, aptly named the *Reprisal*, been taken by an English man-of-war, Franklin would have gone to prison as a rebel. Captain Wickes, however, not only eluded the British navy, but also, as Franklin proudly recounted to Congress, "took two prizes (brigantines) one belonging to Cork, laden with staves, pitch, tar, turpentine, and claret; the other to Hull, with a cargo of flaxseed and brandy." [2] Entering Quiberon Bay, the *Reprisal* was unable to sail up the Loire because of adverse winds. Franklin was therefore taken by a fishing boat the six miles to Auray. From there, feeling weakened by the "tedious passage," but sure "that the good air which I breathe on land will soon reestablish me," with his two grandsons he traveled overland to Nantes, where he was greeted as a hero. But that was only the beginning of a rough two hundred and fifty mile journey to Paris, where excited rumors of his coming preceded him.

For years the French intelligentsia had been unconsciously preparing the nation to welcome just such a figure as Benjamin Franklin. The European Enlightenment was a period of faith in Nature and Reason. Natural laws ruled the universe, and they were discoverable by human reason. They were analogous to mechanical laws obeyed by machines. Deism, the religion of many philosophes, and to some degree subscribed by Franklin, posited a God, who having created the universal machine, withdrew in the contemplation of perfection. Nature was the only true revelation. Through the use of reason, Newton had discovered the law of gravity, that law which kept the very stars themselves in shifting universal concord. Franklin was an even more impressive embodiment of Enlightenment philosophy. His discovery of the laws of electricity was accomplished in the woods of America, where pure reason was unaided by the civilizing educational institutions of the Old World.

The philosophes believed implicitly that men, as well as things, were subject to the laws of nature. But these laws had been thwarted by the unreasonable restraints placed upon man by centuries of encrusted tradition. Church, State, and social custom denied the natural equality of men, a concept of which Franklin was the perfect symbol. Unrestrained by artificial social distinctions, the once obscure printer had attained world renown. With Reason his only support, he became a benefactor of mankind. He was not only a natural, but also a moral philosopher. His prudential maxims discovered those liberating laws of human nature by which men could better their station in life. Poor Richard had infinite appeal to a people emerging from an age of aristocratic institutions.

With the celebration of Nature and Reason, emerged a cult of primitivism for which the writings of Rousseau were chiefly responsible. Once again, Franklin fit the model. Out from the virgin forests of the New World, so went the myth, emerged the unadorned philosopher voicing the eternal truths of nature. Primitive man was far superior to his domesticated brother, for he was uncorrupted by the artificial trappings of civilization. The American's unaffected simplicity was contrasted to the degeneracy of European manners and morals. City bred Benjamin Franklin, who had as well stocked a wine cellar as any grandee of France, became the unlikely embodiment of the Noble Savage.

Voltaire, another moulder of the European Enlightenment, thought he had discovered in Pennsylvania, and in Quakerism, humanity's most glorious virtues: political freedom, religious toleration, and honest dealings among men. Again, Franklin of Pennsylvania seemed to fulfill the philosophic ideal. The physiocrats, since Franklin's previous visits to France, had believed him to be one of their own. Now they viewed the American War of Independence, which he represented, as a justification of their views on free trade. One of them, the radical reformer Turgot, who from 1774 until May, 1776, held the key post of French minister of finance, coined the famous epigram describing Franklin: "He seized the lightning from the sky, and the sceptre from tyrants." These words summed up the meaning of the American for the philosophes of France. Franklin had become the symbol of a new age dawning in the New World. He did not disabuse the French of their notion that he was of the much-admired sect of Quakerism. Clad in a simple black coat, with grey hair stringing down beneath a fur cap ("Think," wrote Franklin, "how this must appear among the powdered heads of Paris,"), Franklin seemed to many the secular messiah come to rid the Old World of all its sins and follies. His reputation as a moralist and scientist had preceded him. His most popular work in France, then preparing for a middle class revolution, was *The Way to Wealth*. Franklin's *Bonhomme Richard* ("Pauvre Richard" in French represents a contradiction in terms) perfectly suited the spirit of the rising bourgeoisie. "His name," wrote John Adams,

> was familiar to government and people, to kings, courtiers, nobility, clergy, and philosophers, as well as plebeians, to such a degree that there was scarcely a peasant or a citizen, a *valet de chambre*, coachman or footman, a lady's chambermaid or a scullion in a kitchen, who was not familiar with it, and who did not consider him a friend to human kind. When they spoke of him, they seemed to think he was to restore the golden age. . . . He was thought to be the magician who had excited the ignorant Americans to resistance. His mysterious wand had separated the Colonies from Great Britain. He had framed and established all the American constitutions of government, especially the best of them, i.e. the most democratical. His plans and his example were to abolish monarchy, aristocracy, and hierarchy throughout the world.[3]

During the years of the Franklin cult in Europe, possibly not even Voltaire eclipsed his fame. When the two sages met and

ERIPUIT CAELO FULMEN SCEPTRUMQUE TIRANNIS

AU GENIE DE FRANKLIN

Honoré Frangonard, *To the Genius of Franklin*, 1780.
Courtesy the Philadelphia Museum of Art.

embraced in the name of humanity ("Solon and Sophocles," exclaimed the French), the nation vibrated with sympathetic adoration.

Almost immediately upon his arrival, Franklin medallions became the rage among the French public. Some were "set in the lids of snuffboxes, and some so small as to be worn in rings; and the numbers sold," Franklin wrote his daughter, "are incredible. These, with the pictures, busts, and prints, (of which copies of copies are spread everywhere,)" he continued, "have made your father's face as well known as that of the moon . . . . It is said by learned etymologists, that the name *doll,* for the images children play with, is derived from the word IDOL. From the number of *dolls* now made of him, he may be truly said *in that sense,* to be *i-doll-ized* in this country." [4] Franklin's emphasizing *"in that sense"* was unduly modest. Great crowds gathered wherever he appeared. He was named a member of the Academy of Medicine and the masonic lodge of the Nine Sisters, where he assisted at the initiation of Voltaire and met many future leaders of the French Revolution. Recognition came from outside France as well. He was made a member of the Academy of Sciences, Letters, and Arts of Padua; an Honorary Fellow of the Royal Society of Edinburgh; and a member of the Royal Academy at Madrid. Both for what he was, and for what he symbolized, Franklin was the perfect emissary to represent the United States in France, and in a larger sense, to be America's ambassador to Europe.

Of the various European powers who thought they might benefit by a rift in the British Empire, the Netherlands, Spain, and France were the most likely candidates for an American alliance. The Netherlands, having long been reduced to second-rate status by her dependence upon England for protection, saw new channels of trade opening up with the emergence of the United States as an independent nation. Inspired

by hopes of wartime profits and later commercial relations
with America, the Netherlands allowed her West Indian island possession, St. Eustatius, to become a center for the
contraband trade to the beleaguered new nation. Later, she
also made essential loans to the United States, loans that
helped assuage America's chronic financial crisis.

The Netherlands viewed America's struggle chiefly in the
light of its possible economic benefits. France and Spain, also,
conceived of economic benefits from trade with the new
American states, but they also took a larger view of the
matter. The civil war in the British Empire offered them, at
last, the chance for revenge for which they had been waiting.
The two Bourbon powers had suffered an overwhelming defeat in the last war. Their objective was to undo the humiliating Treaty of Paris of 1763, by which England had become
mistress of the world. In the breakup of the British Empire,
they believed, lay their salvation.

But there were dangers inherent in a precipitate interference on the American side. Spain desired the security of her
own American Empire which the new nation might threaten.
Also, beneath the fragile surface of eighteenth century life
there stirred those revolutionary impulses, inspired by the
American example, that were shortly to explode forth in the
French Revolution. Ultimately they would reverberate back
across the water to Spanish America. Joseph II of Austria
voiced something of the tremulous mood of Europe's rulers.
"The cause in which England is engaged," he said, "is the
cause of all sovereigns, who have a joint interest in the
maintenance of due subordination and obediance to law in
all the surrounding monarchies." [5] For one monarch, Louis
XVI of France, the overcoming of such kingly scruples would
prove to be his undoing. Revolution would be contagious. An
infected France would lead her king to the scaffold.

But lacking the gift of prophecy, the French court sacrificed domestic considerations to foreign policy. England, it was believed, drew her strength from commerce. America was essential to that commerce. Ergo Britain's loss of America would destroy her power. Into the resulting vacuum would reemerge France as arbiter of Europe and the world.

From the inception of the Anglo-American dispute in the sixties, the Duc de Choiseul, French foreign minister, watched closely for signs of American disaffection from England. He even sent secret emissaries to America to sound public opinion and to encourage revolt. The Comte de Vergennes, successor to Choiseul, continued to fish in the increasingly muddy waters of English-American relations. The Revolution came to be viewed by the French court as France's last chance to restore the *grandeur* that was hers under the glorious reign of the Sun King, Louis XIV.

Having arrived in Paris the latter part of December 1776, Franklin remained in the French capitol for two months. During this time, he, Lee and Deane were unofficially received by Vergennes. Unwilling to challenge Britain by open aid to the Americans, Vergennes granted them a secret loan of two million livres and arranged for their permanent headquarters in the charming suburb of Passy, about a half mile from the city. Here, among park-like surroundings, Franklin established his headquarters and residence at the Hôtel Valentinois, offered him by the businessman-idealist, Donatien Le Ray de Chaumont. Passy was a politic choice, for the Hôtel Valentinois not only put Franklin in intimate proximity to Chaumont, who was heavily involved in the contraband trade to America, but it was also situated along the road from Versailles to Paris. He was thus placed near the center of the emerging economic and political Franco-American entente.

If the French ministry was predisposed to weakening England by aiding America, Franklin nevertheless arrived in

France at a perilous time in American affairs. Washington had retreated across New Jersey and Valley Forge was just ahead. French hopes of bringing Spain into alliance with her were dashed against the reefs of Spanish dislike of republican America. Furthermore, the British ambassador Stormont, for whom Franklin was "a very dangerous engine," watched and noted every sign of French aid to the colonists. Vergennes did not wish to be dragged unprepared into war. The French fleet must be brought to readiness and it must have Spanish support, for alone it could not match England's navy.

Throughout the spring and summer of 1777, American military reversals and Spanish caution stayed Vergennes' policy of *revanche*. So timorous did he become that to please Stormont, he ostentatiously held up an important shipment of war materials to America to prove French neutrality. But Stormont correctly divined French intentions. American ships used both French and Spanish ports—in Europe as well as in the West Indies—with impunity. It was French powder and other contraband goods that fed the American war effort.

The American commissioners, for their part soon became ready to go beyond their original instructions in order to bring France into more active support. Their isolationist inclinations were sacrificed to the requirements of the situation. They were ready to offer not only political and military guarantees to France but to suggest a triple alliance if Spain could also be brought in. By the proffered terms, the United States pledged to make no separate peace with Britain. The United States would not only assure to France one half the Newfoundland fisheries and all the sugar islands, but they would also guarantee Florida to Spain and aid her against Portugal, with whom Spain contended in both Europe and America.

Throughout the spring of 1777, the Bourbons proved unresponsive to the commissioners' appeals. Spain would on no account recognize England's rebels. France would continue her policy of secret aid but would not risk war with mighty Britain. But America's military reversals worried the French foreign minister. The reestablishment of the old British Empire must be avoided, lest France's opportunity be lost. During the first few years of the war, therefore, France made saving grants and loans to the Americans amounting to some four million livres.

These loans and the allowing of American shipping in French ports were veritable acts of war on the part of supposedly neutral France. Munitions and supplies were made available to the Americans through governmental subsidies to the fictitious Roderigue Hortalez and Company. The "Company" was the brainchild of the brilliant courtier-dramatist Caron de Beaumarchais, who achieved a greater fame as the author of *The Barber of Seville* and *The Marriage of Figaro*. Many legitimate French mercantile houses, of which Franklin's host Chaumont's was one, freely traded with England's enemies while American ships were given access to French ports.

England was well aware of French activity through the surveillance of her navy and thanks to the espionage activity of a network of spies. A principal channel of information was the learned and devious Dr. Edward Bancroft, who was for a time secretary to the American mission. Bancroft found a willing accomplice in the ambitious Silas Deane. It was a period when public office was frequently conceived as a private as well as a public trust, and Deane was quick to sense the heady opportunities for personal gain created by the conditions of war. He and Dr. Bancroft manipulated news in order to capitalize on insurance and stock deals. They took commercial advantage of Deane's position as an agent through whom passed French shipments bound for America. The two men, in fact, were intertwined in a labyrinth of duplicity.[6]

Franklin evidently did not suspect Bancroft, who like himself was a member of the Royal Society, and with whom he had been friendly in England. And he misjudged Deane, whose activity in sending supplies to America made an important contribution during the war's early years. But Franklin was aware that England had sources of information close to the American mission. To the vast annoyance of Arthur Lee, however, he refused to be ruffled by English espionage. Franklin was a worldly philosopher who had practiced diplomacy from the Indian long house to Thomas Penn's Spring Garden and Whitehall itself. He alone understood that the more England learned of French activity in support of America, the closer she would be to a rupture with France. The more circuitous the routes by which England received her information, the more significant such news would seem. Franklin was therefore understandably serene when complaints from Vergennes or others came to him with dire warnings of the successful activities of spies at Passy. "I have long observ'd one Rule which prevents any Inconvenience from such Practices," wrote the old diplomat. "It is simply this:"

> to be concern'd in no Affairs that I should blush to have made publick, and to do nothing but what Spies may see & welcome. When a Man's Actions are just & honourable, the more they are known, the more his Reputation is increas'd & establish'd. If I was sure therefore that my Valet de Place was a Spy, as probably he is, I think I should not discharge him for that, if in other Respects I lik'd him.[7]

Franklin's attitude appeared treasonous or worse to the splenetic Lee. He believed the philosopher to be an accomplice of Deane, whom Lee rightly suspected, though for the wrong reasons. To Congress, he accused Deane of falsely reporting aid obtained through Rodrigue Hortalez and Company as loans rather than gifts. Lee thought that Franklin, who defended Deane in this particular, had connived at the alleged falsification of accounts. Congress recalled Deane, who sought an audit, and instead was faced with more accusations at home. Returned to Europe, Deane ultimately completed the destruction of his own reputation by urging upon his countrymen a conciliation with England. In America, Deane's name, like that of his fellow Connecticut citizen Benedict Arnold, became synonymous with the name of traitor.

Though Lee wrongly viewed Franklin as an accomplice in Deane's profiteering, the two men were linked in another affair that also affronted the Virginian. This was the Vandalia scheme in which they, as well as Dr. Bancroft, were stockholders, and which encroached on Virginia's western lands. With the United States Congress having replaced the authority of Whitehall, their hopes now centered in Philadelphia rather than London. Franklin found time to compose and send to the Congress a long memorial recounting the history of the Vandalia project and arguing for his company's right to the disputed area—a claim which, of course, Lee and his friends contested. In his eagerness, Franklin even went so far as to enter into an indiscreet correspondence with his English associates, though none of his or his partners' efforts met with success.

Franklin was not only an associate of Deane in the Vandalia venture. He also sincerely believed the younger man to be steadfast in the American cause, and he supported Deane in his struggle with Arthur Lee. He was consequently shocked when Deane later advised the Americans to compromise their differences with Britain. But even then he seems to have considered Deane guilty of poor judgment, rather than of treason: a not unreasonable construction during the difficult months before Yorktown.

To Lee, however, Franklin's benign attitude meant collusion. The man who refused to condemn wrongdoing was also suspiciously calm about spies. Therefore, throughout the dark days of 1777, Lee continued his vendetta. It was wrong for Franklin's grandson Temple to be in the commission's pay. Franklin's grandnephew Jonathan Williams, an American agent at Nantes, was guilty of peculation. In spite of such charges, Temple was retained, and a Congressional committee cleared Williams. (Later, Williams was named by President Jefferson the first Superintendent of West Point.) There was also the affair of the incompetent Captain Pierre Landais, whom the Lee-Adams group in Congress favored over John Paul Jones, who was an admirer of Franklin. When Franklin relieved the mentally unstable Landais from command of the *Alliance,* Landais, with Lee's support, refused to step down. Lee and Landais defied both Commodore Jones and Franklin, against whom Landais was guilty of insubordination, if not mutiny.

Though Lee failed to impugn Franklin's loyalty, he did succeed in earning an almost unique distinction: that of arousing Franklin to indignation. To his accusing colleague, Franklin wrote a letter:

> Sir
> It is true I have omitted answering some of your Letters. I do not like to answer angry Letters. I hate Disputes. I am old, cannot have long to live, have much to do and no time for Altercation. If I have often receiv'd and borne your Magisterial Snubbings and Rebukes without Reply, ascribe it to the right Causes, my Concern for the Honour & Success of our Mission, which would be hurt by our Quarrelling, my Love of Peace, my Respect for your good Qualities, and my Pity of your Sick Mind, which is forever tormenting itself, with its Jealousies, Suspicions & Fancies that others mean you ill, wrong you, or fail in Respect for you.—If you do not cure your

self of this Temper it will end in Insanity, of which it is the Symptomatick Forerunner, as I have seen in several Instances. God preserve you from so terrible an Evil: and for his sake pray suffer me to live in quiet.[8]

Having given vent to his real feelings, Franklin decided his letter could be of little purpose. The next day he included a toned-down version of it as part of a longer letter in which he attempted to answer Lee's charges. Lee, nevertheless, continued to sow seeds of doubt regarding Franklin's patriotism.

Though Franklin was aware that the Lees—Arthur, Richard Henry, and Francis Lightfoot—and their followers were attempting to influence Congress against him, he had little time to be concerned. There were, for instance, the hundreds of applicants for service in America that Franklin was forced to entertain. It seemed that everyone with influence or who knew someone with influence wanted an introduction to the Congress in Philadelphia. Franklin could ill afford to antagonize such persons by refusal to see them. But he did amuse himself by composing a model letter of recommendation to cover all contingencies:

SIR:—The bearer of this, who is going to America, presses me to give him a Letter of Recommendation, tho' I know nothing of him, not even his Name. This may seem extraordinary, but I assure you it is not uncommon here. Sometimes, indeed one unknown Person brings another equally unknown, to recommend him; and sometimes they recommend one another! As to this Gentleman, I must refer you to himself for his Character and Merits, with which he is certainly better acquainted than I can possibly be. I recommend him however to those Civilities, which every Stranger, of whom one knows no Harm, has a Right to; and I request you will do him all the good Offices, and show him all the Favour that, on further Acquaintance, you shall find him to deserve.[9]

Not all applicants received such cavalier treatment. Fortunately, among those Franklin took seriously were Baron von Steuben and Casimir Pulaski, both of whom Franklin recommended to Washington and the Congress. Von Steuben, whom Franklin and Deane in their letters promoted to lieutenant-general of the Prussian service in order to impress Congress, would play an essential role in building the army's morale. The heroic Count Pulaski would die of wounds suffered during the seige of British-held Savannah. Though the nineteen year old Marquis de Lafayette, burning for revenge upon the English for the death of his father in the last war, had left for America before Franklin's arrival in France, it was Franklin's correspondence with Washington that brought the General and the nobleman together.

Franklin was busy also in publishing effective propaganda pieces for the American cause. Some of his earlier political satires were translated into French and disseminated for the public's amusement. If the French were delighted with the *Edict of the King of Prussia*, they were brought to indignation against the British by Franklin's newly composed *The Sale of the Hessians*. In this Swiftian satire, a fictitious German prince exults over the massacre of his troops in America. Not only does he receive from the English payment for each of his soldiers killed, but he may now sell more men to replenish the supply.

Franklin was frequently as effective in conversation as he was in writing. The French were delighted with his bon mot upon hearing of General Howe's entrance into Philadelphia. Howe had not taken Philadelphia, said Franklin, it was "Philadelphia who had taken him." Once when asked if a certain recounting of American reverses as told by British Ambassador Stormont were true, Franklin replied, "Non, Monsieur, ce n'est pas vérité, c'est seulement un Stormont." [10] ("No sir, it is not the truth, it is only a Stormont.") The phrase caught on, and within the French court circle the word Stormont became the equivalent for lie.

Ambassador Stormont's situation in France became in fact increasingly untenable. The more courtesies shown Franklin, the more strained became Anglo-French relations. To Stormont, France's "whole system with reference to the rebels was so knavish, so mean, and so paltry as well odious" that England's course in contrast, was the very epitome of dignity. It was with some pique that he returned to Franklin the American commissioner's letter with regard to the cruel treatment by Britain of American prisoners of war, prisoners viewed by England as traitors to be tried on the charge of treason. "The King's Ambassador," wrote Stormont, "receives no Letters from Rebels but when they come to implore his Majesty's Mercy." [11]

Although the British Ambassador chose not to recognize the existence of Franklin in his official capacity, British soldiers across the seas were learning, to their dismay, the reality of American determination. On October 17, 1777, General Burgoyne was forced to surrender his entire force of seven thousand men to Generals Gates and Arnold at Saratoga. The result in England was a new wave of revulsion against the war. The Parliamentary opposition increased its drive for a reconciliation shortly to eventuate in the Carlisle Peace Commission, which would be no more successful than the Staten Island conference had been. The effect of Saratoga in France was renewed admiration for American military prowess, an admiration that Franklin turned into active support.

Franklin's diplomacy was consistent with his strategy with regard to spies. He would now see that France was apprised of England's secret attempts to win a negotiated peace. In the fall of 1777, Paul Wentworth, an English emissary, arrived in Paris for confidential talks with the Americans. His mission was to learn their conditions for peace short of independence. It was an effort that played directly into Franklin's hands. He made no attempt to conceal from the French his meetings with Wentworth, meetings which he knew would frighten Vergennes. Independence, of course, had become America's one nonnegotiable demand, but of this fact, France had no absolute assurance. France, after all, was deeply committed to American success. Her aid had sustained the American war effort. It had also brought forth the threat of British retaliation in the Caribbean. Were America to reunite with England, France's remaining imperial possessions would be gravely imperiled. American independence had become the cardinal principle of French foreign policy.

Franklin deliberately played upon French fears. He passed to Vergennes a written offer of conciliation with America from the English. Quickly, Vergennes requested from the American commissioners their price for cutting off further negotiations with Britain. Franklin's answer was clear and to the point. America would cease talking with the British if France would join her in treaties of alliance and commerce. The strategy worked. In return for the American disavowal of reconciliation with England, France was ready, even without Spain, openly to avow her alliance with the young republic across the sea.

Franklin's diplomacy was crowned with success on February 6, 1778. On that day, the American commissioners and French representatives signed two treaties: one of friendship and commerce and one of political alliance in which France recognized the "liberty, sovereignty, and Independence absolute" of the United States. For the signing, Franklin wore the same blue coat he wore at the Cockpit during the Hutchinson letters affair when Wedderburn humiliated him—"to give it a little revenge." The political alliance was kept secret by Vergennes, who perhaps preferred to await Congressional ratification; it may also have indicated even at this late date some reticence on the foreign minister's part. But the commercial alliance, and with it recognition of the new nation, was immediately announced in England by the French ambassador there, in order to forestall the objectives of the Carlisle Peace Commission, shortly to embark for America. On March 20, the American commissioners were officially received at the court of Louis XVI, where Queen Marie Antoinette found it difficult to accept the eminent Benjamin Franklin, who had once been a humble tradesman.

Franklin's triumph at Versailles was the European counterpart of Gates' victory at Saratoga. From the moment of the signing of the treaties, England had to contend not only with the new American states but with her ancient enemy as well. A civil war was becoming a world war. Saratoga and the French alliance turned the tide from the depths of Valley Forge toward the climactic battle of Yorktown. "Tho' the Wickedness of the English Court, & its Malice against us is as great as ever," Franklin commented, "its Horns are shortened; its Strength diminishes daily; and we have formed an Alliance here, & shall form others, that will help to keep the Bull quiet and make him orderly." [12]

One repercussion of the French alliance was a new status for Franklin. John Adams, Deane's replacement, believed, as did the other commissioners, that the commission should be replaced by one minister plenipotentiary. Although Lee thought himself to be the outstanding candidate, Congress, on September 14, named Franklin to the post. Notification of the appointment came, appropriately enough, from Lafayette, returned from America in February 1779. The infuriated Lee ("in creating misunderstandings and quarrels, in malice, subtility, and indefatigable industry, he has I think no equal," wrote Franklin), refused to turn over official papers to the newly named minister, and was later recalled. He sailed in the ill-fated *Alliance* in a wild voyage which forced even Lee to recognize the incompetence of Captain Pierre Landais, whom Congress soon dismissed from the service. In 1781, Lee was elected to the Virginia House of Delegates and then to the Continental Congress, where he represented Virginia until 1784. Adams, taking with him the future statesman, eleven year old John Quincy, for whom Franklin had developed a strong attachment, also returned to America. Like Lee, Adams had resented Franklin's defense of Deane. He believed the old man too yielding to French demands, and he disapproved of Franklin's easygoing manners.

The withdrawal of Lee and Adams left Franklin undisputed master in his own house. For six years he would represent the United States of America at the most influential court in Europe. For much of that time, he would work to bring to fruition the high promise of the French alliance of 1778, the promise of victory for the cause of American independence.

XII Independence Won

WITH FRANKLIN'S APPOINTMENT as minister plenipotentiary, his residence at the Hôtel Valentinois in Passy became in everything but name the first American embassy in Europe. In reality America's first ambassador, the seventy-two year old Franklin, with his young grandson William Temple as secretary, performed consular and military functions besides his ministerial duties. His pioneering efforts took place not during a period of peace, but during tempestuous years of war. He was "in his own person the American Government in Europe and obliged to act not merely as an Ambassador but as a War Department, a Treasury Department, a Navy Department, a Prize Court, a Bureau for the Relief and Exchange of Prisoners, a Consul and a dealer in cargoes which came from America." [1] To these tasks would shortly be added the responsibility of helping bring about a treaty of peace. Such an office would have taxed an ordinary man thirty years younger, but Franklin's equanimity was extraordinary. It was a rare day which found him depressed or unequal to the tasks at hand.

Franklin's ministerial duties extended from dancing the court ritual at Versailles to the obtaining of loans and contracting for war materials. His naval responsibilities included not only acting as judge of admiralty in prize cases, but also in the commissioning of privateers for action on the high seas. Franklin recognized the naval genius of John Paul Jones and commended him to Congress. Jones, who named his ship for Franklin, planned with the older man his daring raids on the English coast. In the bloody battle between the *Bonhomme*

Richard and the ill-fated *Serapis,* Jones gave the weak American navy its most famous Revolutionary victory.

Franklin's multifarious labors did not deter him, however, from the pursuit of his many other interests, including the opposite sex. Indeed, the more onerous his duties, the more in need was the old man for relaxation in the companionship of his friends and neighbors at Passy. It was this side of Franklin that the puritan John Adams could not understand. The delights of the table and the glass, of witty conversation and charming company; these the dour New Englander viewed with deep suspicion and distaste. "The Life of Dr. Franklin," Adams commented, "was a Scene of continual discipation." He breakfasted late, Adams explained, and breakfast over,

> a crowd of Carriages came to his Levee or if you like the term better to his Lodgings, with all Sorts of People; some Phylosophers, Accademicians and Economists; some of his small tribe of humble friends in the litterary Way . . . . but by far the greater part were Women and Children, come to have the honour to see the great Franklin, and to have the pleasure of telling Stories about his Simplicity, his bald head and scattering strait hairs, among their Acquaintances.

Franklin's afternoons, Adams went on, were taken up with dinner—"Mr. Lee said it was the only thing in which he was punctual"—after which came tea, music, chess, and checkers. "In these Agreeable and important Occupations and Amusements," concluded Adams, "the Afternoon and Evening was spent, and he came home at all hours from Nine to twelve O Clock at night." [2] There was more than a modicum of truth in Adam's acid account of Franklin's life in Passy. But in fact, Adams notwithstanding, Franklin's pleasures actually augmented his business. They invariably refreshed him so that he brought renewed energy to his many tasks. His *succés fou* in the French salons not only gave him pleasure but also lent him prestige with those families of wealth and name who wielded definitive influence in the France of the *Ancien Regime*.

Among his neighbors at Passy was the lovely Madame Brillon, forty years his junior, a fine musician who found in "Mon Cher Papa" the father figure who fulfilled her life. Wednesdays and Saturdays Franklin dined at the Brillon home where he found relaxation in conversation, romantic dalliance, music and chess. For eight years Franklin played the suitor and Madame Brillon the virtuous daughter. Once she lightly accused him of inconstancy. "It is clear as the clearest Euclidian proposition," he explained. "He who is constant to many shows more constancy than he who is constant to only one." [3]

Franklin was more serious in his attentions to Mme. Catherine Helvétius, who lived near Passy at Auteuil. The charming and witty widow of the famous philosopher, Claude Adrien Helvétius, only thirteen years younger than Franklin, friend of Voltaire, Turgot and the circle of philosophes in which her husband had been a leading light, she had been one of the great beauties of the age. To her salon continued to come the great of France. Franklin fell into the habit of dining at Auteuil at least once a week. "Statesmen, philosophers, historians, poets and men of learning of all sorts are drawn around you," Franklin told his hostess. "In your company we are not only pleased with you but better pleased with one another and with ourselves." There was humor and there was romance in Franklin's relationship with the woman he called "Notre Dame de Auteuil." He could play the satyr: when once she reproved him for putting off an expected visit, he replied, "Madame, I am waiting till the nights are longer." But beneath the banter, Franklin's intentions were serious:

he wanted to marry her. Her refusal left their relationship unchanged. It was perhaps the greatest friendship of Franklin's life.

The reappearance of John Adams in France marked a new phase in the diplomacy of the Revolution. Adams, who found Franklin "so fond of the fair sex that one was not enough for him, but he must have one on each side, and all the ladies both old and young were ready to eat him up," had returned to Europe as a special peace emissary in 1779. The appointment was in part due to Congress' learning of Spain's efforts to end the war by mediation. In return for Gibraltar, she offered England Spanish neutrality and a peace by which England would retain the principal American ports then in her possession. With England's refusal to countenance Spanish interference, however, Spain joined France in the secret treaty of April, 1779, at Aranjuez. Her price for entering the war against England was high. She would turn the Gulf of Mexico into a Spanish lake with the reconquest of the Floridas. She wished to expel the English from Campeche Bay and the Bay of Honduras, where their presence was an affront to Spain's imperial grandeur. She wanted the return of Minorca, and above all, "that pile of stones," Gibraltar, lost to Britain since 1713. Withal, she would not recognize the United States for fear of the example set before her own American colonies.

The French agreement to continue the war until Gibraltar fell to Spain tied the American cause to the fulfillment of Spanish ambitions. Furthermore, the Treaty of Aranjuez stipulated that France would gain full sovereignty over Dunkirk, presently shared with Britain. France also desired to expel the British from the Newfoundland fisheries which she would share with Spain. She wished as well to take the island of Dominica in the West Indies and Senegal in West Africa, where she wanted full liberty to trade.

Following Aranjuez, Spain entered the war as an ally of

France in June, 1779. Their plans, concerning which they did not so much as consult the United States, included an invasion of England. The invasion, however, was a humiliating fizzle. It was at this time, August, 1779, that Congress sent John Adams back to Europe as a special peace commissioner. It also sent John Jay to Madrid to try to bring Spain into open alliance with the United States. Spain, however, though now allied with France, quietly reopened negotiations with Britain, still hoping to win her objectives if not by war, then by diplomacy.

Fortunately for the new nation, Spain's mediation offer, which would have sacrificed America's territorial integrity, if not her independence, was refused by England. Jay's presence at Madrid, nevertheless, could in itself be used by Spain as a bargaining counter against the English enemy. Yet a Spanish-American alliance proved unobtainable. Spain's price was too high. In return for recognition of the United States, she demanded the east bank of the Mississippi and exclusive navigation of that mighty river below the thirty-first parallel. American acquiescence would have left the new nation cooped up between the Alleghenies and the Atlantic seaboard. Though the Congress was ready to make concessions, Jay hedged. Franklin's support must have been particularly welcome. "Poor as we are," he wrote Jay from Paris, "yet as I know we shall be rich, I would rather agree with them to buy at a great price the whole of their right on the Mississippi than sell a drop of its waters. A neighbor might as well ask me to sell my street door." [4] Even John Adams admired the old doctor's forthright stand. He nevertheless unintentionally threatened the Franco-American alliance, so laboriously built by Franklin, in his outspoken suspicions of both the French and the Spanish. Adams believed, according to Franklin, that "America has been too free in expressions of gratitude to France. . . ." On the other hand, Franklin, convinced that Adams "mistakes his ground," believed "that this court is to be treated with decency and delicacy. The king, a young and virtuous prince," Franklin related to the president of the Congress,

> has, I am persuaded, a pleasure in reflecting on the generous benevolence of the action in assisting an oppressed people, and proposed it as a part of the glory of his reign. I think it right to increase this pleasure by our thankful acknowledgements, and that such an expression of gratitude is not only our duty, but our interest. A different conduct seems to me what is not only improper and unbecoming, but what may be hurtful to us.[5]

Franklin was sensitive, as Adams was not, to the subtleties of European diplomacy. He applied his mastery of human relationships to international relations and succeeded, whereas Adams' bulldog aggressiveness only served to anger the French and endanger the American position.

It was fortunate that the wily Franklin, rather than the impolitic Adams, was at the helm. The military situation in the winter of 1780–81 seemed desperate with the English southern campaign in full swing. Jay's mission to Spain was an abysmal failure, and Congress neared bankruptcy. The usually intrepid Washington had written "that our present situation makes one of two things essential to us: a peace, or the most vigorous aid of our allies, particularly in the article of *money.*" Artfully, Franklin included these lines of Washington in his request to Vergennes for funds. He appealed to the French foreign minister's humanity. "I am grown old," wrote Franklin, "and it is probable I shall not long have any more concern in these affairs." In consequence, the American could frankly state, "that the present conjuncture is critical." Without further aid, the American government might collapse. A conquered America will afford England a "broad basis for future greatness," so that she will become "*the terror of Europe.*" Franklin's appeal brought forth a French response in the form of a gift of six million livres which was as important a victory for America as Yorktown. From the Netherlands, to which he had gone to seek help following the failure of Spanish mediation, John Adams, for the moment forgetting his animus against Franklin, sent congratulations to the old man for "the noble aid obtained from the French court . . . ." [6]

Franklin's diplomatic success marked a turning point both for America and for his own prospects. During the fall of 1780, a severe attack of gout (Franklin wondered if the illness were "a disease or a remedy") had suddenly made him feel his age. At home, the Lee faction attacked him in Congress as too old for his job. He was again accused of nepotism for having his grandson as secretary. His reply was to submit his resignation to Congress, along with the news of the successful negotiation with Vergennes. "I have been engaged in public affairs and enjoyed public confidence, in some shape or other, during the long term of fifty years," Franklin wrote to Congress. He had not "the least doubt of their success in the glorious cause," but his only personal ambition now was for repose. Franklin was undoubtedly ready to retire from public life, but he also may have hoped for some exoneration from the jealous calumnies of his enemies. If that is what he wished, his success was overwhelming. Congress refused to accept his resignation. "I call this continuance an honor," wrote Franklin, "and I really esteem it to be a greater than my first appointment, when I consider that all the interests of my enemies, united with my own request, were not sufficient to prevent it." [7]

Franklin's success in both foreign and domestic diplomacy as well as his recovery from the gout coincided with brightened prospects for the United States. The English were running into unexpected difficulties in the Carolinas. The loyalists were not so numerous or so active as had been hoped, and the brilliance of Nathaniel Greene, with the guerilla tactics of Francis Marion and Thomas Sumter, crippled Cornwallis' progress. In Europe, French diplomacy had been successful in bringing together most of the powers of the continent in resisting threats to neutral commerce. The resultant Armed Neutrality may have been an "armed nullity" as Catherine of Russia put it, but this alliance served to point up the increasing isolation of proud Albion. English possessions from Gibraltar to the West Indies seemed in deadly jeopardy. A soaring national debt, bread riots in London and a vociferous Parliamentary opposition to the North regime all compromised the British government's ability to prosecute what had become an increasingly unpopular war.

Yorktown, "a great and important event," wrote Franklin, provided the crowning blow. Recalling the victory at Saratoga, Franklin quipped, "The infant Hercules has strangled his second serpent that attacked him in his cradle, and," he continued, "I hope his future history will be conformable." [8] The cry in Britain for the resignation of the North ministry became irresistible. Now the logic of events worked to the new nation's benefit. France wanted her independent of Britain; Britain wanted the United States independent of France. Here, as Franklin realized, lay America's opportunity. He would labor to satisfy both English and French desires, and in so doing, make America independent of both.

In June 1781, at the behest of Vergennes, who disliked John Adams, Congress appointed Franklin one of five men to join the latter in writing a peace. However, the recent death of his wife caused Thomas Jefferson, one of the appointees, to refuse the mission. Henry Laurens, another of the new ministers, was captured on his way to France by a British frigate and imprisoned in the tower of London for high treason. He was released the next year and arrived in France at the moment of the signing of the preliminary treaty of peace. The fifth commissioner was the minister to Spain, John Jay, who with Franklin and Adams would share the burdens of peace making.

During the previous months, America's position had been endangered by a renewed suggestion of outside mediation. Russia and Austria, without consulting the United States, suggested a peace that would have created a partitioned America. Fortunately for the new nation, England again rejected mediation by European powers. At the same time, Franklin received numerous English appeals for a solution short of independence. His erstwhile English friends became increasingly concerned that the Franco-American alliance be broken. Yet Franklin was adamant. Independence was of course the *sine qua non* of any negotiations. The king's ministers were furious when Edmund Burke of the opposition read to the House a letter from the rebel Franklin: "Since the foolish part of mankind will make wars from time to time with each other, . . . it certainly becomes the wiser part . . . to alleviate as much as possible the calamities attending them." [9]

Franklin feared that although the English were "somewhat humbled at present, a little success may make them as insolent as ever. I remember," he wrote to the financier Robert Morris, "that, when I was a boxing boy, it was allowed, even after an adversary said he had enough, to give him a rising blow. Let ours be a douser." [10] England, in fact, was down but far from out. In spite of Yorktown, she still held the Carolinas and the principal ports of the nation. America's financial embarrassment—the recent French gift had proven but a stopgap—was chronic. Her morale reached low ebb during the winter of 1781–82. But in Parliament the opposition's incessant attacks upon the government culminated in the March passage of the Conway resolutions by which persons desiring further aggressive war in America were declared enemies to king and country. In the same month occurred the news of Lord North's resignation, while the king prepared to abdicate.

The new ministry—the king was persuaded to stay—was formed of a coalition under the Marquis of Rockingham, who previously headed the government at the time of the repeal of the Stamp Act. Within the coalition, Franklin's old friend, the Earl of Shelburne, emerged as the actual leader, ultimately taking Rockingham's place at the head of the ministry upon the latter's death. Shelburne's policy, not unlike that of Lord North, was reconciliation with America somewhere short of independence. Yet in order to wean America from the French connection, he would use persuasion rather than force.

In line with this policy, Shelburne replaced General Glinton, commander of the British forces in America, with Sir Guy Carleton, long known for his conciliatory stance. Carleton proceeded with the evacuation of most American ports, concentrating his men at New York in readiness to embark for action against the French and Spanish. Shelburne directed that under no circumstances was Carleton to pursue an offensive war against the Americans.

Shelburne's efforts at reconciliation with America were meant not only to retain the old colonies within the British sphere, but also to separate them from Bourbon influence. Having pacified the American war, he now took the diplomatic offensive by sending an old friend of America, the Scottish merchant Richard Oswald, to Passy. He arrived unexpectedly at the American minister's door in April, 1782. It was a time when Franklin was the only American peace commissioner then in Paris. John Jay, for whom Franklin sent when he realized the high significance of the Oswald mission, would not arrive in Paris from Madrid until the end of June. Adams, at The Hague successfully negotiating a Dutch loan, did not join in the peace talks until October.

For several months Franklin carried on the negotiations alone. He made it clear to Oswald that America would not consider a separate peace. To do so would play into the hands of England, who sought to divide and conquer. Franklin stipulated that America must have an acknowledgement of independence. Furthermore, if the Shelburne government truly desired a reconciliation, it ought to cede Canada and Nova Scotia to the American confederation. Their cession would remove the seeds of future contention. They would be appropriate reparation for Britain to pay a despoiled America; at the same time America might set aside a portion of the newly gained Canada as compensation for American loyalists whose property the states had confiscated. Franklin was to regret this last hint in that it introduced into the negotiations the concept that American tories should be compensated for their sufferings.

Franklin had good reason to believe that England was ready for a peace upon advantageous terms. She was desperately anxious to remove America from the French orbit, and her financial situation was critical. The ingenuous Oswald let fall that, if necessary, England would stop payment on the public debt and apply the interest thereon to further military expenditures. Shrewdly, Franklin was delighted at the prospect, which he "considered as cutting the throat of the public credit and a means of adding fresh exasperation against them with the neighboring nations . . . . *They who threaten,*" Franklin recalled, *"are afraid.*"[11]

The Franklin-Oswald negotiations culminated in the American minister's presentation of four "necessary" and four "advisable" articles as the basis for a treaty of peace between England and America. These articles included in the "necessary" category:

1. Independence
2. Settlement of the boundaries of the new nation.
3. Confinement of Canada's boundaries at least to their status before the Quebec Act.
4. Freedom to fish off the Newfoundland Banks.

The "advisable" articles included:

1. British reparations for destruction wrought during the war.
2. British acknowledgement of "error" in prosecuting a war against America.
3. An Anglo-American commercial agreement providing for reciprocal trading privileges.
4. The cession of Canada to the United States.

With some modification, the first four of these became the basis for the definitive peace.

In looking toward the future, Franklin made further suggestions for incorporation into an Anglo-American peace treaty. One of these was to outlaw privateering in the course of future wars. (As judge in prize court, Franklin had ample opportunities to witness the inequities in such proceedings.) He would also render war less cruel by guaranteeing the safety of such noncombatants as fishermen, farmers, unarmed artisans and manufacturers in unfortified locations. Believing war to be brutal and inhumane, Franklin hoped that by treaty agreements, its worst cruelties might at least be contained. *"There never was,"* he later wrote, *"a good War, or a bad Peace."* [12]

Franklin's unilateral exchange with Oswald went considerably beyond the previous years' Congressional instructions to the effect that the American ministers should do nothing without the advice of France. Yet Franklin reasoned that the appointment of more than one peace commissioner indicated that Congress had meant for its ministers to exercise judgment, since, as he later put it, "one could have made a treaty by direction of the French ministry as well as twenty." [13] France could hardly take umbrage at an assertion of an American independence which was the very basis of her foreign policy. She had gone too far to risk a break that might see America back again within the English fold.

Yet in spite of the fact that Franklin was the first to deal unilaterally with England, John Adams believed he was too much under the thumb of Vergennes. John Jay, on the other hand, though he differed from the older man in tactics, respected Franklin's great abilities. Yet both Jay and Adams shared a deep distrust of France and Spain, whom they suspected of attempting to deny to the United States the Newfoundland fisheries, Canada, and the lands lying west of the Alleghenies to the Mississippi. Spain, of course, was no ally of the United States and assuredly had pretensions to the Mississippi Valley that conflicted with the territorial ambitions of the new nation. But there was no reason to expect France to uphold American ambitions in Canada, or for her to back American claims to the fisheries, or the hinterland. From the French point of view, Canada would be better left in English hands so that the United States, with an enemy on its northern border, would feel the need to continue the French alliance. Furthermore, in abetting Spanish ambitions in the Mississippi Valley, France could recompense Spain for her inability to wrest Gibraltar from Britain. France had guaranteed the independence of the thirteen colonies, but she had not agreed to enter into the dispute as to the ownership of the trans-Allegheny west nor to support American territorial aggrandizement in Canada.

The suspicions of Jay, who arrived in Paris before Adams, were further roused by Franklin's acquiescence in treating with Oswald, who was commissioned only to negotiate with representatives of the "said colonies or plantations." Vergennes agreed with Franklin that so long as the final peace treaty included independence the wording of Oswald's commission was unimportant. To Franklin, the lawyer Jay "saw things that other people didn't see. . . . It is a pity," he believed, "to keep three or four million people in war for the sake of form." To Jay, however, it seemed that Vergennes was attempting to postpone American independence for his own devious purposes. More likely, Vergennes was anxious for a quick peace. Its effect upon the United States, however, was of less importance to him than the fact that peace would relieve him of his embarrassing obligations to Spain.

When Vergennes' secretary, Gérard de Rayneval, made a secret trip to London evidently to press French and Spanish claims to the fisheries and the American hinterland, Jay became thoroughly alarmed. Without informing Franklin, he sent an emissary to Shelburne to state that if Oswald were empowered to treat with commissioners of the United States, he was ready for bilateral negotiations in spite of Congress' instructions to act in consultation with France. Shelburne was delighted to see a rift opening up between France and the United States. He complied, and Jay took over the negotiations with the now satisfactorily commissioned Oswald. Franklin, bedridden with bladder stone, agreed with Jay's decision to continue negotiations, a decision strongly concurred in by Adams, when he arrived in Paris following his successful mission to the Netherlands.

Meanwhile, the fortunes of war had strengthened Shelburne's hand. Admiral Rodney's great victory over de Grasse in the West Indies and the lifting of the three-year siege of Gibraltar meant, to the despair of Franklin, that Canada was out of the question. The compliant Oswald was now joined by the tough-minded Henry Strachey, undersecretary of state in the colonial office, who would move America's northern boundary back to the Quebec Act line of the Ohio River. The new English proposals reduced the American claim of fishing rights off Newfoundland to a restricted privilege granted by England. Strachey was also instructed to take a firm stand on the matter of compensating American loyalists as well as on the payment of prewar colonial debts to British claimants.

Franklin, recovered from his recent illness, joined Adams and Jay at the end of October for the climactic negotiations with Oswald and Strachey. Temple Franklin acted as secretary to the American commission. Adams, good New England man, fought mightily for American fishing rights in Newfoundland waters. He was successful with regard to the all-important Grand Banks, but obtained only the "liberty," —not "right,"—for Americans to fish off the coast of Newfoundland itself. He also gained permission for Americans to cure their fish in the unsettled bays and creeks of Nova Scotia, the Magdalen Islands, and Labrador. The fisheries article in the final treaty represented a compromise, the interpretation of which would provide cause of future disputes. The matter of prewar debts, likewise, remained indefinite with the Americans merely guaranteeing to introduce no obstacle to their future settlement.

The problem of the indemnification of the American loyalists proved almost insurmountable. To the American commissioners, compensation for the loyalists was tantamount to betrayal of the Revolution. To the British, abandonment of the American tories could weaken loyalist sentiment in the remaining colonies. On this issue Franklin proved particularly resourceful. The old doctor drew up a list of counter-claims in the form of a letter to Oswald. Should the British demand compensation for the tories, Franklin was prepared to insist upon reparations for a long list of deprivations suffered by the patriots. Franklin's associates were delighted with the maneuver. According to Jay, "Dr. Franklin's firmness and exertions on the subject of the Tories did us much service." Franklin's letter to Oswald, Jay continued, "is written with a degree of acuteness and spirit seldom to be met with in persons of his age." [14] The result was that in the final treaty, Britain backed down considerably on her previous stand: Congress would turn tory claims for compensation back to the states which were not legally bound by the treaty to act.

The true American triumph occurred, however, in the matter of boundaries. Though the military situation in America hardly warranted British sacrifices, the American commissioners made the most of the British desire to weaken the Franco-American alliance. Spanish pretentions to the west were silenced as the Americans won the Mississippi line to the thirty-first parallel. Spain retained the Floridas, her one military conquest, in return for English retention of Gibraltar. The British agreed to withdraw their claim to the Ohio country, giving the new nation a somewhat vague, if generous northern boundary that would not be finally settled until the Webster-Ashburton Treaty of 1842. The American ministers had won for the United States an imperial domain.

The signing of the preliminary peace treaty, not to take effect until confirmed by Congress and the completion of agreements between England and the other belligerents, took place on November 30. At the last minute, the fourth commissioner, Carolinian Henry Laurens, arrived from England, where he had been released from prison, and introduced the stipulation that evacuating British forces would not carry off

American slaves. The Americans signed the preliminary peace treaty without previous consultation with France. For this breach of confidence, Vergennes upbraided Franklin. The American minister, however, masterfully soothed French sensibilities. He admitted to "neglecting a point of *bienseance* (propriety)." Yet if France, because of this "single indiscretion" refused to grant further aid to America, "the whole edifice sinks to the ground immediately. . . ." Then Franklin played his trump. *"The English,"* he wrote, "I just *now learn, flatter themselves they have already divided us.* I hope this little misunderstanding will therefore be kept a secret, and that they will find themselves totally mistaken." [15] Vergennes was mollified. The ship that carried the news of the preliminary treaty to Congress also carried the first installment of a new French loan of six million livres.

The definitive Treaty of Paris was signed September 3, 1783. Its articles pertaining to the United States were substantially the same as those of the preliminary treaty agreed to the previous year. France, for her part, gained the disruption of the British Empire. Dunkirk was fully restored, and she took the relatively unimportant West Indian Island of Tobago and the slave trading domain of the Senegal River. Spain, beside her failure to regain Gibraltar for which she was recompensed by Florida, received Minorca, but the British remained on the Honduran coast. The Dutch, from whom John Adams had won recognition of the United States as well as a timely loan and the new nation's second treaty of amity and commerce, were completely overwhelmed; they were forced to open their East Indian empire to British traders.

The treaty gave rise to festering resentments among the European nations. It also led to disputes between England and America over interpretation of certain of its articles. But the treaty did ratify American independence, and in its boundary provisions, guaranteed American hegemony in the

Benjamin West, *The Treaty of Paris,* unfinished painting, 1784-85.

Courtesy The Henry Francis du Pont Winterthur Museum.

west, and therefore America's future. America's peacemakers deserved well of the new nation. Franklin looked forward to a reward of retirement either to spend his last years in France, or if he could physically withstand another journey—he was now subject to recurring painful attacks of the stone—to return for the last time to his native land. For America he saw a glorious future. Some years before while the English were pressing their southern campaign, he had written to George Washington a magisterial affirmation of American destiny: "I must soon quit this scene," he began,

> but you may live to see our country flourish, as it will amazingly and rapidly after the war is over, like a field of young Indian corn, which long fair weather and sunshine had enfeebled and discoloured, and which, in that weak state, by a thundergust of violent wind, hail, and rain seemed to be threatened with absolute destruction; yet the storm being past, it recovers fresh verdure, shoots up with double vigour, and delights the eye not of its owner only but of every observing traveller.[16]

Franklin, supremely confident of his nation's future, would have been amused at George III's view of the matter. Nor would he resent giving that luckless monarch the last word. "I cannot conclude," wrote the king to Shelburne,

> without mentioning how sensibly I feel the dismemberment of America from the Empire, and that I should be miserable indeed if I did not feel that no blame on that Account can be laid at my door, and did I not also know that knavery seems to be so much the striking feature of its Inhabitants that it may not in the end be an evil that they become Aliens to this Kingdom.[17]

Such were the ungenerous sentiments of a peevish prince as he noted the loss of an empire.

XIII Sage of Two Worlds

THE SIGNING OF the Treaty of Paris on September 3, 1783, represented the climax of Franklin's career as a diplomat. He was nearing his eightieth year; now, if ever, he had earned a respite from public life. He wanted Congress to release him from his ministerial duties so that while there was still time left, he could return to America and spend his last years in quiet—and private—enjoyment of philosophy and friends. But this was not to be. Congress did not replace Franklin for two years. Furthermore, upon his return to America, he was immediately swept up into Pennsylvania politics, and two years later he participated in the writing of the United States Constitution.

At the same time that Franklin expressed his wish to retire from public life, he was also concerned to protect his public reputation. He had had little time to enjoy the coming of peace when he received notice from a Massachusetts friend that rumors were being whispered concerning his part in the treaty negotiations. He was less than zealous, it was hinted, in securing for America the Newfoundland fisheries, nor did he help to win from England the generous territorial concessions embodied in the treaty of peace. Franklin, heretofore, had done little to answer the calumnies against him of the Lees and the "Braintry focus," the term he used for Adams and his friends. But in the words of La Luzerne, French minister to the United States, Franklin "at last aroused himself from the apathy with which, till now, he seems to have regarded the attacks of his colleagues." Franklin immediately wrote both Jay and Adams requesting from each a refutation of the Massachusetts accusations which he believed fell "little short of treason to my country."

Jay immediately replied with a fulsome vindication of Franklin's role in the treaty negotiations. Adams wrote a somewhat less forthright reply. Franklin saw that the letters of both his colleagues were forwarded to the Congress. At the same time he attempted to obtain a diplomatic post for his grandson, Temple, whose training fitted him for little else but government service. His failure led to his training his other grandson, Benny Bache, as a printer, for as Poor Richard says, "He that hath a Trade hath an Estate." Although Franklin was able to vindicate his reputation, the Lee-Adams interest in Congress successfully blocked his appeals for recognition of Temple's secretarial services, appeals which Franklin made almost to the end of his life.

Concern for his reputation and his grandsons' future occupied Franklin's last years in France, as did his remaining official duties. These involved the drawing of commercial treaties, based on the Plan of 1776, with several European nations. The first such treaty entered into by the United States after the Treaty of Paris was with Sweden, whose ambassador let it be known that his king particularly desired that the negotiations be with Franklin. Franklin, in fact, was sought after by the representatives of many nations. The neglected Adams could hardly contain his jealously. "When all Europe sees that a number of your ministers are kept here as a kind of satellite to Mr. Franklin," he complained to the president of Congress, "they fall in contempt." Franklin was lending himself to a subtle conspiracy, Adams believed, by which he and Jay "may not have an opportunity of suggesting ideas for the preservation of American navigation, transport trade, and nurseries of seamen." [1] Franklin attributed Adams' suspicions to "a disorder in the brain, which, though not constant, has its fits too frequent." Adams, Franklin once informed the president of Congress, believes "that Count de Vergennes and myself are continually plotting against him . . . . I am persuaded, however," Franklin added in a succinct summation of Adams' character, "that he means well for his country, is always an honest man, often a wise one, but sometimes and in some things absolutely out of his senses." [2]

It was a relief to both men when Adams left Paris for Amsterdam, where he once again successfully negotiated an essential loan for the United States. Adams' dark suspicions of the "corrupted and debauched" Europeans turned him into a militant American nationalist. On the contrary, though before the Revolution Franklin had frequently commented upon the corruption of old England, his long years in France had renewed his philosophical cosmopolitanism. He hoped to see the United States lead the world into a new era of peace and free trade. Towards this goal, he made a startling suggestion to his English friend David Hartley, member of Parliament and signer with Franklin of the definitive peace treaty between their two countries. "What would you think of a proposition," he queried Hartley,

of a compact between England, France, and America? America would be as happy as the Sabine girls if she could be the means of uniting in perpetual peace her father and her husband. What repeated follies are those repeated wars! You do not want to conquer and govern one another. Why, then, should you be continually employed in injuring and destroying one another? How many excellent things might have been done to promote the internal welfare of each country; what bridges, roads, canals, and other useful public works and institutions, tending to the common felicity, might have been made and established with the money and men foolishly spent during the last seven centuries by our mad wars in doing one another mischief! You are near neighbors, and each have very respectable qualities. Learn to be quiet and to respect each other's rights. You are all Christians. One is The Most Christian King and the other Defender of the Faith. Manifest the propriety of these titles by your future conduct. 'By this,' says Christ, 'shall all men know that ye are my disciples, if ye love one another.' Seek peace and insure it.[3]

Neither England, France, America, nor any other nation for that matter were—or are—ready "to be quiet and to respect each other's rights." And although Franklin hoped for an open world, he was shrewdly aware of the exigencies of power politics. There was, for instance, the matter of the Barbary states, whose corsairs preyed upon American commerce. "I think it not improbable," he wrote, "that those rovers may be privately encouraged by the English to fall upon us, and to prevent our interference in the carrying trade; for I have in London heard it is a maxim among the merchants that *if there were no Algiers it would be worth England's while to build one.*"[4] Franklin was responsible for writing the first draft of a treaty between America and the North African states. But in spite of these and later negotiations, it was left to Franklin's peace-loving friend Thomas Jefferson, as president, to use force to bring the Mediterranean pirates to heel.

Franklin's suspicions of England's encouragement of the Barbary pirates were consistent with his wary attitude toward the English government. His cosmopolitanism did not exclude distrust of England's motives, a distrust that was, in fact, similar to John Adam's attitude toward the Europeans. Franklin believed that Whitehall prompted the British press to portray a chaotic America, unable to maintain order at home, or credit abroad. In order to counter the ill effects of these aspersions, Franklin composed counter propaganda in the form of letters to oldtime English friends. He also published more formal essays such as the *Retort Courteous,* in which courtesy was not the most noticeable aspect of his satirical reply to the British accusation that Americans refused to honor their prewar debts.

Franklin's propaganda efforts also included seeing to the publication of his friend La Rouchefecauld's translation of the "Book of Constitutions," which was a collection of the constitutions of the thirteen American states. That of Pennsylvania particularly interested the French, both because they mistakenly supposed Franklin was its author, and because of its unusual unicameral legislature. During the French Revolution, John Adams believed that the Pennsylvania example had inspired the creation of the French National Assembly. He blamed unicameralism for the Reign of Terror, during which many of Franklin's friends lost their lives. The French paid dearly, according to the grim New Englander, for their misplaced admiration of Dr. Franklin and his impractical democratic ideas.

Franklin wrote not only to counter anti-American British propaganda, but also to inform would-be European emigrants of what to expect in the New World. "The Truth is," he wrote in *Information to those who would Remove to America,* "that though there are in that Country few People so miserable as the Poor of Europe, there are also very few that in Europe would be called rich; it is rather a general happy Mediocrity that prevails." Franklin particularly warned against the emigration to America of a person "who has no other Quality to recommend him but his Birth. In Europe it has indeed its Value; but it is a Commodity that cannot be carried to a worse Market than that of America, where people do not inquire concerning a Stranger, *What is he?* but, *What can he do?*"[5]

Europeans not only were interested in going to America, but in everything about America, particularly the Indians. To satisfy their curiosity, Franklin composed his *Remarks Concerning the Savages of North America*. The piece describes Indian customs and habits through a series of anecdotes, the underlying moral of which Franklin states at the beginning: "Savages we call them, because their Manners differ from ours, which we think the Perfection of Civility; they think the same of theirs." The *Remarks* constitutes a plea for toleration. It is an essay in comparative cultures, and it told Europeans as much about themselves as about the aboriginal Americans.[6]

Franklin was far more interested in turning his pen to the cause of America than he was to continuing his memoirs, for which his French and English friends eagerly waited. At last, in 1784, he took up work on the *Autobiography* he had begun in 1771 at the home of his friend Jonathan Shipley in Twyford, England. In this second part of the book Franklin set forth his youthful "Project of arriving at moral Perfection." Of his list of virtues, Franklin confessed that order seemed impossible for him to obtain, a statement with which John Adams, who was shocked at Franklin's casual treatment of diplomatic papers, would have heartily concurred. Humility, too, proved illusive. Pride, wrote Franklin, will not down: "disguise it, struggle with it, beat it down, stifle it, mortify it as much as one pleases, it is still alive, and will every now and then peep out and show itself. . . . For even if I could conceive that I had compleatly overcome it, I should probably be proud of my Humility." [7]

Franklin printed many of his writings on the private press he had established in his residence at the Hôtel Valentinois. Here he published much of his pro-American propaganda, and here also he printed many of his bagatelles for the enjoyment of his friends. These short humorous sketches are minor literary masterpieces. They illuminate Franklin's wit far better than does the *Autobiography,* and they reveal, as the more famous work does not, the charm that attracted so many people to him and brought him so many friendships. Among the nineteen bagatelles, are the "Morals of Chess," a classic of the game, and "To Madame Helvétius," in which Franklin brings to courtship a wry and subtle humor. In the "Dialogue between Franklin and the Gout," Franklin is chastised by "Madame Gout" for drinking too much wine and playing chess instead of getting exercise. A few of the bagatelles contain enough ribaldry to have shocked some of Franklin's more puritanical contemporaries. They did nothing, of course, to enhance his reputation among the "Braintry focus."

Something of the spirit of the bagatelles comes out in the innumerable anecdotes that were told of Franklin during his ministry to France. During a game of chess with the Dutchess of Bourbon, for example, Franklin took her king. "Ah," said she, "we do not take kings so." "We do in America," said the Doctor.[8] And there was the story of Franklin's having arrived at a particular inn and hearing of the presence of Edward Gibbon. Franklin wrote a note to Gibbon asking the historian to join him. Gibbon's reply was that he refused to meet with a rebel, to which Franklin returned that when Gibbon sat down to write of the decline and fall of the British Empire, he would be happy to supply him with information.

The Franklin-Gibbon communication may be apocryphal. Better authenticated is Franklin's famous bon mot when he observed the first manned balloon ascension. A friend wondered aloud of what possible use the experiment could be. The sage replied, "What is the use of a new-born babe?" Franklin, in fact, saw several uses of manned flight. He foresaw its military potential, but he was too optimistic in believing that its destructive capabilities would render warfare impractical as a method of settling international disputes. Franklin, suffering from the stone, several times expressed the wish that he could travel by balloon, because transportation over rough roads was painful for him. He was also the recipient of the first airmail letter when a friend from England sent him a note conveyed by the first manned balloon channel crossing.

Franklin's enthusiasm for balloons indicated that his ministerial responsibilities had not dampened his enthusiasm for science and human progress. He theorized on the aurora borealis, correctly attributing this spectacle to the effects of an electrical discharge in the partial vacuum of the upper atmosphere. He continued to defend his single fluid theory of electricity against its few remaining critics, and he sent advice to a young lawyer named Maximilien Robespierre, who was involved in a legal case concerning lightning rods. Franklin was the first individual to suggest daylight saving time, albeit facetiously in a short piece on how to economize on the cost of candles. To a friend, he expressed as a certainty the idea that the Danes had preceded Columbus in the discovery of America. The motive for one of his most famous inventions, bifocal glasses, was social. Watching the lips of his French-speaking friends helped him, Franklin explained, to understand their conversation. Bifocals solved the problem of conversing across the dining table, while at the same time enabling him to see his food. Another of his less known sociable inventions of this period was a string quartet he composed for open strings. Although Franklin could play the violin, the performance of his quartet demanded less of the players than any other work in the same genre, while at the same time the work displayed Franklin's remarkable ingenuity.

As a man of science, Franklin was named by the king to a commission to judge the validity of the new theory of Mesmerism, or animal magnetism, that had become a fad in Paris. Friedrich Anton Mesmer had stumbled onto the new science of hypnotism, but his claims were overdrawn and were pronounced to be quackery by Franklin and his colleagues, one of whom, incidentally, was Dr. Joseph-Ignace Guillotin, who in a few years would be sacrificed to the terrible efficiency of *his* invention.

Surrounded by admiring friends, the most renowned man in Europe, Franklin could have spent his last years basking in fame and friendships at Passy. But he wanted to go home. At last the long awaited release came. In May, 1785, Thomas Jefferson was finally named to represent the United States in Franklin's stead. "No one can replace Benjamin Franklin," said Jefferson. "I am only his successor." The philosophical, cosmopolitan Virginian, however, was an appropriate choice. Though he was less well known than Franklin, the author of the Declaration of Independence held an attraction for French intellectuals similar to that of his older compatriot.

With Jefferson and Adams, who had returned to Paris from the Netherlands, Franklin performed his last official duty, the signing of the first American treaty with Prussia. "I did my last public Act in this country," he wrote his sister in Massachusetts; "I have continu'd to work till late in the Day: tis time I should go home and go to Bed." [9] Three days later, amid the tears of his neighbors of almost ten years, Franklin, riding in a litter supplied by the king, left the Hôtel Valentinois with his two grandsons for the overland journey to Le Havre. "It seemed," wrote Jefferson of Passy, "the village had lost its patriarch." Though Franklin had been concerned that the trip would be too much for him, he need not have worried. The journey revived his spirits; he wrote to Madame Helvétiuis from Le Havre that he felt better than before his departure.

During the channel crossing between Le Havre and Southampton, Franklin was the only passenger that did not become seasick. Many of his English friends including the Bishop of St. Asaph and his family came to Southampton to see him. There was also his loyalist son, William, who had previously written from London in the hope of a reconciliation. Franklin had replied that he could not criticize William for holding political opinions different from his own, but *"there are Natural Duties which precede political ones, and cannot be extinguish'd by them."* [10] The Southampton meeting between father and son, during which William deeded his New Jersey farm to Temple, failed to heal the deep hurt that Franklin felt at his son's apostasy.

Franklin's last ocean crossing, his eighth, took some seven weeks from July 28 to September 14. During this time, the incredible octogenarian wrote three significant scientific works. These included his treatises on the *Cause and Cure of Smoky Chimneys* and on his newly devised stove that consumed its own smoke. The third work composed on the homeward journey was the lengthy *Maritime Observations.* Written in the form of a letter to his French friend, David Le Roy, the *Maritime Observations* expands on a theme that had fascinated Franklin since his boyhood days in Boston. "The garrulity of the old man has got hold of me," he wrote Le Roy, "and, as I may never have another occasion of writing on this subject, I think I may as well now, once for all, empty my nautical budget, and give you all the thoughts that have in my various long voyages occurred to me relating to navigation." These thoughts included methods of rigging and anchoring, the estimation of the rate of leakage and the protection of ships from other accidents at sea, and a discussion of primitive modes of navigation. "It is remarkable, that the people we consider as savages," Franklin mused, "have improved the art of sailing and rowing boats in several points beyond what we can pretend to." The *Maritime Observations* also discusses mechanical means of propelling ships, sea currents, the gulf stream, proper sea stores, the proper shape of plates for the retaining of soups and other spillables on a rolling ship, and finally the good and bad uses of navigation. When navigation is "employed in pillaging merchants and transporting slaves," Franklin remarked, "it is clearly the means of augmenting the mass of human misery." [11]

Franklin's friends would later upbraid him for not having continued his memoirs during the voyage. His reply was that he could write his scientific observations out of his head, but on shipboard he lacked the necessary papers and other materials to write the story of his life. He did, however, keep a journal. The last entry reads,

> With the flood in the morning came a light breeze, which brought us above Gloucester Point, in full view of dear Philadelphia! . . ; we landed at Market-Street wharf, where we were received by a crowd of people with huzzas, and accompanied with acclamations quite to my door. Found my family well. God be praised and thanked for all his mercies! [12]

Learning of Franklin's arrival in Pennsylvania, the romantic Lafayette wrote to his American friend, "I have heard of your safe arrival in America, and heartily wished I had been mingled in the happy crowd of your fellow-citizens, when they saw you set your foot on the shore of Liberty." [13]

Franklin, home at last, believed that his diplomatic mission would be his final public duty. To Jan Ingenhousz, friend and noted physican and botanist, Franklin had written, "I shall now be free from politics for the rest of my life. Welcome again my dear Philosophical Amusements!" [14] Yet his "Philosophical Amusements" would once more have to take second place to the demands of the public. He had not been in Philadelphia a week before he became embroiled in Pennsylvania politics.

The Pennsylvania constitution, since its inception in 1776, had been opposed by many individuals who believed the unicameral legislature to be inadequate and the executive too weak. Election to the Executive Council would soon be held and both the Constitutionalists and the Anti-Constitutionalists ran Franklin for the place. Though Franklin, out of weakness as he put it, allowed his name to be put before the public, he bitterly complained: "They eat of my flesh, they pick at my bones." Franklin was overwhelmingly elected; only two votes including his own were cast against him. He was then chosen by his council colleagues and the Assembly as president of the state, an office similar to, though with less power, then present-day governorships.

Franklin was reelected president of Pennsylvania for three consecutive years, the maximum number of terms allowed by the constitution. Perhaps his most important contribution was his opposition to the loyalty oath which the government required of Pennsylvania citizens. Under his guidance this test act was rescinded. During his presidency, he also provided counsel and leadership in helping to settle the conflicting land claims between Connecticut and Pennsylvania, a dispute that had eventuated in near civil war.

In his official capacity as president, Franklin frequently corresponded with officials of other states concerning their domestic problems. To the governor of Georgia, who had apprised him of trouble between his state and the Creek Indians, Franklin replied that "During the Course of a long Life in which I have made Observations on public Affairs, it has appear'd to me that almost every War between the Indians and Whites has been occasion'd by some Injustice of the latter towards the former," [15] Trouble of a different sort came to him from North Carolina. In the western section of that state a group of speculators and settlers had broken away and attempted to form the new state of Franklin. They wrote to the doctor in hopes of his support. Franklin, though expressing appreciation of the honor done his name, urged that the dispute be brought before the Congress. "It is happy for us all," he wrote,

> that we have now in our own Country such a Council to apply to, for composing our Differences, without being oblig'd, as formerly, to carry them across the Ocean to be decided, at an immense Expence, by a Council which knew little of our Affairs. . . . Let us, therefore, cherish and respect our own Tribunal; for the more generally it is held in high Regard, the more able it will be to answer effectually the Ends of its Institution, the quieting of our contentions, and thereby promoting and securing our common Peace and Happiness.[16]

Franklin's commendation of the Congress came at a time when the American government was under increasing attack both at home and abroad. While in France, Franklin had attempted to answer his nation's critics. Having returned home, Franklin now continued to write counter propaganda, including his notable *The Internal State of America,* published in both the English and American press. In this "cool View of the general State of our Affairs," Franklin pointed out that American agriculture and commerce were fundamentally healthy. As for party contentions within the states: "Such will exist wherever there is Liberty; and perhaps they help to preserve it." [17]

Franklin, despite his cheerful appraisal of affairs, was well aware of the nation's shortcomings. Under the Articles of Confederation, Congress, without the power to tax, faced chronic financial embarrassment. Congress' inability to regulate trade impeded her diplomacy and encouraged the states to erect their own commercial systems. During the postwar depression, many of the states, following colonial practice, also experimented with paper money and other debtor-inspired inflationary devices. These, taken as a whole, adversely affected the credit of the union. Franklin, while not unduly alarmed, believed the central government needed modification. "The disposition to furnish Congress with ample Powers," he wrote to Jefferson in France, "augments daily, as People become more enlightened, and," added the author of the *Internal State of America*, "I do not remember ever to have seen during my long Life more signs of Public Felicity than appear at present throughout these States." [18]

Franklin's optimism was not shared by all of America's leaders. George Washington, James Madison, and Alexander Hamilton were only a few of the many individuals who viewed affairs with increasing alarm. Following the rebellion of Daniel Shays in Massachusetts, Washington gave vent to his despair for the Union. "I feel," he wrote, "infinitely more than I can express for the disorders which have arisen in these States. Good God! who besides a tory could have foreseen, or a Briton predicted them!" [19] Mt. Vernon became a center of criticism of the Articles of Confederation. From there arose the idea of a conference at Annapolis to adjust commercial differences among the states. The delegates to the Annapolis conference, however, found that they faced problems so complex that only a greatly strengthened central government could solve them. To this end, Alexander Hamilton and James Madison called for a general convention to amend the Articles of Confederation.

Congress complied with their request and put out a call for a general meeting of the states. Franklin, whose equanimity remained undisturbed by Shays' rebellion, nevertheless accepted a place in the Pennsylvania delegation to the resulting Philadelphia Convention. Eleven other state delegations joined that of Pennsylvania, only Rhode Island refusing representation. The Constitutional Convention met from

May 25 until September 17, 1787, in the old State House in Philadelphia, scene of Franklin's career as a Pennsylvania politician.

On the first day of the Convention, Franklin, since he was the only possible alternative, was to have placed in nomination the name of George Washington as president of the Convention. Bad weather, however, or perhaps his desire to allow Washington the stage to himself, kept Franklin home. His absence—one of the only Convention sessions he missed —also meant that William Temple Franklin was passed over for another applicant to the office of Convention secretary, a post which the old man had hoped to obtain for his grandson.

Franklin's relatively infrequent participation in the Convention's debates was mostly to conciliate rather than to innovate. The weight of his presence alone, like that of Washington, lent great prestige to the gathering. To Benjamin Rush, a fellow delegate, the old man during that hot summer "exhibited daily a spectacle of transcendent benevolence by attending the Convention punctually. . . ." William Pierce of Georgia remarked that although he did not "shine in public council," Franklin was "a most extraordinary man and tells a story in a style more engaging than anything I ever heard. . . ." The philosopher, Pierce found, "possesses an activity of mind equal to a youth of 25 years of age." [20] Yet as in the Second Continental Congress of the previous decade, Franklin was the oldest of all the members.

Franklin's chief contribution to the formation of the Constitution was the part he played in reconciling differences and instilling a spirit of compromise among the delegates. By the end of June, there had emerged a deep cleavage between those delegates who envisioned a consolidated union and the delegates from the smaller states who demanded equality in the newly conceived legislature. Franklin listened to the increasingly acrimonious debate with great concern. James Wilson had just compared the states to the decayed boroughs of England, "the rotten part of the Constitution." Wishing to ward off the inevitably bitter rejoinder and to underline the gravity of the crisis before the Convention, Franklin moved that each days's session be opened with prayer.

Dissension among the delegates, Franklin pointed out, was "a melancholy proof of the imperfection of Human Understanding. . . . How has it happened," Franklin asked, "that we have not hitherto once thought of humbly applying to the Father of lights to illuminate our understandings. . . . I have lived, Sir, a long time," Franklin continued, "and the longer I live, the more convincing proofs I see of this truth—*that God governs in the affairs of men.* And if a sparrow cannot fall to the ground without His notice, is it probable that an empire can rise without his aid. . . ?" [21]

Such sentiments coming from one not known for piety fulfilled their purpose. Tempers cooled; adjournment followed, Franklin's motion having been listened to with respect but not acted upon. (Hamilton, according to one account, is supposed to have quipped that the delegates were not in need of "foreign aid.") But the next day Connecticut moved that states, rather than population as in the lower house, be represented in the Senate. The debate on this motion brought forth Franklin's remark that "when a broad table is to be made, and the edges of the planks do not fit, the artist takes a little from both, and makes a good joint. In like manner here both sides must part with some of their demands, in order that they may join in some accommodating proposition." [22] By Monday, July 2 (Franklin's motion had occurred the previous Thursday), the Convention decided to appoint a "Grand Committee" of one member from each state to come up with a compromise. Franklin was appointed to represent Pennsylvania. On his motion, the committee presented a representational plan for the two houses of Congress substantially identical with that to be finally accepted by the Convention. The dam was broken. Although there yet would be angry debate, by July 16, the Convention had made its Great Compromise. Each state would have an equal vote in the upper house of the legislature. Population would be represented by the lower.

Although in the spirit of compromise Franklin contributed importantly to the establishment of a bicameral legislature, he did so in spite of his own convictions as to the best polity for the union. He favored a unicameral system, a plural executive without the veto power, and frequent elections with no property qualification either for the vote or for holding office. He would do nothing, he said, "to debase the spirit of the common people. . . . Some of the greatest rogues he was ever acquainted with were the richest rogues." [23] His plan for union was very similar to the Pennsylvania Constitution of 1776 which, like the Articles of Confederation, would soon be replaced by a constitution providing for a bicameral system and a strengthened executive.

During the summer's debates, the philosopher revealed other of his political predilections. He would pay little salary to congressmen and none to the executive, in this connection "relating very pleasantly," according to one of the delegates, "the progression in ecclesiastical benefices, from the first departure from the gratuitous provision for the Apostles, to the establishment of the papal system." Yet somewhat inconsistently, he favored raising the salaries of judges during their terms of office should there be inflation in the country or should "the business of the department increase as the Country becomes more populous." Franklin objected to the suggestion of a fourteen year residence requirement for election to Congress because "he should be very sorry to see anything like illiberality in the Constitution." He would tighten the definition of treason because "prosecutions for treason were generally virulent; and perjury too easily made use of against innocence." Franklin also desired that Congress be granted the power to construct canals.[24] Had the Convention acted upon this suggestion, the long disputes over internal improvements that marked the nation's subsequent history would have been moderated or possibly not have occurred at all.

Franklin's final contribution to the Convention occurred in connection with the majority's efforts to get unanimous accord for the Constitution as it finally emerged. Such unanimity would help during the inevitable struggle for ratification when the Constitution was returned to the states. Toward this purpose, Franklin composed an artful speech which was read for him, as were most of his speeches in the Convention, by a younger fellow delegate. Pointing out that "most men as well as most sects in Religion, think themselves in possession of all truth," Franklin asked that every member who objected to aspects of the Constitution, as he did, "would with me, on this occasion doubt a little of his own infallibility —and to make manifest our unanimity, put his name to this instrument."

Franklin's speech was described by Maryland's James McHenry as "plain, insinuating, persuasive—and in any event of the system guarded the Doctor's fame." [25] Whether or not Franklin had posterity in mind, his speech accurately expressed his convictions. His conception of the best form of government was materially different from that defined by the Constitution. He nevertheless supported the document, but in his attempt to win unanimity, he failed. Three of the members present, two of whom took Franklin's remarks personally as being levelled at them, withheld their signatures. Yet his speech, which was widely circulated, undoubtedly did as much as any of the intricate argumentation of *The Federalist* to win ratification in the state Conventions.

It was the last day of the Convention, during the signing of the Constitution, when Franklin turned to several nearby members and pointed to a painting of the sun on back of the president's chair. "Painters," he remarked, "had found it difficult to distinguish in their art a rising from a setting sun. I have," he continued,

> often and often in the course of the Session, and the vicissitudes of my hopes and fears as to its issue, looked at that behind the President without being able to tell whether it was rising or setting: But now at length I have the happiness to know that it is a rising and not a setting Sun.[26]

But for Franklin, it was a setting sun. In January, 1786, he had turned eighty. He lived comfortably in his Market Street house, to which he added a dining room commodious enough for him to entertain the delegates to the Constitutional Convention. Cared for by his daughter Sally Bache and her husband Richard, Franklin delighted in his numerous grandchildren. Benny, Sally's oldest son, attended the College of Philadelphia. Franklin later arranged to set him up as a printer. To Jonathan Shipley in England, Franklin movingly expressed his delight in his family, a delight perhaps tempered by memories of the little four year old Franky, and of William in English exile:

> He that raises a large Family does, indeed, while he lives to observe them, *stand,* as Watts says, *a broader Mark for Sorrow;* but then he stands a broader Mark for Pleasure too. When we launch our little Fleet of Barques into the Ocean, bound to different Ports, we hope for each a prosperous Voyage; but contrary Winds, hidden Shoals, Storms and Enemies come in for a Share in the Disposition of Events; and though these occasion a Mixture of Disappointment, yet, considering the Risque

where we can make no Insurance, we should think ourselves happy if some return with Success.[27]

Franklin was further gratified when in 1786 Polly Stevenson
Hewson from Craven Street in London, her husband having
long since died, removed with her children to Philadelphia
to be near her old friend.

Just as family and friends added to Franklin's happiness
in his declining years, so was he still able to contribute to life's
facilities through his own inventiveness. His last three inventions included a rocking chair that fanned as well as rocked;
a long arm, for removing and replacing books on high library
shelves; and a combination footstool-ladder. Visitors to his
house were also fascinated by a glass figure through which
liquid flowed in patterns illustrating the circulation of the
blood.

For all his satisfactions, however, Franklin had still to cope
with the continuing enmity toward him of the Lee-Adams
clique in Congress, where Arthur Lee sat on the treasury
board. Old rumors still circulated that Franklin had been
involved with Deane in the misappropriation of funds during
their mission to France. Such rumors could be laid to rest
only by a Congressional auditing of Franklin's accounts. Several times Franklin requested such an audit, but his requests
were ignored. It was not till long after his death that the
insubstantial and shadowy suspicions circulated by the Lees
and their friends were finally dissipated. Nor would Congress
take any notice of Temple, in spite of Franklin's plea that his
grandson, who had given up law school to act as secretary
to the American mission in France, deserved some recognition for his services.

Franklin believed that the lawmakers lacked gratitude for
the many services he had rendered, but he accepted the rebuff
philosophically. To his old friend, Charles Thompson, now

Congressional secretary, Franklin wrote that even if he "could have foreseen such unkind treatment from Congress as their refusing me their thanks would not in the least have abated my zeal for the Cause. . . . For I know something of the nature of such changeable Assemblies. . . ." Franklin blamed his difficulties on "the artful and reiterated malevolent insinuations of one or two envious and malicious persons . . . ." He could not blame the present legislators either for listening to such insinuations or for feeling no obligation for services rendered before their admission to Congress. "Therefore," he concluded, "I would pass these reflections into oblivion." [28]

He was less philosophical, however, concerning the educational direction taken by the University of Pennsylvania, which had evolved from the academy he had helped found thirty years previously. Under the guidance of Provost Smith and conservative trustees, the college had failed in its promise to emphasize the practical arts, which had been sacrificed to a more traditional—and aristocratic—curriculum. After a careful researching of the minutes of the academy trustees, Franklin published his *Observations Relative to the Intentions of the Original Founders of the Academy in Philadelphia,* which castigated the Smith administration for breaking faith with the academy's original supporters. The study of Latin and Greek, Franklin believed, could serve no useful purpose. He made his point characteristically with a homely comparison. With the advent of the wig, Franklin wrote, the European carries rather than wears his hat. No longer used to cover the head, although still considered a mark of the gentleman, the useless hat has become a *chapeau bras,* an arm hat. So with Latin and Greek, Franklin concluded, which should be considered "in no other light than as the *chapeau bras* of modern literature." [29]

The idea of the uselessness of Latin and Greek appears also

in the third part of the *Autobiography* which Franklin completed at about the same time as he wrote his *Observations* on the Academy. In this section which comprises some forty percent of the entire work, Franklin recounts his continuing self-education, including modern languages. Most of the section deals, however, with his civic and political career and includes his discoveries in the science of electricity. "This is the Age of Experiments," wrote Franklin—a phrase particularly appropriate for the eighteenth century as well as for his own approach to the problems of his time. His experimental philosophy caused him to appreciate the absence of dogma in Quakerism, the modesty of which, Franklin believed,

> is perhaps a singular Instance in the History of Mankind, every other Sect supposing itself in Possession of all Truth, and that those who differ are so far in the Wrong: Like a Man travelling in foggy Weather: Those at some Distance before him on the Road he sees wrapt up in the Fog, as well as those behind him, and also the People in the Fields on each side; but near him all appears clear, Tho' in truth he is as much in the Fog as any of them.[30]

The third part of the *Autobiography* ends with Franklin's arrival in London on his first agency for the Pennsylvania Assembly. Only months before his death, Franklin once again took his memoirs in hand, but he was able to compose only a few more pages, these dealing with his efforts to gain the principle of the liability of the proprietary estates to taxation. It is fortunate that Franklin found time to bring his biography to the moment that it became a matter of public record. Though incomplete and written in fits and starts over a period of eighteen years in England, France, and America, the *Autobiography* displays a remarkable unity that attests to Franklin's literary ability which he maintained to the end of his life.

Only one month before his death, Franklin turned that

ability for the last time to a public cause, the cause of antislavery. As president of the Pennsylvania Society for Promoting the Abolition of Slavery, he had been actively engaged in making appeals for funds and in signing on behalf of the society a memorial which was placed before Congress. Then in March, 1790, he penned his biting satire, *On the Slave Trade,* which parodies the words of a southern congressman by putting them in the mouth of a fictitious Algerian prince who uses them to justify the enslavement of Christians. The parody was doubly effective in that the Americans at this time were deeply angered by the attacks of the Barbary corsairs against their ships and seamen.

Franklin's mental activity belied his deteriorating physical condition. In January 1788, he had suffered a severe fall, badly spraining his wrist and arm. At about the same time, the stone became so excrutiatingly painful that he was forced to take opium, which provided relief but also exhausted him. Sensing that the end was near, Franklin revised his will. Though providing well for the other members of his family, Franklin left only a small bequest to William, stating that "The part he acted against me in the late war, which is of public notoriety, will account for my leaving him no more of an estate he endeavoured to deprive me of." [31] Franklin carried his bitterness against his son to the grave.

But Franklin's will also carried his philosophy of good works beyond the grave. With the salary he had received as president of Pennsylvania, he set up two endowment trusts, one for Boston and one for Philadelphia. Worthy young men could borrow the funds at interest. From the original amount of one thousand pounds granted each city, the trust has increased in value several hundred times, even with withdrawals for public works, and it has helped innumerable individuals.

On April 8, 1790, Franklin sent the last letter he ever wrote

to Thomas Jefferson, who had returned from France to enter
Washington's cabinet as Secretary of State. As clear-headed
as ever, in answer to a query of Jefferson, he exactly recalled
the map by which the peace commissioners in Paris had
delineated the Maine-Nova Scotia boundary. On April 17, a
lung abcess from which he had been suffering several weeks
suddenly burst. Slowly he weakened. He lapsed into a coma.
That evening, with William Temple and Benny Bache at his
bedside, the eighty-four year old Franklin breathed his last.
Hearing the news, Jefferson included it in a letter he sent to
Ferdinand Grand, a French banking agent for the American
government whom Franklin had known during the Passy
years. "The good old Dr. Franklin," Jefferson wrote, "so long
the ornament of our country and I may say of the world, has
at length closed his eminent career." [32]

XIV The Verdict of History

THOMAS JEFFERSON'S quiet eulogy was the modest beginning of an ever growing flood of commentary on the life and works of Benjamin Franklin. His death sent waves of shock throughout the world of the Atlantic Civilization, that eighteenth century world whose aspirations he so perfectly embodied. It marked the end of an era in American history. By chronology, he was the last of the great colonials, though in spirit he was closer to those new men whose destiny was entwined with the nation rather than with a particular state. Unlike some of these men, however, his vision did not stop at the nation's borders. He was truly an international figure. His passing marked the end of the period of the Enlightenment, when men still believed in their ability to create the good society in harmony with the natural order of the universe.

Nowhere in the Old World or the New was Franklin's death felt more deeply than in France, then in the throes of Revolution. By 1790, the new National Assembly had asserted itself against the power of the king. Yet it was still a time of moderation; the red tide had not yet begun to flow. The Assembly was under the leadership of constitutionalists like Mirabeau, Brissot and Bailly, men whom Franklin had known as fellow Masons during his diplomatic mission in France. To them, Franklin's name had become synonymous with the idea of government based upon consent and operating through a fundamental law to which all subscribed. The American constitutional republic was the shining example and Franklin was its foremost representative.

The Washington Franklin. Staffordshire pottery circa 1793, after the statuette by François Marie Suzanne. *Courtesy the American Philosophical Society.*

Standing before the French National Assembly, the Comte de Mirabeau pronounced his famous eulogy. "Franklin is dead. The genius that freed America and poured a flood of light over Europe has returned to the bosom of the Divinity." [1] In an unprecedented gesture, the Assembly declared three days of mourning for one who was a private citizen of a foreign state. Mirabeau's words were echoed throughout France. Before the Academy of Sciences the great philosophe Condorcet (soon to be guillotined when the Revolution turned from constitutionalism to dictatorship) praised Franklin's concept of a unicameral legislature and claimed that the great American had pointed the way to "the moral perfection of the human species." At the Academy of Medicine of which Franklin had been an associate, Vicq d'Azyrs' eulogy began, "A man is dead, and two worlds are in mourning." As the great physician rang the changes on Franklin's philosophy, so did the printers of Paris introduce the theme of success: "Franklin was born as poor as the poorest among us," they noted, "but he was never ashamed of his poverty." [2] To France, struggling to enter the modern era, Franklin was both guide and mentor, teacher and example.

Ironically, the American reaction to Franklin's death was somewhat less overwhelming than that of the French. It is true that on a motion of James Madison the House of Representatives voted a month of mourning. But no such resolution passed the Senate, presided over by Vice President John Adams. Jefferson suggested to Washington that the executive department wear mourning, but Washington, evidently fearful of establishing a precedent, refused. Philadelphia, however, made up for the federal government's parsimonious acknowledgement of Franklin's accomplishments. More than twenty thousand persons—the greatest assemblage in that city's history—either witnessed or took part in the great funeral procession of which each segment symbolized an aspect

of Franklin's manifold activities. There were the assembly-
men, the judges, the mayor, the printers, the professors, the
doctors, the lawyers. "No other town burying its great man,"
it has been said, "ever buried more of itself than Philadelphia
with Franklin."[3]

Yet even here there were individuals who disapproved
Franklin's political and unorthodox religious principles and
his seeming easy morality. With the growing violence of the
French Revolution, Franklin's well-known sympathy for
France further damaged his reputation in conservative cir-
cles. The contrasting responses of the House of Representatives and the Senate to Franklin's death may have been an
indication of the growing division within the country between
Jefferson and his pro-French following and the more conservative Federalists. Jefferson undoubtedly spoke the majority
view when he praised Franklin as "the greatest man and
ornament of the age and country in which he lived . . . whose
name will be like a star of the first magnitude in the firmament
of heaven, when the memory of those who have surrounded
and obscured him, will be lost in the abyss of time."[4] Though
most Americans would have heartily agreed, there nevertheless remained an undercurrent of dissent from Jefferson's
appraisal.

Many conservatives in both Franklin's native New England and in his adopted Pennsylvania distrusted their most
famous compatriot. Philadelphia aristocrats harbored anti-
Franklin feelings in part because they never quite accepted
the tradesman who flaunted his obscure beginnings. They
also resented Franklin's support of the radical Pennsylvania
Constitution of 1776. To some, Franklin had appeared as an
opportunist and a demagogue. They had come to fear Franklin, in Thomas Penn's words, as a "tribune of the people."

In New England, John Adams' Federalist followers held
opinions similar to their Philadelphia counterparts. Adams'

dislike of Franklin reached back at least as far as their joint mission to France during the American Revolution, when he believed Franklin too friendly toward that ally. His enmity toward Franklin sprang also in part from jealousy of the older man's prestige as well as from puritan shock at his easy manners. But as the voice of New England Federalism, Adams expressed differences more profound than matters of policy or temperament.

Unlike Franklin, Adams thoroughly distrusted the democratic tendencies of the time, tendencies with which he equated his old colleague. With every new report of the triumph of radicalism in France, Adams' conservatism became more truculent. He fulminated at the "popularity of all insurrections against the ordinary authority of government during the last century . . . When, where, and in what manner all this will end," Adams worried, "God only knows. To this cause Mr. Franklin owed much of his popularity." Adams admitted that Franklin "contributed largely to the progress of the human mind," but his "excellence as a legislator, a politician, or a negotiator most certainly never appeared . . . What shall we do," he somewhat petulantly asked, "with these gentlemen of great souls and vast views, who, without the least tincture of vanity, *bona fide* believe themselves the greatest men in the world. . . ?" [5]

The Adams view of Franklin, a view that allowed his scientific genius but disavowed his political and moral character, was reinforced when Franklin's grandson, Benjamin Franklin Bache, as editor of the Jeffersonian *Aurora,* condemned Federalism and all its works. Bache even went so far as to accuse Washington of peculation or worse and publicly to vilify the first president upon his retirement from office. Bache's intemperate polemics did nothing to enhance his grandfather's reputation among those already disposed against him. Nevertheless, it could not be denied that Franklin was one of the founders of the nation. "Because all readers would not say *ay* to his statesmanship," as one of his biographers put it, "he was cried up exceedingly as an economist. As a natural philosopher and as a fireside sage, the digester of the minor morals into a code of every-day ethics; as the man with the kite, and as Poor Richard with an almanac full of wise saws, he is celebrated. . . ." [6]

Franklin himself was partially responsible for the small but significant current of dissent that added a dissonant note to the general chorus of praise. The nineteenth century came to know him principally by the *Autobiography* and the *Way to Wealth.* At a time when the main body of his writings remained inaccessible to the public, these two works obtained enormous popularity. But from them alone, it is not possible to take the full measure of the man. In an increasingly romantic age, they offended the sensibilities of a few men of letters who preferred poetry and mystery to a plain prose tale of worldly success with its attendant manual of counting house wisdom. To some minds, the two works for which Franklin became best known, depict a sententious old maxim monger who valued wealth and success more than he valued the good life. This was a mistaken impression of a man who retired from a lucrative business career at age forty-two to devote the rest of his long life to friendships, intellectual pursuits, and public service, in short, to enjoying life.

The changing climate of opinion also did much to create misunderstanding of Franklin's character. It was inevitable that a tide would set in against the primary assumptions of the Age of Enlightenment of which Franklin was so typical an example. Nature, orderly and rational to men of Franklin's generation, became to the mind of the nineteenth century something wild and ineffable, mysterious and unknowable. Franklin would have been stunned by the romantic statement of Emerson, who wrote in his essay *Nature,* "I become a transparent eyeball. . . . The currents of the Universal Being circulate through me." The incongruity between such a sentiment and Franklin's rational philosophy is a measure of the distance between his age and that which followed.

It is plain that the age of Emerson would find Franklin wanting in poetic sensibility. The poet John Keats' opinion of the "philosophical Quaker full of mean and thrifty maxims," was but a foretaste of the storm of abuse that would fall upon Franklin from romantic temperaments of later generations. But in spite of such criticism, most Americans chose Franklin next only to Washington in the pantheon of the country's heroes. The obscure tradesman who rose to world stature was above all an inspiring model worthy of emulation. At the same time, in Europe Franklin's reputation as a revolutionary statesman remained great.

Particularly was this true in Germany and Italy, countries which like France and the United States struggled against ancient tradition to gain the constitutional liberty for which Franklin was a prime symbol. His life gave inspiration to the German revolutionaries of 1848. Likewise, the Italian patriot Giuseppe Garibaldi, finding precedent in America's successful fight for national independence, viewed Franklin as an embodiment of the liberal aims of the *risorgimento*.

Where revolutionary activity seethed in Europe, Franklin's political reputation soared. In America on the other hand, where revolution gave way to relatively stable political and social institutions, Franklin's revolutionary image was popularly superseded by that of the archetypal self-made man. American writers emphasized Franklin's sobriety, thrift, and perseverence—prudential virtues which explained his emergence from obscurity to world fame. If aspects of Franklin's life had to be neglected or even falsified in constructing the myth, there was enough truth in it to support the model. Both Parson Weems, who fixed the cherry tree on Washington, and

Samuel Goodrich, alias Peter Parley, made of Franklin's life a moral sermon on hard work and thrift.[7]

It was a prim and prudish Franklin that came down to American youth through such writings as these and in the tremendously popular McGuffey Readers, first appearing in the 1830's and molding generations of young Americans. It is estimated that by the 1920's Americans had purchased one hundred and twenty-five million of its successive editions. Nor did the early historians, in spite of the appearance of Jared Sparks' ten volume edition of Franklin's papers, help very much in rescuing Franklin from the empyreal regions to which his biographers had condemned him. "His hope was steadfast, like that hope which rests on the Rock of Ages, and his conduct was as unerring as though the light that led him was a light from heaven," hymned George Bancroft in 1844. "He, from the highest abodes of ideal truth, brought down and applied to the affairs of life the sublimest principles of goodness, as noiselessly and unostentatiously as became the man who, with a kite and a hempen string, drew the lightning from the sky." [8] It is symbolic of the effort to dehumanize Franklin that Bancroft requested that the warts on Franklin's face be omitted from the picture which he intended to use as the frontispiece to the third volume of his history.

The zenith of pre Civil War adoration occurred in Boston in 1856, the one hundred-fiftieth anniversary of Franklin's birth. For the occasion, the city was festooned with flowers, decorations and banners setting forth such Franklinisms as "He that hath a trade, hath an estate," and "Knowledge is Power." Flags and streamers fluttered everywhere. Kites dotted the skies. A great procession five miles long including floats depicting aspects of Franklin's life (upon one of the floats there was an electrical apparatus whose dangling knobs transmitted a shock to such of Franklin's devotees who volunteered a finger) culminated at City Hall for the climactic unveiling of the Franklin statue by the American sculptor Horatio Greenough. "And now behold him," the orator proclaimed, "by the magic power of native genius, once more restored to our sight!" To the cheers of the populace the draping flags were whisked from in front of the great bronze Franklin. "May the visible presence of the GREAT BOSTONIAN," the oration concluded, "impress afresh, day by day . . . a deeper sense of the value of that Liberty, that Independence, that Union, and that Constitution, for all of which he was so early, so constant, and so successful a laborer!" There was one cavil, however. The speaker regretted that "Franklin had not been a more earnest student of the Gospel of Christ." [9]

That Franklin had ended his days as an activist in the anti-slavery movement commended him to many northerners who might otherwise be prone to find him lacking in spirituality. The transcendentalists could make their peace with the unromantic printer, although Emerson gently reproved him. "Transcendentalism says, the Man is all," wrote Emerson. "Franklin says, the tools: riches, old age, land, health; the tools. . . . A master *and* tools,—is the lesson I read in every shop and farm and library. There must be both. . . ." Although Emerson believed that Franklin had only half the truth, he nevertheless could be fulsome in his praise of the man whose "good offices reach through a thousand years to posterity unborn. . . ." [10] So could Theodore Parker, the great transcendentalist abolitionist divine. "What a farewell it was!" wrote Parker of Franklin's satirical *On the Slave Trade*. Parker, like Emerson, found Franklin "underrating the beautiful and the sublime." The abolitionist leader, nevertheless, rated Franklin "the greatest man that America ever bore in her bosom or set eyes upon. Beyond all question. . . . Benjamin Franklin had the largest mind that has shone this side of the sea. . . ." [11]

Franklin's deficiencies in the realm of "the beautiful and the sublime" were not so easy for some of Emerson's and Parker's contemporaries to forgive. For James Russell Lowell, Franklin's presidency of the Pennsylvania Abolition Society was evidently inadequate absolution. On the eve of the Boston commemoration, the poet-professor wrote to a friend that the morrow's oratory will tell us that Franklin "invented being struck with lightning and printing and the Franklin medal, and that he had to move to Philadelphia because great men were so plenty in Boston that he had no chance, and that he revenged himself on his native town by saddling it with the Franklin stove, and that he discovered the almanac, and that a penny saved is a penny lost, or something of the kind. So we put him up a statue. *I* mean to invent something—in order to encourage sculptors." [12]

Lowell's disparagement of Franklin's achievements were paralleled by Nathaniel Hawthorne's belief that Poor Richard's proverbs "all about getting money or saving it" were responsible for Franklin's great fame. Yet these, Hawthorne believed, "taught men but a very small portion of their duties." Hawthorne's younger friend and neighbor Herman Melville portrayed Franklin in his historical novel *Israel Potter* in a more complex way. Nevertheless, even if Melville had ambiguous feelings about Franklin, he left us a superb summation of the man: "Printer, postmaster, almanac maker, essayist, chemist, orator, tinker, statesman, humorist, philosopher, parlor man, political economist, professor of housewifery, ambassador, projector, maxim-monger, herb-doctor, wit:—Jack of all trades, master of each and mastered by none—the type and genius of his land, Franklin was everything but a poet." [13]

If Franklin was, in Thomas Carlyle's words, "the father of all the Yankees," (to the French critic Sainte-Beuve, he was the most French of all Americans) it is little wonder that his name failed to evoke universal admiration in the ante-bellum South. School boys were given Franklin as an object lesson in self-reliance in *The Southern Reader and Speaker.* But some southerners viewed Franklin in a more sinister light. He was the unlovely product of northern materialism. George Fitzhugh, Virginia lawyer and apologist for the planter class, in his *Sociology for the South,* contrasted the "monstrous abortion" that was the free society of the North with "the healthy, beautiful and natural" civilization of the South. "In whatever is purely utilitarian and material," wrote Fitzhugh, "free society incites invention and stimulates industry. Benjamin Franklin," he continued, "is the best exponent of the working of the system. His sentiments and his philosophy are low, selfish, atheistic and material. They tend directly to make a man a mere 'featherless biped'." [14] Although such antislavery writers as James Russell Lowell would have agreed with George Fitzhugh about little else, they were one with him in condemning the doctrine of materialism and Franklin's supposed adherence to it.

The victory of free society in the United States ushered in a period of American history in which materialism did appear to reign supreme. Just as the Horatio Alger stories did obeisance before the Goddess Success, so Franklin emerged as the high priest of the new religion. There sprang up in the Gilded Age a veritable Franklin cult. He was the principal figure of American biography in those years. At the same time his *Autobiography* and *The Way to Wealth* continued to roll from presses which seemed never to satiate the public demand for these works.

In the age of Rockefeller and Carnegie, Franklin provided a model and a manual for ambitious American youth. The experience of Thomas Mellon, who founded a great banking house in 1869, must have been repeated many times over. "The reading of Franklin's biography was the turning point in my life," wrote Mellon. Franklin's example influenced the future tycoon to leave the family farm to climb the ladder of financial success. Once there, Mellon distributed 1000 copies of the *Autobiography* to young men in need of advice. His son Andrew Mellon, secretary of the treasury during the Republican twenties, called Franklin "the Father of Thrift in America." "It is due to his influence," the treasury secretary believed, "that America early learned to spend her surplus earnings on further production rather than selfish enjoyment." [15]

While Franklin remained a popular idol in the years following the Civil War, scholars began the long task of rescuing him from the myths that smothered him. In 1864, James Parton, the inexhaustible biographer of Andrew Jackson, Aaron Burr and other American figures, brought out his splendid two-volume life of Franklin. Believing that Franklin had been by some "misunderstood and undervalued," Parton wanted to render Franklin's "wisdom and goodness more available as a means of influence upon the character of the American people." [16] Although in his view, Franklin's life was still a kind of moral allegory, Parton's was among the best of the flood of Franklin biographies that appeared in the postwar decades.

Following Parton, there was an increasing emphasis upon the immense variety of Franklin's career. Two new editions of his papers led scholars to renewed appreciation of Franklin's many-sidedness. The first of these, edited by John Bigelow, who while serving as American minister to France discovered the original manuscript of the *Autobiography,* appeared in the late 1880's. Bigelow's was the first Franklin collection that followed a chronological rather than a topical format. The next edition, that of Albert Henry Smyth, appeared in 1906 to coincide with the two-hundredth anniversary of Franklin's birth. Its ten volumes included many items hitherto unavailable to the reading public. With the appearance of these great collections of Frankliniana, it became easier to penetrate the myth to the real Franklin.

Bigelow's and Smyth's achievements stimulated numerous studies devoted to one or another aspect of Franklin's life. These include J. B. McMaster, *Benjamin Franklin as a Man of Letters* (1887), J. F. Sache, *Benjamin Franklin as a Free Mason* (1906), Theodore Diller, *Franklin's Contributions to Medicine* (1912), J. C. Oswald, *Benjamin Franklin, Printer* (1917), Ruth Butler, *Doctor Franklin: Postmaster General* (1928), Gerald Stourzh, *Benjamin Franklin and American Foreign Policy* (1954), and I. Bernard Cohen, *Franklin and Newton* (1956). Hardly any facet of Franklin's life has not had a special study devoted to it.

At the same time, even biographers who attempt to tell the whole story have nevertheless emphasized one or another of his attributes. Phillips Russell called his book, *Benjamin Franklin, The First Civilized American,* while Bernard Faÿ viewed Franklin as "The Apostle of Modern Times." More recently, Verner Crane in *Benjamin Franklin and a Rising People* has shown that Franklin's life paralleled the coming to maturity of the American people. Crane believed that Franklin applied the empirical method to politics, a "method which American leaders have generally adopted." [17] In 1938, Carl Van Doren, effected to rescue Franklin from "the dry, prim people who regard him as a treasure shut up in a savings bank to which they have the lawful key. I herewith give him back," wrote Van Doren, "in his grand dimensions, to his nation and the world." He concluded that Franklin "seems to have been more than any single man: a harmonious human multitude." [18]

As Franklin studies proliferated, so scholars other than Franklinists continued after the Civil War to assess his historical significance. A new rise of nationalism brought forth the frontier theory of American history. This theory lent professorial sanction to the growing idealization of the American West, alleged seedbed of such admirable qualities as democracy, individualism, and resourcefulness. Frederick Jackson Turner, author of this gratifying point of view, credited Franklin as being among the first to recognize the importance of the West "for enlarged activities of the American people." [19] Likewise, the super-patriot Henry Cabot Lodge in his *Life of Washington* saw Franklin as the archetype of virile Americanism. Franklin was American, thought the not immodest scholar-politician, "by the character of his genius, by his versatility, the vivacity of his intellect, and his mental dexterity." [20]

During the Progressive Era, intellectuals subjected American institutions to a critical scrutiny. The historian Charles Beard, for example, viewed the Constitution as the result of the machinations of a group of self-interested American speculators, i.e., the founding fathers. But Beard's iconoclasm did not extend to Franklin. According to *The Rise of American Civilization* (co-authored by Mary Beard), "It is no exaggeration to say that Franklin, who stood head and shoulders above his countrymen in versatility and intelligence, was one of the first men of his epoch in the world and would have been an ornament to any nation." Beard believed that "Franklin, in the age of George II, almost divined the drift of the twentieth century." [21] Vernon Parrington, who subscribed to a social philosophy similar to that of Beard, also had high praise for Franklin. Contrary to many Franklin critics who found him too puritanical, Parrington believed that "the Calvinism in which he was bred left not the slightest trace upon him. In his modesty, his willingness to compromise, his openmindedness, his clear and luminous understanding, his charity—above all, in his desire to subdue the ugly facts of society to some more rational scheme of things—he proved himself a great and useful man, one of the greatest and most useful whom America has produced." [22]

For all this chorus of praise, there still remained a strong tradition of dissent. Just as he became a symbol of northern materialism to George Fitzhugh, so after the Civil War Franklin was frequently made a whipping boy for the acquisitiveness allegedly inherent in American character. His critics still came mainly from the ranks of the literati. Mark Twain, for instance, whose Tom Sawyer was hardly a disciple of Poor Richard, believed that "Franklin's maxims were full of animosity toward boys." For instance, a boy may be "robbed of natural rest because Franklin said once in one of his inspired flights of malignity,"

> Early to bed and early to rise
> Make a man healthy and wealthy and wise. [23]

Then there was the perennial boy Theodore Roosevelt, for whom Franklin, whose historical significance he recognized, was yet a bit confining. "The second greatest Revolutionary figure," wrote Roosevelt to a southern correspondent, "Franklin, to my mind embodied just precisely the faults which are most distrusted in the average American of the North today." [24] Another scholar-president, Woodrow Wilson, though in the main an admirer of Franklin, showed in the introduction he wrote for the Century Classics edition of the *Autobiography* a rather similar attitude. Franklin was simply not idealistic enough for the man who would "make the world safe for democracy."

But it was left for an Englishman to bring the theme of dissent to a climax. Basing his criticism upon an altogether unimaginative reading of the *Autobiography,* particularly the section describing "the bold and arduous Project of arriving at moral Perfection," D. H. Lawrence proceeded to annihi-

late the straw man he had manufactured. Franklin's list of
virtues is a "barbed-wire fence" with which "Doctor Franklin, snuff-coloured little man! . . . fenced off" the soul of
man. But "the soul of man is a dark vast forest, with wild
life in it. Think of Benjamin fencing it off." Lawrence, reveal-
ing the anti-Americanism that lay at the base of his animosity
toward Franklin, blamed the latter for the invidious influence
he believed America exercised upon Europe. "The pattern
American, the dry, moral, utilitarian little democrat, has
done more to ruin old Europe than any Russian nihilist." [25]

Something of the same animus may unconsciously have
motivated the great German sociologist Max Weber's assessment of Franklin. In his immensely influential book, *The
Protestant Ethic and the Spirit of Capitalism,* Franklin is given
a central place as expressing "the spirt of modern capitalism." [26] *The Way to Wealth* signified to Weber the Puritan
doctrine of the calling without its accompanying theology.
Ironically Karl Marx had already given Franklin credit for
being "one of the first economists . . . who saw through the
nature of value. . . ." [27] In his recognition that the value of
a product resulted from the amount of labor expended upon
it, Franklin became to Marx an intellectual forerunner of
socialism.

Franklin's life was so multifarious that he can be said to
belong to everyone. Labor declared him its "Patron Saint." [28]
Businessmen find in him the prototype of "the American
doer—the energetic, cheerful, sail-in-and-get-it-done kind of
person." [29] At least one contemporary historian believes him
to have been a "philosophical revolutionist." [30] Whatever the
assessment, there has long been a belief that somehow the
character of Franklin helps explain the character of American civilization. A not always friendly critic of America, the
English socialist Harold Laski, expressed this view: Franklin exemplified "the supreme symbol of the American spirit

. . . In his shrewdness, his sagacity, his devotion to making this world the thing that a kindly and benevolent soul would wish it to be, Franklin seems to summarize in a remarkable way the American idea of a good citizen." [31]

Today, Franklin is newly honored by yet another edition of his papers. Unlike the earlier editions, this time a team of distinguished scholars is utilizing the great resources of Yale University and the American Philosophical Society to publish an exhaustive collection. Copious notes carefully identify persons, places, and events; and letters to as well as from Franklin are included. The Franklin scholars' search for materials has been world wide. This edition, like the earlier ones, will stimulate fresh appraisals of Franklin's historical significance. Leonard Labaree, first editor of the project, has already suggested one such view: "After a life like Franklin's had become possible and could be described matter-of-factly, the Declaration of Independence seems understandable and much less revolutionary." [32]

That Franklin's life prefigured the great Declaration suggests the definition of history as philosophy teaching by example. His life and the nature of his contribution typify the thought of the eighteenth century Enlightenment, a time when enlightened men celebrated reason over emotion, law over men, ability over privilege, cosmopolitanism over nationalism, intellect over passion, order over confusion, and observation over revelation. The charge that Franklin lacked romantic sensibility reflects as much upon his times as it does upon him. But neither he nor his century lacked faith.

Only four months before his death, Franklin summed up the aspirations of the Age of the Enlightenment. "God grant," he wrote, "that not only the Love of Liberty, but a thorough Knowledge of the Rights of Man, may pervade all the Nations of the Earth, so that a Philosopher may set his Foot anywhere on its Surface, and say, 'This is my

Country.'" [33] In the verdict of history, Franklin's reputation rests secure in his contribution to the founding of his nation, and in his personification of his generation's faith in the progress of mankind.

XV Epilogue

FRANKLIN DIED almost two centuries ago. He was a representative of his times, yet his life and works retain striking relevance for the present day.

Shortly after the publication of his essays on stoves and chimneys, Franklin received a letter from England stating that his essays "arrived very seasonably." Franklin's correspondent described his intention to suggest "the expediency and necessity of adopting some measures to purify the air of Manchester. . . ." The writer was aware that the solution to the problem of dirty air demanded interference with private enterprise. Persons engaged in manufactures, he believed, "should be induced or compelled to conduct them in a manner as little injurious as possible to the public." [1] The letter undoubtedly pleased Franklin, for he had several times yearned to get out of Philadelphia and into the fresh air of the country.

Franklin furthermore would not have been averse to "compelling" the industrialists of Manchester or of America to consider the effect of their activities on the environment. Though he was conservative on the issue of welfare, believing it sapped the initiative of the individual, he was radical in his attitude toward the fundamentally public nature of private property. Angered over a suggestion that the Pennsylvania constitution be modified to include an upper legislative chamber to represent property, Franklin asked, "Is it supposed that Wisdom is the necessary concomitant of Riches? . . . The accumulation of Property and its Security to Individuals in every Society," Franklin insisted,

> must be an Effect of the Protection afforded to it by the joint Strength of the Society, in the Execution of its

Laws. Private Property, therefore is a Creature of Society, and is subject to the Calls of that Society, whenever its necessities shall require it, even to its last Farthing; its Contributions therefore to the public Exigencies [are to be considered] . . . as the Payment of a just Debt.[2]

Private property, Franklin believed, must be the servant, not the master of society.

Many of Franklin's activities were concerned with the improvement of urban life. He solved some of his city's problems by combining voluntary efforts with governmental support as in his dollar-matching plan for the hospital. His example has relevance today when the achievement of a livable urban environment has become vital to the nation's survival.

Franklin's attitude toward war is also relevant to the present age. He opposed war on humanitarian grounds. Moreover, he clearly saw its domestic consequences. "An army is a devouring monster," he wrote,

and, when you have raised it, you have, in order to subsist it, not only the fair charges of pay, clothing, provisions, arms, and ammunition, . . . but you have all the additional knavish charges of the numerous tribe of contractors to defray, with those of every other dealer who furnishes the articles wanted for your army, and takes advantage of that want to demand exorbitant prices.[3]

To the nation that today finds well over half its budget going to the "military-industrial complex," these words have special significance.

Franklin's contributions to the establishment of schools for black Americans and his observation of their success led him to believe—far ahead of his time—in the intellectual equality of the races. In his leadership of the Pennsylvania Abolition Society he put this belief into action. It is altogether appropriate for him to have devoted his last published essay less than a month before his death to the cause of antislavery.

In the natural and the social sciences, many of Franklin's ideas still retain a remarkable validity. He laid the foundations for the science of electricity. He anticipated modern trends, particularly in his education theories. In his theory of the relation of population growth to the available natural resources, he touched upon another problem that today is critical. He also envisioned the later history of America in its ongoing rush to the west.

Franklin's early life embodied the archetypal American success story. Yet in spite of the accusations of certain modern critics, he was not satisfied with the attainment of material success. His civic and philosophical activities brought him to the forefront of public affairs. His career as a Pennsylvania politician perfectly illustrates the "quest for power" on the part of the colonial assemblies against external control. As a world statesman, Franklin symbolized the Age of the Democratic Revolution for which his nation would set the precedent.

He was among the earliest colonials to think in continental terms. As a Bostonian removed to Philadelphia, as deputy postmaster-general of North America, as the author of the Albany Plan, Franklin was more of an American than a Pennsylvanian. At first he entertained an imperial vision whereby Great Britain would transfer the seat of empire to the American continent. Later, as unofficial ambassador to the court of St. James, this vision was slowly replaced by the idea of a separate American nation.

During the first few years of Franklin's mission for the Pennsylvania Assembly in England, he undoubtedly tried to moderate the political differences between England and the colonies. Later, disillusioned by the social and political failures of the mother country, Franklin's attitude hardened. His program for reconciliation, unacceptable to the British, included the rescinding of all English colonial legislation since the end of the Great War for the Empire. Nor was his concept of the imperial constitution any more acceptable, for Franklin had been among the first to consider the colonial assemblies as "so many Parliaments," autonomous, and tied to the mother country only through a tenuous loyalty to the Crown. Franklin's was a dominion concept almost a century before its time.

It was also a federal concept. Yet when he returned from England to America, he remained a continentalist. In England, he had argued for the autonomy of the colonial assemblies. Now in the second Continental Congress, he favored strengthening the union of the states. He was, in consequence, the first to suggest that Congress draw up articles of confederation for the new nation.

Franklin's contributions to the founding of the United States of America were many. He was the only man to sign four of the basic documents of American independence: the Declaration, the Franco-American Treaty of 1778, the Treaty of Paris, and the Constitution. No man in America was better suited than Franklin to represent the new nation in Europe, where he was universally admired as a scientist, statesman, and moralist. Welcomed in France as a virtual embodiment of the Enlightenment, Franklin successfully won that nation to America's cause. Later, with John Jay and John Adams, he negotiated the peace settlement. Winning an extensive landed domain for the United States, the negotiators guaranteed the new nation's future.

Returned home once again, Franklin was called to the highest office in his state, the presidency of Pennsylvania.

And in 1787, in his eighty-first year, he served in the Philadelphia Convention to write a new constitution for his nation. His approbation of the completed document served to convince many of its propriety. Its ratification and the institution of the new government which Franklin lived to witness completed the Revolution begun in 1776.

In all, during the latter half of his life, Franklin spent almost twenty-five years in England and France. In America, he was a continentalist; at the last, he was a citizen of the world. He believed that the example of America might well be copied in Europe. If the Constitution succeeds, he wrote to a French friend during the struggle for ratification, "I do not see why you might not in Europe carry the Project of good Henry the 4th into Execution, by forming a Federal Union and One Grand Republick of all its different States and Kingdoms, by means of a like Convention, for we had many Interests to reconcile." [4]

Franklin, it has been said, was a child of the eighteenth century. So too was the nation he helped to found. To that extent, an understanding of Franklin helps us to understand the character of America. But Franklin was also an individual with a uniquely powerful intellect combined with great warmth and human sympathy. It was the latter characteristics that drew to him individuals of all ages. He was always, for example, a great favorite of children. And it was the combination of his penetrating intelligence and humanity that gave to Franklin his special qualities of humor and wit.

In 1780, when he was seventy-four years old, Franklin replied from Passy to a letter of his old friend, Dr. Thomas Bond, with whom he had founded the Philadelphia Hospital. "Being arrived at seventy," Franklin wrote, "and considering that by travelling further in the same road I should probably be led to the grave, I stopped short, turned about, and walked back again; which having done these four years, you may now call me sixty-six." [5] Franklin continued to "walk back" for ten years, and although he could not forestall the physical depredations of old age, his mind retained its youthful vigor.

Some seven months before his death, Franklin wrote his last letter to George Washington. "For my own personal Ease," Franklin said, "I should have died two Years ago; but tho' those Years have been spent in excruciating Pain, I am pleas'd that I have liv'd them, since they have brought me to see our present Situation." The president replied:

> Would to God, my dear Sir, that I could congratulate you upon the removal of that excruciating pain, under which you labour, and that your existence might close with as much ease to yourself, as its continuance has been beneficial to our country and useful to mankind. . . .
>
> If to be venerated for benevolence, if to be admired for talents, if to be esteemed for patriotism, if to be beloved for philanthropy, can gratify the human mind, you must have the pleasing consolation to know, that you have not lived in vain. [6]

It would also have consoled Franklin to have known that even as the nation entered its third century, his thought, as well as his example, would be useful still.

Appendix: DOCUMENTS

1. Printer

Franklin, reflecting his New England background, was ever mindful of his calling. He was a printer by trade, and it was as a printer that according to his last will and testament he wanted first to be remembered.

It was not unusual for a colonial printer to publish an almanac. If popular, almanacs added considerably to the profitability of a printing establishment. Franklin's *Poor Richard,* which he composed and published from 1733 to 1758, attained the remarkable annual circulation of 10,000. Its popularity resulted from its adroit combination of wit, wisdom, and usefulness. Richard Saunders, Franklin's pen name, became a household word in colonial America. Most famous for its aphorisms, *Poor Richard's Almanac,* Franklin wrote, "contained the Wisdom of many Ages and Nations." Some of its sayings are Franklin's own; many he improved over the original. They were used by Franklin as fillers among such usual almanac material as astronomical and historical statistics, monthly calendars, announcements of various court sittings and the like—material excluded from the sampling below from *Poor Richard* for 1736.

Franklin's readers had to wait an anxious year for the explanations to his concluding "enigmatic prophecies." The present reader is spared the suspense by the inclusion here of the explanations from *Poor Richard's Almanac* for 1737.

POOR RICHARD'S ALMANAC (1736) [1]

Loving Readers,

Your kind Acceptance of my former Labours, has encouraged me to continue writing, tho' the general Approbation you have been so good as to favour me with, has excited the Envy of some, and drawn upon me the Malice of others. These Ill-willers of mine, despited at the great Reputation I gain'd by exactly predicting another Man's Death, have endeavour'd to deprive me of it all at once in the most effectual Manner, by reporting that I my self was never alive. They say in short, *That there is no such a Man as I am;* and have spread this Notion so thoroughly in the Country, that I have been frequently told it to my Face by those that don't know me. This is not civil Treatment, to endeavour to deprive me of my very Being, and reduce me to a Non-entity in the Opinion of the publick. But so long as I know my self to walk about, eat, drink and sleep, I am satisfied that *there is really such a Man as I am,* whatever they may say to the contrary: And the World may be satisfied likewise; for if there were no such Man as I am, how is it possible I should appear publickly to hundreds of People, as I have done for several Years past, in print? I need not, indeed, have taken any Notice of so idle a Report, if it had not been for the sake of my Printer, to whom my Enemies are pleased to ascribe my Productions; and who it seems is as unwilling to father my Offspring, as I am to lose the Credit of it. Therefore to clear him entirely, as well as to vindicate my own Honour, I make this publick and serious Declaration, which I desire may be believed, to wit, *That what I have written heretofore, and do now write, neither was nor is written by any other Man or Men, Person or Persons whatsoever.* Those who are not satisfied with this, must needs be very unreasonable.

My Performance for this Year follows; it submits itself, kind Reader, to thy Censure, but hopes for thy Candor, to forgive its Faults. It devotes itself entirely to thy Service, and will serve thee faithfully: And if it has the good Fortune to please its Master, 'tis Gratification enough for the Labour of Poor R. SAUNDERS

> Presumptuous Man! the Reason wouldst thou find
> Why form'd so weak, so little, and so blind?
> First, if thou canst, the harder reason guess
> Why form'd no weaker, blinder, and no less?
> Ask of thy Mother Earth, why Oaks are made,
> Taller or stronger than the Weeds they shade?
> Or ask of yonder argent Fields above,
> Why JOVE's Satellites are less than JOVE?

XI Mon. January hath xxxi days.

> Some have learnt many Tricks of sly Evasion,
> Instead of Truth they use Equivocation,
> And eke it out with mental Reservation,
> Which to good Men is an Abomination.
> Our Smith of late most wonderfully swore,
> That whilst he breathed he would drink no more;
> But since, I know his Meaning, for I think
> He meant he would not breath whilst he did drink.

He is no clown that drives the plow, but he that doth clownish things.

If you know how to spend less than you get, you have the Philosophers-Stone.

The good Paymaster is Lord of another man's Purse.

Fish and Visitors stink in 3 days.

XII Mon. February hath xxix days.

> Sam's Wife provok'd him once; he broke her Crown,
> The Surgeon's Bill amounted to Five Pound;
> *This Blow* (she brags) *has cost my Husband dear,*
> *He'll ne'er strike more.* Sam chanc'd to over-hear.
> Therefore before his Wife the Bill he pays,
> And to the Surgeon in her Hearing says:
> *Doctor, you charge Five Pound, here e'en take Ten;*
> *My Wife may chance to want your Help again.*

He that has neither fools, whores nor beggars among his kindred, is the son of a thunder gust.

Diligence is the Mother of Good-Luck.

He that lives upon Hope, dies farting.

Do not do that which you would not have known.

I Mon. March hath xxxi days.

> Whate'er's desired, Knowledge, Fame, or Pelf,
> Not one will change his Neighbour with himself,
> The learn'd are happy Nature to explore,

The Fool is happy that he knows no more.
The Rich are happy in the Plenty given;
The Poor contents him with the Care of Heav'n.
Thus does some Comfort ev'ry State attend,
And Pride's bestow'd on all, a common Friend.

Never praise your Cyder, Horse, or Bedfellow.

Wealth is not his that has it, but his that enjoys it.

Tis easy to see, hard to foresee.

In a discreet man's mouth, a publick thing is private.

II Mon. April hath xxx days.

By nought is Man from Beast distinguished
More than by Knowledge in his learned Head.
Then Youth improve thy Time, but cautious see
That what thou learnest some how useful be.
Each Day improving, Solon waxed old;
For Time he knew was better far than Gold:
Fortune might give him Gold which would decay,
But Fortune cannot give him Yesterday.

Let thy maidservant be faithful, strong, and homely.

Keep flax from fire, youth from gaming.

Bargaining has neither friends nor relations.

Admiration is the Daughter of Ignorance.

There's more old Drunkards than old Doctors.

III Mon. May hath xxxi days.

Lalus who loves to hear himself discourse
    Keeps talking still as if he frantick were,
And tho' himself might no where hear a worse,
    Yet he no other but himself will hear.
Stop not his Mouth, if he be troublesome,
But stop his Ears, and then the Man is dumb.

She that paints her Face, thinks of her Tail.

Here comes Courage! that seiz'd the lion absent, and run
away from the present mouse.

He that takes a wife, takes care.

Nor Eye in a letter, nor Hand in a purse, nor Ear in the secret of another.

He that buys by the penny, maintains not only himself, but other people.

IV Mon. June hath xxx days.

Things that are bitter, bitterer than Gall
Physicians say are always physical:
Now Women's Tongues if into Powder beaten,
May in a Potion or a Pill be eaten,
And as there's nought more bitter, I do muse,
That Women's Tongues in Physick they ne'er use.
My self and others who lead restless Lives,
Would spare that bitter Member of our Wives.

He that can have Patience, can have what he will.

Now I've a sheep and a cow, every body bids me good morrow.

God helps them that help themselves.

Why does the blind man's wife paint herself?

V Mon. July hath xxxi days.

Who can charge Ebrio with Thirst of Wealth?
See he consumes his Money, Time and Health,
In drunken Frolicks which will all confound,
Neglects his Farm, forgets to till his Ground,
His Stock grows less that might be kept with ease;
In nought but Guts and Debts he finds Encrease.
In Town reels as if he'd shove down each Wall,
Yet Walls must stand, poor Soul, or he must fall.

None preaches better than the ant, and she says nothing.

The absent are never without fault, nor the present without excuse.

Gifts burst rocks.

If wind blows on you thro' a hole,
Make your will and take care of your soul.

The rotten Apple spoils his Companion.

VI Mon. August hath xxxi days.

> The Tongue was once a Servant to the Heart,
> And what it gave she freely did impart;
> But now Hypocrisy is grown so strong
> The Heart's become a Servant to the Tongue.
> Virtue we praise, but practise not her good,
> (Athenian-like), we act not what we know,
> As many Men do talk of Robin Hood
> Who never did shoot Arrow in his Bow.

He that sells upon trust, loses many friends, and always
wants money.

Don't throw stones at your neighbours, if your own
windows are glass.

The excellency of hogs is fatness, of men virtue.

Good wives and good plantations are made by good
husbands.

Pox take you, is no curse to some people.

VII Mon. September hath xxx days.

> Briskcap, thou'st little Judgment in thy Head,
> More than to dress thee, drink and go to Bed:
> Yet thou shalt have the Wall, and the Way lead,
> Since Logick wills that simple Things precede.
> Walking and meeting one not long ago,
> I ask'd who 'twas, he said, he did not know.
> I said, I know thee; so said he, I you;
> But he that knows himself I never knew.

Force shites upon Reason's Back.

Lovers, Travellers, and Poets, will give money to be
heard.

He that speaks much, is much mistaken.

Creditors have better memories than debtors.

Forwarn'd, forearm'd, unless in the case of Cuckolds, who are often forearm'd before warn'd.

VIII Mon. October hath xxxi days.

> Whimsical Will once fancy'd he was ill,
> The Doctor's call'd, who thus examin'd Will;
> *How is your Appetite?* O, as to that
> I eat right heartily, you see I'm fat.
> *How is your Sleep anights?* 'Tis sound and good;
> I eat, drink, sleep as well as e'er I cou'd.
> *Well,* says the Doctor, clapping on his Hat;
> *I'll give you something shall remove all that.*

Three things are men most liable to be cheated in, a Horse, a Wig, and a Wife.

He that lives well, is learned enough.

Poverty, Poetry, and new Titles of Honour, make Men ridiculous.

He that scatters Thorns, let him not go barefoot.

There's none deceived but he that trusts.

IX Mon. November hath xxx days.

When you are sick, what you like best is to be chosen for a Medicine in the first Place; what Experience tells you is best, is to be chosen in the second Place; what Reason (i.e. Theory) says is best, is to be chosen in the last Place. But if you can get Dr. Inclination, Dr. Experience and Dr. Reason to hold a Consultation together, they will give you the best Advice that can be given.

God heals, and the Doctor takes the Fees.

If you desire many things, many things will seem but a few.

Mary's mouth costs her nothing, for she never opens it but at others expence.

Receive before you write, but write before you pay.

I saw few die of Hunger, of Eating 100000.

X Mon. December hath xxxi days.

☉ nearer the Earth in Winter than in Summer 15046 miles, *(his Lowness and short Appearance making Winter cold.)* ☽ nearer in her *Perigeon* than *Apogeon* 69512 miles: ♄ nearer 49868 miles; ♃ nearer 38613 miles: ♂ nearer 80608 miles: ♀ nearer 6209 miles: ☿ 181427 miles. And yet ☿ is never distant from the ☉ a whole Sign, nor ♀ above two: You'll never find a ✳ ☉ ☿, nor a ☐ ☉ ♂.

Maids of America, who gave you bad teeth?
Answ. Hot Soupings: and frozen Apples.

Marry your Daughter and eat fresh Fish betimes.

If God blesses a Man, his Bitch brings forth Pigs.

> He that would live in peace and at ease,
> Must not speak all he knows, nor judge all he sees.

Adieu.

Of the ECLIPSES, 1736

There will be this Year six Eclipses, four of the Sun, and two of the Moon; those of the Moon both visible and total.

The first is a small Eclipse of the Sun, March the first, 35 minutes past 9 in the Morn. Scarcely visible in these Parts.

The second is an Eclipse of the Moon, March 15, beginning 30 minutes after 4 a Clock, P. M. the Moon being then beneath our Horizon, and rises totally dark, and continues so till 25 minutes after 7, and the Eclipse is not entirely ended till 20 minutes after 8. This Eclipse falls in Libra, or the Balance. Poor Germania! *Mene, mene, tekel upharsin!*

The Third is of the Sun, March 31. 30 minutes past 2 in the Morning. Invisible here.

The Fourth is of the Sun likewise, Aug. 25. 35 minutes after three in the Morning; no more to be seen than the former; the Sun at the Conjunction being under the Horizon.

The Fifth is of the Moon, Sept. 8. 18 minutes after 8 at Night; Beginning of total Darkness 18 min. after 9. Time of Emergence 57 min. after 10. End of the Eclipse at midnight.

The 6th and last, is of the Sun, September 23 at Noon: Invisible here tho' the Sun itself be visible. For there is this Difference between Eclipses of the Moon and of the Sun, viz. All Lunar Eclipses are universal, i.e. visible in all Parts of the Globe which have the Moon above their Horizon, and are every where of the same Magnitude: But Eclipses of the Sun do not appear the same in all Parts of the Earth where they are seen; being when total in some Places, only partial in others; and in other Places not seen at all, tho' neither Clouds nor Horizon prevent the Sight of the Sun it self.

As to the Effects of these two great Eclipses, suffer me to observe, that whoever studies the Eclipses of former Ages, and compares them with the great Events in the History of the Times and Years in which they happened (as every true Astrologer ought to do) shall find, that the Fall of the Assyrian, Persian, Grecian and Roman Monarchies, each of them, was remarkably preceded by great and total Eclipses of the Heavenly Bodies. Observations of this kind, join'd with the ancient and long-try'd Rules of our Art, (too tedious to repeat here) make me tremble for an Empire now in being. O Christendom! why art thou so fatally divided against thy self? O Poland! formerly the Bulwark of the Christian Faith, wilt thou become the Flood-gate to let in an Inundation of Infidelity? O mischievous Crescent! when shall we see thee at the Full, and rejoice at thy future Waning? May Heaven avert these presag'd Misfortunes, and confound the Designs of all wicked and impious Men!

COURTS.

For Gratitude there's none exceed 'em,
(Their Clients know this when they bleed 'em).
Since they who give most for their Laws,
Have most return'd, and carry th' Cause.
All know, except an arrant Tony,

That Right and Wrong's meer Ceremony.
It is enough that the Law Jargon,
Gives the best Bidder the best Bargain.

In my last Year's Almanack I mention'd, that the visible Eclipses of this Year, 1736, portended some great and surprizing Events relating to these Northern Colonies, of which I purposed this Year to speak at large. But as those Events are not to happen immediately this Year, I chuse rather, upon second Thought, to defer farther Mention of them, till the Publication of my Almanack for that Year in which they are to happen. However, that the Reader may not be entirely disappointed, here follow for his present Amusement a few

ENIGMATICAL PROPHECIES

Which they that do not understand, cannot well explain.

1. Before the middle of this Year, a Wind at N. East will arise, during which the *Water of the* Sea and Rivers will be in such a manner raised, that great part of the Towns of Boston, Newport, NewYork, Philadelphia, the low Lands of Maryland and Virginia, and the Town of Charlstown in South Carolina, will be *under Water.* Happy will it be for the Sugar and Salt, standing in the Cellars of those Places, if there be tight Roofs and Cielings overhead; otherwise, without being a Conjurer, a Man may easily foretel that such Commodities will receive Damage.

2. About the middle of the Year, great Numbers of Vessels fully laden will be taken out of the Ports aforesaid, by a *Power* with which we are not now at War, and whose Forces shall not be *descried or seen* either coming or going. But in the End this may not be disadvantageous to those Places.

3. However, not long after, a visible Army of 20000 *Musketers* will land, some in Virginia and Maryland, and some in the lower Counties on both sides of Delaware, who will over-run the Country, and sorely annoy

the Inhabitants: But the Air in this Climate will agree with them so ill towards Winter, that they will die in the beginning of cold Weather like rotten Sheep, and by Christmas the Inhabitants will get the better of them.

Note, In my next Almanack these Enigmatical Prophecies will be explained. R. S.

FROM POOR RICHARD'S ALMANAC (1737) [2]

In my last I published some *Enigmatical Prophecies,* which I did not expect any one would take for serious Predictions. The Explanation I promised, as follows, viz.

1. The Water of the Sea and Rivers is raised in Vapours by the Sun, is form'd into Clouds in the Air, and thence descends in Rain. Now when there is Rain overhead, (which frequently happens when the Wind is at N.E.) the Cities and Places on the Earth below, are certainly *under Water.*

2. The Power with which *we were not then at War,* but which, it was said, would take many full laden Vessels out of our Ports before the End of the Year, is THE WIND, whose Forces also *are not descried either coming or going.*

3. The Army which it was said would *land* in Virginia, Maryland, and the Lower Counties on Delaware, were not *Musketeers* with Guns on their Shoulders as some expected; but their Namesakes, in Pronunciation, tho' truly spelt *Moschitos,* arm'd only with a sharp Sting. Every one knows they are Fish before they fly, being bred in the Water; and therefore may properly be said *to land* before they become generally troublesome.

2. Civic Leader

In the third part of his *Autobiography,* Franklin recounted his role as a civic leader in Philadelphia during the middle years of the century. Franklin composed this part of his memoirs in his eighty-second year, the year following his participation in the Constitutional Convention.

The following selections include Franklin's projects concerning the city watch, fire protection, education, medical care for the poor, and city streets. The selections provide insight into the manner in which Franklin exercised leadership among his fellow citizens. They particularly illustrate his keen sense of human psychology, and they are also a valuable source for the social history of eighteenth century Philadelphia.

THE CITY WATCH AND FIRE PROTECTION [3]

. . . I began now to turn my Thoughts a little to public Affairs, beginning however with small Matters. The City Watch was one of the first Things that I conceiv'd to want Regulation. It was managed by the Constables of the respective Wards in Turn. The Constable warn'd a Number of Housekeepers to attend him for the Night. Those who chose never to attend paid him Six Shillings a Year to be excus'd, which was suppos'd to be for hiring Substitutes; but was in reality much more than was necessary for that purpose, and made the Constableship a Place of Profit. And the Constable for a little Drink often got such Ragamuffins about him as a Watch, that reputable Housekeepers did not chuse to mix with. Walking the rounds too was often neglected, and most of the Night spent in Tippling. I thereupon wrote a Paper to be read in Junto, representing these Irregularities, but insisting more particularly on the Inequality of this Six Shilling Tax of the Constables, respecting the Circumstances of those who paid it, since a poor Widow Housekeeper, all whose Property to be guarded by the Watch did not perhaps exceed the Value of Fifty Pounds, paid as much as the wealthiest Merchant who had Thousands of Pounds-worth of Goods in his Stores. On the whole I proposed as a more effectual Watch, the Hiring of proper Men to serve constantly in that Business; and as a more equitable Way of supporting the Charge, the levying a Tax that should be proportion'd to Property. This idea being approv'd by the Junto, was communicated to the other Clubs, but as arising in each of them. And tho' the Plan was not immediately carried into Execution, yet by preparing the Minds of People for the Change, it paved the Way for the Law obtain'd a few

Years after, when the Members of our Clubs were grown into more Influence.

About this time I wrote a Paper, (first to be read in Junto but it was afterwards publish'd) on the different Accidents and Carelessnesses by which Houses were set on fire, with Cautions against them, and Means proposed of avoiding them. This was much spoken of as a useful Piece, and gave rise to a Project, which soon followed it, of forming a Company for the more ready Extinguishing of Fires, and mutual Assistance in Removing and Securing of Goods when in Danger. Associates in this Scheme were presently found amounting to Thirty. Our Articles of Agreement oblig'd every Member to keep always in good Order and fit for Use, a certain Number of Leather Buckets, with strong Bags and Baskets (for packing and transporting of Goods) which were to be brought to every Fire; and we agreed to meet once a Month and spend a social Evening together, in discoursing and communicating such Ideas as occur'd to us upon the Subject of Fires as might be useful in our Conduct on such Occasions.

The Utility of this Institution soon appear'd, and many more desiring to be admitted than we thought convenient for one Company, they were advised to form another, which was accordingly done. And this went on, one new Company being formed after another, till they became so numerous as to include most of the Inhabitants who were Men of Property; and now at the time of my Writing this, tho' upwards of Fifty Years since its Establishment, that which I first formed, called the Union Fire Company, still subsists and flourishes, tho' the first Members are all deceas'd but myself and one who is older by a Year than I am. The small Fines that have been paid by Members for Absence at the Monthly Meetings, have been apply'd to the Purchase of Fire Engines, Ladders, Firehooks, and other useful Implements for each Company, so that I question whether there is a City in the World better provided with the Means of putting a Stop to beginning Conflagrations; and in fact since those Institutions, the City has never lost by Fire more than one or two Houses at a time, and the Flames have often been extinguish'd before the House in which they began has been half consumed.

THE ACADEMY [4]

[Franklin has just described his establishment of a military association for defense during the War of the Austrian Succession. The building to which Franklin alludes was erected during the Great Awakening particularly for the use of George Whitefield.]

Peace being concluded, and the Association Business therefore at an End, I turn'd my Thoughts again to the Affair of establishing an Academy. The first Step I took was to associate in the Design a Number of active Friends, of whom the Junto furnished a good Part: the next was to write and publish a Pamphlet intitled, *Proposals relating to the Education of Youth in Pennsylvania.* This I distributed among the principal Inhabitants gratis; and as soon as I could suppose their Minds a little prepared by the Perusal of it, I set on foot a Subscription for Opening and Supporting an Academy; it was to be paid in Quotas yearly for Five Years; by so dividing it I judg'd the Subscription might be larger, and I believe it was so, amounting to no less (if I remember right) than Five thousand Pounds. In the Introduction to these Proposals, I stated their Publication not as an Act of mine, but of some *publick-spirited Gentlemen;* avoiding as much as I could, according to my usual Rule, the presenting myself to the Publick as the Author of any Scheme for their Benefit.

The Subscribers, to carry the Project into immediate Execution chose out of their Number Twenty-four Trustees, and appointed Mr. Francis, then Attorney General, and myself, to draw up Constitutions for the Government of the Academy, which being done and signed, a House was hired, Masters engag'd and the Schools opened I think in the same Year 1749. The Scholars Encreasing fast, the House was soon found too small, and we were looking out for a Piece of Ground properly situated, with Intention to build, when Providence threw into our way a large House ready built, which with a few Alterations might well serve our purpose, this was the building before mentioned erected by the Hearers of Mr. Whitefield, and was obtain'd for us in the following Manner.

It is to be noted, that the Contributions to this Building being made by People of different Sects, Care was taken in the Nomination of Trustees, in whom the Building and Ground was to be vested, that a Predominancy should not be given to any Sect, lest in time that Predominancy might be a means of appropriating the whole to the Use of such Sect, contrary to the original Intention; it was therefore that one of each Sect was appointed, viz. one Church-of-England-man, one Presbyterian, one Baptist, one Moravian, &c. those in case of Vacancy by Death were to fill it by Election from among the Contributors. The Moravian happen'd not to please his Colleagues, and on his Death, they resolved to have no other of that Sect. The Difficulty then was, how to avoid having two of some other Sect, by means of the new Choice. Several Persons were named and for that reason not agreed to. At length one mention'd me, with the Observation that I was merely an honest Man, and of no Sect at all; which prevail'd with them to chuse me. The Enthusiasm which existed when the House was built, had long since abated, and its Trustees had not been able to procure fresh Contributions for paying the Ground Rent, and discharging some other Debts the Building had occasion'd, which embarrass'd them greatly. Being now a Member of both Sets of Trustees, that for the Building and that for the Academy, I had good Opportunity of negociating with both, and brought them finally to an Agreement, by which the Trustees for the Building were to cede it to those of the Academy, the latter undertaking to discharge the Debt, to keep forever open in the Building a large Hall for occasional Preachers according to the original Intention, and maintain a Free School for the Instruction of poor Children. Writings were accordingly drawn, and on paying the

Debts the Trustees of the Academy were put in Possession of the Premises, and by dividing the great and lofty Hall into Stories, and different Rooms above and below for the several Schools, and purchasing some additional Ground, the whole was soon made fit for our purpose, and the Scholars remov'd into the Building. The Care and Trouble of agreeing with the Workmen, purchasing Materials, and superintending the Work fell upon me, and I went thro' it the more chearfully, as it did not then interfere with my private Business, having the Year before taken a very able, industrious and honest Partner, Mr. David Hall, with whose Character I was well acquainted, as he had work'd for me four Years. He took off my Hands all Care of the Printing-Office, paying me punctually my Share of the Profits. This Partnership continued Eighteen Years, successfully for us both.

The Trustees of the Academy after a while were incorporated by a Charter from the Governor; their Funds were increas'd by Contributions in Britain, and Grants of Land from the Proprietaries, to which the Assembly has since made considerable Addition and thus was established the present University of Philadelphia. I have been continued one of its Trustees from the Beginning, now near forty Years, and have had the very great Pleasure of seeing a Number of the Youth who have receiv'd their Education in it, distinguish'd by their improv'd Abilities, serviceable in public Stations, and Ornaments to their Country.

THE HOSPITAL, ADVICE TO A PROJECTOR, AND CITY STREETS [5]

In 1751. Dr. Thomas Bond, a particular Friend of mine, conceiv'd the Idea of establishing a Hospital in Philadelphia, for the Reception and Cure of poor sick Persons, whether Inhabitants of the Province or Strangers. A very beneficent Design, which has been ascrib'd to me, but was originally his. He was zealous and active in endeavouring to procure subscriptions for it; but the Proposal being a Novelty in America, and at first not well understood, he met with small Success. At length he came to me, with the Compliment that he found there was no such thing as carrying a public Spirited Project through, without my being concern'd in it; "for, says he, I am often ask'd by those to whom I propose Subscribing, Have you consulted Franklin upon this Business? and what does he think of it? And when I tell them that I have not, (supposing it rather out of your Line) they do not subscribe, but say they will consider of it." I enquir'd into the Nature, and probable Utility of his Scheme, and receiving from him a very satisfactory Explanation, I not only subscrib'd to it myself, but engag'd heartily in the Design of Procuring Subscriptions from others. Previous however to the Solicitation, I endeavoured to prepare the Minds of the People by writing on the Subject in the Newspapers, which was my usual Custom in such Cases, but which he had omitted.

The Subscriptions afterwards were more free and generous, but beginning to flag, I saw they would be insufficient without some Assistance from the Assembly, and therefore propos'd to petition for it, which was done. The Country Members did not at first relish the Project. They objected that it could only be serviceable to the City, and therefore the Citizens should alone be at the Expence of it; and they doubted whether the Citizens themselves generally approv'd of it: My Allegation on the contrary, that it met with such Approbation as to leave no doubt of our being able to raise £2000 by voluntary Donations, they considered as a most extravagant Supposition, and utterly impossible. On this I form'd my Plan; and asking Leave to bring in a Bill, for incorporating the Contributors according to the Prayer (of their) Petition, and granting them a blank Sum of Money, which Leave was obtain'd chiefly on the Consideration that the House could throw the Bill out if they did not like it, I drew it so as to make the important Clause a conditional One, viz. "And be it enacted by the Authority aforesaid That when the said Contributors shall have met and chosen their Managers and Treasurer, *and shall have raised by their Contributions a Capital Stock of* £2000 *Value,* (the yearly Interest of which is to be applied to the Accommodating of the Sick Poor in the said Hospital, free of Charge for Diet, Attendance, Advice and Medicines) and *shall make the same appear to the Satisfaction of the Speaker of the Assembly* for the time being; that *then* it shall and may be lawful for the said Speaker, and he is hereby required to sign an Order on the Provincial Treasurer for the Payment of Two Thousand Pounds in two yearly Payments, to the Treasurer of the said Hospital, to be applied to the Founding, Building and Finishing of the same." This Condition carried the Bill through; for the Members who had oppos'd the Grant, and now conceiv'd they might have the Credit of being charitable without the Expence, agreed to its Passage; And then in soliciting Subscriptions among the People we urg'd the conditional Promise of the Law as an additional Motive to give, since every Man's Donation would be doubled. Thus the Clause work'd both ways. The Subscriptions accordingly soon exceeded the requisite sum, and we claim'd and receiv'd the Public Gift, which enabled us to carry the Design into Execution. A convenient and handsome Building was soon erected, the Institution has by constant Experience been found useful, and flourishes to this Day. And I do not remember any of my political Manoeuvres, the Success of which gave me at the time more Pleasure. Or that in after-thinking of it, I more easily excus'd my-self for having made some Use of Cunning.

It was about this time that another Projector, the Revd. Gilbert Tennent, came to me, with a Request that I would assist him in procuring a Subscription for erecting a new Meeting-house. It was to be for the Use of a Congregation he had gathered among the Presbyterians who were originally Disciples of Mr. Whitefield. Unwilling to make myself disagreable to my fellow Citizens, by too frequently soliciting their Contributions, I absolutely refus'd. He then desir'd I would furnish him with a List of the Names of Persons I knew by Experience to be generous and public-spirited. I thought it would be unbecoming in me, after their kind Compliance with my Solicitations, to mark them out to be worried by other Beggars, and therefore refus'd also to give such a List. He then desir'd I would at least give him my Advice. That I will readily do, said I; and, in the first Place, I advise you to apply to all those whom you know will give something; next to those whom you are uncertain whether they will given any thing or not; and show them the List of those who have given: and lastly, do not neglect those who you are sure will give nothing; for in some of them you may be mistaken. He laugh'd, thank'd me, and said he would take my Advice. He did so, for he ask'd of *every body;* and he obtain'd a much larger Sum than he expected, with which he erected the capacious and very elegant Meeting-house that stands in Arch Street.

Our City, tho' laid out with a beautifull Regularity, the Streets large, strait, and crossing each other at right Angles, had the Disgrace of suffering those Streets to remain long unpav'd, and in wet Weather the Wheels of heavy Carriages plough'd them into a Quagmire, so that it was difficult to cross them. And in dry Weather the Dust was offensive. I had liv'd near the Jersey Market, and saw with Pain the Inhabitants wading in Mud while purchasing their Provisions. A Strip of Ground down the middle of the Market was at length pav'd with Brick, so that being once in the Market they had firm Footing, but were often over Shoes in Dirt to get there. By talking and writing on the Subject, I was at length instrumental in getting the Street pav'd with Stone between the Market and the brick'd Foot-Pavement that was on each Side next the Houses. This for some time gave an easy Access to the Market, dry-shod. But the rest of the Street not being pav'd, whenever a Carriage came out of the Mud upon this Pavement, it shook off and left its Dirt upon it, and it was soon cover'd with Mire, which was not remov'd, the City as yet having no Scavengers. After some Enquiry I found a poor industrious Man, who was willing to undertake keeping the Pavement clean, by sweeping it twice a week and carrying off the Dirt from before all the Neighbours Doors, for the Sum of Sixpence per Month, to be paid by each

House. I then wrote and printed a Paper, setting forth the Advantages to the Neighbourhood that might be obtain'd by this small Expence; the greater Ease in keeping our Houses clean, so much Dirt not being brought in by People's Feet; the Benefit to the Shops by more Custom, as Buyers could more easily get at them, and by not having in windy Weather the Dust blown in upon their Goods, &c. &c. I sent one of these Papers to each House, and in a Day or two went round to see who would subscribe an Agreement to pay these Sixpences. It was unanimously sign'd, and for a time well executed. All the Inhabitants of the City were delighted with the Cleanliness of the Pavement that surrounded the Market, it being a Convenience to all; and this rais'd a general Desire to have all the Streets paved; and made the People more willing to submit to a Tax for that purpose.

After some time I drew a Bill for Paving the City, and brought it into the Assembly. It was just before I went to England in 1757. and did not pass till I was gone, and then with an Alteration in the Mode of Assessment, which I thought not for the better, but with an additional Provision for lighting as well as Paving the Streets, which was a great Improvement. It was by a private Person, the late Mr. John Clifton, his giving a Sample of the Utility of Lamps by placing one at his Door, that the People were first impress'd with the Idea of enlightning all the City. The Honour of this public Benefit has also been ascrib'd to me, but it belongs truly to that Gentleman. I did but follow his Example; and have only some Merit to claim respecting the Form of our Lamps as differing from the Globe Lamps we at first were supply'd with from London. Those we found inconvenient in these respects; they admitted no Air below, the Smoke therefore did not readily go out above, but circulated in the Globe, lodg'd on its Inside, and soon obstructed the Light they were intended to afford; giving, besides, the daily Trouble of wiping them clean; and an accidental Stroke on one of them would demolish it, and render it totally useless. I therefore suggested the composing them of four flat Panes, with a long Funnel above to draw up

the Smoke, and Crevices admitting Air below, to facilitate the Ascent of the Smoke. By this means they were
kept clean, and did not grow dark in a few Hours as the
London Lamps do, but continu'd bright till Morning;
and an accidental Stroke would generally break but a
single Pane, easily repair'd. I have sometimes wonder'd
that the Londoners did not, from the Effect Holes in the
Bottom of the Globe Lamps us'd at Vauxhall, have in
keeping them clean, learn to have such Holes in their
Street Lamps. But those Holes being made for another
purpose, viz. to communicate Flame more suddenly to
the Wick, by a little Flax hanging down thro' them, the
other Use of letting in Air seems not to have been
thought of. And therefore, after the Lamps have been
lit a few Hours, the Streets of London are very poorly
illuminated.

The Mention of these Improvements puts me in mind
of one I propos'd when in London, to Dr. Fothergill,
who was among the best Men I have known, and a great
Promoter of useful Projects. I had observ'd that the
Streets when dry were never swept and the light Dust
carried away, but it was suffer'd to accumulate till wet
Weather reduc'd it to Mud, and then after lying some
Days so deep on the Pavement that there was no Crossing but in Paths kept clean by poor People with Brooms,
it was with great Labour rak'd together and thrown up
into Carts open above, the Sides of which suffer'd some
of the Slush at every jolt on the Pavement to shake out
and fall, some times to the Annoyance of Foot-Passen-
gers. The Reason given for not sweeping the dusty
Streets was, that the Dust would fly into the Windows
of Shops and Houses. An accidental Occurrence had
instructed me how much Sweeping might be done in a
little Time. I found at my Door in Craven Street one
Morning a poor Woman sweeping my Pavement with
a birch Broom. She appeared very pale and feeble as just
come out of a Fit of Sickness. I ask'd who employ'd her
to sweep there. She said, "Nobody; but I am very poor
and in Distress, and I sweeps before Gentlefolkeses
Doors, and hopes they will give me something." I bid

her sweep the whole Street clean and I would give her a Shilling. This was at 9 a Clock. At 12 she came for the Shilling. From the slowness I saw at first in her Working, I could scarce believe that the Work was done so soon, and sent my Servant to examine it, who reported that the whole Street was swept perfectly clean, and all the Dust plac'd in the Gutter which was in the Middle. And the next Rain wash'd it quite away, so that the Pavement and even the Kennel were perfectly clean. I then judg'd that if that feeble Woman could sweep such a Street in 3 Hours, a strong active Man might have done it in half the time. And here let me remark the Convenience of having but one Gutter in such a narrow Street, running down its Middle instead of two, one on each Side near the Footway. For where all the Rain that falls on a Street runs from the Sides and meets in the middle, it forms there a Current strong enough to wash away all the Mud it meets with: But when divided into two Channels, it is often too weak to cleanse either, and only makes the Mud it finds more fluid, so that the Wheels of Carriages and Feet of Horses throw and dash it up on the Foot Pavement which is thereby rendered foul and slippery, and sometimes splash it upon those who are walking. My Proposal communicated to the good Doctor, was as follows.

"For the more effectual cleaning and keeping clean the Streets of London and Westminister, it is proposed,

"That the several Watchmen be contracted with to have the Dust swept up in dry Seasons, and the Mud rak'd up at other Times, each in the several Streets and Lanes of his Round.

"That they be furnish'd with Brooms and other proper Instruments for these purposes, to be kept at their respective Stands, ready to furnish the poor People they may employ in the Service.

"That in the dry Summer Months the Dust be all swept up into Heaps at proper Distances, before the Shops and Windows of Houses are usually opened: when the Scavengers with close-covered Carts shall also carry it all away.

"That the Mud when rak'd up be not left in Heaps to be spread abroad again by the Wheels of Carriages and Trampling of Horses; but that the Scavengers be provided with Bodies of Carts, not plac'd high upon Wheels, but low upon Sliders; with Lattice Bottoms, which being cover'd with Straw, will retain the Mud thrown into them, and permit the Water to drain from it, whereby it will become much lighter, Water making the greatest Part of its Weight. These Bodies of Carts to be plac'd at convenient Distances, and the Mud brought to them in Wheelbarrows, they remaining where plac'd till the Mud is drain'd, and then Horses brought to draw them away."

I have since had Doubts of the Practicability of the latter Part of this Proposal, on Account of the Narrowness of some Streets, and the Difficulty of placing the Draining Sleds so as not to encumber too much the Passage: But I am still of Opinion that the former, requiring the Dust, to be swept up and carry'd away before the Shops are open, is very practicable in the Summer, when the Days are long: For in Walking thro' the Strand and Fleetstreet one Morning at 7 a Clock I observ'd there was not one shop open tho' it had been Day-light and the Sun up above three Hours. The Inhabitants of London chusing voluntarily to live much by Candle Light, and sleep by Sunshine; and yet often complain a little absurdly, of the Duty on Candles and the high Price of Tallow.

Some may think these trifling Matters not worth minding or relating. But when they consider, that tho' Dust blown into the Eyes of a single Person or into a single Shop on a windy Day, is but of small Importance, yet the great Number of the Instances in a populous City, and its frequent Repetitions give it Weight and Consequence; perhaps they will not censure very severely those who bestow some of Attention to Affairs of this seemingly low Nature. Human Felicity is produc'd not so much by great Pieces of good Fortune that seldom happen, as by little Advantages that occur every Day. Thus if you teach a poor young Man to shave himself and keep his Razor in order, you may contribute more to the Happiness of his Life than in giving him a 1000 Guineas. The Money may be soon spent, the Regret only remaining of having foolishly consum'd it. But in the other Case he escapes the frequent Vexation of waiting for Barbers, and of their some times, dirty Fingers, offensive Breaths and dull Razors. He shaves when most convenient to him, and enjoys daily the Pleasure of its being done with a good Instrument. With these Sentiments I have hazarded the few preceding Pages, hoping they may afford Hints which some time or other may be useful to a City I love, having lived many Years in it very happily; and perhaps to some of our Towns in America.

3. Scientist

The incisive quality of Franklin's mind is best exemplified by his scientific writing. Without a sampling from his *Experiments and Observations on Electricity,* no collection of Frankliniana is complete. Franklin's first scientific letter to Peter Collinson (May or June, 1747) opens with his doctrine of points which was to lead to the lightning rod. The letter proceeds with the Franklinian theory that electricity is a "common element," whose presence in various objects could be described in terms of positive or negative electrification. The "Mr. Watson" to whom Franklin refers was William Watson, the foremost English electrician of the period. Franklin's miscellaneous scientific writings cover an incredible array of subjects. His letter of February 13, 1749, to Jared Eliot, Connecticut physician and agriculturalist, on the course of northeast storms typifies his method from observation and verification of data to the formulation of a reasonable hypothesis appropriately illustrated by familiarly simple images.

TO PETER COLLINSON [6]

Philadelphia, May or June, 1747.

Sir

In my last I informed you that In pursuing our Electrical Enquiries, we had observ'd some particular Phaenomena, which we lookt upon to be new, and of which I promised to give you some Account; tho' I apprehended they might possibly not be new to you, as so many Hands are daily employed in Electrical Experiments on your Side the Water, some or other of which would probably hit on the same Observations.

The first is the wonderful Effect of Points both in *drawing* off and *throwing* off the Electrical Fire. For Example,

Place an Iron Shot of three or four Inches Diameter on the Mouth of a clean dry Glass Bottle. By a fine silken Thread from the Ceiling, right over the Mouth of the Bottle, suspend a small Cork Ball, about the Bigness of a Marble: the Thread of such a Length, as that the Cork Ball may rest against the Side of the Shot. Electrify the Shot, and the Ball will be repelled to the Distance of 4 or 5 Inches, more or less according to the Quantity of Electricity. When in this State, if you present to the Shot the Point of a long, slender, sharp Bodkin at 6 or 8 Inches Distance, the Repellency is instantly destroy'd, and the Cork flies to it. A blunt Body must be brought within an Inch, and draw a Spark to produce the same Effect. To prove that the Electrical Fire is drawn off by the Point: if you take the Blade of the Bodkin out of the wooden Handle, and fix it in a Stick of Sealing Wax, and then present it at the Distance aforesaid no such Effect follows; but slide one Finger long the Wax till you touch the Blade, and the Ball flies to the Shot immediately. If you present the Point in the Dark, you will see, sometimes at a Foot Distance and more, a Light gather upon it like that of a Fire-Fly or Glow-Worm; the less sharp the Point, the nearer you must bring it to observe this Light: and at whatever Distance you see the Light, you may draw off the Electrical Fire, and destroy the Repellency. If a Cork Ball, so suspended, be repelled by the Tube, and a Point be presented quick to it, tho' at a considerable Distance, tis surprizing to see how suddenly it flies back to the Tube. Points of Wood do as well as those of Metal, provided the Wood is not dry.

To shew that Points will *throw* off, as well as *draw* off the Electrical Fire: Lay a long sharp Needle upon the

Shot, and you can not electrise the Shot, so as to make it repel the Cork Ball. Fix a Needle to the End of a suspended Gun Barrel, so as to point beyond it like a little Bayonet, and while it remains there, the Gun Barrel can not be electrised (by the Tube applied to the other End) so as to give a Spark; the Fire is continually running out silently at the Point. In the Dark you may see it make the same Appearance as it does in the Case before mentioned. . . .

We had for some Time been of Opinion, that the Electrical Fire was not created by Friction, but collected, being an Element diffused among, and attracted by other Matter, particularly by Water and Metals. We had even discovered and demonstrated its Afflux to the Electrical Sphere, as well as its Efflux, by Means of little light Wind-Mill Wheels made of stiff Paper Vanes, fixt obliquely, and turning freely on fine Wire Axes. Also by little Wheels of the same Matter, but formed like Water Wheels. Of the Disposition and Application of which Wheels, and the various Phaenomena resulting, I could, if I had Time, and it were necessary, fill you a Sheet.

The Impossibility of Electrising one's self (tho' standing on Wax) by Rubbing the Tube and drawing the Fire from it: and the Manner of doing it by passing the Tube near a Person, or Thing standing on the Floor &c. had also occurred to us some Months before Mr. Watsons ingenious *Sequel* came to hand; and these were some of the new Things I intended to have communicated to you: But now I need only mention some Particulars not hinted in that Piece, with our Reasonings thereon; tho' perhaps the latter might well enough be spared.

1. A Person standing on Wax and rubbing the Tube; and another Person on Wax drawing the Fire, they will both of them (provided they do not stand so as to touch one another) appear to be electrised to a Person standing on the Floor; that is, he will perceive a Spark on approaching each of them.

2. But if the Persons standing on Wax touch one another during the exciting of the Tube, neither of them will appear to be electrised.

3. If they touch one another after exciting the Tube, and drawing the Fire as aforesaid, there will be a stronger Spark between them than was between either of them and the Person on the Floor.

4. After such strong Spark, neither of them discovers any Electricity.

These Appearances we attempt to account for thus. We suppose as aforesaid, That Electrical Fire is a common Element, of which every one of the three Persons abovementioned has his equal Share before any Operation is begun with the Tube. *A* who stands on Wax, and rubs the Tube, collects the Electrical Fire from himself into the Glass; and his Communication with the common Stock being cut off by the Wax, his Body is not again immediately supply'd. *B,* who stands upon Wax likewise, passing his Knuckle along near the Tube, receives the Fire which was collected by the Glass from *A;* and his Communication with the common Stock being likewise cutt off, he retains the additional Quantity received. To *C,* standing on the Floor, both appear to be electrised; for he having only the middle Quantity of Electrical Fire receives a Spark on approaching *B,* who has an over-quantity, but gives one to *A,* who has an under-quantity. If *A* and *B* touch each other, the Spark between them is stronger, because the Difference between them is greater. After such Touch, there is no Spark between either of them and *C;* because the Electrical Fire in all is reduced to the original Equality. If they touch while Electrising, the Equality is never destroyed, the Fire only circulating. Hence have arisen some new Terms among us. We say *B* (and other Bodies alike circumstanced) are electrised *positively; A negatively:* Or rather *B* is electrised *plus* and *A minus.* And we daily in our Experiments electrise Bodies *plus* or *minus* as we think proper. *These Terms* we may use till your Philosophers give us better. To electrise *plus* or *minus,* no more needs to be known than this; that the Parts of the Tube of Sphere, that are rub'd, do, in the Instant of the Friction, attract the Electrical Fire, and therefore take it from the Thing rubbing: the same Parts immediately, as the Friction upon them ceases, are disposed to give the Fire they have received, to any Body that has less. Thus you may circulate it, as Mr. Watson has shewn; You may also accumulate or subtract it upon, or from any Body, as you connect it with the Rubber or with the Receiver; the Communication with the common Stock being cut off. We think that ingenious Gentleman was deceived, when he imagined (Page [64] of the Sequel) that the Electrical Fire came down the Wire from the Cieling to the Gun Barrel, thence to the Sphere and so electrised the Machine, the Man turning the Wheel &c. We suppose it was *driven off* and not *brought on* thro' that Wire; and that the Machine and Man &c. were electrized *minus,* i.e. had less electrical Fire in them than Things in common. . . .

To Jared Eliot [7]

                                   Philadelphia, February 13, 1749

Dear Sir

You desire to know my Thoughts about the N.E. Storms beginning to Leeward. Some Years since there was an Eclipse of the Moon at 9 in the Evening, which I intended to observe, but before 8 a Storm blew up at N E. and continued violent all Night and all next Day, the Sky thick clouded, dark and rainy, so that neither Moon nor Stars could be seen. The Storm did a great deal of Damage all along the Coast, for we had Accounts of it in the News Papers from Boston, Newport, New York, Maryland and Virginia. But what surpriz'd me, was to find in the Boston Newspapers an Account of an Observation of that Eclipse made there: For I thought, as the Storm came from the N E. it must have begun sooner at Boston than with us, and consequently have prevented such Observation. I wrote to my Brother about it, and he inform'd me, that the Eclipse was over there, an hour before the Storm began. Since which I have made Enquiries from time to time of Travellers, and of my Correspondents N Eastward and S. Westward, and observ'd the Accounts in the Newspapers from N England, N York, Maryland, Virginia and South Carolina, and I find it to be a constant Fact, that N East Storms begin to Leeward, and are often more violent there than farther to Windward. Thus the last October Storm, which with you was on the 8th. began on the 7th in Virginia and N Carolina, and was most violent there. As to the Reason of this, I can only give you my Conjectures. Suppose a great Tract of Country, Land and Sea, to wit Florida and the Bay of Mexico, to have clear Weather for several Days, and to be heated by the Sun and its Air thereby exceedingly rarified; Suppose the Country North Eastward, as Pensilvania, New England, Nova Scotia, Newfoundland, &c. to be at the same time cover'd with Clouds, and its Air chill'd and condens'd. The rarified Air being lighter must rise, and the Dense Air next to it will press into its Place; that will be follow'd by the next denser Air, that by the next, and so on. Thus when I have a Fire in my Chimney, there is a Current of Air constantly flowing from the Door to the Chimney: but the beginning of the Motion was at the Chimney, where the Air being rarified by the Fire, rising, its Place was supply'd by the cooler Air that was next to it, and the Place of that by the next, and so on to the Door. So the Water in a long Sluice or Mill Race, being stop'd by a Gate, is at Rest like the Air in a Calm; but as soon as you open the Gate at one End to let it out, the Water next the Gate begins first to move, that which is next to it follows; and so tho' the Water proceeds forward to the Gate, the Motion which began there runs backwards, if one may so speak, to the upper End of the Race, where the Water is last in Motion. We have on this Continent a long Ridge of Mountains running from N East to S. West; and the Coast runs the same Course. These may, perhaps, contribute towards the Direction of the winds or at least influence them in some Degree. If these Conjectures do not satisfy you, I wish to have yours on the Subject.

4. Pennsylvania Politician

During the middle decades of the eighteenth century, Franklin played a central role in the politics of his adopted colony of Pennsylvania. At first Franklin retained his independence of both the proprietary and assembly factions. Soon, however, he was drawn into open enmity to the proprietors because of their desire for immunity of their Pennsylvania estates from taxation. Franklin was annually reelected to the Pennsylvania Assembly from 1751 to 1764. In the latter election year, the issue involved Franklin's campaign for petitioning the Crown to take the colony away from the Penns and turning it into a royal colony.

The march of the Paxton boys provided Franklin with a central argument for royalization: the proprietors could not keep the peace in Pennsylvania. Franklin movingly describes the brutal massacre of friendly Indians by frontiersmen from Paxton and Donnegal townships. His *Narrative* is a masterpiece of moral indignation, heightened by the fact that the proprietary faction in Philadelphia allied itself with the frontier elements in its efforts to unseat Franklin's so-called Quaker Party in the Assembly.

In *Cool Thoughts,* written in the form of an answer to an inquiry, Franklin summed up his reasons for preferring royal to proprietary government for Pennsylvania. His allusion to the proprietor's "turning to the Church," refers to Thomas Penn's conversion from Quakerism to Anglicanism.

Though Franklin narrowly lost the election of 1764, his party kept a majority in the Assembly, which promptly sent him to England with the petition for royalization which he had drafted. The petition never received a hearing, however, as Pennsylvania's problems became overshadowed by the growing dispute between England and America.

NARRATIVE
OF THE LATE MASSACRES,
IN LANCASTER COUNTY,

OF A

NUMBER OF INDIANS, FRIENDS OF THIS
PROVINCE,

BY PERSONS UNKNOWN.

WITH SOME OBSERVATIONS ON THE SAME.

Printed in the Year

MDCCLXIV.[8]

THESE *Indians* were the Remains of a Tribe of the *Six Nations,* settled at *Conestogoe,* and thence called *Conestogoe Indians.* On the first Arrival of the *English* in *Pennsylvania,* Messengers from this Tribe came to welcome them, with Presents of Venison, Corn, and Skins; and the whole Tribe entered into a Treaty of Friendship with the first Proprietor, William Penn, which was to last "as long as the Sun should shine, or the Waters run in the Rivers."

This Treaty has been since frequently renewed, and the *Chain brightened,* as they express it, from time to time. It has never been violated, on their Part or ours, till now. As their Lands by Degrees were mostly purchased, and the Settlements of the White People began to surround them, the Proprietor assigned them lands on the Manor of *Conestogoe,* which they might not part with; there they have lived many years in Friendship with their White Neighbours, who loved them for their peaceable inoffensive Behaviour.

It has always been observed, that *Indians,* settled in the Neighbourhood of White People, do not increase, but diminish continually. This Tribe accordingly went on diminishing, till there remained in their Town on the Manor, but 20 persons, viz. 7 Men, 5 Women, and 8 Children, Boys and Girls.

Of these, *Shehaes* was a very old Man, having assisted at the second Treaty held with them, by Mr. Penn, in 1701, and ever since continued a faithful and affectionate

Friend to the *English;* He is said to have been an exceeding good Man, considering his Education, being naturally of a most kind, benevolent Temper.

Peggy was *Shehaes's* Daughter; she worked for her aged Father, continuing to live with him, though married, and attended him with filial Duty and Tenderness.

John was another good old Man; his Son *Harry* helped to support him.

George and *Will Soc* were two Brothers, both young Men.

John Smith, a valuable young Man of the *Cayuga* Nation, who became acquainted with *Peggy, Shehaes's* Daughter, some few Years since, married her, and settled in that Family. They had one Child, about three Years old.

Betty, a harmless old Woman; and her son *Peter,* a likely young Lad.

Sally, whose *Indian* name was *Wyanjoy,* a Woman much esteemed by all that knew her, for her prudent and good Behaviour in some very trying situations of Life. She was a truly good and an amiable Woman, had no Children of her own, but, a distant Relation dying, she had taken a Child of that Relation's, to bring up as her own, and performed towards it all the Duties of an affectionate Parent.

The Reader will observe, that many of their Names are *English.* It is common with the *Indians* that have an affection for the *English,* to give themselves, and their Children, the Names of such *English* Persons as they particularly esteem.

This little Society continued the Custom they had begun, when more numerous, of addressing every new Governor, and every Descendant of the first Proprietor, welcoming him to the Province, assuring him of their Fidelity, and praying a Continuance of that Favour and Protection they had hitherto experienced. They had accordingly sent up an Address of this Kind to our present Governor, on his Arrival; but the same was scarce delivered, when the unfortunate Catastrophe happened, which we are about to relate.

On *Wednesday,* the 14th of *December,* 1763, Fifty-seven Men, from some of our Frontier Townships, who had projected the Destruction of this little Commonwealth, came, all well mounted, and armed with Firelocks, Hangers and Hatchets, having travelled through the Country in the Night, to *Conestogoe* Manor. There they surrounded the small Village of *Indian* Huts, and just at Break of Day broke into them all at once. Only three Men, two Women, and a young Boy, were found at home, the rest being out among the neighbouring White People, some to sell the Baskets, Brooms and Bowls they manufactured, and others on other Occasions. These poor defenceless Creatures were immediately fired upon, stabbed, and hatcheted to Death! The good *Shehaes,* among the rest, cut to Pieces in his Bed. All of them were scalped and otherwise horribly mangled. Then their Huts were set on Fire, and most of them burnt down. When the Troop, pleased with their own Conduct and Bravery, but enraged that any of the poor *Indians* had escaped the Massacre, rode off, and in small Parties, by different Roads, went home.

The universal Concern of the neighbouring White People on hearing of this Event, and the Lamentations of the younger *Indians,* when they returned and saw the Desolation, and the butchered half-burnt Bodies of their murdered Parents and other Relations, cannot well be expressed.

The Magistrates of *Lancaster* went out to collect the remaining *Indians,* brought them into the Town for their better Security against any farther Attempt; and it is said condoled with them on the Misfortune that had happened, took them by the Hand, comforted and *promised them Protection.* They were all put into the Workhouse, a strong Building, as the Place of greatest Safety.

When the shocking News arrived in Town, a Proclamation was issued by the Governor, in the following Terms, viz.

"WHEREAS I have received Information, that on *Wednesday,* the Fourteenth Day of this Month, a Number of People, armed, and mounted on Horseback, unlawfully assembled together, and went to the *Indian* Town in the *Conestogoe* Manor, in *Lancaster County,* and without the least Reason or Provocation, in cool Blood, barbarously killed six of the *Indians* settled there, and burnt and destroyed all their Houses and Effects: And whereas so cruel and inhuman an Act, committed in the Heart of this Province on the said *Indians,* who have lived peaceably and inoffensively among us, during all our late Troubles, and for many Years before, and were justly considered as under the Protection of this Government and its Laws, calls loudly for the vigorous Exertion of the civil Authority, to detect the Offenders, and bring them to condign Punishment; I have therefore, by and with the Advice and Consent of the Council, thought fit to issue this Proclamation, and do hereby strictly charge and enjoin all Judges, Justices, Sheriffs, Constables, Officers Civil and Military, and all other His Majesty's liege Subjects within this Province, to make diligent Search and Enquiry after the Authors and Perpetrators of the said Crime, their Abettors and Accomplices, and to use all possible Means to apprehend and secure them in some of the publick Goals of this Province, that they may be brought to their Trials, and be proceeded against according to Law.

"And whereas a Number of other *Indians,* who lately lived on or near the Frontiers of this Province, being willing and desirous to preserve and continue the ancient Friendship, which heretofore subsisted between them and the good People of this Province, have, at their own earnest Request, been removed from their Habitations, and brought into the County of *Philadelphia* and seated for the present, for their better Security, on the *Province Island,* and in other places in the Neighbourhood of the City of *Philadelphia,* where Provision is made for them at the public Expence; I do therefore hereby strictly forbid all Persons whatsoever, to molest or injure any of the said *Indians,* as they will answer the contrary at their Peril.

"Given under my Hand, and the Great Seal of the said Province, at Philadelphia, *the Twenty-second Day of*

December, *Anno Domini. One Thousand Seven Hundred and Sixty-three, and in the Fourth Year of His Majesty's Reign.*

"JOHN PENN.

"By his Honour's Command,
"JOSEPH SHIPPEN, *Jun., Secretary.*
"God save the King."

Notwithstanding this Proclamation, those cruel Men again assembled themselves, and hearing that the remaining fourteen *Indians* were in the Workhouse at *Lancaster,* they suddenly appeared in that Town, on the 27th of *December.* Fifty of them, armed as before, dismounting, went diretly to the Workhouse, and by Violence broke open the Door, and entered with the utmost Fury in their Countenances. When the poor Wretches saw they had *no Protection* nigh, nor could possibly escape, and being without the least Weapon for Defence, they divided into their little Familes, the Children clinging to the Parents; they fell on their Knees, protested their Innocence, declared their Love to the *English,* and that, in their whole Lives, they had never done them Injury; and in this Posture they all received the Hatchet! Men, Women and little Children were every one inhumanly murdered!—in cold Blood!

The barbarous Men who committed the atrocious Fact, in defiance of Government, of all Laws human and divine, and to the eternal Disgrace of their Country and Colour, then mounted their Horses, huzza'd in Triumph, as if they had gained a Victory, and rode off—*unmolested!*

The Bodies of the Murdered were then brought out and exposed in the Street, till a Hole could be made in the Earth to receive and cover them.

But the Wickedness cannot be covered, the Guilt will lie on the whole Land, till Justice is done on the Murderers. THE BLOOD OF THE INNOCENT WILL CRY TO HEAVEN FOR VENGEANCE.

It is said that, *Shehaes* being before told, that it was to be feared some *English* might come from the Frontier into the Country, and murder him and his People; he replied, "It is impossible: there are *Indians*, indeed, in the Woods, who would kill me and mine, if they could get at us, for my Friendship to the *English;* but the *English* will wrap me in their Matchcoat, and secure me from all Danger." How unfortunately was he mistaken!

Another Proclamation has been issued, offering a great Reward for apprehending the Murderers, in the following Terms, *viz.*

"WHEREAS on the Twenty-second Day of *December* last, I issued a Proclamation for the apprehending and bringing to Justice, a Number of Persons, who, in Violation of the Public Faith, and in Defiance of all Law, had inhumanly killed six of the *Indians*, who had lived in *Conestogoe* Manor, for the Course of many Years, peaceably and inoffensively, under the Protection of this Government, on Lands assigned to them for their Habitation; notwithstanding which, I have received Information, that on the Twenty-seventh of the same Month, a large Party of armed Men again assembled and met together in a riotous and tumultuous Manner, in the County of *Lancaster*, and proceeded to the Town of *Lancaster*, where they violently broke open the Workhouse, and butchered and put to Death fourteen of the said *Conestogoe Indians*, Men, Women and Children, who had been taken under the immediate Care and Protection of the Magistrates of the said County, and lodged for their better Security in the said Workhouse, till they should be more effectually provided for by Order of the Government; and whereas common Justice loudly demands, and the Laws of the Land (upon the Preservation of which not only the Liberty and Security of every Individual, but the Being of the Government itself depend) require, that the above Offenders should be brought to condign Punishment; I have therefore, by and with the Advice of the Council, published this Proclamation, and do hereby strictly charge and command all Judges, Justices, Sheriffs, Constables, Officers Civil and Military, and all other His Majesty's faithful and liege

Subjects within this Province, to make diligent Search and Enquiry after the Authors and Perpetrators of the said last-mentioned Offence, their Abettors and Accomplices, and that they use all possible Means to apprehend and secure them in some of the public Goals of this province, to be dealt with according to Law.

"And I do hereby further promise and engage, that any Person or Persons, who shall apprehend and secure, or cause to be apprehended and secured, any Three of the Ringleaders of the said Party, and prosecute them to Conviction, shall have and receive for each, the public Reward of *Two Hundred Pounds;* and any Accomplice, not concerned in the immediate shedding the Blood of the said *Indians,* who shall make Discovery of any or either of the said Ringleaders, and apprehend and prosecute them to Conviction, shall, over and above the said Reward, have all the Weight and Influence of the Government, for obtaining His Majesty's Pardon for his Offence.

"Given under my Hand, and the Great Seal of the said Province, at Philadelphia, *the Second Day of January, in the Fourth Year of His Majesty's Reign, and in the Year of our Lord One Thousand Seven Hundred and Sixty-four.*

"JOHN PENN.

"By his Honour's command,
   "JOSEPH SHIPPEN, Jun., *Secretary.*
      "God save the King."

These Proclamations have as yet produced no Discovery; the Murders having given out such Threatenings against those that disapprove their Proceedings, that the whole Country seems to be in Terror, and no one durst speak what he knows; even the Letters from thence are unsigned, in which any Dislike is expressed of the Rioters.

There are some, (I am ashamed to hear it,) who would extenuate the enormous Wickedness of these Actions, by saying, "The Inhabitants of the Frontiers are exasperated with the Murder of their Relations, by the

Enemy *Indians,* in the present War." It is possible;—but though this might justify their going out into the Woods, to seek for those Enemies, and avenge upon them those Murders, it can never justify their turning into the Heart of the Country, to murder their Friends.

If an *Indian* injures me, does it follow that I may revenge that Injury on all *Indians?* It is well known, that *Indians* are of different Tribes, Nations and Languages, as well as the White People. In *Europe,* if the *French,* who are White People, should injure the *Dutch,* are they to revenge it on the *English,* because they too are White People? The only Crime of these poor Wretches seems to have been, that they had a reddish-brown Skin, and black Hair; and some People of that Sort, it seems, had murdered some of our Relations. If it be right to kill Men for such a Reason, then, should any Man, with a freckled Face and red Hair, kill a Wife or Child of mine, it would be right for me to revenge it, by killing all the freckled red-haired Men, Women and Children, I could after-wards anywhere meet with.

But it seems these People think they have a better Justification; nothing less than the *Word of God.* With the Scriptures in their Hands and Mouths, they can set at nought that express Command, *Thou shalt do no Murder;* and justify their Wickedness by the Command given *Joshua* to destroy the Heathen. Horrid Perversion of Scripture and of Religion! To father the worst of Crimes on the God of Peace and Love! Even the *Jews,* to whom that particular Commission was directed, spared the *Gibeonites,* on Account of their Faith once given. The Faith of this Government has been frequently given to those *Indians;* but that did not avail them with People who despise Government.

We pretend to be *Christians,* and, from the superior Light we enjoy, ought to exceed *Heathens, Turks, Saracens, Moors, Negroes* and *Indians,* in the Knowledge and Practice of what is right. I will endeavour to show, by a few Examples from Books and History the Sense those People have had of such Actions. . . .

Now I am about to mention someting of *Indians,* I

beg that I may not be understood as framing Apologies for *all Indians.* I am far from desiring to lessen the laudable Spirit of Resentment in my Countrymen against those now at War with us, so far as it is justified by their Perfidy and Inhumanity. I would only observe, that the *Six Nations,* as a Body, have kept Faith with the *English* ever since we knew them, now near an Hundred Years; and that the governing Part of those People have had Notions of Honour, whatever may be the Case with the Rum-debauched, Trader-corrupted Vagabonds and Thieves on the *Sasquehannah* and *Ohio,* at present in Arms against us. As a Proof of that Honour, I shall only mention one well-known recent Fact. When six *Catawba* Deputies, under the Care of Colonel *Bull,* of *Charlestown,* went by Permission into the *Mohawks* Country, to sue for and treat of Peace for their Nation, they soon found the *Six Nations* highly exasperated, and the Peace at that Time impracticable: They were therefore in Fear for their own Persons, and apprehended that they should be killed in their Way back to *New York;* which being made known to the *Mohawk Chiefs* by Colonel *Bull,* one of them, by Order of the Council, made this Speech to the *Catawbas;*

"Strangers and Enemies,
"While you are in this Country, blow away all Fear out of your Breasts; change the black Streak of Paint on your Cheek for a red One, and let your Faces shine with Bear's Grease: You are safer here than if you were at home. The *Six Nations* will not defile their own Land with the Blood of Men that come unarmed to ask for Peace. We shall send a Guard with you, to see you safe out of our Territories. So far you shall have Peace, but no farther. Get home to your own Country, and there take Care of yourselves, for there we intend to come and kill you."

The *Catawbas* came away unhurt accordingly.
It is also well known, that just before the late War broke out, when our Traders first went among the *Piankeshaw Indians,* a Tribe of the *Twightwees,* they found

the Principle of giving Protection to Strangers in full Force; for, the *French* coming with their *Indians* to the *Piankeshaw* Town, and demanding that those Traders and their Goods should be delivered up; the *Piankeshaws* replied, the *English* were come there upon their Invitation, and they could not do so base a Thing. But the *French* insisting on it, the *Piankeshaws* took Arms in Defence of their Guests, and a Number of them, with their old Chief, lost their Lives in the Cause; the *French* at last prevailing by superior Force only.

I will not dissemble that numberless Stories have been raised and spread abroad, against not only the poor Wretches that are murdered, but also against the Hundred and Forty christianized *Indians,* still threatened to be murdered; all which Stories are well known, by those who know the *Indians* best, to be pure Inventions, contrived by bad People, either to excite each other to join in the Murder, or since it was committed, to justify it; and believed only by the Weak and Credulous. I call this publickly on the Makers and Venders of these Accusations to produce their Evidence. Let them satisfy the Public that even *Will Soc,* the most obnoxious of all that Tribe, was really guilty of those Offences against us which they lay to his Charge. But if he was, ought he not to have been fairly tried? He lived under our Laws, and was subject to them; he was in our Hands, and might easily have been prosecuted; was it *English Justice* to condemn and execute him unheard? Conscious of his own Innocence, he did not endeavour to hide himself when the Door of the Workhouse, his Sanctuary, was breaking open. "I will meet them," says he, "for they are my Brothers." These Brothers of his shot him down at the Door, while the Word Brothers was between his Teeth.

But if *Will Soc* was a bad Man, what had poor old *Shehaes* done? What could he or the other poor old Men and Women do? What had little Boys and Girls done? What could Children of a Year old, Babes at the Breast, what could they do, that they too must be shot and hatcheted? Horrid to relate! And in their Parents Arms!

This is done by no civilized Nation in *Europe*. Do we come to *America* to learn and practise the Manners of *Barbarians?* But this, *Barbarians* as they are, they practise againt their Enemies only, not against their Friends.

These poor People have been always our Friends. Their Fathers received ours, when Strangers here, with Kindness and Hospitality. Behold the Return we have made them! When we grew more numerous and powerful, they put themselves under our *Protection*. See, in the mangled Corpses of the last Remains of the Tribe, how effectually we have afforded it to them!

Unhappy People! to have lived in such Times, and by such Neighbours! We have seen, that they would have been safer among the ancient *Heathens,* with whom the Rites of Hospitality were *sacred*. They would have been considered as *Guests* of the Publick, and the Religion of the Country would have operated in their Favour. But our Frontier People call themselves *Christians!* They would have been safer, if they had submitted to the *Turks;* for ever since *Mahomet's* Reproof to *Khaled,* even the cruel *Turks* never kill Prisoners in cold Blood. These were not even Prisoners. But what is the Example of *Turks* to Scripture *Christians?* They would have been safer, though they had been taken in actual War against the *Saracens,* if they had once drank Water with them. These were not taken in War against us, and have drank with us, and we with them, for Fourscore Years. But shall we compare *Saracens* to *Christians?*

They would have been safer among the *Moors* in *Spain,* though they had been Murderers of Sons; if Faith had once been pledged to them, and a Promise of Protection given. But these have had the Faith of the *English* given to them many times by the Government, and, in Reliance on that Faith, they lived among us, and gave us the Opportunity of murdering them. However, what was honourable in *Moors,* may not be a Rule to us; for we are *Christians!* They would have been safer it seems among *Popish Spaniards,* even if Enemies, and delivered into their Hands by a Tempest. These were not Enemies; they were born among us, and yet we have killed them all. But shall we imitate *idolatrous Papists,* we that are *enlightened Protestants?* They would have even been safer among the *Negroes* of *Africa,* where at least one manly Soul would have been found, with Sense, Spirit and Humanity enough, to stand in their Defence. But shall *Whitemen* and *Christians* act like a *Pagan Negroe?* In short it appears, that they would have been safe in any Part of the known World, except in the Neighbourhood of the CHRISTIAN WHITE SAVAGES of *Peckstang* and *Donegall!*

O, ye unhappy Perpetrators of this horrid Wickedness! reflect a Moment on the Mischief ye have done, the Disgrace ye have brought on your Country, on your Religion, and your Bible, on your Families and Children! Think on the Destruction of your captivated Countryfolks (now among the wild *Indians*) which probably may follow, in Resentment of your Barbarity! Think on the Wrath of the United *Five Nations,* hitherto our Friends, but now provoked by your murdering one of their Tribes, in Danger of becoming our bitter Enemies. Think of the mild and good Government you have so audaciously insulted; the Laws of your King, your Country, and your God, that you have broken; the infamous Death that hangs over your Heads; for Justice, though slow, will come at last. All good People everywhere detest your Actions. You have imbrued your Hands in innocent Blood; how will you make them clean? The dying Shrieks and Groans of the Murdered, will often sound in your Ears: Their Spectres will sometimes attend you, and affright even your innocent Children! Fly where you will, your Consciences will go with you. Talking in your Sleep shall betray you, in the Delirium of a Fever you yourselves shall make your own Wickedness known.

One Hundred and Forty peaceable *Indians* yet remain in this Government. They have, by *Christian* Missionaries, been brought over to a *Liking,* at least, of our Religion; some of them lately left their Nation which is now at War with us, because they did not chuse to join with them in their Depredations; and to shew their Confidence in us, and to give us an equal Confidence in them, they have brought and put into our Hands their Wives and Children. Others have lived long among us in *Northampton* County, and most of their Children have been born there. These are all now trembling for their Lives. They have been hurried from Place to Place for Safety, now concealed in Corners, then sent out of the Province, refused a Passage through a neighbouring Colony, and returned, not unkindly perhaps, but disgracefully, on our Hands. O *Pennsylvania!* Once renowned for Kindness to Strangers, shall the Clamours of a few mean Niggards about the Expence of this *Publick Hospitality,* an Expence that will not cost the noisy Wretches *Sixpence* a Piece, (and what is the Expence of the poor Maintenance we afford them, compared to the Expence they might occasion if in Arms against us) shall so senseless a Clamour, I say, force you to turn out of your Doors these unhappy Guests, who have offended their own Country-folks by their Affection for you, who, confiding in your Goodness, have put themselves under your Protection? Those whom you have disarmed to satisfy groundless Suspicions, will you leave them exposed to the armed Madmen of your Country? Unmanly Men! who are not ashamed to come with Weapons against the Unarmed, to use the Sword against Women, and the Bayonet against young Children; and who have already given such bloody Proofs of their Inhumanity and Cruelty.

Let us rouze ourselves, for Shame, and redeem the Honour of our Provnce from the Contempt of its Neighbours; let all good Men join heartily and unanimously in Support of the Laws, and in strengthening the Hands of Government; that JUSTICE may be done, the Wicked punished, and the Innocent protected; otherwise we can, as a People, expect no Blessing from Heaven; there will be no Security for our Persons or Properties; Anarchy and Confusion will prevail over all; and Violence without Judgment, dispose of every Thing.

When I mention the Baseness of the Murderers, in the Use they made of Arms, I cannot, I ought not to forget, the very different Behaviour of *brave Men* and *true Soldiers,* of which this melancholy Occasion has afforded us fresh Instances. The *Royal Highlanders* have, in the Course of this War, suffered as much as any other Corps, and have frequently had their Ranks thinn'd by an *Indian* Enemy; yet they did not for this retain a brutal undistinguishing Resentment against *all Indians,* Friends as well as Foes. But a Company of them happening to be here, when the 140 poor *Indians* above mentioned were thought in too much Danger to stay longer in the Province, chearfully undertook to protect and escort them to *New York,* which they executed (as far as that Government would permit the *Indians* to come) with Fidelity and Honour; and their captain *Robinson,* is justly applauded and honoured by all sensible and good People, for the Care, Tenderness and Humanity, with which he treated those unhappy Fugitives, during their March in this severe Season.

General *Gage,* too, has approved of his Officer's Conduct, and, as I hear, ordered him to remain with the *Indians* at *Amboy,* and continue his Protection to them, till another Body of the King's Forces could be sent to relieve his Company, and escort their Charge back in Safety to *Philadelphia,* where his Excellency has had the Goodness to direct those Forces to remain for some Time, under the Orders of our Governor, for the Security of the *Indians;* the Troops of this Province being at present necessarily posted on the Frontier. Such just and generous Actions endear the Military to the Civil Power, and impress the Minds of all the Discerning with a still greater Respect for our national Government. I shall conclude with observing, that *Cowards* can handle Arms, can strike where they are sure to meet with no Return, can wound, mangle and murder; but it belongs to *brave* Men to spare and to protect; for, as the Poet says,

"Mercy still sways the Brave."

COOL THOUGHTS
ON THE
PRESENT SITUATION
OF OUR
PUBLIC AFFAIRS.

IN A LETTER TO A FRIEND IN THE COUNTRY.[9]

SIR,

Your Apology was unnecessary. It will be no *Trouble,* but a *Pleasure,* if I can give you the Satisfaction you desire. I shall therefore immediately communicate to you my Motives for approving the Proposal of endeavouring to obtain a *Royal Government,* in Exchange for this of the Proprietaries; with such Answers to the Objections you mention, as, in my Opinion, fully obviate them.

I do not purpose entering into the Merits of the Disputes between the Proprietaries and the People. I only observe it as a Fact known to us all, that such Disputes there are, and that they have long subsisted, greatly to the Prejudice of the Province, clogging and embarrassing all the Wheels of Government, and exceedingly obstructing the publick Defence, and the Measures wisely concerted by our Gracious Sovereign, for the common Security of the Colonies. I may add it as another Fact, that *we are all heartily tired of these Disputes.*

It is very remarkable, that Disputes of the same Kind have arisen in *All* Proprietary Governments, and subsisted till their Dissolution; All were made unhappy by them, and found no Relief but in recurring finally to the immediate Government of the Crown. *Pennsylvania* and *Maryland,* are the only Two of the Kind remaining, and both at this Instant agitated by the same Contentions between Proprietary Interest and Power, and Popular Liberty. Thro' these Contentions the good People of that Province are rendered equally unhappy with ourselves, and their Proprietary, perhaps, more so than our's; for he has no *Quakers* in his Assembly to saddle with the Blame of those Contentions, nor can he justify himself with the Pretence, that turning to the Church has made his People his Enemies.

Pennsylvania had scarce been settled Twenty Years, when these Disputes began between the first Proprietor and the original Settlers; they continued, with some Intermissions, during his whole Life; his Widow took them up, and continued them after his Death. Her Sons resum'd them very early, and they still subsist. Mischievous and distressing as they have been found to both Proprietors and People, it does not appear that there is any Prospect of their being extinguish'd, till either the Proprietary Purse is unable to support them, or the Spirit of the People so broken, that they shall be willing to submit to any Thing, rather than continue them. The first is not very likely to happen, as that immense Estate goes on increasing.

Considering all Circumstances, I am at length inclin'd to think, that the Cause of these miserable Contentions is not to be sought for merely in the Depravity and Selfishness of human Minds. For tho' it is not unlikely that in these, as well as in other Disputes, there are *Faults on both Sides,* every glowing Coal being apt to inflame its Opposite; yet I see no Reason to suppose that all Proprietary Rulers are worse Men than other Rulers, nor that all People in Proprietary Governments are worse People than those in other Governments. I suspect therefore, that the Cause is radical, interwoven in the Constitution, and so become of the very Nature, of Proprietary Governments; and will therefore produce its Effects, as long as such Governments continue. And, as some Physicians say, every Animal Body brings into the World among its original Stamina the Seeds of that Disease that shall finally produce its Dissolution; so so the Political Body of a Proprietary Government, contains those convulsive Principles that will at length destroy it.

I may not be Philosopher enough to develop those Principles, nor would this Letter afford me Room, if I had Abilities, for such a Discussion. The *Fact* seems sufficient for our Purpose, and the *Fact* is notorious, that such Contentions have been in all Proprietary Governments, and have brought, or are now bringing, them all to a Conclusion. I will only mention one Particular common to them all. Proprietaries must have a Multitude of private Accounts and Dealings with almost all the People of their Provinces, either for Purchase money or Quit-rents. Dealings often occasion Differences, and Differences produce mutual Opinions of Injustice. If Proprietaries do not insist on small Rights, they must on the Whole lose large Sums; and if they do insist on small Rights, they seem to descend, their Dignity suffers in the Opinion of the People, and with it the Respect necessary to keep up the Authority of Government. The People, who think themselves injured in Point of Property, are discontended with the Government, and grow turbulent; and the Proprietaries using their Powers of Government to procure for themselves what they think Justice in their Points of Property, renders those Powers odious. I suspect this has had no small Share in producing the Confusions incident to those Governments. They appear, however, to be, *of all others,* the most unhappy.

At present we are in a wretched Situation. The Government that ought to keep all in Order, is itself weak, and has scarce Authority enough to keep the common Peace. Mobs assemble and kill (we scarce dare say *murder*) Numbers of innocent People in cold Blood, who were under the Protection of the Government. Proclamations are issued to bring the Rioters to Justice. Those Proclamations are treated with the utmost Indignity and Contempt. Not a Magistrate dares wag a Finger towards discovering or apprehending the *Delinquents,* (we must not call them *Murderers.*) They assemble again, and with Arms in their Hands approach the Capital. The Government truckles, condescends to cajole them, and drops all Prosecution of their Crimes; whilst honest Citizens, threatened in their Lives and Fortunes, flie the Province, as having no Confidence in the Publick Protection. We are daily threatened with more of these Tumults; and the Government, which in its Distress call'd aloud on the sober Inhabitants to come with Arms to its Assistance, now sees those who afforded that Assistance daily libell'd, abus'd, and menac'd by its Partizans for so doing; whence it has little Reason to expect such Assistance on another Occasion:—

In this Situation, what is to be done? By what Means is that Harmony between the two Branches of Government to be obtain'd, without which the internal Peace of the Province cannot be well secured? One Project is, to turn all *Quakers* out of the Assembly; or, by obtaining more Members for the Back Counties, to get a Majority in, who are not *Quakers.* This, perhaps, is not very difficult to do; and more Members for those Counties may, on other Accounts, be proper; but I much question if it would answer this End, as I see among the Members, that those who are not *Quakers,* and even those from the Back Counties, are as hearty and unanimous in opposing what they think Proprietary Injustice, as the *Quakers* themselves, if not more so. Religion has happily nothing to do with our present Differences, tho' great Pains is taken to lug it into the Squabble. And even were the *Quakers* extirpated, I doubt whether the Proprietaries, while they pursue the same Measures, would be a Whit more at their Ease.

Another Project is, to chuse none for Assembly-men but such as are Friends to the Proprietaries. The Number of Members is not so great, but that I believe this Scheme may be practicable, if you look for Representatives among Proprietary Officers and Dependants. Undoubtedly it would produce great Harmony between Governor and Assembly: But how would both of them agree with the People? Their Principles and Conduct must greatly change, if they would be elected a second Year. But that might be needless. Six Parts in Seven agreeing with the Governor, could make the House perpetual. This, however, would not probably establish Peace in the Province. The Quarrel the People now have with the Proprietaries, would then be with both the Proprietaries and Assembly. There seems to remain, then, but one Remedy for our Evils, a Remedy approved by Experience, and which has been tried with Success by other Provinces; I mean that of an immediate *Royal Government,* without the Intervention of Proprietary Powers, which, like unnecessary Springs and Movements in a Machine are so apt to produce Disorder. . . .

[Franklin here answers several arguments against royalization by citing examples of other colonies that originally were proprietaries, but had later been royalized. In none of these, Franklin avers, were religious or political liberties abridged as a result of the institution of royal government.]

In fine, it does not appear to me, that this *Change of Government* can possibly hurt us; and I see many Advantages that may flow from it. The Expression, *Change of Government,* seems, indeed, to be too extensive; and is apt to give the Idea of a general and total Change of our Laws and Constitution. It is rather and only a *Change of Governor,* that is, instead of self-interested Proprietaries, a gracious King! His Majesty who has no Views but for the Good of the People, will thenceforth appoint the Governor, who, unshackled by Proprietary Instructions, will be at Liberty to join with the Assembly in enacting wholesome Laws. At present, when the King requires Supplies of his faithful Subjects, and they are willing and desirous to grant them, the Proprietaries intervene and say, *unless our private Interests in certain Particulars are served,* NOTHING SHALL BE DONE. This insolent Tribunitial VETO has long encumbered all our Publick Affairs, and been productive of many Mischiefs. By the Measure proposed, not even the Proprietaries can justly complain of any Injury. The being oblig'd to fulfill a fair Contract is no Injury. The Crown will be under no Difficulty in compleating the old Contract made with their Father, as there needs no Application to Parliament for the necessary Sum, since half the Quit-Rents of the Lower Counties belongs to the King, and the many Years Arrears in the Proprietaries' Hands, who are the Collectors, must vastly exceed what they have a Right to demand, or any Reason to expect.

On the whole, I cannot but think, the more the

Proposal is considered, of *an humble Petition to the* KING *to take this Province under his Majesty's immediate Protection and Government,* the more unanimously we shall go into it. We are chiefly People of *three Countries: British* Spirits can no longer bear the Treatment they have received, nor will they put on the Chains prepared for them by a Fellow Subject. And the *Irish* and *Germans* have felt too severely the Oppressions of *hard-hearted Landlords and arbitrary Princes,* to wish to see, in the Proprietaries of *Pennsylvania,* both the one and the other united.

PETITION TO THE KING,[10]

FOR CHANGING THE PROPRIETARY GOVERNMENT OF PENNSYLVANIA INTO A ROYAL GOVERNMENT.

To the King's most excellent Majesty, in Council,

The Petition of the Representatives of the Freemen of the Province of Pennsylvania, in General Assembly met,

Most humbly sheweth;

That the Government of this Province by Proprietaries has by long Experience been found inconvenient, attended with many Difficulties and Obstructions to your Majesty's Service, arising from the Intervention of Proprietary private Interests in publick Affairs and Disputes concerning those Interests.

That the said Proprietary Government is weak, unable to support its own Authority, and maintain the common internal Peace of the Province; great Riots have lately arisen therein, armed Mobs marching from Place to Place, and committing violent Outrages and Insults on the Government with Impunity, to the great Terror of your Majesty's Subjects. And these Evils are not likely to receive any Remedy here, the continual Disputes between the Proprietaries and People, and their mutual Jealousies and Dislikes preventing.

We do, therefore, most humbly pray, that your

Majesty would be graciously pleased to resume the Government of this Province, making such Compensation to the Proprietaries for the same as to your Majesty's Wisdom and Goodness shall appear just and equitable, and permitting your dutiful Subjects therein to enjoy under your Majesty's more immediate Care and Protection, the Privileges that have been granted to them by and under your Royal Predecessors.

5. Continentalist

The Albany Plan of Union, the product of the Albany Congress of 1754, was chiefly the work of Franklin. The Congress had been called at the beginning of the Great War for the Empire to provide for the general defense against the French and Indians. In the Albany Plan, Franklin composed a first essay in federalism, while at the same time he tried to bring the imperial constitution into line with American realities. The Plan, though rejected both by the Crown and the various colonies, signified an awareness on the part of Franklin and many other colonial leaders of the need for colonial confederation.

The Albany Congress was a step toward intercolonial cooperation; it provided a precedent for the first Continental Congress. The Albany Plan of Union likewise was a step toward the drafting of an American fundamental law. It was altogether appropriate that Franklin, twenty years after the Albany Congress, would suggest articles of confederation for the emerging new nation, and that he would live to help draft the American Constitution.

THE ALBANY PLAN OF UNION [11]

PLAN of a Proposed Union of the Several Colonies of Masachusets-bay, New Hampshire, Coneticut, Rhode Island, New York, New Jerseys, Pensilvania, Maryland, Virginia, North Carolina, and South Carolina, For their Mutual Defence and Security, and for Extending the British Settlements in North America.

THAT humble Application be made for an Act of the Parliament of Great Britain, by Virtue of which, one

General Government may be formed in America, including all the said Colonies, within and under which Government, each Colony may retain its present Constitution, except in the Particulars wherein a Change may be directed by the said Act, as hereafter follows.

President General

Grand Council.

That the said General Government be administered by a President General, To be appointed and Supported by the Crown, and a Grand Council to be Chosen by the Representatives of the People of the Several Colonies, met in their respective Assemblies.

Election of Members.

That within_____Months after the passing of such Act, The House of Representatives in the Several Assemblies, that Happen to be Sitting within that time or that shall be Specially for that purpose Convened, may and Shall Choose Members for the Grand Council in the following Proportions, that is to say.

Masachusets-Bay .... 7.
New Hampshire .... 2.
Conecticut .... 5.
Rhode-Island .... 2.
New-York .... 4.
New-Jerseys .... 3.
Pensilvania........................... 6.
Maryland .... 4.
Virginia .... 7.
North-Carolina .... 4.
South-Carolina.................... 4.
                                    48.

Place of first meeting.

Who shall meet for the first time at the City of Philadelphia, in Pensilvania, being called by the President General as soon as conveniently may be, after his Appointment.

New Election.

That there shall be a New Election of Members for the Grand Council every three years. And on the Death or Resignation of any Member his Place shall be Supplyed by a New Choice at the next Sitting of the Assembly of the Colony he represented.

Proportion of Members after first 3 years.

That after the first three years, when the Proportion of Money arising out of each Colony to the General Treasury can be known, The Number of Members to be Chosen, for each Colony shall from time to time in all ensuing Elections be regulated by that proportion (yet so as that the Number to be Chosen by any one Province be not more than Seven nor less than Two).

Meetings of Grand Council.

Call.

That the Grand Council shall meet once in every Year, and oftner if Occasion require, at such Time and place as they shall adjourn to the last preceeding meeting, or as they shall be called to meet at by the President General, on any Emergency, he having first obtained in Writing the Consent of seven of the Members to such call, and sent due and timely Notice to the whole.

Speaker.

Continuance.

That the Grand Council have Power to Chuse their Speaker, and shall neither be Dissolved, prorogued nor Continue Sitting longer than Six Weeks at one Time without their own Consent, or the Special Command of the Crown.

Member's Allowance

That the Members of the Grand Council shall be Allowed for their Service ten shillings Sterling per Diem, during their Sessions or Journey to and from the Place of Meeting; Twenty miles to be reckoned a days Journey.

Assent of President General.
His Duty.

That the Assent of the President General be requisite, to all Acts of the Grand Council, and that it be His Office, and

Duty to cause them to be carried into Execution.

That the President General with the Advice of the Grand Council, hold or Direct all Indian Treaties in which the General Interest or Welfare of the Colony's may be Concerned; And make Peace or Declare War with the Indian Nations. That they make such Laws as they Judge Necessary for regulating all Indian Trade. That they make all Purchases from Indians for the Crown, of Lands not within the Bounds of Particular Colonies, or that shall not be within their Bounds when some of them are reduced to more Convenient Dimensions. That they make New Settlements on such Purchases, by Granting Lands in the Kings Name, reserving a Quit Rent to the Crown, for the use of the General Treasury. That they make Laws for regulating and Governing such new Settlements, till the Crown shall think fit to form them into Particular Governments.

That they raise and pay Soldiers, and build Forts for the Defence of any of the Colonies, and equip Vessels of Force to Guard the Coasts and protect the Trade on the Ocean, Lakes, or Great Rivers; But they shall not Impress Men in any Colonies, without the Consent of its Legislature. That for these purposes they have Power to make Laws And lay and Levy such General Duties, Imposts, or Taxes, as to them shall appear most equal and Just, Considering the Ability and other Circumstances of the Inhabitants in the Several Colonies, and such as may be Collected with the least Inconvenience to the People, rather discouraging Luxury, than

Marginal notes:

Power of President and Grand Council.
Peace and War.

Indian Purchases.

New Settlements.

Laws to Govern them.

Raise Soldiers &c.

Lakes.
Not to Impress

Power to make Laws Duties &c.

Treasurer.

Money how
to Issue.

Accounts.

Quorum.

Laws to be
Transmitted.

Death of Presi-
dent General.

Officers how
Appointed.

Loading Industry with unnecessary Burthens. That they may Appoint a General Treasurer and a Particular Treasurer in each Government, when Necessary, And from Time to Time may Order the Sums in the Treasuries of each Government, into the General Treasury, or draw on them for Special payments as they find most Convenient; yet no money to Issue, but by joint Orders of the President General and Grand Council Except where Sums have been Appropriated to particular Purposes, And the President General is previously impowered By an Act to draw for such sums.

That the General Accounts shall be yearly Settled and Reported to the Several Assembly's.

That a Quorum of the Grand Council impower'd to Act with the President General, do consist of Twenty-five Members, among whom there shall be one, or more from a Majority of the Colonies. That the Laws made by them for the Purposes aforesaid, shall not be repugnant but as near as may be agreeable to the Laws of England, and Shall be transmitted to the King in Council for Approbation, as Soon as may be after their Passing and if not disapproved within Three years after Presentation to remain in Force.

That in case of the Death of the President General The Speaker of the Grand Council for the Time Being shall Succeed, and be Vested with the Same Powers, and Authority, to Continue until the King's Pleasure be known.

That all Military Commission Officers Whether for Land or Sea Service, to Act under this General Constituition, shall be

Nominated by the President General But the Approbation of the Grand Council, is to be Obtained before they receive their Commissions, And all Civil Officers are to be Nominated, by the Grand Council, and to receive the President General's Approbation, before they Officiate; But in Case of Vacancy by Death or removal of any Officer Civil or Military under this Constitution, The Governor of the Province, in which such Vacancy happens, may Appoint till the Pleasure of the President General and Grand Council can be known. That the Particular Military as well as Civil Establishments in each Colony remain in their present State, this General Constitution Notwithstanding. And that on Sudden Emergencies any Colony may Defend itself, and lay the Accounts of Expence thence Arisen, before the President General and Grand Council, who may allow and order payment of the same As far as they Judge such Accounts Just and reasonable.

Vacancies how Supplied.

Each Colony may defend itself on Emergency.

6. Patriot

Franklin's appearance before Parliament at the height of the movement for repeal of the Stamp Act made him the unofficial American ambassador to England. His examination was widely reprinted in England, Europe and America, where it assured his reputation as a patriot. In France, the physiocrats reprinted the examination in their journal because they believed that Frankliln's words verified their economic theories.

A year after the repeal of the Stamp Act, Franklin described to the eminent Scottish jurist Lord Kames his concept of the nature of the imperial constitution.

On the Propriety of Taxing America first appeared in the British press in April, 1767, at the same time that Franklin expressed his concept of the empire to Lord Kames. The piece is one example of the innumerable propaganda essays composed for newspaper distribution by Franklin for the patriot cause. Although it repeats many of the arguments of the Parliamentary examination, its careful organization provides for a more orderly exposition of Franklin's views. Writing as a disinterested Englishman, "Benevolus," Franklin, as in the examination, refers to a supposed American distinction between internal and external taxation. He himself had already discarded this distinction, but he evidently believed that it was still useful in publicly saving something of Parliamentary authority in America. The alleged American acceptance of Parliamentary regulation of trade served to allay British suspicions of the colonists' denial of *all* Parliamentary authority in America.

THE EXAMINATION OF DOCTOR BENJAMIN FRANKLIN
IN THE BRITISH HOUSE OF COMMONS,
RELATIVE TO THE REPEAL OF THE AMERICAN STAMP ACT, IN 1766.[12]

Q. What is your name, and place of abode?

A. Franklin, of Philadelphia. . . .

Q. Do you think the people of America would submit to pay the stamp duty, if it was moderated?

A. No, never, unless compelled by force of arms. . . .

Q. What was the temper of America towards Great Britain before the year 1763?

A. The best in the world. They submitted willingly to the government of the Crown, and paid, in all their courts, obedience to acts of parliament. Numerous as the people are in the several provinces, they cost you nothing in forts, citadels, garrisons, or armies, to keep them in subjection. They were governed by this country at the expence only of a little pen, ink and paper. They were led by a thread. They had not only a respect, but an affection for Great-Britain; for its laws, its customs and manners, and even a fondness for its fashions, that greatly increased the commerce. Natives of Britain were always treated with particular regard; to be an Old-England man was, of itself, a character of some respect, and gave a kind of rank among us.

Q. And what is their temper now?

A. O, very much altered.

Q. Did you ever hear the authority of parliament to make laws for America questioned till lately?

A. The authority of parliament was allowed to be valid in all laws, except such as should lay internal taxes. It was never disputed in laying duties to regulate commerce.

Q. In what proportion hath population increased in America?

A. I think the inhabitants of all the provinces together, taken at a medium, double in about 25 years. But their demand for British manufactures increases much faster, as the consumption is not merely in proportion to their numbers, but grows with the growing abilities of the same numbers to pay for them. In 1723, the whole importation from Britain to Pennsylvania, was but about 15,000 Pounds Sterling; it is now near Half a Million.

Q. In what light did the people of America use to consider the parliament of Great-Britain?

A. They considered the parliament as the great bulwark and security of their liberties and privileges, and always spoke of it with the utmost respect and veneration. Arbitrary ministers, they thought, might possibly, at times, attempt to oppress them; but they relied on it, that the parliament, on application, would always give redress. They remembered, with gratitude, a strong instance of this, when a bill was brought into parliament, with a clause, to make royal instructions laws in the colonies, which the House of Commons would not pass, and it was thrown out.

Q. And have they not still the same respect for parliament?

A. No, it is greatly lessened.

Q. To what causes is that owing?

A. To a concurrence of causes; the restraints lately

laid on their trade, by which the bringing of foreign gold and silver into the Colonies was prevented; the prohibition of making paper money among themselves; and then demanding a new and heavy tax by stamps; taking away, at the same time, trials by juries, and refusing to receive and hear their humble petitions.

Q. Don't you think they would submit to the stamp-act, if it was modified, the obnoxious parts taken out, and the duty reduced to some particulars, of small moment?

A. No; they will never submit to it. . . .

Q. What is your opinion of a future tax, imposed on the same principle with that of the stamp-act? How would the Americans receive it?

A. Just as they do this. They would not pay it.

Q. Have not you heard of the resolutions of this House, and of the House of Lords, asserting the right of parliament relating to America, including a power to tax the people there?

A. Yes, I have heard of such resolutions.

Q. What will be the opinion of the Americans on those resolutions?

A. They will think them unconstitutional and unjust.

Q. Was it an opinion in America before 1763, that the parliament had no right to lay taxes and duties there?

A. I never heard any objection to the right of laying duties to regulate commerce; but a right to lay internal taxes was never supposed to be in parliament, as we are not represented there. . . .

Q. But in case a governor, acting by instruction, should call on an assembly to raise the necessary supplies, and the assembly should refuse to do it, do you not think it would then be for the good of the people of the colony, as well as necessary to government, that the parliament should tax them?

A. I do not think it would be necessary. If an assembly could possibly be so absurd, as to refuse raising the supplies requisite for the maintenance of government among them, they could not long remain in such a situation; the disorders and confusion occasioned by it must soon bring them to reason.

Q. If it should not, ought not the right to be in Great Britain of applying a remedy?

A. A right, only to be used in such a case, I should have no objection to; supposing it to be used merely for the good of the people of the Colony.

Q. But who is to judge of that, Britain or the Colony?

A. Those that feel can best judge.

Q. You say the Colonies have always submitted to external taxes, and object to the right of parliament only in laying internal taxes; now can you shew, that there is any kind of difference between the two taxes to the Colony on which they may be laid?

A. I think the difference is very great. An external tax is a duty laid on commodities imported; that duty is added to the first cost and other charges on the commodity, and, when it is offered to sale, makes a part of the price. If the people do not like it at that price, they refuse it; they are not obliged to pay it. But an internal tax is forced from the people without their consent, if not laid by their own representatives. The stamp act says, we shall have no commerce, make no exchange of property with each other, neither purchase, nor grant, nor recover debts; we shall neither marry nor make our wills, unless we pay such and such sums; and thus it is intended to extort our money from us, or ruin us by the consequences of refusing to pay it.

Q. But supposing the internal tax or duty to be laid on the necessaries of life, imported into your colony, will not that be the same thing in its effects as an internal tax?

A. I do not know a single article imported into the Northern Colonies, but what they can either do without, or make themselves. . . .

Q. Considering the resolutions of parliament, as to the right, do you think, if the stamp act is repealed, that the North Americans will be satisfied?

A. I believe they will.

Q. Why do you think so?

A. I think the resolutions of right will give them very little concern, if they are never attempted to be carried into practice. The Colonies will probably consider themselves in the same situation, in that respect, with Ireland; they know you claim the same right with regard to Ireland, but you never exercise it. And they may believe you never will exercise it in the Colonies, any more than in Ireland, unless on some very extraordinary occasion.

Q. But who are to be the judges of that extraordinary occasion? Is not the parliament?

A. Though the parliament may judge of the occasion, the people will think it can never exercise such right, till representatives from the Colonies are admitted into parliament; and that, when ever the occasion arises, representatives will be ordered. . . .

Q. Did the Americans ever dispute the controuling power of parliament to regulate the commerce?

A. No.

Q. Can any thing less than a military force carry the stamp act into execution?

A. I do not see how a military force can be applied to that purpose.

Q. Why may it not?

A. Suppose a military force sent into America, they will find nobody in arms; what are they then to do? They cannot force a man to take stamps who chuses to do without them. They will not find a rebellion; they may indeed make one.

Q. If the act is not repealed, what do you think will be the consequences?

A. A total loss of the respect and affection the people of America bear to this country, and of all the commerce that depends on that respect and affection.

Q. How can the commerce be affected?

A. You will find, that if the act is not repealed, they will take very little of your manufactures in a short time.

Q. Is it in their power to do without them?

A. I think they may very well do without them.

Q. Is it their interest not to take them?

A. The goods they take from Britain are either necessaries, mere conveniences, or superfluities. The first, as cloth, &c. with a little industry they can make at home; the second they can do without, till they are able to provide them among themselves; and the last, which are much the greatest part, they will strike off immediately. They are mere articles of fashion, purchased and consumed because the fashion in a respected country; but will now be detested and rejected. The people have already struck off, by general agreement, the use of all goods fashionable in mournings, and many thousand pounds worth are sent back as unsaleable.

Q. Is it their interest to make cloth at home?

A. I think they may at present get it cheaper from Britain, I mean of the same fineness and workmanship; but, when one considers other circumstances, the restraints on their trade, and the difficulty of making remittances, it is their interest to make every thing.

Q. Suppose an act of internal regulations connected with a tax; how would they receive it?

A. I think it would be objected to.

Q. Then no regulation with a tax would be submitted to?

A. Their opinion is, that, when aids to the Crown are wanted, they are to be asked of the several assemblies, according to the old established usage; who will, as they always have done, grant them freely. And that their money ought not to be given away, without their consent, by persons at a distance, unacquainted with their circumstances and abilities. The granting aids to the Crown is the only means they have of recommending themselves to their sovereign; and they think it extremely hard and unjust, that a body of men, in which they have no representatives, should make a merit to itself of giving and granting what is not its own, but theirs; and deprive them of a right they esteem of the utmost value and importance, as it is the security of all their other rights.

Q. But is not the post-office, which they have long received, a tax as well as a regulation?

A. No; the money paid for the postage of a letter is not of the nature of a tax; it is merely a quantum meruit for a service done; no person is compellable to pay the money if he does not chuse to receive the service. A man may still, as before the act, send his letter by a servant, a special messenger, or a friend, if he thinks it cheaper and safer. . . .

Q. Supposing the stamp act continued, and enforced, do you imagine that ill humour will induce the Americans to give as much for worse manufactures of their own, and use them, preferably to better of ours?

A. Yes, I think so. People will pay as freely to gratify one passion as another, their resentment as their pride.

Q. Would the people at Boston discontinue their trade?

A. The merchants are a very small number compared with the body of the people, and must discontinue their trade, if nobody will buy their goods.

Q. What are the body of the people in the Colonies?

A. They are farmers, husbandmen or planters.

Q. Would they suffer the produce of their lands to rot?

A. No; but they would not raise so much. They would manufacture more, and plough less.

Q. Would they live without the administration of justice in civil matters, and suffer all the inconveniencies of such a situation for any considerable time, rather than take the stamps, supposing the stamps were protected by a sufficient force, where every one might have them?

A. I think the supposition impracticable, that the stamps should be so protected as that every one might have them. The act requires sub-distributors to be appointed in every county town, district, and village, and they would be necessary. But the principal distributors, who were to have had a considerable profit on the whole, have not thought it worth while to continue in the office; and I think it impossible to find sub-distributors fit to be trusted, who, for the trifling profit that must come to their share, would incur the odium, and run the hazard, that would attend it; and, if they could be found,

I think it impracticable to protect the stamps in so many distant and remote places.

Q. But in places where they could be protected, would not the people use them, rather than remain in such a situation, unable to obtain any right, or recover by law any debt?

A. It is hard to say what they would do. I can only judge what other people will think, and how they will act, by what I feel within myself. I have a great many debts due to me in America, and I had rather they should remain unrecoverable by any law, than submit to the stamp act. They will be debts of honour. It is my opinion the people will either continue in that situation, or find some way to extricate themselves; perhaps by generally agreeing to proceed in the courts without stamps.

Q. What do you think a sufficient military force to protect the distribution of the stamps in every part of America?

A. A very great force; I can't say what, if the disposition of America is for a general resistance.

Q. What is the number of men in America able to bear arms, or of disciplined militia?

A. There are, I suppose, at least. . . .

[*Question objected to. He withdrew. Called in again.*]

Q. Is the American stamp act an equal tax on the country?

A. I think not.

Q. Why so?

A. The greatest part of the money must arise from law-suits for the recovery of debts, and be paid by the lower sort of people, who were too poor easily to pay their debts. It is, therefore, a heavy tax on the poor, and a tax upon them for being poor.

Q. But will not this increase of expence be a means of lessening the number of law-suits?

A. I think not; for as the costs all fall upon the debtor, and are to be paid by him, they would be no discouragement to the creditor to bring his action.

Q. Would it not have the effect of excessive usury?

A. Yes; as an oppression of the debtor. . . .

Q. If the stamp act should be repealed, would not the Americans think they could oblige the parliament to repeal every external tax-law now in force?

A. It is hard to answer questions of what people at such a distance will think.

Q. But what do you imagine they will think were the motives of repealing the act? ·

A. I suppose they will think that it was repealed from a conviction of its inexpediency; and they will rely upon it, that while the same inexpediency subsists, you will never attempt to make such another.

Q. What do you mean by its inexpediency?

A. I mean its inexpediency on several accounts; the poverty and inability of those who were to pay the tax; the general discontent it has occasioned; and the impracticability of enforcing it.

Q. If the act should be repealed, and the legislature should shew its resentment to the opposers of the stamp act, would the Colonies acquiesce in the authority of the legislature? What is your opinion they would do?

A. I don't doubt at all, that if the legislature repeal the stamp act, the Colonies will acquiesce in the authority.

Q. But if the legislature should think fit to ascertain its right to lay taxes, by any act laying a small tax, contrary to their opinion, would they submit to pay the tax?

A. The proceedings of the people in America have been considered too much together. The proceedings of the assemblies have been very different from those of the mobs, and should be distinguished, as having no connection with each other. The assemblies have only peaceably resolved what they take to be their rights; they have taken no measures for opposition by force; they have not built a fort, raised a man, or provided a grain of ammunition, in order to such opposition. The ringleaders of riots, they think ought to be punished; they would punish them themselves, if they could. Every sober, sensible man, would wish to see rioters punished, as, otherwise, peaceable people have no security of person or estate. But as to an internal tax, how small soever, laid by the legislature here on the people there, while they have no representatives in this legislature, I think it will never be submitted to. They will oppose it to the last. . . .

Q. If the stamp act should be repealed, and an act should pass, ordering the assemblies of the Colonies to indemnify the sufferers by the riots, would they obey it?

A. That is a question I cannot answer.

Q. Suppose the King should require the Colonies to grant a revenue, and the parliament should be against their doing it, do they think they can grant a revenue to the King, without the consent of the parliament of Great-Britain?

A. That is a deep question. As to my own opinion, I should think myself at liberty to do it, and should do it, if I liked the occasion.

Q. When money has been raised in the Colonies, upon requisitions, has it not been granted to the King?

A. Yes, always; but the requisitions have generally been for some service expressed, as to raise, clothe, and pay troops, and not for money only.

Q. If the act should pass requiring the American assemblies to make compensation to the sufferers, and they should disobey it, and then the parliament should, by another act, lay an internal tax, would they then obey it?

A. The people will pay no internal tax; and I think an act to oblige the assemblies to make compensation is unnecessary; for I am of opinion, that, as soon as the present heats are abated, they will take the matter into consideration, and if it is right to be done, they will do it of themselves. . . .

Q. If the parliament should repeal the stamp act, will the assembly of Pennsylvania rescind their resolutions?

A. I think not.

Q. Before there was any thought of the stamp act, did they wish for a representation in parliament?

A. No.

Q. Don't you know, that there is, in the Pennsylvania charter, an express reservation of the right of parliament to lay taxes there?

A. I know there is a clause in the charter, by which the King grants, that he will levy no taxes on the inhabitants, unless it be with the consent of the assembly, or by act of parliament.

Q. How, then, could the assembly of Pennsylvania assert that laying a tax on them by the stamp act was an infringement of their rights?

A. They understand it thus; by the same charter, and otherwise, they are entitled to all the privileges and liberties of Englishmen; they find in the great charters, and the petition and declaration of rights, that one of the privileges of English subjects is, that they are not to be taxed but by their common consent; they have therefore relied upon it, from the first settlement of the province, that the parliament never would, nor could, by colour of that clause in the charter, assume a right of taxing them, till it had qualified itself to exercise such right, by admitting representatives from the people to be taxed, who ought to make a part of that common consent.

Q. Are there any words in the charter that justify that construction?

A. "The common rights of Englishmen," as declared by Magna Charta, and the petition of right, all justify it.

Q. Does the distinction between internal and external taxes exist in the words of the charter?

A. No, I believe not.

Q. Then, may they not, by the same interpretation, object to the parliament's right of external taxation?

A. They never have hitherto. Many arguments have been lately used here to shew them, that there is no difference, and that, if you have no right to tax them internally, you have none to tax them externally, or make any other law to bind them. At present they do not reason so; but in time they may possibly be convinced by these arguments.

Q. Do not the resolutions of the Pennsylvania assembly say, all taxes?

A. If they do, they mean only internal taxes; the same words have not always the same meaning here and in the Colonies. By taxes, they mean internal taxes; by duties, they mean customs; these are their ideas of the language. . . .

Q. Can we, at this distance, be competent judges of what favours are necessary.

A. The parliament have supposed it, by claiming a right to make tax-laws for America; I think it impossible.

Q. Would the repeal of the stamp act be any discouragement of your manufactures? Will the people that have begun to manufacture decline it?

A. Yes, I think they will; especially if, at the same time, the trade is opened again, so that remittances can be easily made. I have known several instances that make it probable. In the war before last, tobacco being low, and making little remittance, the people of Virginia went generally into family manufactures. Afterwards, when tobacco bore a better price, they returned to the use of British manufactures. So fullingmills were very much disused in the last war in Pennsylvania, because bills were then plenty, and remittances could easily be made to Britain for English cloth and other goods.

Q. If the stamp act should be repealed, would it induce the assemblies of America to acknowledge the rights of parliament to tax them, and would they erase their resolutions?

A. No, never.

Q. Are there no means of obliging them to erase those resolutions?

A. None that I know of; they will never do it, unless compelled by force of arms.

Q. Is there a power on earth that can force them to erase them?

A. No power, how great soever, can force men to change their opinions. . . .

Q. What used to be the pride of the Americans?

A. To indulge in the fashions and manufactures of Great Britain.

Q. What is now their pride?

A. To wear their old cloaths over again, till they can make new ones.

TO LORD KAMES[13]

London, April 11, 1767

. . . . It becomes a matter of great importance that clear ideas should be formed on solid principles, both in Britain and America, of the true political relation between them, and the mutual duties belonging to that relation. Till this is done, they will be often jarring. I know none whose knowledge, sagacity and impartiality qualify him so thoroughly for such a service, as yours do you. I wish therefore you would consider it. You may thereby be the happy instrument of great good to the nation, and of preventing much mischief and bloodshed. I am fully persuaded with you, that a *Consolidating Union,* by a fair and equal representation of all the parts of this empire in Parliament, is the only firm basis on which its political grandeur and prosperity can be founded. Ireland once wished it, but now rejects it. The time has been, when the colonies might have been pleased with it: they are now *indifferent* about it; and if it is much longer delayed, they too will *refuse* it. But the pride of this people cannot bear the thought of it, and therefore it will be delayed. Every man in England seems to consider himself as a piece of a sovereign over America; seems to jostle himself into the throne with the King, and talks of *our subjects in the Colonies.* The Parliament cannot well and wisely make laws suited to the Colonies, without being properly and truly informed of their circumstances, abilities, temper, &c. This it cannot be, without representatives from thence: and yet it is fond of this power, and averse to the only means of acquiring the necessary knowledge for exercising it; which is desiring to be *omnipotent,* without being *ominiscient.*

I have mentioned that the contest is likely to be revived. It is on this occasion. In the same session with the stamp act, an act was passed to regulate the quartering of soldiers in America; when the bill was first brought in, it contained a clause, empowering the officers to quarter their soldiers in private houses: this we warmly opposed, and got it omitted. The bill passed, however, with a clause, that empty houses, barns, &c., should be hired for them, and that the respective provinces where they were should pay the expense and furnish firing, bedding, drink, and some other articles to the soldiers *gratis*. There is no way for any province to do this, but by the Assembly's making a law to raise the money. The Pennsylvanian Assembly has made such a law: the New York Assembly has refused to do it: and now all the talk here is of sending a force to compel them.

The reasons given by the Assembly to the Governor, for the refusal, are, that they understand the act to mean the furnishing such things to soldiers, only while on their march through the country, and not to great bodies of soldiers, to be fixt as at present, in the province; the burthen in the latter case being greater than the inhabitants can bear: That it would put it in the power of the Captain-General to oppress the province at pleasure, &c. But there is supposed to be another reason at bottom, which they intimate, though they do not plainly express it; to wit, that it is of the nature of an *internal tax* laid on them by Parliament, which has no right so to do. Their refusal is here called *Rebellion,* and punishment is thought of.

Now waving that point of right, and supposing the Legislatures in America subordinate to the Legislature of Great Britain, one might conceive, I think, a power in the superior Legislature to forbid the inferior Legislatures making particular laws; but to enjoin it to make a particular law contrary to its own judgment, seems improper; an Assembly or Parliament not being an *executive* officer of Government, whose duty it is, in lawmaking, to obey orders, but a *deliberative* body, who are to consider what comes before them, its propriety, practicability, or possibility, and to determine accordingly: The very nature of a Parliament seems to be de-

stroyed, by supposing it may be bound, and compelled
by a law of a superior Parliament, to make a law contrary to its own judgment.

Indeed, the act of Parliament in question has not, as
in other acts, when a duty is enjoined, directed a penalty
on neglect or refusal, and a mode of recovering that
penalty. It seems, therefore, to the people in America as
a mere requisition, which they are at liberty to comply
with or not, as it may suit or not suit the different circumstances of different provinces. Pennsylvania has
therefore voluntarily complied. New York, as I said
before, has refused. The Ministry that made the act, and
all their adherents, call for vengeance. The present Ministry are perplext, and the measures they will finally take
on the occasion, are yet unknown. But sure I am, that,
if *Force* is used, great mischief will ensue; the affections
of the people of America to this country will be alienated; your commerce will be diminished; and a total
separation of interests be the final consequence.

It is a common, but mistaken notion here, that the
Colonies were planted at the expence of Parliament, and
that therefore the Parliament has a right to tax them,
&c. The truth is, they were planted at the expence of
private adventurers, who went over there to settle, with
leave of the King, given by charter. On receiving this
leave, and those charters, the adventurers voluntarily
engaged to remain the King's subjects, though in a foreign country; a country which had not been conquered
by either King or Parliament, but was possessed by a free
people.

When our planters arrived, they purchased the lands
of the natives, without putting King or Parliament to
any expence. Parliament had no hand in their settlement, was never so much as consulted about their constitution, and took no kind of notice of them, till many
years after they were established. I except only the two
modern Colonies, or rather attempts to make Colonies,
(for they succeed but poorly, and as yet hardly deserve
the name of Colonies), I mean Georgia and Nova Scotia,
which have hitherto been little better than Parliamen-

tary jobs. Thus all the colonies acknowledge the King as their sovereign; his Governors there represent his person: Laws are made by their Assemblies or little Parliaments, with the Governor's assent, subject still to the King's pleasure to confirm or annul them: Suits arising in the Colonies, and differences between Colony and Colony, are determined by the King in Council. In this view, they seem so many separate little states, subject to the same Prince. The *sovereignty of the King* is therefore easily understood. But nothing is more common here than to talk of the *sovereignty* of PARLIAMENT, and the *sovereignty of* THIS NATION over the Colonies; a kind of sovereignty, the idea of which is not so clear, nor does it clearly appear on what foundation it is established. On the other hand, it seems necessary for the common good of the empire, that a power be lodged somewhere, to regulate its general commerce: this can be placed nowhere so properly as in the Parliament of Great Britain; and therefore, though that power has in some instances been executed with great partiality to Britain, and prejudice to the Colonies, they have nevertheless always submitted to it. Custom-houses are established in all of them, by virtue of laws made here, and the duties constantly paid, except by a few smugglers, such as are here and in all countries; but internal taxes laid on them by Parliament, are still and ever will be objected to, for the reasons that you will see in the mentioned Examination.

Upon the whole, I have lived so great a part of my life in Britain, and have formed so many friendships in it, that I love it, and sincerely wish it prosperity; and therefore wish to see that Union, on which alone I think it can be secured and established. As to America, the advantages of such a union to her are not so apparent. She may suffer at present under the arbitrary power of this country; she may suffer for a while in a separation from it; but these are temporary evils that she will outgrow. Scotland and Ireland are differently circumstanced. Confined by the sea, they can scarcely increase in numbers, wealth and strength, so as to overbalance England. But America, an immense territory, favoured by Nature with all advantages of climate, soil, great navigable rivers, and lakes, &c. must become a great country, populous and mighty; and will, in a less time than is generally conceived, be able to shake off any shackles that may be imposed on her, and perhaps place them on the imposers. In the mean time, every act of oppression will sour their tempers, lessen greatly, if not annihilate the profits of your commerce with them, and hasten their final revolt; for the seeds of liberty are universally found there, and nothing can eradicate them. And yet, there remains among that people, so much respect, veneration and affection for Britain, that, if cultivated prudently, with kind usage, and tenderness for their privileges, they might be easily governed still for ages, without force, or any considerable expence. But I do not see here a sufficient quantity of the wisdom, that is necessary to produce such a conduct, and I lament, the want of it. . . .

ON THE PROPRIETY OF TAXING AMERICA [14]

To the Printer of the London Chronicle.
Sir,
The propriety of taxing America by laws made here, is frequently handled in public papers and pamphlets by writers, who seem not well acquainted with the circumstances of that country, or with the points in dispute. Will you give me leave, through your paper, to offer some information, that may be of use to them in their future discussions. The following positions are generally taken for granted;

1. That the colonies were settled at the expence of parliament.

2. That they received their constitutions from parliament, which could not be supposed to give away its own powers of taxing them.

3. That they have been constantly protected from the Indians, at the expence of money granted by parliament.

4. That the two last wars were entered into for their protection.

5. That they refused to contribute towards the expence of those wars.

6. That they are great gainers by the event of the last war.

7. That they pay no taxes.

8. That they contend the parliament of Great Britain has no authority over them.

Upon these positions assumed as facts, there has been much declamation, on the unreasonableness, selfishness, ingratitude of the Colonists, (some have even used the word *rebellion*) and government is urged to proceed against them by force of arms. Let us coolly consider these positions, one by one.

1. *That the colonies were settled at the expence of parliament.*—If we examine our records, the journals of parliament, we shall not find that a farthing was ever granted for the settling any colonies before the last reign, and then only for Georgia and Nova Scotia, which are still of little value. But the colonies of New-Hampshire, Massachusets, Rhode Island, Connecticut, New-York, (as far as the English were concerned in it) New-Jersey, Pensylvania, Maryland, Virginia, North and South Carolina, &c. were settled at the private expence of the adventurers.

2. *That they received their constitutions from parliament, which could not be supposed to give away its own power of taxing them.*—The charters themselves shew that they were granted by the King; and the truth is, that parliament had no participation in these grants, and was not so much as consulted upon them. The right to the territory in America, was supposed to be in the King, that is, so far as to exclude the claim of any other European Prince; but in reality was in the tribes of Indians who inhabited it, and from whom the settlers were obliged to purchase or conquer it at *their own expence,* without any expence to parliament. But they settled there with the King's leave, promising him their allegiance, which they hold faithfully to this day.

3. *That they have been constantly protected from the Indians at the expence of parliament.*—No grants for

that purpose appear on our records, and the fact is, that they protected themselves, at their own expence, for near 150 years after the first settlement, and never thought of applying to parliament for any aid against the Indians.

4. *That the two last wars were entered into for their protection.*—The truth is, that the war with Spain, 1739, was occasioned by the Spaniards interrupting with their guarda costas the British trade, carried on indeed in the American seas, but in British ships chiefly, and wholly with British manufactures. It was, therefore, a war for the protection of our commerce, and not for the protection of the people of America. The last war began concerning the boundaries of *Acadia,* a country ceded to the crown by the treaty of Aix-la-Chapelle; the lands in dispute belonged to the crown only, and to no colony or Colonist whatever: Another motive was, the security of the Ohio trade with the Indians, a trade carried on chiefly for account of British merchants, members of that company, and wholly with the manufactures of Britain, which had also all the skins and furs produced by that trade. It was, therefore, a British interest, that was to be defended and secured by that war. The colonies were in peace, and the settlers had not been attacked or molested in the least, 'till after the miscarriage of Braddock's expedition to the Ohio.

5. *That the colonies refused to contribute their share towards the expence of those wars.* The fact is, that in the first war, upon requisitions from the crown, the colonies sent between 3 and 4000 men to join our army in the seige of Carthagena; and in the last war they raised and paid 25,000 men, a number equal to those sent from Britain; which was far beyond their proportion. If we examine the journals of the house of commons, we shall there find, that their conduct was approved of by government here; for every year during the war, a message came down from the crown to this purpose, "That his Majesty being highly sensible of the great zeal and vigour with which his faithful subjects in America had exerted themselves in defence of his rights and territories there, recommended it to parliament to enable him to

make them some compensation, &c." The parliament did accordingly grant £200 000 yearly for that purpose, which his Majesty divided among the colonies in honorary gratuities; not to discharge their accounts, for they produced none, and their expence was ten times greater than the money returned to them. But if they had not in our own judgment done their share, and more, there could have been no room or reason for any payment, or any compensation.

6. *That the colonies are great gainers by the event of the last war.* There is to be sure a great extent of country conquered. It was however ceded not to the colonies, but to the crown, which is now granting it away in large tracts to British gentlemen. No colony has more landed property than it had before the war; and though it may be supposed the land the colonists had in possession was increased in value by being rendered more secure, the fact is otherwise; for it is in land as in other commodities, the greater the quantity at market, the lower the price; so that the value of the old possessions is really diminished instead of being increased. Plenty of money was indeed circulated in the colonies by means of the war, but this was a temporary advantage only, and by introducing habits of luxury and expence before unknown there, the money is not only all returned already to Britain, and with it what money there was before in the colonies, but has left them under a load of debt to the British merchants, that they must now labour hard to discharge; besides the heavy public debt incurred by the war itself.

7. *That the colonies pay no taxes.* There cannot be a greater mistake than this. They have their own civil and military establishments to support, and the public debt just mentioned to discharge, for which heavy taxes are and must be levied among themselves. They are besides under great burthens that we are free from. Our ancestors in Britain have long since defrayed the expence of most of our publick buildings, churches, colleges, highways, bridges, and other conveniences, which are left to us as an inheritance: These our people who remove to America cannot enjoy, but as they extend their settle-

ments, are obliged to tax themselves anew for all such publick works: And all who know their circumstances, and the taxes they really pay, are and must be satisfied, that those taxes in proportion to the property in the country, are not only equal but greater than the taxes paid in Britain compared with the property in Britain.

8. *That the colonies contend the parliament of Britain has no authority over them.* The truth is, that all acts of the British legislature, expressly extending to the colonies, have ever been received there as laws, and executed in their courts, the right of parliament to make them being never yet contested, acts to raise money upon the colonies by internal taxes only and alone excepted. In granting their money to the crown, they think their assent is constitutionally necessary; they say that voluntary grants by themselves of what is their own, are the only means they have of manifesting their loyalty and duty, and recommending themselves to the favour of their sovereign. That they have always made such grants chearfully when required, in proportion to their abilities: And they think it hard that a parliament in which they have no representative, should make a merit to itself by granting *their money* to the crown without asking their consent, and deprive them of the privilege of granting it themselves, which they have always enjoyed, never abused, and are always ready and willing to exercise in behalf of the crown when occasion shall require, and the usual requisitions are made to their assemblies. This is the *sole point* that has been in dispute: It is now indeed determined here by an act of parliament, and therefore I say no more of it; and should not have said so much but to obviate mistakes of what the point really was. The colonies submit to pay all external taxes laid on them by way of duty on merchandizes imported into their country, and never disputed the authority of parliament to lay such duties. The distinction indeed between internal and external taxes is here looked upon as groundless and frivolous, and some are apt to wonder how a sensible people should ever advance it. But an American founds it thus; an internal tax to be raised in the colonies by authority of parliament, forces the money out of my

purse without the consent of my representative in assembly: An external tax or duty is added to the first cost and other charges of the commodity on which it is laid, and makes a part of its price: If I do not like it, at that price I refuse it. If I do like it, I pay the price, and do not need to give my consent by my representative for the payment of this tax, because I can consent to it myself in person. However, whether there be validity in this distinction or not, seems to be immaterial; since if they are willing to pay *external* though not *internal* taxes, and we say they are the same, 'tis then the same thing to us, provided we get the same money from them, as much as they ought or are able to pay, and we may let them please themselves with their futile distinction as long as they think proper.

There is however another distinction of theirs, which will here appear less exceptionable. The colonies were originally chartered companies for the purposes of trade and settlement. They joined a more than equal number of troops with ours in the operations of the American war: Advantages were obtained by that war, to wit, greater security of trade and settlement free from the interruptions of the French, and a great extent of territory and dominion. In dividing these advantages they suppose, that the security of trade and settlement only belongs to them, and that the territory and dominion acquired appertain to the crown. They never pretended to lay claim to the least part of either of these latter advantages. Their adversaries, who think *another trading Company* (in exactly *similar* circumstances) have a right to both, must at least allow, on the same principle, that the colonies in this particular are modest, however silly it may have been in them to waive their pretentions in favour of government. And probably, whenever these Gentlemen come again into power, a regard to justice, and a noble disdain to take advantage of the simplicity and ignorance of the colonists, will induce them to give the colonies all the same advantages now claimed for that other company.

I hope, Mr. Printer, that your Readers will, on considering the premises, be a little less hasty in censuring their brethren in America, upon the groundless surmises, and mistaken facts, so frequently delivered as truths in our public papers; and that they will consider the importance of a firm union between the two countries, in affection as well as in government; and not suffer themselves to be exasperated by false insinuations against the *absent* and the *distant*.

I am, yours, &c.   BENEVOLUS.

7. Political Satirist

Franklin was a master of political satire and parody. His work in this genre is reminiscent of the writing of Jonathan Swift, perhaps the greatest satirist in the language. *Rules by which a Great Empire may be reduced to a Small One* is a broad parody of British policies toward her colonies. *An Edict of the King of Prussia* is a burlesque of the mercantilist system. Here Franklin has King Frederick proclaim a Prussian monopoly of the trade of England, a monopoly based upon the ancient migrations there of various Germanic peoples. Both the *Rules* and the *Edict* were written in 1773, the year of the Tea Act when Anglo-American relations had disastrously deteriorated. Franklin wrote *The Sale of the Hessians* during his ministry to France. England paid Germany's rulers for mercenary soldiers to fight in America on the basis of the mercenary mortality rate. The arrangement was ideally suited to the satiric talents of Franklin, who writes as Hesse's Count de Schaumbergh to his military commander in America.

RULES
BY WHICH
A GREAT EMPIRE MAY BE REDUCED TO A
SMALL ONE;
PRESENTED TO A LATE MINISTER,
WHEN HE ENTERED UPON HIS
ADMINISTRATION.[15]

AN ancient Sage boasted, that, tho' he could not fiddle, he knew how to make a *great city* of a *little one*. The science that I, a modern simpleton, am about to communicate, is the very reverse.

I address myself to all ministers who have the management of extensive dominions, which from their very greatness are become troublesome to govern, because the multiplicity of their affairs leaves no time for *fiddling.*

I. In the first place, gentlemen, you are to consider, that a great empire, like a great cake, is most easily diminished at the edges. Turn your attention, therefore, first to your *remotest* provinces; that, as you get rid of them, the next may follow in order.

II. That the possibility of this separation may always exist, take special care the provinces are never incorporated with the mother country; that they do not enjoy the same common rights, the same privileges in commerce; and that they are governed by *severer* laws, all of *your enacting,* without allowing them any share in the choice of the legislators. By carefully making and preserving such distinctions, you will (to keep to my simile of the cake) act like a wise gingerbread-baker, who, to facilitate a division, cuts his dough half through in those places where, when baked, he would have it *broken to pieces.*

III. Those remote provinces have perhaps been acquired, purchased, or conquered, at the *sole expence* of the settlers, or their ancestors, without the aid of the mother country. If this should happen to increase her *strength,* by their growing numbers, ready to join in her wars; her *commerce,* by their growing demand for her manufactures; or her *naval power,* by greater employment for her ships and seamen, they may probably suppose some merit in this, and that it entitles them to some favour; you are therefore to *forget it all, or resent it,* as if they had done you injury. If they happen to be zealous whigs, friends of liberty, nurtured in revolution principles, *remember all that* to their prejudice, and resolve to punish it; for such principles, after a revolution is thoroughly established, are of *no more use;* they are even *odious* and *abominable.*

IV. However peaceably your colonies have submitted to your government, shewn their affection to your interests, and patiently borne their grievances; you are to *suppose* them always inclined to revolt, and treat them accordingly. Quarter troops among them, who by their insolence may *provoke* the rising of mobs, and by their bullets and bayonets *suppress* them. By this means, like the husband who uses his wife ill *from suspicion,* you may in time convert your *suspicions* into *realities.*

V. Remote provinces must have *Governors* and *Judges,* to represent the Royal Person, and execute everywhere the delegated parts of his office and authority. You ministers know, that much of the strength of government depends on the *opinion* of the people; and much of that opinion on the *choice of rulers* placed immediately over them. If you send them wise and good men for governors, who study the interest of the colonists, and advance their prosperity, they will think their King wise and good, and that he wishes the welfare of his subjects. If you send them learned and upright men for Judges, they will think him a lover of justice. This may attach your provinces more to his government. You are therefore to be careful whom you recommend for those offices. If you can find prodigals, who have ruined their fortunes, broken gamesters or stockjobbers, these may do well as *governors;* for they will probably be rapacious, and provoke the people by their extortions. Wrangling proctors and pettifogging lawyers, too, are not amiss; for they will be for ever disputing and quarrelling with their little parliaments. If withal they should be ignorant, wrong-headed, and insolent, so much the better. Attornies' clerks and Newgate solicitors will do for *Chief Justices,* especially if they hold their places *during your pleasure;* and all will contribute to impress those ideas of your government, that are proper for a people *you would wish to renounce it.*

VI. To confirm these impressions, and strike them deeper, whenever the injured come to the capital with complaints of mal-administration, oppression, or injustice, punish such suitors with long delay, enormous expence, and a final judgment in favour of the oppressor. This will have an admirable effect every way. The trouble of future complaints will be prevented, and Governors and Judges will be encouraged to farther acts of oppression and injustice; and thence the people may become more disaffected, and at length desperate.

VII. When such Governors have crammed their coffers, and made themselves so odious to the people that they can no longer remain among them, with safety to their persons, *recall and reward* them with pensions. You may make them *baronets* too, if that respectable order should not think fit to resent it. All will contribute to encourage new governors in the same practice, and make the supreme government, *detestable*.

VIII. If, when you are engaged in war, your colonies should vie in liberal aids of men and money against the common enemy, upon your simple requisition, and give far beyond their abilities, reflect that a penny taken from them by your power is more honourable to you, than a pound presented by their benevolence; despise therefore their voluntary grants, and resolve to harass them with novel taxes. They will probably complain to your parliaments, that they are taxed by a body in which they have no representative, and that this is contrary to common right. They will petition for redress. Let the Parliaments flout their claims, reject their petitions, refuse even to suffer the reading of them, and treat the petitioners with the utmost contempt. Nothing can have a better effect in producing the alienation proposed; for though many can forgive injuries, *none ever forgave contempt.*

IX. In laying these taxes, never regard the heavy burthens those remote people already undergo, in defending their own frontiers, supporting their own provincial governments, making new roads, building bridges, churches, and other public edifices, which in old countries have been done to your hands by your ancestors, but which occasion constant calls and demands on the purses of a new people. Forget the *restraints* you lay on their trade for *your own* benefit, and the advantage a *monopoly* of this trade gives your exacting merchants.

Think nothing of the wealth those merchants and your manufacturers acquire by the colony commerce; their encreased ability thereby to pay taxes at home; their accumulating, in the price of their commodities, most of those taxes, and so levying them from their consuming customers; all this, and the employment and support of thousands of your poor by the colonists, you are *intirely to forget.* But remember to make your arbitrary tax more grievous to your provinces, by public declarations importing that your power of taxing them has *no limits;* so that when you take from them without their consent one shilling in the pound, you have a clear right to the other nineteen. This will probably weaken every idea of *security in their property,* and convince them, that under such a government they *have nothing they can call their own;* which can scarce fail of producing the *happiest consequences!*

X. Possibly, indeed, some of them might still comfort themselves, and say, "Though we have no property, we have yet *something* left that is valuable; we have constitutional *liberty,* both of person and of conscience. This King, these Lords, and these Commons, who it seems are too remote from us to know us, and feel for us, cannot take from us our *Habeas Corpus* right, or our right of trial *by a jury of our neighbours;* they cannot deprive us of the exercise of our religion, alter our ecclesiastical constitution, and compel us to be Papists, if they please, or Mahometans." To annihilate this comfort, begin by laws to perplex their commerce with infinite regulations, impossible to be remembered and observed; ordain seizures of their property for every failure; take away the trial of such property by Jury, and give it to arbitrary Judges of your own appointing, and of the lowest characters in the country, whose salaries and emoluments are to arise out of the duties or condemnations, and whose appointments are *during pleasure.* Then let there be a formal declaration of both Houses, that opposition to your edicts is *treason,* and that any person suspected of treason in the provinces may, according to some obsolete law, be seized and sent to the metropolis of the empire for trial; and pass an act, that those there charged with certain other offences, shall be sent away in chains from their friends and country to be tried in the same manner for felony. Then erect a new Court of Inquisition among them, accompanied by an armed force, with instructions to transport all such suspected persons; to be ruined by the expence, if they bring over evidences to prove their innocence, or be found guilty and hanged, if they cannot afford it. And, lest the people should think you cannot possibly go any farther, pass another solemn declaratory act, "that King, Lords, Commons had, hath, and of right ought to have, full power and authority to make statutes of sufficient force and validity to bind the unrepresented provinces IN ALL CASES WHATSOEVER." This will include *spiritual* with temporal, and, taken together, must operate wonderfully to your purpose; by convincing them, that they are at present under a power something like that spoken of in the scriptures, which can not only *kill their bodies,* but *damn their souls* to all eternity, by compelling them, if it pleases, *to worship the Devil.*

XI. To make your taxes more odious, and more likely to procure resistance, send from the capital a board of officers to superintend the collection, composed of the most *indiscreet, ill-bred,* and *insolent* you can find. Let these have large salaries out of the extorted revenue, and live in open, grating luxury upon the sweat and blood of the industrious; whom they are to worry continually with groundless and expensive prosecutions before the abovementioned arbitrary revenue Judges; *all at the cost of the party prosecuted,* tho' acquitted, because *the King is to pay no costs.* Let these men, *by your order,* be exempted from all the common taxes and burthens of the province, though they and their property are protected by its laws. If any revenue officers are *suspected* of the least tenderness for the people, discard them. If others are justly complained of, protect and reward them. If any of the under officers behave so as to provoke the people to drub them, promote those to better offices: this will encourage others to procure for themselves such profitable drubbings, by multiplying and enlarging such provocations, and *all will work towards the end you aim at.*

XII. Another way to make your tax odious, is to misapply the produce of it. If it was originally appropriated for the *defence* of the provinces, the better support of government, and the administration of justice, where it may be *necessary,* then apply none of it to that *defence,* but bestow it where it is *not necessary,* in augmented salaries or pensions to every governor, who has distinguished himself by his enmity to the people, and by calumniating them to their sovereign. This will make them pay it more unwillingly, and be more apt to quarrel with those that collect it and those that imposed it, who will quarrel again with them, and all shall contribute to your *main purpose,* of making them *weary of your government.*

XIII. If the people of any province have been accustomed to support their own Governors and Judges to satisfaction, you are to apprehend that such Governors and Judges may be thereby influenced to treat the people kindly, and to do them justice. This is another reason for applying part of that revenue in larger salaries to such Governors and Judges, given, as their commissions are, *during your pleasure* only; forbidding them to take any salaries from their provinces; that thus the people may no longer hope any kindness from their Governors, or (in Crown cases) any justice from their Judges. And, as the money thus misapplied in one province is extorted from all, probably *all will resent the misapplication.*

XIV. If the parliaments of your provinces should dare to claim rights, or complain of your administration, order them to be harrassed with *repeated dissolutions.* If the same men are continually returned by new elections, adjourn their meetings to some country village, where they cannot be accommodated, and there keep them *during pleasure;* for this, you know, is your PREROGATIVE; and an excellent one it is, as you may manage it to promote discontents among the people, diminish their respect, and *increase their disaffection.*

XV. Convert the brave, honest officers of your *navy* into pimping tide-waiters and colony officers of the *customs*. Let those, who in time of war fought gallantly in defence of the commerce of their countrymen, in peace be taught to prey upon it. Let them learn to be corrupted by great and real smugglers; but (to shew their diligence) scour with armed boats every bay, harbour, river, creek, cove, or nook throughout the coast of your colonies; stop and detain every coaster, every wood-boat, every fisherman, tumble their cargoes and even their ballast inside out and upside down; and, if a penn'orth of pins is found un-entered, let the whole be seized and confiscated. Thus shall the trade of your colonists suffer more from their friends in time of peace, than it did from their enemies in war. Then let these boats crews land upon every farm in their way, rob the orchards, steal the pigs and the poultry, and insult the inhabitants. If the injured and exasperated farmers, unable to procure other justice, should attack the aggressors, drub them, and burn their boats; you are to call this *high treason and rebellion,* order fleets and armies into their country, and threaten to carry all the offenders three thousand miles to be hanged, drawn, and quartered. *O! this will work admirably!*

XVI. If you are told of discontents in your colonies, never believe that they are general, or that you have given occasion for them; therefore do not think of applying any remedy, or of changing any offensive measure. Redress no grievance, lest they should be encouraged to demand the redress of some other grievance. Grant no request that is just and reasonable, lest they should make another that is unreasonable. Take all your informations of the state of the colonies from your Governors and officers in enmity with them. Encourage and reward these *leasing-makers;* secrete their lying accusations, lest they should be confuted; but act upon them as the clearest evidence; and believe nothing you hear from the friends of the people: suppose all *their* complaints to be invented and promoted by a few factious demagogues, whom if you could catch and hang, all would be quiet.

Catch and hang a few of them accordingly; and the *blood of the Martyers* shall *work miracles* in favour of your purpose.

XVII. If you see *rival nations* rejoicing at the prospect of your disunion with your provinces, and endeavouring to promote it; if they translate, publish, and applaud all the complaints of your discontented colonists, at the same time privately stimulating you to severer measures, let not that *alarm* or offend you. Why should it, since you all mean *the same thing?*

XVIII. If any colony should at their own charge erect a fortress to secure their port against the fleets of a foreign enemy, get your Governor to betray that fortress into your hands. Never think of paying what it cost the country, for that would look, at least, like some regard for justice; but turn it into a citadel to awe the inhabitants and curb their commerce. If they should have lodged in such fortress the very arms they bought and used to aid you in your conquests, seize them all; it will provoke like *ingratitude* added to *robbery.* One admirable effect of these operations will be, to discourage every other colony from erecting such defences, and so your enemies may more easily invade them; to the great disgrace of your government, and of course *the furtherance of your project.*

XIX. Send armies into their country under pretence of protecting the inhabitants; but, instead of garrisoning the forts on their frontiers with those troops, to prevent incursions, demolish those forts, and order the troops into the heart of the country, that the savages may be encouraged to attack the frontiers, and that the troops may be protected by the inhabitants. This will seem to proceed from your ill will or your ignorance, and contribute farther to produce and strengthen an opinion among them, *that you are no longer fit to govern them.*

XX. Lastly, invest the General of your army in the provinces, with great and unconstitutional powers, and free him from the controul of even your own Civil Governors. Let him have troops enow under his command, with all the fortresses in his possession; and who knows but (like some provincial Generals in the Roman empire, and encouraged by the universal discontent you have produced) he may take it into his head to set up for himself? If he should, and you have carefully practised these few *excellent rules* of mine, take my word for it, all the provinces will immediately join him; and you will that day (if you have not done it sooner) get rid of the trouble of governing them, and all the *plagues* attending their *commerce* and connection from henceforth and for ever.   Q. E. D.

AN EDICT
BY THE KING OF PRUSSIA [16]
Dantzic, Sept. 5, [1773.]

We have long wondered here at the supineness of the English nation, under the Prussian impositions upon its trade entering our port. We did not, till lately, know the claims, ancient and modern, that hang over that nation; and therefore could not suspect that it might submit to those impositions from a sense of duty or from principles of equity. The following Edict, just made publick, may, if serious, throw some light upon this matter.

"FREDERIC, by the grace of God, King of Prussia, &c. &c. &c., to all present and to come, *(à ious présens et à venir,)* Health. The peace now enjoyed throughout our dominions, having afforded us leisure to apply ourselves to the regulation of commerce, the improvement of our finances, and at the same time the easing our domestic subjects in their taxes: For these causes, and other good considerations us thereunto moving, we hereby make known, that, after having deliberated these affairs in our council, present our dear brothers, and other great officers of the state, members of the same, we, of our certain knowledge, full power, and authority royal, have made and issued this present Edict, viz.

"Whereas it is well known to all the world, that the first German settlements made in the Island of Britain, were by colonies of people, subject to our renowned ducal ancestors, and drawn from their dominions, under the conduct of Hengist, Horsa, Hella, Uff, Cerdicus, Ida, and others; and that the said colonies have flourished under the protection of our august house for ages past; have never been emancipated therefrom; and yet have hitherto yielded little profit to the same: And whereas we ourself have in the last war fought for and defended the said colonies, against the power of France, and thereby enabled them to make conquests from the said power in America, for which we have not yet received adequate compensation: And whereas it is just and expedient that a revenue should be raised from the said colonies in Britain, towards our indemnification; and that those who are descendants of our ancient subjects, and thence still owe us due obedience, should contribute to the replenishing of our royal coffers as they must have done, had their ancestors remained in the territories now to us appertaining: We do therefore hereby ordain and command, that, from and after the date of these presents, there shall be levied and paid to our officers of the *customs,* on all goods, wares, and merchandizes, and on all grain and other produce of the earth, exported from the said Island of Britain, and on all goods of whatever kind imported into the same, a duty of four and a half per cent *ad valorem,* for the use of us and our successors. And that the said duty may more effectually be collected, we do hereby ordain, that all ships or vessels bound from Great Britain to any other part of the world, or from any other part of the world to Great Britain, shall in their respective voyages touch at our port of Koningsberg, there to be unladen, searched, and charged with the said duties.

"And whereas there hath been from time to time discovered in the said island of Great Britain, by our colonists there, many mines or beds of iron-stone; and sundry subjects, of our ancient dominion, skilful in converting the said stone into metal, have in time past transported themselves thither, carrying with them and communicating that art; and the inhabitants of the said island, presuming that they had a natural right to make the best use they could of the natural productions of their country for their own benefit, have not, only built furnaces for smelting the said stone into iron, but have erected plating-forges, slitting-mills, and steel-furnaces, for the more convenient manufacturing of the same; thereby endangering a diminution of the said manufacture in our ancient dominion;—we do therefore hereby farther ordain, that, from and after the date hereof, no mill or other engine for slitting or rolling of iron, or any plating-forge to work with a tilt-hammer, or any furnace for making steel, shall be erected or continued in the said island of Great Britain: And the Lord Lieutenant of every county in the said island is hereby commanded, on information of any such erection within his county, to order and by force to cause the same to be abated and destroyed; as he shall answer the neglect thereof to us at his peril. But we are nevertheless graciously pleased to permit the inhabitants of the said island to transport their iron into Prussia, there to be manufactured, and to them returned; they paying our Prussian subjects for the workmanship; with all the costs of commission, freight, and risk, coming and returning; any thing herein contained to the contrary notwithstanding.

"We do not, however, think fit to extend this our indulgence to the article of wool; but, meaning to encourage, not only the manufacturing of woollen cloth, but also the raising of wool, in our ancient dominions, and to prevent both, as much as may be, in our said island, we do hereby absolutely forbid the transportation of wool from thence, even to the mother country, Prussia; and that those islanders may be farther and more effectually restrained in making any advantage of their own wool in the way of manufacture, we command that none shall be carried out of one county into another; nor shall any worsted, bay, or woollen yarn, cloth, says, bays, kerseys, serges, frizes, druggets, cloth-serges, shalloons, or any other drapery stuffs, or woollen manufactures whatsoever, made up or mixed with wool in any of the said counties, be carried into any other county, or be waterborne even across the smallest river or creek, on penalty of forfeiture of the same, together with the boats, carriages, horses, &c., that shall be employed in removing them. Nevertheless, our loving subjects there are hereby permitted (if they think proper) to use all their wool as manure for the improvement of their lands.

"And whereas the art and mystery of making hats hath arrived at great perfection in Prussia, and the making of hats by our remoter subjects ought to be as much as possible restrained: And forasmuch as the islanders before mentioned, being in possession of wool, beaver and other furs, have presumptuously conceived they had a right to make some advantage thereof, by manufacturing the same into hats, to the prejudice of our domestic manufacture: We do therefore hereby strictly command and ordain, that no hats or felts whatsoever, dyed or undyed, finished or unfinished, shall be loaded or put into or upon any vessel, cart, carriage, or horse, to be transported or conveyed out of one county in the said island into another county, or to any other place whatsoever, by any person or persons whatsoever; on pain of forfeiting the same, with a penalty of five hundred pounds sterling for every offence. Nor shall any hatmaker, in any of the said counties, employ more than two apprentices, on penalty of five pounds sterling per month; we intending hereby, that such hatmakers, being so restrained, both in the production and sale of their commodity, may find no advantage in continuing their business. But, lest the said islanders should suffer inconveniency by the want of hats, we are farther graciously pleased to permit them to send their beaver furs to Prussia; and we also permit hats made thereof to be exported from Prussia to Britain; the people thus favoured to pay all costs and charges of manufacturing, interest, commission to our merchants, insurance and freight going and returning, as in the case of iron.

"And, lastly, being willing farther to favour our said colonies in Britain, we do hereby also ordain and command, that all the *thieves,* highway and street robbers, house-breakers, forgerers, murderers, s—d—tes, and vil-

lains of every denomination, who have forfeited their
lives to the law in Prussia; but whom we, in our great
clemency, do not think fit here to hang, shall be emptied
out of our goals into the said island of Great Britain, for
the better peopling of that country.

"We flatter ourselves, that these our royal regulations
and commands will be thought just and reasonable by
our much-favoured colonists in England; the said regulations being copied from their statutes of 10 and 11 William III. c. 10, 5 Geo. II. c. 22, 23, Geo. II. c. 29, 4 Geo.
I. c. 11, and from other equitable laws made by their
parliaments; or from instructions given by their Princes;
or from resolutions of both Houses, entered into for the
good government of their *own colonies in Ireland and
America.*

"And all persons in the said island are hereby cau-
tioned not to oppose in any wise the execution of this
our Edict, or any part thereof, such opposition being
high treason; of which all who are suspected shall be
transported in fetters from Britain to Prussia, there to
be tried and executed according to the Prussian law.

"Such is our pleasure.

"Given at Potsdam, this twenty-fifth day of the month
of August, one thousand seven hundred and seventy-
three, and in the thirty-third year of our reign.

"By the King, in his Council.

"RECHTMAESSIG, *Sec.*"

Some take this Edict to be merely one of the King's
Jeux d'Esprit: others suppose it serious, and that he
means a quarrel with England; but all here think the
assertion it concludes with, "that these regulations are
copied from acts of the English parliament respecting
their colonies," a very injurious one; it being impossible
to believe, that a people distinguished for their love of
liberty, a nation so wise, so liberal in its sentiments, so
just and equitable towards its neighbours, should, from
mean and injudicious views of petty immediate profit,

treat its own children in a manner so arbitrary and tyrannical!

THE SALE OF THE HESSIANS

FROM THE COUNT DE SCHAUMBERGH TO THE BARON HOHENDORF, COMMANDING THE HESSIAN TROOPS IN AMERICA.[17]

Rome, February 18, 1777.

MONSIEUR LE BARON:—On my return from Naples, I received at Rome your letter of the 27th December of last year. I have learned with unspeakable pleasure the courage our troops exhibited at Trenton, and you cannot imagine my joy on being told that of the 1,950 Hessians engaged in the fight, but 345 escaped. There were just 1,605 men killed, and I cannot sufficiently commend your prudence in sending an exact list of the dead to my minister in London. This precaution was the most necessary, as the report sent to the English ministry does not give but 1,455 dead. This would make 483,450 florins instead of 643,500 which I am entitled to demand under our convention. You will comprehend the prejudice which such an error would work in my finances, and I do not doubt you will take the necessary pains to prove that Lord North's list is false and yours correct.

The court of London objects that there were a hundred wounded who ought not to be included in the list, nor paid for as dead; but I trust you will not overlook my instructions to you on quitting Cassel, and that you will not have tried by human succor to recall the life of the unfortunates whose days could not be lengthened but by the loss of a leg or an arm. That would be making them a pernicious present, and I am sure they would rather die than live in a condition no longer fit for my service. I do not mean by this that you should assassinate them; we should be humane, my dear Baron, but you may insinuate to the surgeons with entire propriety that a crippled man is a reproach to their profession, and that there is no wiser course than to let every one of them die when he ceases to be fit to fight.

I am about to send to you some new recruits. Don't economize them. Remember glory before all things. Glory is true wealth. There is nothing degrades the soldier like the love of money. He must care only for honour and reputation, but this reputation must be acquired in the midst of dangers. A battle gained without costing the conqueror any blood is an inglorious success, while the conquered cover themselves with glory by perishing with their arms in their hands. Do you remember that of the 300 Lacedæmonians who defended the defile of Thermopylæ, not one returned? How happy should I be could I say the same of my brave Hessians!

It is true that their king, Leonidas, perished with them: but things have changed, and it is no longer the custom for princes of the empire to go and fight in America for a cause with which they have no concern. And besides, to whom should they pay the thirty guineas per man if I did not stay in Europe to receive them? Then, it is necessary also that I be ready to send recruits to replace the men you lose. For this purpose I must return to Hesse. It is true, grown men are becoming scarce there, but I will send you boys. Besides, the scarcer the commodity the higher the price. I am assured that the women and little girls have begun to till our lands, and they get on not badly. You did right to send back to Europe that Dr. Crumerus who was so successful in curing dysentery. Don't bother with a man who is subject to looseness of the bowels. That disease makes bad soldiers. One coward will do more mischief in an engagement than ten brave men will do good. Better that they burst in their barracks than fly in a battle, and tarnish the glory of our arms. Besides, you know that they pay me as killed for all who die from disease, and I don't get a farthing for run-aways. My trip to Italy, which has cost me enormously, makes it desirable that there should be a great mortality among them. You will therefore promise promotion to all who expose themselves; you will exhort them to seek glory in the midst of dangers; you will say to Major Maundorff that I am not at all content with his saving the 345 men who escaped the massacre of Trenton. Through the whole campaign he has not had ten men killed in consequence of his orders. Finally, let it be your principal object to prolong the war and avoid a decisive engagement on either side, for I have made arrangements for a grand Italian opera, and I do not wish to be obliged to give it up. Meantime I pray God, my dear Baron de Hohendorf, to have you in his holy and gracious keeping.

8. Minister to France

Franklin served on a three man ministerial commission to France from 1776 to 1779 when he received appointment as minister plenipotentiary. Later he was joined by John Jay, John Adams and at the last minute Henry Laurens in making peace with Britain. He was not relieved from his diplomatic post until 1785 when he returned at last to Philadelphia.

The following selections provide some idea of the multifarious duties he was called upon to perform during his years in France. They included the procurement of loans from France for the matériel of war which he helped obtain and ship to America. Franklin was frequently called upon to act as banker to cover the expenses of American ministers elsewhere in Europe and of the Congress. He saw to the proper disposition of the prizes of war, and he was concerned in obtaining prisoner exchanges for the release of Americans incarcerated in England. He had constantly to uphold the Franco-American alliance through carefully nurtured relations with the French foreign minister, relations which Franklin feared the tactless John Adams inadvertently threatened. He dealt with the neutral nations of Europe particularly in the matter of prizes and their maintenance of the freedom of the seas. He corresponded with the leaders of Congress, keeping them informed of his affairs as well as of the general political situation and the prospects for peace.

The selections are presented chronologically rather than topically, for Franklin dealt concurrently with all of these matters and more. At the same time, he attended to the requirements of protocol. He dutifully appeared at Versailles when called upon. He was ever studious to present an image of America designed to encourage the French court to extend its aid and support of the cause of American independence.

TO THE MARQUIS DE LAFAYETTE [18]

Passy, March, 1780

[On February 29, Lafayette wrote Franklin of his assurances of supplies which John Paul Jones was to take to America. M. de Chaumont, Franklin's landlord at Passy, was a contractor involved in the American trade. Jonathan Williams, Franklin's nephew, was an American agent at Nantes.]

DEAR SIR,

I receiv'd with Pleasure the Letter you honour'd me with of the 29th past, and am infinitely obliged by the zeal and assiduity with which you have forwarded our affairs at Versailles. The 15,000 Arms and Accoutrements are a great article.

I had written to Capt. Jones that besides the 122 Bales of Cloth, we hoped for that quantity arms which it was suppos'd he might take at Ballast. I think the cloathing, 4,000 suits, was also mentioned to him by M. de Chaumont. In his last letter to me he says he will take as much as possible, and hopes he may be able to cram in the whole, if not your Ship can take the rest. I wish much to know where the Arms are and when they can be render'd at L'Orient.

Mr. Williams I hear is indefatigable in preparing the cloathing, and hopes to have the whole 10,000 suits ready by the End of the Month. I wish they could go with you; but that being impossible, I hope we shall get another Ship of Force to carry them. They are made precisely according to the Directions of the Committee.

If on seeing the accounts, I find I can add a proportion of cloaths for Officers, which you urge so earnestly, I shall do it with Pleasure. But from the large and unexpected Drafts often made upon me by Congress, I am become timid. I must take Care of their Credit and my own, and cannot take hazardous steps, as protesting or not paying one of their Bills would be attended with great Mischief on both sides the Water; and when I consider the vast Expence occasioned to this nation by the War, I am asham'd to be repeatedly worrying the Ministers by applications for more Money.

I ought to let Capt. Jones know as soon as Possible whether the Arms are to go with him, as he would stow them low to serve partly for Ballast. If a Ship can be obtain'd for them and what shall remain of the Cloathing, perhaps it may be as well to excuse the *Alliance* from that article and let her take more of the Cloathing.

I am told the 122 Bales of Cloth to be shipt by Mr. Ross for the Congress will by Computation make 7 or 8000 Suits. These will be in addition to the 10,000 making by Mr. Williams. Those Suits will be compos'd of Coat, Wastecoat, Breeches, Overalls, 2 pair of Stockings, 2 pair of Shoes, two Shirts, two Stocks, and a Hat for each man. I think there will also be Buckles. If there be any further information that you want, let me know and I will give what I can. . . .

NOTE FOR HIS EXCELLENCY, MONSIEUR LE COMTE DE VERGENNES [19]

May 16, 1780

[Franklin here informs French Foreign Minister Vergennes of the capture of the *Serapis* by the *Bonhomme Richard* and discusses the problem of arranging a cartel (agreement) for prisoner exchange. M. de Sartine was French Minister of Marine. Following is Franklin's request to the French admiralty for the sale of the *Serapis* as a prize of war.]

WHEN the *Alliance* Frigate arrived in France, Mr. Franklin was desirous of employing her in annoying the English Trade, and obtaining Prisoners to Exchange for the Americans who had long languished in the Prisons of England.

A Cruise with a small Squadron, under Commodore Jones round the Coast of Britain being about that time intended, Mr. Franklin was requested by his Excellency the Minister of the Marine to join the *Alliance* to that squadron. He chearfully complied with that Request, and in his instructions to Capt. Jones he encouraged him by the hopes of his being useful to his Country in delivering so many poor Prisoners from their Captivity.

As the Squadron acted under American Commission and Colours, was commanded by an American Chief, and was thence understood to be American, our Countrymen in the British Prisons rejoiced to hear of its Success, and that 500 English were made Prisoners in the Cruise, by an Exchange with whom they hoped to obtain their Liberty, and to return to their families and Country.

The *Alliance* alone took Vessels containing near 200 of those English Prisoners. The *Bonhomme Richard,* which was mann'd chiefly by Americans, took in the *Serapis* a great part of the Remainder.

The ambassador of France at the Hague applied to Comm^e Jones for the Prisoners in order to execute a Cartel entered into with the Ambassador of England. Comm^e Jones declined delivering them without Orders from Mr Franklin. The Ambassador did Mr. F. the honour of writing to him on the subject acquainting him that Mr Jones had urged the Exchanging them for Americans, and promising to use his Endeavours for that Purpose.

Mr. Franklin thereupon immediately sent the Orders desired, expressing at the same time his Confidence in the Ambassadors Promise.

The Prisoners were accordingly delivered, but they were actually exchanged for French.

His Excellency M. de Sartine afterwards acquainting Mr. Franklin that he had not English Prisoners enough at L'Orient to fill an English Cartel then there, Mr. F. gave Orders that 48 he had in that Port should be deliver'd up for that Purpose, 38 others at Brest to be employed in the same manner.

Mr. Franklin was afterwards informed by M. de Chaumont that M. de Sartine had assured him that other English Prisoners should be furnished to exchange for those so given up, in Holland and in France.

Mr. Franklin wrote accordingly to England, and a Cartel Vessel was thereupon ordered from Plymouth to Morlaix with 100 Americans. As soon as Mr. F. was acquainted with this he apply'd thro' M. de Chaumont to M. de Sartine for an Equal Number of English, who readily agreed to furnish them, and promised to send Orders immediately to march 100 from Saumur to Morlaix.

The Cartel arrived, landed the 100 Americans, but was sent back empty, with only a Receipt from the Commissary of the Port, no English being arrived for the Exchange.

Mr. F. has since received Letters from England, acquainting him that he is charged with Breach of Faith, and with deceiving the Board which had the Charge of Managing the Exchange of Prisoners, and a Stop is put to that Exchange in consequence.

The poor American Prisoners there, many of whom have been confined two or three Years, and have bravely resisted all the Temptations, accompanied with Threats, and follow'd by ill Usage, to induce them to enter into the English Service, are now in Despair, seeing their hopes of speedy liberty ruined by this failure.

His Excellency M. de Sartine has kindly and repeatedly promised, by M. de Chaumont, to furnish the number wanted—about 400—for exchanging the said Americans.

But it is now said that the king's Order is necessary to be first obtained.

Mr. Franklin therefore earnestly requests his Excellency M. Le Comte de Vergennes to support the proposition in Council, and thereby obtain liberty for those unfortunate People.

TO THE OFFICERS OF THE ADMIRALTY OF VANNES [20]

Passy, May 18, 1780.

GENTLEMEN, By the Declaration and Report to me made by the Honourable Commodore Jones, a Copy of which Declaration I herewith send you, it appears to me that the British Ship of War (the *Serapis*) therein mentioned to be met with, when convoying a fleet of the same Nation from the Baltic and taken by the *Bonhomme Richard,* which was commissioned by the Congress and commanded by the aforesaid Commodore, is undoubtedly a good Prize, being taken from the Enemies of the United States of America. And I do accordingly hereby desire of you that you would proceed to the Sale of the above said Prize, in Conformity to his Majesty's Regulation of September 27, 1778.

I have the Honour to be, etc.,

B. FRANKLIN.

TO SAMUEL HUNTINGTON [21]

Passy, May 31, 1780

[The following letter to the president of Congress illustrates the range of Franklin's concerns and responsibilities. Mr. Ross was John Ross, Scottish merchant acting as an American agent at Nantes. William Bingham was American agent in French Martinique in the West Indies. The Marquis de Fleury, who fought in America, was the recipient of one of the eight congressional medals authorized by Congress during the Revolution. M. Dumas was Franklin's scholarly friend and American agent at The Hague.]

SIR,

I wrote to your Excellency the 4th of March past, to go by this Ship, the *Alliance,* then expected to sail immediately. But the Men refusing to go till paid their Shares of Prize Money, and sundry Difficulties arising with regard to the Sale and Division, she has been detain'd thus long, to my great Mortification, and I am yet uncertain when I shall be able to get her out. The Trouble and Vexation these Maritime Affairs give me is inconceivable. I have often express'd to Congress my Wish to be reliev'd from them, and that some Person better acquainted with them, and better situated, might be appointed to manage them: Much Money as well as Time would, I am sure, be saved by such an Appointment.

The *Alliance* is to carry some of the Cannon long since ordered, and as much of the Powder, Arms, and Cloathing (furnished by Government here), as she, together with a Frigate, the *Ariel,* we have borrowed, can take. I hope they may between them take the whole, with what has been provided by Mr. Ross. This Gentleman has, by what I can learn, served the Congress well in the Quality and Prices of the Goods he has purchas'd. I wish it had been in my Power to have discharg'd his Ballance here, for which he has importun'd me rather too much. We furnish'd him with about £20,000 Sterling to discharge his first Accounts, which he was to replace as soon as he receiv'd Remittances from the Committee of Commerce: This has not been done, and he now demands another nearly equal Sum, urging as before, that the Credit of the States as well as his own will be hurt by my Refusal.

Mr. Bingham too complains of me for refusing some of his Drafts, as very hurtful to his Credit, tho' he owns he had no Orders from Congress to authorize those Drafts. I never undertook to provide for more than the Payment of the Interest Bills of the first Loan. The Congress have drawn on me very considerably for other Purposes, which has sometimes greatly embarrass'd me, but I have duly accepted and found means to pay their Drafts; so that their Credit in Europe has hitherto been well supported. But, if every Agent of Congress in different Parts of the World is permitted to run in Debt, and draw upon me at pleasure to support his Credit, under the Idea of its being necessary to do so for the Honour of Congress, the Difficulty upon me will be too great, and I may in fine be obliged to protest the Interest Bills. I therefore beg that a Stop may be put to such irregular Proceedings.

Had the Loans proposed to be made in Europe succeeded, these Practices might not have been so inconvenient: But the Number of Agents from separate States running all over Europe, and asking to borrow Money, has given such an Idea of our Distress and Poverty as makes everybody afraid to trust us. I am much pleas'd to find, that Congress has at length resolv'd to borrow of our own People, by making their future Bills bear Interest. This Interest duly paid in hard Money, to such as require hard Money, will fix the Interest in such Money for the most part unnecessary, provided always that the Quantity of Principal be not excessive.

A great Clamour has lately been made here by some Merchants, who say, they have large Sums in their Hands of Paper Money in America, and that they are ruin'd by some Resolution of Congress, which reduces its Value to One Part in Forty. As I have had no Letter explaining this Matter, I have only been able to say, that it is probably misunderstood, and that I am confident the Congress have not done, nor will do, any thing unjust towards Strangers, who have given us Credit. I have indeed been almost ready to complain, that I hear so little and so seldom from Congress, or from the Committee of Correspondence; but I know the Difficulty of Communication, and the frequent Interruption it meets in this Time of War. I have not yet receiv'd a Line this Year, and the Letters wrote by the *Confederacy,* (as I suppose some must have been written by her,) have not yet come to hand.

I mention'd in a former Letter, my having communicated to Mr. Johnson of Nantes, the Order of Congress appointing him to examine the accounts, and his Acceptance of the Appointment. Nothing, however, has yet been done in pursuance of it; for, Mr. Deane having wrote that he might be expected here by the middle of March, and as his Presence would be very useful in explaining the mercantile Transactions, I have waited his Arrival to request Mr. Johnson's coming to Paris, that his Detention here from his affairs at Nantes might be as short as possible. Mr. Dean *(sic)* is not yet come; but, as we have heard of the Arrival of the *Fendant* in Martinique, in which Ship he took his Passage, we imagine he may be here in some of the first Ships from that Island.

The medal for M. Fleury is done and deliver'd to his Order, he being absent; I shall get the others prepar'd' as soon as possible, by the same hand, if I cannot find a cheaper equally good, which I am now enquiring after. 2000 Livres appearing to me a great sum for the Work.

With my last I sent a Copy of my Memorial to the Court of Denmark. I have since receiv'd an Answer from the Minister of that Court for Foreign Affairs, a Copy of which I enclose. It referr'd me to the Danish Minister here, with whom I have had a Conference on the Subject. He was full of Professions of the Good will of his Court to the United States, and would excuse the Delivery of our Prizes to the English, as done in Conformity to Treaties, which it was necessary to observe. He had not the Treaty to show me, and I have not been able to find such a Treaty on Enquiry. After my Memorial, our People left at Bergen were treated with the greatest Kindness by an Order from Court, their Expences during the Winter that they had been detain'd there all paid, Necessaries furnished to them for their voyage to Dunkerque, and a passage thither found for them all at the King's Expence. I have not dropt the Application for a Restitution, but shall continue to push it, not without some Hopes of Success. I wish, however, to receive Instructions relating to it, and I think a Letter from Congress to that Court might forward the Business; for I believe they are sensible they have done wrong, and are apprehensive of the Inconveniencies that may follow. With this I send the Protests taken at Berghen against the Proceeding.

The *Alliance,* in her last Cruize, met with and sent to America a Dutch Ship, suppos'd to have on board an English Cargo. The Owners have made Application to me. I have assur'd them, that they might depend on the Justice of our Courts, and that, if they could prove their Property there, it would be restor'd. M. Dumas has written to me about it. I inclose his Letter. and wish Dispatch may be given to the Business, as well to prevent the Inconveniencies of a Misunderstanding with Holland, as for the sake of Justice.

A Ship of that Nation has been brought in here by the *Black Prince,* having an English Cargo. I consulted with Messrs. Adams and Dana, who inform'd me, that it was an established Rule with us in such cases to confiscate the Cargos, but to release the Ship, paying her Freight, &c. This I have accordingly ordered in the Case of this Ship, and hope it may be satisfactory. But it is a critical Time with respect to such Cases; for, whatever may formerly have been the Law of Nations, all the Neutral Powers at the Instance of Russia seem at present dispos'd to change it, and to inforce the Rule that *free Ships shall make free Goods,* except in the Case of Contraband. Denmark, Sweden, and Holland have already acceded to the Proposition, and Portugal is expected to follow. France and Spain, in their Answers, have also express'd their Approbation of it. I have, therefore, instructed our Privateers to bring in no more neutral Ships, as such Prizes occasion much Litigation, and create ill Blood.

The *Alliance,* Capt. Landais, took two Swedes in coming hither, who demand of us for Damages, one upwards of 60,000 Livres, and the other near £500 Sterling; and I cannot well see how the Demand is to be settled. In the Newspapers that I send, the Congress will see authentic Pieces expressing the Sense of the European Powers on the Subject of Neutral Navigation. I hope to receive the Sense of Congress for my future Government, and for the Satisfaction of the Neutral Nations now entering into the Confederacy, which is considered here as a great Stroke against England.

In Truth, that Country appears to have no Friends on this Side the Water; no other Nation wishes it Success in its present War, but rather desires to see it effectually humbled; no one, not even their old Friends the Dutch, will afford them any assistance. Such is the mischievous Effect of Pride, Insolence, and Injustice on the Affairs of Nations, as well as on those of private Persons!

The English Party in Holland is daily diminishing, and the States are arming vigorously to maintain the Freedom of their Navigation. The Consequences may possibly be a War with England, or a serious Disposition in that mad Nation to save what they can by a timely Peace.

Our Cartel for the Exchange of American Prisoners has been some time at a Stand. When our little Squadron brought near 500 into Holland, England would not at first exchange Americans for them there, expecting to take them in their Passage to France. But at length an Agreement was made between the English and French Ambassadors, and I was persuaded to give them up, on a Promise of having an equal Number of English delivered to my Order at Morlaix. So those were exchang'd for Frenchmen. But the English now refuse to take any English in Exchange for Americans, that have not been taken by American Cruisers. They also refuse to send me any Americans in Exchange for their Prisoners releas'd, and sent home by the two Flags of Truce from Boston. Thus they give up all Pretensions to Equity and Honour, and govern themselves by Caprice, Passion, and transient Views of present Interest. . . .

TO JOHN JAY [22]

Passy, June 13, 1780

[Franklin frequently wrote to John Jay, American minister to Spain. In this letter there is a personal note as Franklin complies with Mrs. Jay's request for pictures of him.]

DEAR SIR,

Yesterday, and not before, is come to hand your Favour of April 14, with the Pacquets and Dispatches from Congress, etc., which you sent me by a French Gentleman to Nantes.

Several of them appear to have been opened; the Paper round the Seals being smok'd and burnt, as with the Flame of a Candle us'd to soften the wax, and the impression defac'd. The Curiosity of People in this Time of War is unbounded. Some of them only want to see the news; but others want to find, (thro' interested Views,) what Chance there is of a speedy Peace. Mr. Ross has undertaken to forward the Letters to England.

I have not seen them; but he tells me they have all been opened. I am glad, however, to receive the Despatches from Congress, as they communicate to me Mr. Adams's Instructions, and other Particulars of which I have been long ignorant.

I am very sensible of the Weight of your Observation, "that a constant Interchange of Intelligence and Attentions, between the public Servants at the different courts, are necessary to procure to their Constituents all the Advantages capable of being derived from their Appointment." I shall endeavour to perform my Part with you, as well to have the Pleasure of your Correspondence, as from a Sense of Duty, But my Time is more taken up with matters extraneous to the Function of a Minister, than you can possibly imagine. I have written often to the Congress to establish Consuls in the Ports, and ease me of what relates to maritime and mercantile Affairs; but no Notice has yet been taken of my Request.

A number of Bills of Exchange, said to be drawn by Order of Congress on Mr. Laurens, are arrived in Holland. A Merchant there has desired to know of me, whether, if he accepts them, I will engage to reimburse him. I have no Orders or Advice about them from Congress. Do you know to what Amount they have drawn? I doubt I cannot safely meddle with them.

Mrs. Jay does me much Honour in desiring to have one of the Prints, that have been made here of her Countryman. I send what is said to be the best of 5 or 6 engraved by different hands, from different Paintings. The Verses at the bottom are truly extravagant. But you must know, that the Desire of pleasing, by a perpetual rise of Compliments in this polite Nation, has so us'd up all the common Expressions of Approbation, that they are become flat and insipid, and to use them almost implies Censure. Hence Musick, that formerly might be sufficiently prais'd when it was called *bonne,* to go a little farther they call'd it *excellente,* then *superbe, magnifique, exquise, céleste,* all which being in their turns worn out, there only remains *divine;* and, when that is grown as insignificant as its Predecessors, I think they must return to common Speech and common Sense; as from vying with one another in fine and costly Paintings on their Coaches, since I first knew the Country, not being able to go farther in that Way, they have returned lately to plain Carriages, painted without Arms or Figures, in one uniform Colour.

The League of neutral Nations to protect their Commerce is now established. Holland, offended by fresh Insults from England, is arming Vigorously. That Nation has madly brought itself into the greatest Distress, and has not a Friend in the World. With great and sincere esteem, &c.

B. FRANKLIN.

[The following two letters to the French foreign minister concern first the establishment of American consuls in French ports, an event desired particularly by Franklin to relieve him of consular duties. M. de la Luzerne was French minister to the United States. The second letter is an example of Franklin's diplomacy in winning additional loans from France.]

TO COMTE DE VERGENNES [23]

Passy, Sept. 7, 1780.

SIR,

I received the Letter your Excellency did me the Honour of writing to me, the 4th instant, on the appointment of Consuls. I have not yet received any Orders or Instructions from the Congress relating to that Object. I shall transmit to that Body a Copy of your Excellency's Letter, but as the Office of Consul has not been heretofore in use in America, and they may therefore not be so well acquainted with the usual Functions and Powers of such an Officer in Europe as to send me Instructions equally compleat and perfect with those your Excell^y. could send to M. de la Luzerne, if the Convention were to be treated there, I would submit it to your Judgement whether that Method may not be the best and shortest. As it is a Matter of the same general Nature with others that are enumerated among the Powers of Congress in the Articles of Confederation, tho' not particularly mentioned; and as the Grant in the 29th Article of the Treaty is to the *States United,* and not to each separately; and farther, as the having a Consul for each State, or thirteen American Consuls, in each Port of France would be of more Expence and Inconvenience than of real Unity, I cannot imagine that the Authority of Congress to make the necessary Convention will be disputed by the particular States. With the greatest Respect, I have the honour to be, Sir, your Excellency's most obedient and most humble Servant,

B. FRANKLIN.

TO COMTE DE VERGENNES [24]

Passy, Sept. 20. 1780

SIR

Since I had the Honour of speaking to your Excellency on the Subject of a farther Loan of Money to the United States, our Banker Mr Grand has given me a State of the Funds necessary to be provided, which I beg Leave to lay before you.

I have frequently written to Congress to draw no farther upon me, but to make me Remittances; for that the inevitable Expences of France in this War were immense, and that I could not presume to make repeated Applications for more Money with any Prospect of Success. Your Excellency will see this acknowledg'd in their late Letters to me; of which I inclose Copies; and that they would have avoided drawing on me any more, if the present Conjuncture in which they were oblig'd to make vast Preparations to act effectually with your Troops, had not laid them under the absolute Necessity.

The present State of their Currency rendring it insufficient for the Maintaining of their Troops, they provide for a great Part of the Expence by furnishing Provisions in kind: but some more hard Money than came in by Taxes, was wanted, and could only be obtain'd by these fresh Drafts.

Their former unexpected Drafts had already absorb'd much of the Money put into my hands, and I am now put into a Situation that distresses me exceedingly. I dread the Consequences of protesting their Bills. The Credit of the Congress being thereby destroy'd at home, the People will be unable to act or exert their Force. The Enemy will find them in a State similar to that of being bound hand and foot.

We have had Hopes of some Aid from Spain; but they are vanished.

The Expectation of a Loan in Holland, has also failed.—

I submit these important Circumstances to your Excellency's wise Consideration. The States will be well able in a few Years of Peace, to repay all that shall be advanc'd to them in this time of Difficulty: and they will repay it with Gratitude. The Good Work of establishing a free Government *for them,* and a free Commerce with them *for France,* is nearly compleated. It is pity it should now miscarry for want of 4 or 5 millions of Livres, to be furnished, not immediately but in the Course of the ensuing Year. . . .

TO ROBERT R. LIVINGSTON [25]

Passy, April 8, 1782

[In this letter Franklin informs the American secretary of foreign affairs of the fall of the North ministry in England.]

Sir,

Since my last an extraordinary Revolution has taken place in the Court of England. All the old Ministers are out, and the Chiefs of the Opposition are in their places. The Newspapers that I send will give you the names as correctly as we yet know them. Our last advices mention their kissing hands, but they had yet done nothing in their respective Offices, by which one might judge of their projected Measures; as whether they will ask a Peace, of which they have great need, the Nation having of late suffered many losses, men grown extreamly scarce, and Lord North's new Taxes proposed as funds

for the Loan meeting with great Opposition; or whether
they will stive to find new resources and obtain Allies
to enable them to please the King and Nation by some
vigorous Exertions against France, Spain, and Holland.

With regard to America, having, while in Opposition
carried the Vote for making no longer an offensive War
with us, they seem to have tied their own hands from
acting against us. Their Predecessors had been tamper-
ing with this Court for a separate Peace. The King's
Answer gave me great pleasure. It will be sent to M. de
la Luzerne, and by him communicated to Congress.
None of their Attempts to divide us meet with the least
Encouragement, and I imagine the present Set will try
other measures.

My Letters from Holland give pleasing Accounts of
the rapid Progress our Affairs are making in that
Country. The Packet from M. Dumas, which I forward
with this, will give you the particulars. The Prince de
Broglie will do me the favour of delivering this to you.
He goes over to join the French Army with the more
Pleasure, as it is employed in the Cause of Liberty, a
Cause he loves, and in establishing the Interests of
America, a Country for which he has much regard and
affection. I recommend him earnestly to the Civilities
and Services it may be in your Power to render him, and
I request you would introduce him to the President of
Congress, and to the principal Members, civil and mili-
tary.

Our excellent Friend, the Marquis de la Fayette, will
sail in about three Weeks. By that time we may have
more interesting Intelligence from England, and I shall
write you fully. . . .

TO ROBERT R. LIVINGSTON [26]

Paris, October 14, 1782

[Peace negotiations began in April, 1782, when the Shelburne
ministry sent Richard Oswald to confer with Franklin. In this
letter Franklin informs Secretary Livingston of the progress
of the negotiations. He also discusses the payment of minis-

ters' salaries. Lewis R. Morris, a nephew of Gouverneur Morris, was one of Secretary Livingston's two clerks.]

SIR,

I have but just received information of this opportunity, and have only time allowed to write a few lines.

In my last of the 26th past, I mentioned that the negotiation for peace had been obstructed by the want of due form in the English commissions appointing their plenipotentiaries. In that for treating with us, the mentioning our States by their public name had been avoided, which we objected to; another is come, of which I send a copy enclosed. We have now made several preliminary propositions, which the English minister, Mr. Oswald, has approved, and sent to his court. He thinks they will be approved there, but I have some doubts. In a few days, however, the answer expected will determine. By the first of these articles, the King of Great Britain renounces, for himself and successors, all claim and pretension to dominion or territory within the Thirteen United States; and the boundaries are described as in our instructions, except that the line between Nova Scotia and New England is to be settled by commissioners after the peace. By another article, the fishery in the American seas is to be freely exercised by the Americans, wherever they might formerly exercise it while united with Great Britain. By another, the citizens and subjects of each nation are to enjoy the same protection and privileges in each others' ports and countries, respecting commerce, duties, &c., that are enjoyed by native subjects. The articles are drawn up very fully by Mr. Jay, who I suppose sends you a copy; if not, it will go by the next opportunity If these articles are agreed to, I apprehend little difficulty in the rest. Something has been mentioned about the refugees and English debts, but not insisted on; as we declared at once, that, whatever confiscations had been made in America, being in virtue of the laws of particular States, the Congress had no authority to repeal those laws, and therefore could give us none to stipulate for such repeal.

I have been honoured with the receipt of your letters, Nos. 14 and 15. I have also received two letters from Mr. Lewis R. Morris, both dated the 6th of July, and one dated the 10th of August, enclosing bills for

$$68,290 \text{ livres,}$$
$$71,380$$
$$9,756$$
$$\overline{}$$

In all 149,426 livres, being intended for the payment of ministers' salaries for the two first quarters of this year. But, as these bills came so late, that all those salaries were already paid, I shall make no use of the bills, but lay them by till further orders; and, the salaries of different ministers not having all the same times of falling due, as they had different commencements, I purpose to get all their accounts settled and reduced to the same period, and send you the state of them, that you may be clear in future orders. I see in one of the estimates sent me, that a quarter's salary of a minister is reckoned at 14,513 livres, in the other it is reckoned 16,667 livres, and the bill for 9,756 livres is mentioned as intended to pay a balance due on the remittance of the 68,290 livres. Being unacquainted with the state of your exchange, I do not well comprehend this, and therefore leave the whole for the present, as I have said above. Permit me only to hint for your consideration, whether it may not be well hereafter to omit mention of sterling in our appointments, since we have severed from the country to which that denomination of money is peculiar; and also to order the payment of your ministers in such a manner, that they may know exactly what they are to receive, and not be subject to the fluctuations of exchange. If it is that, which occasions the difference between 14,513 for the first quarter, and the 16,667 for the second, it is considerable. I think we have no right to any advantage by the exchange, nor should we be liable to any loss from it. Hitherto we have taken 15,000 for a quarter, (subject however to the allowance or disallowance of Congress,) which is lower than the medium between those two extremes.

The different accounts given of Lord Shelburne's character, with respect to sincerity, induced the ministry here to send over M. de Rayneval, Secretary to the Council, to converse with him, and endeavour to form by that means a more perfect judgment of what was to be expected from the negotiations. He was five or six days in England, saw all the ministers, and returned quite satisfied, that they are sincerely desirous of peace, so that the negotiations now go on with some prospect of success. But the court and people of England are very changeable. A little turn of fortune in their favour sometimes turns their heads; and I shall not think a speedy peace to be depended on, till I see the treaties signed. I am obliged to finish. With great esteem, &c.

B. Franklin

TO CHARLES THOMSON [27]

Passy, May 13, 1784

[To his old friend Charles Thomson, secretary of the Congress, Franklin wrote of the exchange of the American and British ratifications of the definitive treaty of peace. His English friend David Hartley had signed the treaty for Britain. Franklin also expresses his wish to be recalled and his concern for the future of his grandson, William Temple Franklin.]

DEAR SIR,

Yesterday evening Mr. Hartley met with Mr. Jay and myself when the ratifications of the Definitive Treaty were exchanged. I send a copy of the English Ratification to the President.

Thus the great and hazardous enterprize we have been engaged in is, God be praised, happily compleated; an event I hardly expected I should live to see. A few years of Peace, will improve, will restore and encrease our strength; but our future safety will depend on our union and our virtue. Britain will be long watching for advantages, to recover what she has lost. If we do not convince the world, that we are a Nation to be depended on for fidelity in Treaties; if we appear negligent in paying our Debts, and ungrateful to those who have served and befriended us; our reputation, and all the strength it is capable of procuring, will be lost, and fresh attacks upon us will be encouraged and promoted by better prospects of success. Let us therefore beware of being lulled into a dangerous security; and of being both enervated and impoverished by luxury; of being weakened by internal contentions and divisions; of being shamefully extravagant in contracting private debts, while we are backward in discharging honorably those of the public; of neglect in military exercises and discipline, and in providing stores of arms and munitions of war, to be ready on occasion; for all these are circumstances that give confidence to enemies, and diffidence to friends; and the expenses required to prevent a war are much lighter than those that will, if not prevented, be absolutely necessary to maintain it.

I am long kept in suspense without being able to learn the purpose of Congress respecting my request of recall, and that of some employment for my secretary, William Temple Franklin. If I am kept here another winter, and as much weakened by it as by the last, I may as well resolve to spend the remainder of my days here; for I shall be hardly able to bear the fatigues of the voyage in returning. During my long absence from America, my friends are continually diminishing by death, and my inducements to return in proportion. But I can make no preparations either for going conveniently, or staying comfortably here, nor take any steps towards making some other provision for my grandson, till I know what I am to expect. Be so good, my dear friend, as to send me a little private information. With great esteem, I am ever yours, most affectionately

                                                    B. FRANKLIN.

9. Abolitionist

In his last years, Franklin was president of the *Pennsylvania Society for Promoting the Abolition of Slavery, and the Relief of Free Negroes Unlawfully held in Bondage.* In earlier years, he had promoted schools for Negroes in Philadelphia. He was perhaps the first notable American to believe that the mental capacity of Negro children was equal to that of white children. In November, 1789, he addressed to the public an appeal for funds for the abolition society, which sent to the first Congress an antislavery memorial which he signed. Writing as "Historicus," Franklin's last published writing, composed only three weeks before his death and entitled *On the Slave-Trade,* was a biting parody of proslavery arguments given in Congress by Georgia's James Jackson. Herein, the hypothetical "Sidi Mehemet Ibrahim," member of the Algerian Council of State, utilizes Jackson's arguments against the abolitionist "Erika," (Quakers) and in support of white slavery in North Africa.

AN ADDRESS TO THE PUBLIC; [28]

FROM THE PENNSYLVANIA SOCIETY FOR PROMOTING THE ABOLITION OF SLAVERY, AND THE RELIEF OF FREE NEGROES UNLAWFULLY HELD IN BONDAGE.

IT is with peculiar satisfaction we assure the friends of humanity, that, in prosecuting the design of our association, our endeavours have proved successful, far beyond our most sanguine expectations.

Encouraged by this success, and by the daily progress of that luminous and benign spirit of liberty, which is diffusing itself throughout the world, and humbly hoping for the continuance of the divine blessing on our labours, we have ventured to make an important addition to our original plan, and do therefore earnestly solicit the support and assistance of all who can feel the tender emotions of sympathy and compassion, or relish the exalted pleasure of beneficence.

Slavery is such an atrocious debasement of human nature, that its very extirpation, if not performed with solicitous care, may sometimes open a source of serious evils.

The unhappy man, who has long been treated as a

brute animal, too frequently sinks beneath the common standard of the human species. The galling chains, that bind his body, do also fetter his intellectual faculties, and impair the social affections of his heart. Accustomed to move like a mere machine, by the will of a master, reflection is suspended; he has not the power of choice; and reason and conscience have but little influence over his conduct, because he is chiefly governed by the passion of fear. He is poor and friendless; perhaps worn out by extreme labour, age, and disease.

Under such circumstances, freedom may often prove a misfortune to himself, and prejudicial to society.

Attention to emancipated black people, it is therefore to be hoped, will become a branch of our national policy; but, as far as we contribute to promote this emancipation, so far that attention is evidently a serious duty incumbent on us, and which we mean to discharge to the best of our judgment and abilities.

To instruct, to advise, to qualify those, who have been restored to freedom, for the exercise and enjoyment of civil liberty, to promote in them habits of industry, to furnish them with employments suited to their age, sex, talents, and other circumstances, and to procure their children an education calculated for their future situation in life; these are the great outlines of the annexed plan, which we have adopted and which we conceive will essentially promote the public good, and the happiness of these our hitherto too much neglected fellow-creatures.

A plan so extensive cannot be carried into execution without considerable pecuniary resources, beyond the present ordinary funds of the Society. We hope much from the generosity of enlightened and benevolent freemen, and will gratefully receive any donations or subscriptions for this purpose, which may be made to our treasurer, James Starr, or to James Pemberton, chairman of our committee of correspondence.

Signed, by order of the Society,

B. FRANKLIN, *President.*

ON THE SLAVE-TRADE [29]

TO THE EDITOR OF THE FEDERAL GAZETTE

March 23d, 1790.

SIR,

Reading last night in your excellent Paper the speech of Mr. Jackson in Congress against their meddling with the Affair of Slavery, or attempting to mend the Condition of the Slaves, it put me in mind of a similar One made about 100 Years since by Sidi Mehemet Ibrahim, a member of the Divan of Algiers, which may be seen in Martin's Account of his Consulship, anno 1687. It was against granting the Petition of the Sect called *Erika,* or Purists, who pray'd for the Abolition of Piracy and Slavery as being unjust. Mr. Jackson does not quote it; perhaps he has not seen it. If, therefore, some of its Reasonings are to be found in his eloquent Speech, it may only show that men's Interests and Intellects operate and are operated on with surprising similarity in all Countries and Climates, when under similar Circumstances. The African's Speech, as translated, is as follows.

"Allah Bismillah, &c. God is great, and Mahomet is his Prophet.

"Have these *Erika* considered the Consequences of granting their Petition? If we cease our Cruises against the Christians, how shall we be furnished with the Commodities their Countries produce, and which are so necessary for us? If we forbear to make Slaves of their People, who in this hot Climate are to cultivate our Lands? Who are to perform the common Labours of our City, and in our Families? Must we not then be our own Slaves? And is there not more Compassion and more Favour due to us as Mussulmen, than to these Christian Dogs? We have now above 50,000 Slaves in and near Algiers. This Number, if not kept up by fresh Supplies, will soon diminish, and be gradually annihilated. If we then cease taking and plundering the Infidel Ships, and making Slaves of the Seamen and Passengers, our Lands will become of no Value for want of Cultivation; the Rents of Houses in the City will sink one half; and the Revenues of Government arising from its Share of Prizes be totally destroy'd! And for what? To gratify the whims of a whimsical Sect, who would have us, not only forbear making more Slaves, but even to manumit those we have.

"But who is to indemnify their Masters for the Loss? Will the State do it? Is our Treasury sufficient? Will the *Erika* do it? Can they do it? Or would they, to do what they think Justice to the Slaves, do a greater Injustice to the Owners? And if we set our Slaves free, what is to be done with them? Few of them will return to their Countries; they know too well the greater Hardships they must there be subject to; they will not embrace our holy Religion; they will not adopt our Manners; our People will not pollute themselves by intermarrying with them. Must we maintain them as Beggars in our Streets, or suffer our Properties to be the Prey of their Pillage? For Men long accustom'd to Slavery will not work for a Livelihood when not compell'd. And what is there so pitiable in their present Condition? Were they not Slaves in their own Countries?

"Are not Spain, Portugal, France, and the Italian states govern'd by Despots, who hold all their Subjects in Slavery, without Exception? Even England treats its Sailors as Slaves; for they are, whenever the Government pleases, seiz'd, and confin'd in Ships of War, condemn'd not only to work, but to fight, for small Wages, or a mere Subsistence, not better than our Slaves are allow'd by us. Is their Condition then made worse by their falling into our Hands? No; they have only exchanged one Slavery for another, and I may say a better; for here they are brought into a Land where the Sun of Islamism gives forth its Light, and shines in full Splendor, and they have an Opportunity of making themselves acquainted with the true Doctrine, and thereby saving their immortal Souls. Those who remain at home have not that Happiness. Sending the Slaves home then would be sending them out of Light into Darkness.

"I repeat the Question, What is to be done with them? I have heard it suggested, that they may be planted in the Wilderness, where there is plenty of Land for them to subsist on, and where they may flourish as a free State; but they are, I doubt, too little dispos'd to labour without Compulsion, as well as too ignorant to establish a good government, and the wild Arabs would soon molest and destroy or again enslave them. While serving us, we take care to provide them with every thing, and they are treated with Humanity. The Labourers in their own Country are, as I am well informed, worse fed, lodged, and cloathed. The Condition of most of them is therefore already mended, and requires no further Improvement. Here their Lives are in Safety. They are not liable to be impress'd for Soldiers, and forc'd to cut one another's Christian Throats, as in the Wars of their own Countries. If some of the religious mad Bigots, who now teaze us with their silly Petitions, have in a Fit of blind Zeal freed their Slaves, it was not Generosity, it was not Humanity, that mov'd them to the Action; it was from the conscious Burthen of a Load of Sins, and Hope, from the supposed Merits of so good a Work, to be excus'd Damnation.

"How grossly are they mistaken in imagining Slavery to be disallow'd by the Alcoran! Are not the two Precepts, to quote no more, *'Masters, treat your Slaves with kindness; Slaves, serve your Masters with Cheerfulness and Fidelity,'* clear Proofs to the contrary? Nor can the Plundering of Infidels be in that sacred Book forbidden, since it is well known from it, that God has given the World, and all that it contains, to his faithful Mussulmen, who are to enjoy it of Right as fast as they conquer it. Let us then hear no more of this detestable Proposition, the Manumission of Christian Slaves, the Adoption of which would, by depreciating our Lands and Houses, and thereby depriving so many good Citizens of their Properties, create universal Discontent, and provoke Insurrections, to the endangering of Government and producing general Confusion. I have therefore no doubt, but this wise Council will prefer the Comfort and Happiness of a whole Nation of true Believers to the Whim of a few *Erika,* and dismiss their Petition."

The Result was, as Martin tells us, that the Divan came to this Resolution; "The Doctrine, that Plundering and Enslaving the Christians is unjust, is at best *problematical;* but that it is the Interest of this State to continue the Practice, is clear; therefore let the Petition be rejected."

And it was rejected accordingly.

And since like Motives are apt to produce in the Minds of Men like Opinions and Resolutions, may we not, Mr. Brown, venture to predict, from this Account, that the Petitions to the Parliament of England for abolishing the Slave-Trade, to say nothing of other Legislatures, and the Debates upon them, will have a similar Conclusion? I am, Sir, your constant Reader and humble Servant,   HISTORICUS.

10. Conciliator

Franklin's role in the Constitutional Convention was not to innovate but to conciliate. He accordingly acted a central part in bringing about the Great Compromise, by which the small states accepted proportional representation in the House of Representatives in return for equality in the Senate. Firmly convinced of the need to strengthen the federal union, Franklin pled for the unanimous adoption of the Constitution. In spite of his artful address, three of the forty-one delegates present refused to put their signatures to the document. Franklin's speech, his last, was widely circulated during the struggle for ratification following the submission of the Constitution to the states. His approbation of the document did much to allay the suspicions of many individuals and helped gain the victory for the federalist cause.

SPEECH IN THE CONVENTION,[30]

MR. PRESIDENT,

I confess, that I do not entirely approve of this Constitution at present; but, Sir, I am not sure I shall never approve it; for, having lived long, I have experienced many instances of being obliged, by better information or fuller consideration, to change my opinions even on important subjects, which I once thought right, but found to be otherwise. It is therefore that, the older I grow, the more apt I am to doubt my own judgment of others. Most men, indeed, as well as most sects in religion, think themselves in possession of all truth, and that wherever others differ from them, it is so far error. Steele, a Protestant, in a dedication, tells the Pope, that the only difference between our two churches in their opinions of the certainty of their doctrine, is, the Romish Church is *infallible,* and the Church of England is *never in the wrong.* But, though many private Persons think almost as highly of their own infallibility as of that of their Sect, few express it so naturally as a certain French Lady, who, in a little dispute with her sister, said, "But I meet with nobody but myself that is *always* in the right." *"Je ne trouve que moi qui aie toujours raison."*

In these sentiments, Sir, I agree to this Constitution, with all its faults,—if they are such; because I think a general Government necessary for us, and there is no *form* of government but what may be a blessing to the people, if well administered; and I believe, farther, that this is likely to be well administered for a course of years, and can only end in despotism, as other forms have done before it, when the people shall become so corrupted as to need despotic government, being incapable of any other. I doubt, too, whether any other Convention we can obtain, may be able to make a better constitution; for, when you assemble a number of men, to have the advantage of their joint wisdom, you inevitably assemble with those men all their prejudices, their passions, their errors of opinion, their local interests, and their selfish views. From such an assembly can a *perfect* production be expected? It therefore astonishes me, Sir, to find this system approaching so near to perfection as it does; and I think it will astonish our enemies, who are waiting with confidence to hear, that our councils are confounded like those of the builders of Babel, and that our States are on the point of separation, only to meet hereafter for the purpose of cutting one another's throats. Thus I consent, Sir, to this Constitution, because I expect no better, and because I am not sure that it is not the best. The opinions I have had of its *errors* I sacrifice to the public good. I have never whispered a syllable of them abroad. Within these walls they were born, and here they shall die. If every one of us, in returning to our Constituents, were to report the objections he has had to it, and endeavour to gain Partisans in support of them, we might prevent its being generally received, and thereby lose all the salutary effects and great advantages resulting naturally in our favour among foreign nations, as well as among ourselves, from our real or apparent unanimity. Much of the strength and efficiency of any government, in procuring and securing happiness to the people, depends on *opinion,* on the general opinion of the goodness of that government, as well as of the wisdom and integrity of its governors. I hope, therefore, for our own sakes, as a part of the people, and for the sake of our posterity, that we shall act heartily and unanimously in recommending this Constitution, wherever our Influence may extend, and turn our future thoughts and endeavours to the means of having it *well administered.*

On the whole, Sir, I cannot help expressing a wish, that every member of the Convention who may still have objections to it, would with me on this occasion doubt a little of his own infallibility, and, to make *manifest* our *unanimity,* put his name to this Instrument.

Footnotes

Chapter I

1 *The Autobiography of Benjamin Franklin,* ed. by Leonard Labaree *et al.,* (New Haven, 1964), pp. 54–55.
2 *Ibid.,* p. 54.
3 *Ibid.,* pp. 59–60.
4 Previous papers were *The Boston News-Letter* (1704), *The Boston Gazette* (1719), and *The American Weekly Mercury* (Philadelphia, 1719). *Public Occurences* (Boston, 1690), though preceding these, ran only one issue.
5 Leonard Labaree, ed., *The Papers of Benjamin Franklin* (New Haven, 1959—), 1:17, 40.
6 *Autobiography,* ed. by Labaree *et al.,* p. 71
7 *Ibid.,* p. 76.

Chapter II

1 *Autobiography,* ed. by Labaree *et al.,* p. 124.
2 Oscar Handlin and John Clive, eds., *Journey to Pennsylvania* (Cambridge, 1960), pp. 48, 86.
3 *Autobiography,* ed. by Labaree *et al.,* p. 78.
4 *Ibid.,* p. 79.
5 *Ibid.,* p. 80.
6 *Ibid.,* p. 82.
7 *Ibid.,* p. 85.
8 *Ibid.,* p. 86.
9 *Ibid.,* pp. 87–88.
10 *Ibid.,* p. 95.
11 Labaree, ed., *Papers of Franklin,* 1:100.
12 *Ibid.,* 1:112.
13 *Ibid.,* 1:124.
14 *Ibid.,* 1:161, 184, 165, 169–170.
15 *Ibid.,* 2:226–227.
16 Lawrence C. Wroth, *Typographic Heritage* (New York, 1949), p. 116.

17 *Autobiography,* ed. by Labaree *et al.,* pp. 129, 282.
18 Labaree, ed., *Papers of Franklin,* 2:14.

Chapter III

1   Labaree, ed., *Papers of Franklin,* 1:101–109.
2   *Autobiography,* ed., by Labaree *et al.,* pp. 148–152, 156.
3   *Ibid.,* pp. 161–162, 153.
4   *Ibid.,* pp. 116–117; Labaree, ed., *Papers of Franklin,* 1:257.
5   *Autobiography,* ed. by Labaree *et al.,* pp. 175, 202, 203, 204, 192–193.
6   Labaree, ed., *Papers of Franklin,* 3:404, 397–421.
7   *Autobiography,* ed. by Labaree *et al.,* p. 178.
8   *Ibid.,* p. 201.
9   Labaree, ed., *Papers of Franklin,* 4:62.
10 *Autobiography,* ed. by Labaree *et al.,* p. 201.
11 Labaree, ed., *Papers of Franklin,* 3:381–382.
12 *Autobiography,* ed. by Labaree *et al.,* p. 192.
13 Labaree, ed., *Papers of Franklin,* 3:118–119, 127, 129–130, 131.
14 *Autobiography,* ed. by Labaree *et al.,* p. 244 n.
15 Labaree, ed., *Papers of Franklin,* 4:505; 2:27.
16 *Ibid.,* 2:204.
17 Albert Henry Smyth, ed., *The Writings of Benjamin Franklin,* (New York, 1905–07), 10:84.

Chapter IV

1   *Autobiography,* ed. by Labaree, *et al.,* pp. 171, 172.
2   *Ibid.,* p. 184.
3   Labaree, ed., *Papers of Franklin,* 3:199, 186 n.
4   *Ibid.,* 4:132.
5   *Ibid.,* 5:107.
6   *Ibid.,* 4:229, 233.
7   *Ibid.,* 4:119.
8   *Autobiography,* ed. by Labaree, *et al.,* p. 212.
9   Labaree, ed., *Papers of Franklin,* 5:444, 445, 447, 417.
10 *Ibid.,* 5:460.
11 *Ibid.,* 6:86–88; *Autobiography,* ed. by Labaree *et al.,* pp. 215–216.

12 *Ibid.,* pp. 221, 228, 224; Labaree, ed., *Papers of Franklin,* 6:21–22, 14, 210.
13 *Ibid.,* 6:162, 194, 242. For Franklin's break with the Penns, see James H. Hutson, "Benjamin Franklin and Pennsylvania Politics, 1751–1755: A Reappraisal," *Pennsylvania Magazine of History and Biography,* 93 (1969), 303–371.
14 *Autobiography,* ed. by Labaree, *et al.,* p. 238.
15 Labaree, ed., *Papers of Franklin,* 7:73, 13–14.
16 *Autobiography,* ed. by Labaree *et al.,* p. 232.
17 Labaree, ed., *Papers of Franklin,* 7:73–74.
18 *Ibid.,* 7:110–111 n.
19 *Ibid.,* 7:116.

Chapter V

1 Labaree, ed. *Papers of Franklin,* 7:250.
2 *Autobiography,* ed. by Labaree *et al.,* pp. 264, 264 n; Labaree, ed., *Papers of Franklin,* 7:179.
3 *Ibid.,* 7:374.
4 *Ibid.,* 10:11.
5 Quoted in I. Bernard Cohen, *Franklin and Newton* (Philadelphia, 1956), p. 310.
6 Labaree, ed., *Papers of Franklin,* 9:251.
7 *Ibid.,* 10:59–100.
8 *Ibid.,* 10:81–82, 133.
9 *Ibid.,* 10:161.
10 Smyth, ed. *Writings of Franklin,* 4:309, 298.
11 *Ibid.,* 4:229, 230, 231.
12 Labaree, ed., *Papers of Franklin,* 4:234.
13 Quoted in J. Philip Gleason, "A Scurrilous Colonial Election and Franklin's Reputation," *William and Mary Quarterly,* 3d. Ser., 18 (1961), 74.
14 Smyth, ed., *Writings of Franklin,* 4:347.
15 James H. Hutson, "The Campaign to Make Pennsylvania a Royal Province, 1764–1770, Part I," *Pennsylvania Magazine of History and Biography,* 94 (1970), 427–463.
16 Smyth, ed., *Writings of Franklin,* 4:273–285.
17 *Ibid.,* 4:241, 349.

Chapter VI

1 Smyth, ed., *Writings of Franklin,* 4:243–244.
2 Quoted in Alfred Aldridge, *Benjamin Franklin, Philosopher and Man* (New York, 1965), p. 168.
3 Smyth, ed., *Writings of Franklin,* 4:246.
4 *Ibid.,* 4:390.
5 Samuel Eliot Morison, ed., *Sources and Documents Illustrating the American Revolution, 1764–1788* (2nd. ed., New York, 1965), p. 18.
6 Smyth, ed., *Writings of Franklin,* 4:392.
7 Quoted in J. A. Cochrane, *Dr. Johnson's Printer: The Life of William Strahan* (Cambridge, 1964), p. 113.
8 Verner Crane, ed., *Benjamin Franklin's Letters to the Press, 1758–1775* (Chapel Hill, 1950), p. 63.
9 *Ibid.,* pp. 33–34.
10 Merrill Jensen, ed., *Tracts of the American Revolution, 1763–1776* (New York, 1967), p. 122.
11 Verner Crane, "Benjamin Franklin and the Stamp Act," Colonial Society of Massachusetts, *Publications,* 32 (1937), 71, 73.
12 *The Parliamentary History of England . . .* (London, 1813), 16:97, 108.
13 *Ibid.,* 16:141, 147, 158–159.
14 Crane, ed., *Letters,* pp. 73–74.
15 Smyth, ed., *Writings of Franklin,* 4:400.

Chapter VII

1 Smyth, ed., *Writings of Franklin,* 4:411.
2 *Ibid.,* 4:212.
3 *Ibid.,* 4:290, 25, 41.
4 Henry Steele Commager, ed., *Documents of American History* (7th ed., New York, 1963), p. 63.
5 Smyth, ed., *Writings of Franklin,* 5:21–22.
6 *Ibid.,* 5:197.
7 *Ibid.,* 5:115.
8 Crane, ed., *Letters,* p. 158.
9 Smyth, ed., *Writings of Franklin,* 5:288, 296, 319.
10 *Ibid.,* 5:132–133.

11 Labaree, ed., *Papers of Franklin,* 6:468, 469.
12 Smyth, ed., *Writings of Franklin,* 5:508.
13 *Ibid.,* 5:117.
14 Quoted in Jack Sosin, *Whitehall and Wilderness* (Lincoln, 1961), p. 187.
15 Smyth, ed., *Writings of Franklin,* 5:314.
16 *Ibid.,* 6:33–34.
17 *Ibid.,* 5:117.
18 *Ibid.,* 5:260.
19 *Ibid.,* 5:295.
20 *Ibid.,* 5:90, 148, 133.
21 *Ibid.,* 5:299.
22 Crane, ed., *Letters to the Press,* p. 167.

Chapter VIII

1 Smyth, ed., *Writings of Franklin,* 5:202.
2 *Ibid.,* 5:367.
3 *Ibid.,* 5:368.
4 *Ibid.,* 5:362.
5 *Ibid.,* 5:363–4.
6 Crane, ed., *Letters,* pp. 186–192.
7 *Ibid.,* pp. 222–223.
8 Smyth, ed., *Writings of Franklin,* 6:222.
9 *Autobiography,* ed. by Labaree *et al.,* pp. 43, 131.
10 Smyth, ed., *Writings of Franklin,* 5:439.
11 *Ibid.,* 5:272–280.
12 *Ibid.,* 4:386, 96.
13 *Ibid.,* 6:63, 67.
14 *Ibid.,* 6:43–44.
15 *Ibid.,* 6:311–12.

Chapter IX

1 Smyth, ed., *Writings of Franklin,* 4:4; 8:453.
2 *Ibid.,* 6:57.
3 *Ibid.,* 5:452.
4 Quoted in Benjamin Labaree, *The Boston Tea Party* (New York, 1964), p. 145.
5 Smyth, ed., *Writings of Franklin,* 4:179.

6   *Ibid.,* 6:127–137.
7   *Ibid.,* 6:118–124.
8   *Ibid.,* 6:145, 146.
9   Israel Maudit, ed., *The Letters of Governor Hutchinson . . . Together with the Substance of Mr. Wedderburn's Speech* (London, 1774), pp. 3, 18, 15–17, 25, 41.
10 Smyth, ed., *Writings of Franklin,* 6:284, 263.
11 *Ibid.,* 6:186.
12 Crane, ed., *Letters to the Press,* p. 239.
13 Smyth, ed., *Writings of Franklin,* 6:188–189.
14 Maudit, ed., *Letters of Governor Hutchinson,* pp. 87, 90, 115; Benjamin Vaughan, ed., *Political, Miscellaneous, and Philosophical Pieces . . . by Benj. Franklin* (London, 1779), p. 341; Smyth, ed., *Writings of Franklin,* 6:189.
15 *Ibid.,* 6:254.
16 *Ibid.,* 6:372.
17 Crane, ed., *Letters,* pp. 232–233.
18 Smyth, ed., *Writings of Franklin,* 6:394.
19 *Ibid.,* 6:370.
20 *Ibid.,* 6:392.
21 *Ibid.,* 6:312.
22 *Ibid.,* 6:312.

Chapter X

1   Smyth, ed., *Writings of Franklin,* 6:446.
2   Carl Van Doren, ed., *Benjamin Franklin's Autobiographical Writings* (New York, 1945), pp. 407, 409.
3   Smyth, ed., *Writings of Franklin,* 6:407.
4   Lyman H. Butterfield, ed., *Adams Family Correspondence* (Cambridge, 1963—), 1:253.
5   Smyth, ed., *Writings of Franklin,* 6:420–425.
6   *Ibid.,* 6:431.
7   Quoted in Edmund Cody Burnett, *The Continental Congress* (New York, 1964), p. 106.
8   Smyth, ed., *Writings of Franklin,* 6:447, 448, 438–439.
9   Quoted in Burnett, *Congress,* p. 113.
10 Smyth, ed., *Writings of Franklin,* 6:450.
11 Moncure Daniel Conway, ed., *The Writings of Thomas Paine* (New York, 1894–96), 1:84–101.

12 Van Doren, ed., *Autobiographical Writings,* pp. 417–418.
13 Smyth, ed., *Writings of Franklin,* 6:458–462.
14 *Ibid.,* 6:437.
15 Quoted in Samuel Flagg Bemis, *The Diplomacy of the American Revolution* (Washington: American Historical Association, 1935; Bloomington: Indiana University Press, 1957), p. 47. Reprinted by permission.
16 Francis Wharton, ed., *Revolutionary Diplomatic Correspondence of the United States* (Washington, 1889), 2: 298.

Chapter XI

1 Smyth, ed., *Writings of Franklin,* 9:696; 7:289.
2 Wharton, ed., *Diplomatic Correspondence,* 2:223, 217.
3 Charles Francis Adams, ed., *The Works of John Adams* (Boston, 1852–1856), 1:660–663.
4 Smyth, ed., *Writings of Franklin,* 7:347.
5 Quoted in Richard B. Morris, *The Peacemakers: the Great Powers and American Independence* (New York, 1965), p. 153.
6 Julian P. Boyd, "Silas Deane: Death by a Kindly Teacher of Treason," *William and Mary Quarterly,* 3d. Ser., 16 (1959), 165–187, 319–342, 515–550.
7 Smyth, ed., *Writings of Franklin,* 7:11.
8 *Ibid.,* 7:132.
9 *Ibid.,* 7:36.
10 Quoted in Alfred Owen Aldridge, *Benjamin Franklin, Philosopher and Man* (Philadelphia, 1965), p. 275.
11 *Ibid.;* Richard W. Van Alstyne, *Empire and Independence* (New York, 1965), p. 183.
12 Smyth, ed., *Writings,* 7:112.

Chapter XII

1 J. H. Choate quoted in Beckles Willson, *America's Ambassadors to France: (1777–1927)* (New York, 1928), p. 9.
2 Lyman H. Butterfield, ed., *Diary and Autobiography of John Adams* (New York, 1964), 4:118–119.

3 Quoted in Claude-Anne Lopez, *Mon Cher Papa: Franklin and the Ladies of Paris* (New Haven, 1966), p. 85.
4 Wharton, ed., *Diplomatic Correspondence,* 4:75.
5 *Ibid.,* 4:23.
6 *Ibid.,* 4:255, 403.
7 *Ibid.,* 4:283, 659.
8 *Ibid.,* 5:121.
9 *Ibid.,* 4:780.
10 Smyth, ed., *Writings of Franklin,* 8:396–397.
11 Wharton, ed., *Diplomatic Correspondence,* 5:540.
12 Smyth, ed., *Writings of Franklin,* 9:96.
13 Wharton, ed., *Diplomatic Correspondence,* 6:581.
14 *Ibid.,* 6:130.
15 *Ibid.,* 6:144.
16 *Ibid.,* 3:537–538.
17 Sir John Fortescue, ed., *The Correspondence of King George the Third* (London, 1927–1928), 6:154.

Chapter XIII

1 Wharton, ed., *Diplomatic Correspondence,* 6:649.
2 *Ibid.,* 6:744, 582.
3 *Ibid.,* 3:587.
4 *Ibid.,* 6:587.
5 Smyth, ed., *Writings of Franklin,* 8:603–614.
6 *Ibid.,* 10:97–104.
7 *Autobiography,* ed., by Labaree *et al.,* p. 160.
8 Paul Leicester Ford, ed., *The Writings of Thomas Jefferson* (New York, 1892–1899), 10:119.
9 Smyth, ed., *Writings of Franklin,* 9:364.
10 *Ibid.,* 9:252.
11 *Ibid.,* 9:372–413.
12 *Ibid.,* 10:471.
13 John Bigelow, ed., *The Works of Benjamin Franklin* (New York, 1887–89), 11:228.
14 Smyth, ed., *Writings of Franklin,* 11:228.
15 *Ibid.,* 9:625.
16 *Ibid.,* 9:535.
17 *Ibid.,* 10:116–122.
18 *Ibid.,* 9:499.

19   John C. Fitzpatrick, ed., *The Writings of George Wash-
      ington* (Washington, 1931–44), 29:122.
20   Max Farrand, ed., *The Records of the Federal Conven-
      tion of 1787* (rev. ed., New Haven, 1966), 3:33, 91.
21   *Ibid.,* 1:451.
22   *Ibid.,* 1:488.
23   *Ibid.,* 2:249.
24   *Ibid.,* 1:216; II:44–45, 236, 348, 615.
25   *Ibid.,* 2:643, 649.
26   *Ibid.,* 2:648.
27   Smyth, ed., *Writings of Franklin,* 9:491.
28   *Ibid.,* 9:694.
29   *Ibid.,* 10:31.
30   *Autobiography,* ed. by Labaree *et al.,* p. 191.
31   Smyth, ed., *Writings of Franklin,* 10:494.
32   Julian P. Boyd, ed., *The Papers of Thomas Jefferson*
      (Princeton, 1950—), 16:369.

Chapter XIV

1   Charles Moulton, ed., *The Library of Literary Criticism
     of English and American Authors* (Buffalo, 1901–1905),
     4:83.
2   Gilbert Chinard, "The Apotheosis of Benjamin Frank-
     lin: Paris, 1790–1791," *Proceedings of the American Phil-
     osophical Society,* 98-99 (1954–55), 440–473.
3   Carl Van Doren, *Benjamin Franklin* (New York, 1938),
     p. 779.
4   Quoted in Dixon Wecter, *The Hero in America* (New
     York, 1941), p. 70.
5   Charles Francis Adams, *The Works of John Adams,* 1:
     660–664.
6   Reverend H. Hastings Weld, *Benjamin Franklin, his Au-
     tobiography, with a Narrative of his Public Life and Serv-
     ices* (New York, 1849) pp. vii–viii.
7   Mason Locke Weems, *The Life of Benjamin Franklin*
     (Philadelphia, 1829); Peter Parley, *The Lives of Franklin
     and Washington* (London, 1839).
8   George Bancroft, *History of the United States* (Boston,
     1844), 3:378.

9 James Parton, *Life and Times of Benjamin Franklin* (Boston, 1864), 2:633–638.

10 Edward Waldo Emerson and Waldo Emerson Forbes, *Journals of Ralph Waldo Emerson* (Boston and New York, 1909), 7:268; 1:376.

11 Theodore Parker, *Historic Americans* (Boston, 1878), pp. 35, 38, 14.

12 Moulton, ed., *Library of Literary Criticism,* 4:87.

13 Hawthorne, *Works* (Boston, 1883), 12:202; Melville, *Works* (New York, 1963), 11:62.

14 Harvey Wish, ed., *Ante-Bellum: Writings of George Fitzhugh and Hinton Rowan Helper on Slavery* (New York, 1969), pp. 92–93.

15 *Autobiography,* ed. by Labaree *et al.,* Introduction, p. 10; J. Henry Smyth, ed., *The Amazing Benjamin Franklin* (New York, 1929), p. 39.

16 Parton, *Benjamin Franklin,* p. 8.

17 Crane, *Franklin* (Boston: Little, Brown & Co., 1954), p. 206. Reprinted by permission.

18 Van Doren, *Franklin,* pp. viii, 782.

19 Turner, *The Frontier in American History* (New York, 1920), p. 182.

20 Richard D. Miles, "The American Image of Benjamin Franklin," *American Quarterly,* 9 (1957), 142.

21 Charles and Mary Beard, *The Rise of American Civilization* (New York, 1933), pp. 158–159.

22 *Main Currents in American Thought,* Vol. 1: *The Colonial Mind* (New York, 1927), pp. 165, 178.

23 "The Late Benjamin Franklin," *The Galaxy,* 10 (1870), p. 139.

24 *The Letters of Theodore Roosevelt,* ed. by Elting E. Morison *et al.* (Cambridge, 1951–1954), 2:224.

25 D. H. Lawrence, *Studies in Classic American Literature* (Garden City, 1953), pp. 10–11, 22.

26 Talcott Parsons, trans. (New York, 1958), p. 52.

27 *Capitol* (New York, 1967), 1:54 n.

28 Smyth, ed., *The Amazing Benjamin Franklin,* p. 93.

29 The Rotarian, 88 #1 (January, 1956), p. 4.

30 Bernard Knollenberg in *Meet Dr. Franklin* (Philadelphia, 1943), p. 127.

31 *The American Democracy* (New York, 1948), p. 39.
32 *Autobiography,* ed. by Labaree *et al.,* Introduction, p. 4.
33 Smyth, ed., *Writings of Franklin,* 10:72.

Chapter XV

1 Bigelow, ed., *The Works of Benjamin Franklin,* 11:286.
2 Smyth, ed., *Writings of Franklin,* 10:59.
3 *Ibid.,* 9:612–613.
4 *Ibid.,* 9:619.
5 *Ibid.,* 8:37.
6 *Ibid.,* 10:41–42.

APPENDIX: DOCUMENTS

1 Labaree, ed., *Papers of Franklin,* 2:136–145
2 *Ibid.,* 2:172.
3 *Autobiography,* ed., by Labaree *et al.,* pp. 173–175.
4 *Ibid.,* pp. 192–196.
5 *Ibid.,* 199–208.
6 Labaree, ed., *Papers of Franklin,* 3:126–132.
7 *Ibid.,* 3:463–465.
8 Smyth, ed., *Writings of Franklin,* 4:389–315.
9 *Ibid.,* 4:226–241.
10 *Ibid.,* 4:314.
11 Labaree, ed., *Papers of Franklin,* 5:387–392.
12 Smyth, ed., *Writings of Franklin,* 4:413–448.
13 *Ibid.,* 5:16–22.
14 Crane, ed., *Letters,* pp. 87–92.
15 Smyth, ed., *Writings of Franklin,* 6:118–124.
16 *Ibid.,* 6:127–137.
17 *Ibid.,* 8:27–29.
18 *Ibid.,* 8:20–21.
19 *Ibid.,* 8:66–69.
20 *Ibid.,* 8:69.
21 *Ibid.,* 8:72–78.
22 *Ibid.,* 8:92–94.
23 *Ibid.,* 8:138–139.
24 *Ibid.,* 8:139–140.
25 *Ibid.,* 8:420–422.

26 *Ibid.*, 8:614–617.
27 *Ibid.*, 9:212–214.
28 *Ibid.*, 10:66–68.
29 *Ibid.*, 10:87–91.
30 *Ibid.*, 10:607–609.

Bibliography

I. PRIMARY SOURCES

a. Collected Works and Documents

*Adams, John. *Diary and Autobiography of John Adams.* Edited by Lyman H. Butterfield and others. 4 vols. New York: Atheneum, 1964.

————. *The Works of John Adams.* Edited by Charles Francis Adams. 10 vols. Boston: Little, Brown & Co., 1852–1856.

* Butterfield, Lyman H., ed. *Adams Family Correspondence.* The Belknap Press of Harvard University Press, 1963.

* Commager, Henry Steele, ed. *Documents of American History.* 7th ed. New York: Appleton-Century-Crofts, 1963.

* Farrand, Max, ed. *The Records of the Federal Convention of 1787.* Revised edition. 4 vols. New Haven: Yale University Press, 1966.

Fortescue, Sir John, ed. *The Correspondence of King George the Third from 1760 to December, 1783.* 6 vols. London: Macmillan & Co., 1927–28.

* Franklin, Benjamin. *The Autobiography of Benjamin Franklin.* Edited by Leonard Labaree and others. New Haven: Yale University Press, 1964.

————. *Benjamin Franklin's Autobiographical Writings.* Edited by Carl Van Doren. New York: Viking Press, 1945.

————. *Benjamin Franklin's Letters to the Press, 1758–1775.* Edited by Verner Crane. Chapel Hill: University of North Carolina Press, 1950.

————. *The Papers of Benjamin Franklin.* Edited by Leonard Labaree and others. 13 vols. to date. New Haven: Yale University Press, 1959—.

* Available in paperback

———. *Political, Miscellaneous, and Philosophical Pieces.* . . . Edited by Benjamin Vaughan. London: J. Johnson, 1779.

———. *The Works of Benjamin Franklin.* Edited by John Bigelow. 10 vols. New York: G. P. Putnam's Sons, 1887–89.

———. *The Works of Benjamin Franklin.* Edited by Jared Sparks. 10 vols. Boston: Hilliard, Gray & Co., 1840.

———. *The Writings of Benjamin Franklin.* Edited by Albert Henry Smyth. 10 vols. New York: Macmillan Co., 1905–07.

Jefferson, Thomas. *The Papers of Thomas Jefferson.* Edited by Julian P. Boyd. Princeton: Princeton University Press, 1950—.

———. *The Writings of Thomas Jefferson.* Edited by Paul Leicester Ford. 10 vols. New York: G. P. Putnam's Sons, 1892–99.

*Jensen, Merrill, ed. *Tracts of the American Revolution.* Indianapolis: The Bobbs-Merrill Co., 1967.

* Jorgenson, Chester E. and Frank Luther Mott, eds. *Benjamin Franklin: Representative Selections with Introduction, Bibliography, and Notes.* Revised edition. New York: Hill and Wang, 1962.

Mauduit, Israel, ed. *The Letters of Governor Hutchinson, and Lieutenant Governor Oliver.* . . . 2d. ed. London: J. Wilkie, 1774.

Mittelberger, Gottlieb. *Journey to Pennsylvania.* Edited and translated by Oscar Handlin and John Clive. Cambridge: The Belknap Press of Harvard University Press, 1960.

* Edmund S. Morgan, ed. *Prologue to Revolution: Sources and Documents on the Stamp Act Crisis, 1764–1766.* Chapel Hill: University of North Carolina Press, 1959.

* Morison, Samuel Eliot, ed. *Sources and Documents Illustrating the American Revolution, 1764–1788 and the Formation of the Federal Constitution.* 2d. ed. New York: Oxford University Press, 1965.

Paine, Thomas. *The Writings of Thomas Paine.* Edited by

Moncure Daniel Conway. 4 vols. New York: G. P. Putnam's Sons, 1894–96.

Parliamentary History of England . . . . Vol. XVI. London, 1813.

Washington, George. *The Writings of George Washington.* Edited by John C. Fitzpatrick. 39 vols. Washington: Government Printing Office, 1931–44.

Wharton, Francis, ed. *Revolutionary Diplomatic Correspondence of the United States.* Washington: Government Printing Office, 1889.

b. Sources for Chapter XIV, "The Verdict of History."

Bancroft, George. *History of the United States.* 10 vols. Boston: Little, Brown & Co. 1860–74.

Beard, Charles and Mary. *The Rise of American Civilization.* New York: Macmillan Co., 1933.

Clemens, Samuel. *Contributions to the Galaxy, 1868–1871, by Mark Twain (Samuel Clemens).* Edited by Bruce R. McEdlerry. Gainsville, Fla.: Scholars' Facsimiles and Reprints, 1961.

Diller, Theodore. *Franklin's Contributions to Medicine.* Brooklyn: A. T. Huntington, 1912.

Emerson, Ralph Waldo. *Journals of Ralph Waldo Emerson.* Edited by Edward Waldo Emerson and Waldo Emerson Forbes. 12 vols. Boston: Houghton, Mifflin & Co., 1903–04.

Goodrich, Samuel Griswold [Peter Parley]. *The Life of Benjamin Franklin.* Philadelphia: Thomas, Cowperthwait & Co., 1838.

Hawthorne, Nathaniel. *Tales, Sketches, and other Papers. The Complete Works of Nathaniel Hawthorne.* Vol. XII. Boston: Houghton, Mifflin & Co. Riverside edition, 1883.

Laski, Harold. *The American Democracy.* New York: Viking Press, 1948.

* Lawrence, D. H. *Studies in Classic American Literature.* Garden City: Doubleday, 1953.

* Marx, Karl. *Capitol.* Edited by Frederick Engels. Translated by Samuel Moore and Edward Aveling. 3 vols. New York: International Publishers, 1967.

McMaster, John Bach. *Benjamin Franklin as a Man of Letters.* Boston: Houghton, Mifflin & Co., 1887.

Meet Dr. Franklin. Philadelphia: The Franklin Institute, 1943.

* Melville, Herman. *Israel Potter. The Works of Herman Melville.* Vol. XI. New York: Russell & Russell, 1963.

Moulton, Charles, ed. *The Library of Literary Criticism of English and American Authors.* 8 vols. Buffalo: The Moulton Publishing Co., 1901–05.

Parker, Theodore. *Historic Americans.* Boston: H. B. Fuller, 1870.

* Parrington, Vernon Lewis. *Main Currents in American Thought.* New York: Harcourt, Brace & Co., 1930.

Roosevelt, Theodore. *The Letters of Theodore Roosevelt.* Edited by Elting E. Morison and others. 8 vols. Cambridge: Harvard University Press, 1951–54.

The Rotarian. LXXXVIII #1 (January, 1956): p. 4.

* Sanford, Charles L., ed. *Benjamin Franklin and the American Character.* Boston: Heath, 1955.

Smyth, J. Henry, Jr., ed. *The Amazing Benjamin Franklin.* New York: Frederick A. Stokes Co., 1929.

* Turner, Frederick Jackson. *The Frontier in American History.* New York: Henry Holt & Co., 1921.

* Weber, Max. *The Protestant Ethic and the Spirit of Capitalism.* Translated by Talcott Parsons. New York: Charles Scribner's Sons, 1958.

Weems, Mason Locke. *The Life of Benjamin Franklin.* Philadelphia: U. Hunt, 1829.

Weld, Horatio Hastings. *Benjamin Franklin, his Autobiography, with a Narrative of his Public Life and Services.* New York: Harper & Brothers, 1849.

* Wish, Harvey, ed. Ante-Bellum: *Writings of George*

Fitzhugh and Hinton Rowan Helper on Slavery. New York: Capricorn Books, 1960.

II. SECONDARY WORKS

Aldridge, Alfred Owen. *Benjamin Franklin, Philosopher and Man.* Philadelphia: J. B. Lippincott Co., 1965.
_____. *Franklin and his French Contemporaries.* New York: New York University Press, 1957.
Becker, Carl. "Benjamin Franklin." *Dictionary of American Biography.* III: 585–598. New York: Charles Scribner's Sons, 1958.
* Bemis, Samuel Flagg. *The Diplomacy of the American Revolution.* Bloomington: Indiana University Press, 1957.
Boyd, Julian P. "Silas Deane: Death by a Kindly Teacher of Treason." *William and Mary Quarterly,* 3d. S., XVI (1959), 165–187, 319–342, 515–550.
* Bridenbaugh, Carl and Jessica. *Rebels and Gentlemen: Philadelphia in the Age of Franklin.* New York: Oxford University Press, A Hesperides Book, 1962.
* Burnett, Edmund Cody. *The Continental Congress.* New York: W. W. Norton & Co., The Norton Library, 1964.
Butler, Ruth. *Doctor Franklin: Postmaster General.* Garden City: Doubleday, Doren & Co., 1928.
Cheyney, Edward Potts. *History of the University of Pennsylvania.* Philadelphia: University of Pennsylvania Press, 1940.
Chinard, Gilbert. "The Apotheosis of Benjamin Franklin: Paris, 1790–1791." *Proceedings of the American Philosophical Society,* XCVIII–XCIX (1954–55): 440–473.
Cochrane, James A. *Dr. Johnson's Printer: The Life of William Strahan.* Cambridge: Harvard University Press, 1964.
Cohen, I. Bernard. *Franklin and Newton.* Philadelphia: The American Philosophical Society, 1956.
* Crane, Verner W. *Benjamin Franklin and a Rising People.* Boston: Little, Brown & Co., 1954.

_____. "Benjamin Franklin and the Stamp Act." *Publications of the Colonial Society of Massachusetts*, XXXII (1937): 56–77.

_____. *"The Club of Honest Whigs: Friends of Science and Liberty."* William and Mary Quarterly, 3d. S., XXIII (1966): 210–233.

Faÿ, Bernard. *Franklin: the Apostle of Modern Times.* Boston: Little, Brown & Co., 1929.

* Gipson, Lawrence Henry. *The Coming of the Revolution.* New York: Harper & Row, 1954.

Gleason, J. Philip. "A Scurrilous Colonial Election and Franklin's Reputation." *William and Mary Quarterly,* 3d. S., XVIII (1961): 68–84.

Greene, Jack P. *The Quest for Power: The Lower Houses of Assembly in the Southern Royal Colonies, 1689–1776.* Chapel Hill: University of North Carolina Press, 1963.

Hanna, William S. *Benjamin Franklin and Pennsylvania Politics.* Stanford: Stanford University Press, 1964.

Hindle, Brooke. "The March of the Paxton Boys." *William and Mary Quarterly,* 3d. S., III (1964): 461–486.

*_____. *The Pursuit of Science in Revolutionary America.* Chapel Hill: University of North Carolina Press, 1956.

Hutson, James E. "The Campaign to Make Pennsylvania a Royal Province, 1764–1770." *Pennsylvania Magazine of History and Biography,* XCIV (1970), 427–463, XCV (1971), 28–49.

_____. *Pennsylvania Politics, 1746–1770: The Movement for Royal Government and Its Consequences.* Princeton: Princeton University Press, 1972.

Jaffe, Bernard. *Men of Science in America.* New York: Simon and Schuster, 1958.

Jensen, Merrill. *The Founding of a Nation: A History of the American Revolution, 1763–1776.* New York: Oxford University Press, 1968.

Kammen, Michael. *A Rope of Sand: The Colonial Agents, British Politics, and the American Revolution.* Ithaca: Cornell University Press, 1968.

* Knollenberg, Bernard. *Origin of the American Revolution, 1759–1766.* New York: Collier Books, 1961.

* Labaree, Benjamin. *The Boston Tea Party.* New York: Oxford University Press, 1964.

Labaree, Leonard. "Benjamin Franklin's British Friendships." *Proceedings of the American Philosophical Society,* CVIII (1964): 423–428.

Lopez, Claude-Anne. *Mon Cher Papa: Franklin and the Ladies of Paris.* New Haven: Yale University Press, 1966.

McMurtrie, Douglas C. *A History of Printing in the United States.* Vol. II: *Middle and South Atlantic States.* New York: R. R. Bowker Co., 1936.

Miles, Richard D. "The American Image of Benjamin Franklin." *American Quarterly,* IX (1957): 117–145.

Morison, Samuel Eliot. *John Paul Jones, a Sailor's Biography.* Boston: Little, Brown & Co., 1959.

Morris, Richard B. *The Peacemakers: the Great Powers and American Independence.* New York: Harper & Row, 1965.

Newbold, Richard C. *The Albany Congress and the Plan of Union of 1754.* New York: Vantage Press, 1955.

Oswald, John Clyde. *Benjamin Franklin, Printer.* Garden City: Doubleday, Page & Co., 1917.

Pace, Antonio. *Benjamin Franklin and Italy.* Philadelphia: American Philosophical Society, 1958.

* Palmer, Robert. *The Age of the Democratic Revolution; A Political History Of Europe and America, 1760–1800.* 2 vols. Princeton: Princeton University Press, 1959–1964.

Parton, James. *Life and Times of Benjamin Franklin.* 2 vols. Boston: James R. Osgood & Co., 1864.

Riddell, W. R. "Benjamin Franklin's Mission to Canada and the Causes of its Failure." *Pennsylvania Magazine of History and Biography,* LIV (1930): 52–64.

Sayre, Robert F. "The Worldly Franklin and the Provincial Critics." *Texas Studies in Literature and Language, a Journal of the Humanities,* IV (1963): 512–24.

Sosin, Jack. *Agents and Merchants: British Colonial Policy and the Origins of the American Revolution, 1763–1775.* Lincoln: University of Nebraska Press, 1965.

————. *Whitehall and Wilderness: the Middle West in British Colonial Policy, 1760–1775.* Lincoln: University of Nebraska Press, 1961.

* Stourzh, Gerald. *Benjamin Franklin and American Foreign Policy.* Chicago: University of Chicago Press, 1954.

Thayer, Theodore. *Pennsylvania Politics and the Growth of Democracy, 1740–1776.* Harrisburg: Pennsylvania Historical and Museum Commission, 1953.

* Van Alstyne, Richard W. *Empire and Independence.* New York: John Wiley & Sons, 1965.

* Van Doren, Carl. *Benjamin Franklin.* New York: The Viking Press, 1938.

* Wecter, Dixon. *The Hero in America: a Chronicle of Hero-Worship.* New York: Charles Scribner's Sons, 1941.

Willson, Beckles. *America's Ambassadors to France (1777–1927): a Narrative of Franco-American Diplomatic Relations.* New York: Frederick A. Stokes Co., 1928.

Wroth, Lawrence C. *Typographic Heritage.* New York: The Typophiles, 1949.

Zimmerman, John J. "Benjamin Franklin and the Quaker Party, 1755–56." *William and Mary Quarterly,* 3d. S., XVII (1960): 291–313

Index

207–08; his "hang separately" quip, 208; elected president of Pennsylvania's constitutional convention, 208; his letter to Admiral Howe, 209–10; and Staten Island Conference, 210–11; diplomatic correspondence of, 211; appointed to ministerial commission, 212; distrusts foreign entanglements, 213; sails for France, 214–15; reception of, in France, 215–19; and Voltaire, 218–19; international recognition of, 219; chooses Passy as his French residence, 221; on spies, 224; his angry letter to Arthur Lee, 226–27; composes model letter of recommendation, 227; publishes pro-American propaganda, 228; recommends Von Steuben and Pulaski, 228; aphorisms of, concerning Stormont and General Howe, 228–29; and American prisoners of war, 229; signs French treaty of alliance, 230–31; appointed minister plenipotentiary, 231, 233–34; social life of, at Passy, 234–36; praises Louis XVI, 237–38; on Spanish pretensions to the Mississippi, 237; his successful plea to Vergennes for funds, 238–39; Congress refuses resignation of, 239; Congress appoints to peace commission, 240; writes to Edmund Burke, 241; negotiates peace terms, 242–45; relinquishes Oswald negotiations to Jay, 246; with Jay and Adams, negotiates preliminary peace treaty, 247–48; soothes French sensibilities, 249; confidence of, in America's future, 252; obtains refutations of calumnies against him, 253–54; signs commercial treaties, 254; on Adams' character, 254–55; antiwar letter of, 255; on Barbary states, 256; publishes pro-American propaganda, 256–58; aphorisms of, 259; various scientific interests of, and new inventions, 260; judges Mesmer's theories, 260–61; succeeded by Jefferson as minister to France, 261; signs treaty with Prussia, 261; leaves Passy, 261; last meeting with son, 262; last voyage of, 262–63; duties of, as president of Pennsylvania, 264–65; delegate to Constitutional Convention, 266–71; his last inventions, 272; criticizes college trustees, 273; active in antislavery movement, 275; suffers a fall, 275; his will, 275; last letter of, 275–76; death of, 276; reputation of, in revolutionary France, 278–79; reaction to death of, in America, 279–80; reputation of, in revolutionary Germany and Italy, 283, in nineteenth century America, 282, 284–89, in the twentieth century, 289–93; and the nature of private property, 260–61; warning of, concerning armies, 296; and slavery, 296–97; contributions of, to physical and social sciences, 297; his political career: summary, 297–99

Franklin, Benjamin: Works
Account of Negotiations in London, 192
Articles of Confederation and Perpetual Union, 198
Autobiography, 163, 258, 274, 282
Bagatelles, 258–59
Busy-Body, The, 25